Breaking the Shackles:
Deregulating Canadian Industry

Breaking the Shackles: Deregulating Canadian Industry

edited by Walter Block and George Lermer

Proceedings of a Conference on Economics of Regulation and Deregulation held September 21-23, 1989, in Lethbridge, Alberta. This conference was organized by Walter Block, Senior Research Fellow, the Fraser Institute, and George Lermer, Dean, Faculty of Management, the University of Lethbridge. The Faculty of Management gratefully acknowledges the financial support of the Burns Foods Endowment Fund.

Canadian Cataloguing in Publication Data

Main entry under title:

Breaking the Shackles

> Based on a conference held in Lethbridge, Alta., Sept. 21-23, 1989.
> Includes bibliographical references.
> ISBN 0-88975-131-5
> 1. Deregulation—Canada—Congresses. 2.
> Trade regulation—Canada—Congresses. I.
> Block, Walter, 1941-   II. Lermer, George.
> III. Fraser Institute (Vancouver, B.C.)
> HD3616.C23B74 1991   338.971   C91-091240-8

Printed in Canada.

Contents

Preface

These papers were commissioned for presentation at a conference held at the University of Lethbridge from September 21 to 23, 1989. The editors, Walter Block of the Fraser Institute and George Lermer of the University of Lethbridge Faculty of Management, designed the conference for analysts of heavily regulated sectors of the Canadian economy to assess the success of the Mulroney government's deregulatory program. That program is outlined here in an essay by Anthony Campbell. As a senior civil servant with the Nielson Task Force on Program Review which examined and reported on the scope of federal regulatory activities in 1984 and 1985, and later as head of the Office of Deregulation, he was well placed to review the aims and objectives of the federal government.

The authors of these conference papers, critiques, and discussions applaud the incomplete yet significant deregulation achieved especially in the transportation, communication, and energy fields. Though Canadian deregulation of transportation and communication continues to lag American experience, the record is bleaker in other industries. The massive apparatus of agricultural regulation, much of it installed as recently as the late 1970s (200 years after Adam Smith's *Wealth of Nations*), remains unreformed. Also, the process of reforming the regulatory system governing the financial sector strikes some as a long running farce with little prospect for addressing the fundamental problems of the regulatory regime presently in place. Finally, rent control, a massive political intrusion into the market allocation system, has become deeply rooted in Ontario during the 1980s. Because of the scope and significance of rent control, the editors commissioned a paper on the subject despite the fact that it falls outside federal jurisdiction.

We asked each author to provide a capsule review of the regulatory regime in their field, to emphasize any recent changes, and to contrast developments with the U.S experience. Thus, this volume provides a timely and convenient summary of regulatory regimes in telecommunications, agriculture, energy, finance, housing, and in rail, truck, and airline transportation modes. In addition, each author was asked to evaluate the extent to which the economic benefits expected of deregulation have been realized, especially in the United States where post-deregulation experience is greater. Finally, the authors were expected to describe the interest group politics that helps explain the shifting regulatory environment in each field. In other words, the authors were asked to explain the process of deregulation and, if possible, to link those changes to one of several positive theories of regulation and by implication reregulation or deregulation.

We planned the conference with a belief in the importance of encouraging politicians to maintain and intensify a deregulatory program and to resist the special pleading of those groups that had lost from deregulation, especially in the United States but also in Canada. Such groups have been actively presenting alleged negative evidence of the impacts of deregulation, most vociferously in the airline industry. In our opinion the possibility of a political counter-action to the feeble deregulatory initiatives of the past decade ought not to be dismissed, and given the little that has been achieved, such a counter-action might reverse policies in some sectors and stall the deregulatory initiatives being considered in others. We wanted to set the record straight on the slow pace of deregulation and the benefits that have followed.

Moreover, we realized that conventional rhetoric about the downsizing of government masks its enormous expansion in allocating resources in social, environmental, and health portfolios. But here it was apparent from the outset that no group of economists could agree on where government responsibility starts and finishes. Because in these sectors poorly defined property rights and consequent externalities are recognizable, an economic case for some types of governmental interference has merit. When property rights are poorly defined, analysts may continue to disagree about what constitutes efficient government interference. That disagreement might turn on technical questions of how government should establish and enforce property rights where problems of appropriability, information asymmetry, and contract enforcement seem to eliminate the possibility for private means of clearly and sufficiently specifying property rights. Or the disagreement might turn at a deeper level to the degree of which analysts differ on the extent to which it is legitimate for governments to attenuate individuals' freedoms even when there exists a bona fide economic efficiency rationale for intervention. Finally, many analysts would argue that failure is endemic if not characteristic in the political process that leads to the assignment of property rights by governments and regulatory authorities.

For the above reasons we decided to focus the conference's attention on the traditional areas of economic regulation in which it is difficult to maintain that regulation today corrects a "market failure." Market failure is said to result from the existence of a natural monopoly, inadequately specified property rights, information asymmetry, and the associated excessive transaction costs of contract enforcement. In some of the sectors examined, a market failure rationale due to natural monopoly might once have had some plausibility, though as Herb Grubel points out, market failure is not a sufficient condition for introducing regulation which itself might be prone to the broader problem of government failure. Whatever the merits of that dispute, the fact is that technological change has since undermined the "market failure" rationale, so that for all the areas examined herein few economists claim that a market failure can rationalize the continuation of current levels of regulation. In most areas no "market failure" argument had any credibility at the time that regulation was introduced. Before the conference began, therefore, we anticipated writing an introduction to this book that would list the gains from recent deregulation, bemoan the slow pace of deregulation, and help strengthen the resolve of government to stand firm behind the deregulation that has been achieved and to speed up the deregulatory process where it has bogged down. We hoped that this book, like the conference from which it is derived, would produce a simple to read scorecard rating the degree of success or failure achieved by the authorities in extracting costly and unnecessary regulation.

In general, the conference's aim has been achieved and is recorded in this book. Like virtually all previous serious examinations of the morass of regulation in these traditional economic sectors, these studies cannot find economic benefits that outweigh the economic costs of regulation. Examined on a sector by sector basis, the deadweight losses in the form of reduced social wealth is in each case considerable, and the U.S. experience since deregulation is in line with prior economic predictions about the merits of deregulation. Moreover, the efficiency losses reported do not generally include quantitative estimates of the resource cost associated with the rent-seeking efforts of special interest groups in organizing to bring pressure on politicians and regulators.

At the same time, the essays and commentaries in this volume show how difficult it is with our present knowledge to sort out all issues involved in trying to rate the performance of governments on effective regulatory policy. The editors would stand accused by many of holding the naïve belief that political forces can be directed in favour of economically efficient policies through presentation of data on economic cost-benefits of regulation. From this point of view, economists' evaluations of regulation matter only as propaganda that can be used by a rent-seeking or rent-defending lobby on behalf of a special interest group. Because politicians did not introduce regulation in response to demonstrated market failures, they will not deregulate in response to demonstrations that the market is robust. According to this view, politicians supplied regulation under pressure from and in a form of exchange with special interests, and they will alter regulations only in response to a shift in the relative effectiveness of special interests to outflank their adversaries.

But this is the least serious of attacks on the endeavours of academic economists with no apparent "special interest" to grind to enlist in the debate and present data on regulation and deregulation. At least those in favour of regulation may be forced to confront the economists' analysis, and that analysis might carry additional weight with some of the politicians' and regulators' constituencies because it comes from an independent source. A more serious attack is mounted on the partial equilibrium cost-benefit analyses of regulatory regimes reported in this volume by those who argue that economists often misspecify the alternative to regulation. Implicit in many of the studies presented here is the notion that deregulation, in the form of less onerous controls on entry, exit, price, service level, and profit rate, will not be replaced by explicit subsidies and benefits previously delivered through regulation. But, as is most evident in the case of agriculture, tariff protection, non-tariff barriers, and various forms of subsidies may often be as effective a means of conferring a benefit to a special interest group as is a regulatory instrument that directly controls entry, price, service level, and profit rate.

A possibly more important criticism of the cost-benefit approach is that the administrative process surrounding much industrial regulation has emerged as an efficient alternative to direct regulation by legislative fiat. Since legislatures cannot be bound in advance to avoid introducing regulatory policies when circumstances change, as in the case of the National Energy Policy, administrative regulation provides some measure of protection for private investors from expropriation by legislatures. In a similar vein, it is argued that politicians have opted for administrative regulation as a means of educating special interest groups and the public about the limits of government power with the purpose of diffusing intense political pressure to provide benefits. From the latter point of view, whatever level of regulation we observe at any moment may well be an equilibrium in the political marketplace, even if economists observe only disequilibrium and waste in the economic domain. Moreover, a threat to an existing regulatory regime may in turn invite later legislative reaction and the expropriation of all those who invested in anticipation that government would stay out of the field.

It is beyond the scope of this volume to evaluate the force of these criticisms. For those that warn that special interest groups might seek benefits from government outside the umbrella of economic regulation, we respond that at least those benefits might have more immediate and transparent implications for governments' budgets and might therefore be more costly for politicians to rationalize to taxpayers. It is more difficult to counter the argument that the regulatory process has emerged as a means of channelling special interest group pressures for governmental interference in the economy in order to protect both private investors and politicians from the ex post facto opportunism demanded from politicians by a short-sighted electorate. We find it difficult to respond because the status of the argument is untested. Baldwin shows how regulation emerged in several U.S. industries as a response to legislative opportunism and how similar circumstances in Canada led instead to Crown corporations replacing private investors. By contrast, the rent control case examined by Smith suggests that the regulatory mechanism of rent control is a means of implementing ex post facto opportunistic behaviour and does not divert demand for rent control to a less economically damaging political channel. Nor, as Stanbury stresses, does the rent control mechanism seem to educate any of the players in the drama to the economic and social deterioration it causes. Moreover, it is well within the scope of the position we advance that deregulation proceed without causing governments to eliminate the responsibilities for regulatory authorities to provide administrative machinery for restraining demands for new and more onerous regulatory regimes. As Campbell points out, government has moved in this direction by establishing a regulatory budgeting procedure. Alternatively, the government might choose to make increased use of its inquiry powers to inform the public of the costs and consequences of regulatory processes for allocating resources. The government has acted this way in the cases of textiles, footwear, and corn by referrals to the Canadian Import Tribunal (known today as the Canadian International Trade Tribunal). It may be said to have acted similarly by establishing the Royal Commission on Corporate Concentration in response to pressure for merger legislation following the Power Corporation's threat to acquire the Argus Corporation. Regardless of the outcome of this comparatively new debate over the merits of regulatory procedures, all participants in and students of public affairs should find interesting the economic responses to deregulation where it has occurred, recorded herein, as well as the economic consequences of those sectors in which deregulation has been stalled.

Theories of Regulation

Not surprisingly, many non-specialists may be unfamiliar with the debate over the value of cost-benefit analyses of regulatory regimes because the debate hinges on competing theories that economists and political scientists have offered to help explain the often bewildering array of regulatory interventions in the economy. Accordingly, Don McFetridge was asked to write an introductory level survey article about how recent deregulatory experience fits into the cosmology of theories of regulation. As a by-product of his main assignment, McFetridge has also succeeded in writing an exceptionally fine non-specialist summary of the important theories of regulation, and he evaluates how competing regulatory theories have fared as models for recent deregulatory incidents in both Canada and the United States.

McFetridge emphasizes that both the public interest and special interest group models of regulation are incomplete because they fail to convincingly exhibit the political decision-making process. This situation permits advocates of various models to interpret the fragmentary deregulatory record in favour of their own preferred model and makes it difficult to choose empirically between models. McFetridge cannot identify any obvious shift during the 1970s and 1980s in special interest group structure or power that might explain the moves toward deregulation. Instead, the disappearance of a regulatory surplus to be shared between the regulatees and other politically favoured constituents does have some explanatory power. But the absence of a taxable regulatory surplus may have been present on other occasions without having led to deregulation, so evidence of the absence of a surplus cannot be used to argue conclusively that in the absence of a surplus the public and special interest group models will always agree that regulation is superfluous. Nevertheless, from the point of view of the public interest model, there is no further political capital in regulation when cross-subsidies are impossible, and from the point of view of the special interest group model, the special interests might well seek a return to their political capital through a policy other than regulation.

After canvassing the literature on the efficacy of cost-benefit analysis for evaluation of regulation and deregulation, McFetridge concludes that "the effect of deregulation has been salutary in the sense that it has resulted in welfare gains from both the restoration of cost-based pricing and from real savings." More importantly, he concludes that "ideas matter and that there is political opportunity in introducing new ones or repackaging old ones." In other words, books like this one that report on the economic cost-benefits of regulation contribute to the political process through which regulatory and deregulatory policies are forged because the parties to the process may otherwise fail to identify all the relevant consequences of regulatory policies.

The authors and other participants in the conference have worked in the spirit that McFetridge recommends, and we are confident that both the specialist and the informed lay person will learn something valuable from the essays and commentaries that follow. In the remainder of this introductory essay, we offer a condensed review of each paper in an executive summary style, and end with a brief editorial that acts as a summary of the papers and seeks to draw conclusions for the totality of deregulatory policy from these separate studies.

Telecommunications

The pace of deregulation of telecommunications in Canada lags U.S., Japanese, and U.K. experiences. In Canada regulation has been relaxed only on the subscriber freedom to privately own telephone equipment that is connected to a network. Otherwise, regulations continue to govern conditions of entry, tariffs, rates of return, and new service offerings. Competition is totally excluded from the provision of the switched voice telephone service which accounts for 90 percent of telephone traffic. The largest burden imposed by Canadian regulators today is the cross-subsidy of local telephone service by long distance users. Globerman estimates that the deadweight loss of this policy stands at $2 billion (in 1984 dollars) per annum. Those who do not use long distance service enjoy low local monthly flat rates that fail to ration local telephone usage. Demand for this service is highly inelastic, whereas the demand for long distance services is elastic. Rules for efficient pricing under natural monopoly (Ramscy prices) require that local prices should be high and long distance rates low, which also conform with the relative marginal costs of providing the two types of service. Therefore, even if the combined long distance and local services were a natural monopoly, the present regulatory scheme creates large inefficiencies. Globerman examines the natural monopoly argument and finds that it has some transient credibility only for the local exchange networks. In the near future, cable television systems and cellular telephone networks threaten entry into the local telephone network market.

The persistence of a cross-subsidy for local telephone users at the expense of business users who make greater use of long distance services challenges the interest group model of regulation. On its face, local users are diffuse and disorganized, whereas business users are well organized. Globerman speculates that the interest group model may not be contradicted. The model's forecast, that concentrated special interests always win at the expense of widely scattered special users for whom the consequences of even a doubling of local rates would hardly be noticed as a percentage of income, may not describe the reality of the telephone industry. Politicians face immediate pressures from local users who have no difficulty observing the immediate benefit from lower local telephone rates but are ignorant of the higher prices they pay for goods and services because long distance telephone charges are incorporated in the price of virtually every good and service they buy. At the same time, the largest telephone users who would be well placed to pressure politicians make use of specialized services to avoid high rates. Medium and small businesses, and government service organizations are left to pay the burden, and some of these groups may be able to pass part of the additional cost on to consumers. Moreover, these groups are diverse and not particularly well organized.

Rate rebalancing between local and long distance services is slowly occurring and might be largely achieved under the auspices of the regulator since the regulator is aware of the speciousness of arguments for maintaining the present cross-subsidy. Globerman would welcome that action, but rate rebalancing would not win all the efficiency gains for society that competition has to offer. After careful cross-section analysis of telephone industry performance in various countries and time series investigations of performance before and after regulation in several countries, Globerman concludes that "competition has played an important role in stimulating producers to take advantage of available technology and to pass a large portion of available benefits on to consumers." In addition, it "encouraged a greater convergence between prices and costs, i.e., allocative efficiency, a proliferation of new products and services, and a faster adaptation of new cost-saving technologies, i.e., dynamic efficiencies."

Truck and Rail

While allowing the two railways to quote jointly determined fares, deregulation of railway tariffs occurred in 1967 in order to permit the railroads to earn a sufficient surplus to compensate for the burden of the Crow Rate tariff on grain transportation from the Prairies. But intermodal competition between trucking and rail, despite the coalition of the two trunk railways, did not permit a sufficient surplus to be generated for the purpose. In the 1980s the Crow Rate was finally dismantled by transferring the burden of the subsidy to prairie land-owning grain producers from the railways to the general taxpayer. In 1987 railway deregulation proceeded in light of the absence of a surplus available for the public finance of prairie grain producers, the effects of intermodal competition, and the demonstrated effect of and competition from lower tariffs on the deregulated U.S. rail network. Under the recent legislation, railways are unable to avoid negotiating confidential contracts, captive shippers have access to negotiating for access to the closest transfer point to another railway though there is some uncertainty about how that provision is operating in practice, and railway route abandonment is easier than it once was.

The data will not permit the calculation of the effects or gains from Canadian railway deregulation. United States data indicate that rates have fallen on those routes where intermodal competition was previously not binding. Also, Canadian railways seem to be concentrating more heavily on long distance hauling and offering a larger variety of specialized services.

Truck deregulation is partial because intraprovincial trucking is under provincial control. In 1967 the federal government reasserted its regulatory authority over interprovincial trucking that it had previously ceded to provincial authorities. On its face, the restrictive truck regulation should be relatively easy to avoid through "pseudo-leasing arrangements, freight forwarding, and private trucking," but control over tariff setting and entry to the public trucking industry continues to provide some measure of protection. The evidence for this conclusion is the higher rates charged in provinces with more onerous protection and the price commanded by operating authorities. As a result, provincial authorities encountered the well-known regulatory trap by which it becomes difficult to eliminate regulation without first buying up operating authorities.

On balance it seems that the partial deregulation in the railway and truck industries has brought much of the gains that might be expected from deregulation. Since the value added in this sector is about 2 percent of GDP, the potential gains may be considerable and, like telecommunications, may be an important potential source of cost reduction for other industries.

In Canada railway regulation was a means of financing the Crow Rate subsidy, and regulation disappeared with the disappearance of the opportunity for off-budget financing. The special interest group served was the prairie land owner. In the United States the Interstate Commerce Commission regulated both trucking and the railways. As Richard Schwindt emphasizes, railway rate control was justified as a means of controlling a natural monopoly, and trucking regulation was necessary in order to protect the railway from competition. This ludicrous tale taught to all undergraduates in countless economics courses according to Schwindt lost credibility, and the misregulation became unsustainable. Palmer is less sanguine about the influence of rational analysis and he notes that deregulation coincided with the fact that "rapidly changing fuel prices in the 1970s made rate regulation a dog's breakfast." He suggests that bureaucrats in the Interstate Commerce Commission could not cope with the situation and slowly permitted deregulation to emerge. Another interpretation is that heightened political awareness of high fuel costs, sensitivity to the environmental impact of empty trucks uselessly burning fuel on circuitous routes, and the drive to fight inflation all raised the political costs of continued regulation and strengthened the political position of shippers relative to truck owners.

Possibly the most controversial point that Palmer makes is that safety might be compromised somewhat by the emergence of competitive trucking, but he speculates that, like anything else, safety must be paid for, and there is no evidence that the level of safety is below the optimal level. If U.S. experience is to be followed in Canada, competition is usually accompanied by an increase in the average size of trucking firms which makes attention to safety more likely because bankruptcy is less likely and the firm remains liable for losses attributable to unsafe operation of its trucks.

Airlines

Airline deregulation is examined separately from rail and truck. Based on its minor contribution to GDP, this might indicate that the editors have misallocated space in this book. The rationale for this choice is that airline deregulation has received much media and scholarly attention possibly because airlines are so often used by academics, media people, lawyers, and politicians. Nevertheless, Canada's recent steps toward deregulation of its airline industry is incomplete and is far from secure from a political reaction.

Though reduced labour costs accompanied U.S. deregulation and explains the Canadian airline personnel's opposition to deregulation, the main gains from deregulation are stimulated by improved route planning and the better matching of plane sizes and types to passenger volume. Though the gains experienced in the United States from the "hub-and-spoke" route systems may be less prevalent in Canada because of the linear nature of Canada's main traffic routes, Canada's regulatory system created a great deal of waste because large jets were diverted to smaller communities. In the two short years since deregulation in Canada, any traveller can observe the huge expansion in the fleets of various sized turbo-prop and small jet liners that link smaller communities to major airports.

Grubel reports that "non-fuel" operating costs per passenger seat mile flown dropped in the United States by 43 percent in 1985 from their 1981 peak and by 21 percent from the pre-deregulation level in 1978. By contrast, the same index in Canada was 10 percent higher in 1985 than in 1978. Clearly, this is strong evidence that deregulation in the United States has caused performance to improve there faster than in Canada. As a result, fares in the United States fell by 14 percent and traffic skyrocketed. In Canada fares fell by just 4 percent and traffic stagnated.

Grubel also addresses safety, quality, and concentration issues. On safety, he notes that because of the possibility of bankruptcy, a risk prone entrepreneur might theoretically skimp on safety and walk away from the firm's liabilities should safety experience be poor, but pocket additional revenues should safety experience be positive. Grubel points out, however, that safety and maintenance remain regulated activities. Any airline operator would be aware of the rapid loss of clientele that follows a government report of any systematic effort to avoid safety procedures. Grubel examines the rate of accidents before and after deregulation in the United States and observes a continued trend toward improved safety performance despite the far greater congestion in the skies and the effects of the air traffic controllers' strike. He also notes that increased air travel has reduced intercity automobile travel with a subsequent savings in accident costs of $1.9 billion per year and a savings in lives by 1,700 per year. He dismisses the quality and product differentiation issue as being a red herring. Regulation diverted competition from price to quality to the especial satisfaction of business travellers whose fares were paid by their employers. Post-regulation competition is forcing airlines to search for the mix of differentiated services and price premiums that best serve significant groups of travellers. Insofar as travellers are suffering from increased congestion and the lagged organizational response to rapid traffic growth, Grubel suggests that the fault lies with the absence of deregulation in the operations of airports and runways. In the short run, he recommends increased use of pricing mechanisms to ration access to airports at peak periods, and in the long run, he calls for private ownership or franchise operation of airports. Grubel accepts that concentration may be an emerging problem despite the observation by many that there are few sunk-costs in airline operations because an airliner is the classic example of a capital item that is not a sunk-cost and can be transferred easily to better uses. It may be that much of the cost in establishing a hub-and-spoke system is in the nature of a sunk-cost that creates protection for incumbents already established at a particular hub. But Grubel is sceptical about the potential application of competition policy to the airline concentration issue and he recommends instead that competition in Canada be strengthened by allowing foreign airlines to operate between two points in Canada.

Finance

The traditional four pillars of financial regulation have been crumbling for several decades, but the federal government's efforts to reform financial regulation in recognition of those changes are stalled. Past regulation separated institutions into banking, trust, insurance, and securities; it also limited the ownership of a major domestic bank to 10 percent for a single owner and prevented a real sector firm from acquiring control of a bank. The old order has been battered by the internationalization of the financial services industry, the absence of ownership restrictions and separation rules on foreign institutions, including some that are operating in Canada, the shift of corporate financing away from banks towards securities markets, and competition between federal and provincial regulators with overlapping jurisdictions over the financial sector.

The effort to reform financial regulation in an orderly way seems to have been outpaced by events. Internationalization of financial markets is proceeding quickly and the international legal structure is expanding to cover trade in services taking the form of the Canada-U.S. Free Trade Agreement and discussions at GATT concerning services including financial services. For example, Courchene documents how Canada's international commitments place it presently in the uncomfortable position of disallowing the acquisition of a Canadian financial institution by a major Canadian conglomerate firm, while being forced to authorize the acquisition of the same target by a subsidiary of a similar foreign owned conglomerate.

The complexity of financial market regulation rules out a summary of Courchene's paper that does justice to the range of his rich ideas, especially as he has essentially written three different papers. The first outlines the reasons why the four-pillar model of regulation is dead. The second paper reviews the several federal proposals for reform that have floundered after publication. That review is less concerned with the detail of the proposals than with the politics that has stymied reform. The last paper considers the link between financial structure and ownership and government industrial policy. In particular, Courchene demonstrates that Quebec has proceeded quite far toward subordinating regulatory concerns of a traditional nature in favour of building protected domestically owned institutions to be permanently headquartered in Quebec. Courchene believes that, like Quebec, federal authorities will be forced into using financial regulation as an instrument of nationalism and industrial policy.

Lermer agrees that financial regulation is being caught up in geopolitical strategies and nationalist politics. He thinks this is unfortunate because there is only one rationale for financial sector regulation and that is protection of the deposit insurer. Lermer, Chant, and Courchene would prefer that the deposit insurance scheme be reformed directly so that financial regulation would become of secondary concern. Unfortunately, recent large bank failures make it more likely that the deposit insurance system will be expanded rather than contracted. This makes it imperative that the financial system reform proceed in a way that will reduce the potential for moral hazard behaviour (taking the form of the financial institution holding a risky portfolio of assets in relation to the type of liabilities that they have issued in order to finance the assets) by managers and owners of insured institutions. In this connection, Chant suggests that one way to proceed is to insure only the deposits of certain institutions that are also required to hold safe assets. This proposal has much in common with Milton Friedman's and James Tobin's recommendations for a 100 percent reserve banking system. Chant further proposes that no other financial institution would receive a government guarantee, and therefore all non-insured institutions would be free to operate outside the control of government administered financial regulation.

Block points out in connection with his radical proposal for privatization of all roads, that government regulation and ownership prevent the market from searching out alternative methods of providing safety and otherwise better managing assets. However radical that idea may appear in the case of the public road system, or for environmental concerns, it certainly deserves attention of the financial sector. In the financial industry, there are no "market failure" concerns that give government, even in principle if not in practice, an advantage in the regulation of financial institutions.

Oil and Gas

Watkins summarizes the events of 1985 that dismantled the National Energy Policy (NEP). The NEP and earlier policies allowed the federal government to appropriate a large part of the wealth of owners of oil and gas reserves between 1974 and 1985, including the province of Alberta (some estimates run as high as $50 billion (1980) dollars. Those policies diverted revenues from domestic crude oil production to subsidize imported oil in order to bring the average price of crude oil and refined petroleum products in Canada well below the world market price. The high tax on domestic crude oil was a disincentive to further exploration which led the government to expand the role of Petro-Canada and to subsidize up to 100 percent of exploration costs on Crown lands but not on provincial territory. The federal government's power to regulate against the interests of Alberta was derived from its ability to tax and control provincial export of oil and gas from Alberta and from Canada. The National Energy

Board was able to disallow exports for a variety of reasons having to do with alleged future Canadian requirements or for insufficient price.

Unfortunately for the owners of oil and gas reserves, the Western Accord of March 1985 which "emasculated the NEP," coincided with a rapid drop in the price of oil and gas. Though some might ask about the fairness of expropriating the value of oil and gas reserves in the boom and deregulating in the trough of the cycle, the main legacy of the NEP, as Watkins points out, is the Alberta government's fear that despite the apparent protection in the Canada-U.S. Free Trade Agreement the federal government may again behave opportunistically if energy prices rise once more. Another legacy is the existence of long-term take-or-pay gas contracts between TransCanada PipeLine Limited and several natural gas producers that TransCanada has been unable to live up to in the post-regulation world.

Watkins emphasizes that we observe different rates of adjustment to deregulation in oil and gas markets: there has been continued provincial and federal intervention in natural gas markets while the crude oil market is free of intervention. This difference can be traced to differences in downstream market structures for both products. Upstream, at the exploration and production levels, there are many oil and gas producers in Canada, and gas reserve ownership is less highly concentrated than oil reserves. Both oil and gas must move through pipeline systems to markets in the United States and eastern Canada. Large sunk-cost investments are needed in pipeline and production facilities, and when these assets are owned by distinct parties the threat of opportunistic behaviour exists. The regulation of pipelines is one response to the natural monopoly of the pipeline and the bargaining problem associated with a single pipeline serving a small number of producers. However, the regulation of pipelines does not eliminate the problem as is seen by the dispute between natural gas producers and Canadian gas distributors and users about the toll to be applied in order to permit pipeline expansion, which is mainly to expand sales to the United States.

Further downstream the markets for oil and gas differ fundamentally. Canadian crude oil refined in Ontario and Quebec must meet the price of imported crude oil and imported refined petroleum. Because the world market for crude oil and refined products is highly competitive there are active spot and futures markets from which price information can be freely and openly acquired. It is therefore impossible for Alberta crude oil to sell in Edmonton at a price other than the net back price calculated as the price of foreign crude landed in eastern Canada minus the cost of delivery from Edmonton to the East. Watkins demonstrates that this is in fact the case under present market conditions.

In one significant segment of the natural gas market there is a rent that can be earned from the fact that the next best alternative fuel to natural gas is generally far more expensive and because in response to a price increase buyers would take some time to shift from burning natural gas to burning an alternative fuel like heating oil or propane. That segment of the market is the household user of natural gas that is served by a local distributor by pipeline. The pipeline is a natural monopoly and is regulated. If the local distributing company (LDC) can access alternative sources of natural gas, it would of course have the best poker hand and could negotiate the lowest possible price and hope its regulator would allow it to hold on to the higher profit stream. (Because the LDCs are regulated, consumer provinces like Ontario and Manitoba have become embroiled in negotiations with Alberta over the pricing of natural gas.) In eastern Canada, however, the LDCs are highly dependent upon shipments from Alberta via the TransCanada PipeLine. This is largely because natural gas was until recently heavily regulated in the United States so that American sources of supply were not reasonably priced in Canada and a pipeline infrastructure linking the U.S. sources of supply and southern Ontario does not exist. Moreover, pipeline links will only be built when the investor can be assured that there will be sufficient flow of gas to warrant construction. Under these circumstances, natural gas distributors and pipeline companies seek assurances through contract, and sometimes with the assistance of a regulator, that long-term supplies will be available and at reasonable prices. Much of the gas is therefore committed under long-term contracts with a range of different prices applying to different sales. Watkins reports that recent sales to "core" Ontario markets by Alberta producers through TransCanada PipeLine is at a substantial premium price only part of which can be explained as compensation for the long-term commitment of reserves for sales to Ontario. The remainder of the premium reflects some leverage retained by TransCanada PipeLine and the Government of Alberta. This market power will assuredly disappear as new pipeline construction makes it possible to sell more natural gas in the United States and Alberta's producers compete for Ontario's business.

In a nutshell, there are no characteristics of the oil and gas business that invite government regulation except possibly at the level of ensuring that pipelines remain common carriers. In the oil business the March 1985 deregulation is complete, and the market is operating as would be expected. In the natural gas market deregulation has not gone quite as smoothly because of provincial regulators and long-term sales contracts. None the less, the natural gas industry has responded rapidly to deregulation, many spot and new contract sales are at marginal cost, and the role of regulation is likely to disappear with the development of new sales opportunities for western Canadian gas in the United States.

Agriculture

Loyns, Carter, and Peters indicate that in agriculture there is such a high degree of substitutability between tax, subsidy, and regulatory policies that it becomes more convenient for analytic purposes to group these together and to measure the degree of government intervention in several different ways. One such way, used extensively by trade negotiators, is a single numerical measure to capture the degree of government interference. That measure is called the "producer subsidy equivalent," which measures the rise in price that would be needed to leave farm income unchanged despite the removal of all applicable farm programs. For 13 agricultural commodities, that producer subsidy equivalent for Canada averaged 31 percent between 1982 and 1986. Though there are numerous problems with measuring the extent of intervention and of separating regulatory interventions from subsidies and taxes, this figure does convey the extent to which Canadian agriculture has become a government dependent.

Loyns and Carter describe the pro-interventionist environment of the 1970s, review the Economic Council of Canada's extensive recommendations for reform published in 1981, and document for each product the limited progress made to step back from intervention during the 1980s. Put plainly, there is no significant deregulatory experience to report with the exception of the moves made to deregulate grain transportation. Loyns and Carter see some signs that the 1990s may be the period of deregulation for agriculture in Canada.

Not having deregulatory experience to examine, the authors ambitiously attempt a cross-sectional analysis over 12 crops pooled with time series data for the period 1965-87. Their study is designed to test the validity of the Peltzman-Becker formulation of the interest group model of political influence. The results are ambiguous, and do not seem to support the notion that agricultural support conforms to an "efficient redistribution" through regulation hypothesis. For example, elasticity measures and production concentration measures do not seem to have a significant impact on the extent of public support, whereas the retail/farm price ratio and production variability index are both highly significant. There is, therefore, some support for the interest group model but not the model in the form proposed by Becker. The retail farm price ratio result indicates that the lower the farm share of the retail price, the lower is the degree of subsidy, presumably because downstream processors and distributors have insufficient political power to resist producer initiatives. The production variability index indicates that the more regions of the country in which a crop is produced, the larger the level of that crop's subsidy, presumably reflecting the greater ease with which a political coalition around a new program proposal can be formed within the agricultural community.

The joint influence of GATT and the Canada-U.S. Free Trade Agreement may bring reform to Canadian agricultural support in its regulatory and subsidy modes. There is no indication that domestic political forces will provoke change, though Canadian consumers are aware of the disparity between Canadian and American food prices, especially for dairy and feathered product prices, and the heavy budgetary burden of agricultural programs on the taxpayer. At the same time, it must be acknowledged that agricultural regulation is in part a product of international conflict and negotiation strategies, and that unilateral retreat from agricultural support may be strategically and politically difficult. Still, agriculture is a clear case in which the consumer and taxpayer is generally poorer than those producers earning the largest share of government support. For this reason subsidy programs can be attacked both for the deadweight losses they generate and for the distributional consequences of the programs that transfer income from poorer to richer households.

Rent Control

Rent control, more than any other form of regulation, demonstrates a flaw in the argument that regulation somehow responds to inherent weaknesses in the market allocation system. Rent control attenuates the property rights of landlords and creates property rights for tenants by expropriating those from the landlord. Setting aside the unfairness attached to the *ex post facto* opportunism that takes the wealth of those unfortunate enough to have invested in rental housing rather than in something else, the impact of rent control is to destroy incentives for maintaining existing housing stocks and adding to that stock. Larry Smith documents how Ontario's experience has followed down the slope that destroyed the rental housing stock of so many other cities. Though rent control causes rental housing stock to erode, it is the erosion of the social contract that does the most harm. First, potential investors lose all confidence in a government that continually changes the rules, initially to entice new construction, then to expropriate from the investor. Second, thousands of persons violate and evade the law with impunity, a behaviour that allows rent control programs to operate without immediate catastrophic damage but that hardly entrenches respect for civic responsibilities.

Rent control is a negative sum game. The short-term winners gain at the expense of others, but the costs of administering the rent control system and the costly long-term incentive effects cause virtually everyone to lose in the long run. Larry Smith documents that just the costs imposed by the rent control system on the Ontario taxpayer totalled about $300 million in 1988. But this is just the tip of the iceberg and it overlooks the legal costs of private parties, the dispute costs between landlords and tenants, the deterioration of the rental housing stock, the rise in the price of close substitutes, search costs, and the loss in respect for law and government.

Despite these demonstrated problems many communities introduce rent control. Stanbury examines the politics of rent control, with pessimistic implications for the possible triumph of long-term economic and social rationality over the power of the political appeal to transferring wealth from an allegedly undeserving minority of landlords to a deserving majority of tenants. Denton Marks is more diffident, with more confidence than Stanbury and Smith that the market continues to work surreptitiously and thus mitigates the worst consequences of rent control, and that a flexible rent control system may be a reasonable substitute for a rental subsidy system or a negative income tax. But Larry Smith reports several studies that show a comprehensive shelter allowance program in Ontario could be funded at far less cost than the administrative and tax cost of the rent control program and without the negative incentive effects on rental housing stock.

The puzzle, therefore, is why an expensive and erosive rent control system emerges and a comprehensive shelter subsidy system does not. Why has a better mechanism not emerged for controlling the tendency for legislative *ex post facto* opportunism in the rental housing market? Evidently, rent control is not a form of contract that protects landlords from expropriation, but it is the vehicle for giving some semblance of order to the process of expropriation. It may be inevitable that a Crown corporation will emerge as the mechanism for building, owning, and maintaining rental housing in Toronto. The record of public housing programs around the world demonstrates that government failure should be a greater concern than any alleged market failure, but ironically the only failure in the rental housing market is our inability to bind government from politically opportunistic behaviour in the form of rent control legislation.

Summary

Is it accurate to describe the past decade as the decade of deregulation? Has Canada embraced the traditional liberal or today's neo-conservative program for reliance on market solutions in the industries examined here?

Our review identifies progress in rail and truck transportation, incomplete but valuable deregulation of the airline industry, modest improvements in telecommunications, substantial progress in the oil and gas industry, and a confused and potentially damaging situation in the finance industry. The deregulatory process has barely begun in agriculture, but there are signs that international trade negotiations will force Canada to move away from the extensive regulatory system currently in place. Finally, all news is bad regarding Ontario's rental housing market which seems to have entered a rigid and permanent regulatory regime.

One approach for selling deregulation might be for government to publish a regulatory budget that would show the billions of consumer dollars saved through deregulation. Deregulation would release resources that could be applied to reducing of the budget without damaging the standard of living of most Canadians. We cannot place a precise figure on the savings available, but it is certainly in the range of tens of billions of dollars each year. Globerman's estimate of the savings from rebalancing long distance and local telephone rates accounts for a substantial chunk of the total, and many more gains are potentially available especially as the sector is poised to expand. Agricultural deregulation would bring a saving of many more billions of dollars since over 32 percent of farm income presently comes through government programs. Rent control in Ontario costs $300 million per year in tax losses and administrative costs and many more millions in private costs that have not been measured. In transportation deregulation has proceeded sufficiently to have generated the majority of the gains we are likely to see. We do not have an estimate of the costs of misregulation in the finance sector, but the contingent liabilities of government as deposit insurer are enormous, and as we have seen in the savings and loan crisis in the United States, these potential losses can be enormous.

The benefits from deregulation are difficult to measure with precision because they are cumulative and accrue through the speed of innovation—they are the effective management of resources with prices reflecting costs and with management intensifying its search to package goods and services that respond to the requirements of consumers.

Walter Block
George Lermer

About the Authors

John Baldwin

Professor of economics at Queen's University, John Baldwin is presently on leave as a research fellow at Statistics Canada and the Economic Council of Canada. With research interests concentrating on the nature of the regulatory process in industrial economics, he has written two books in this area—*The Regulatory Agency and the Public Corporation* and *Regulatory Failure and Renewal: The Evolution of the Natural Monopoly Contract*. Other publications include *The Role of Scale in Canada/U.S. Productivity Differences in the Canadian Manufacturing Sector in the 1970s*, a study of the relationship between trade flows and market structure, and *Structural Change and the Adjustment Process: Perspectives on Firm Growth and Worker Turnover*, which examines the effect of adjustment of labour markets. He is completing a monograph that measures the dynamics of the market system.

Walter Block

Walter Block is Adjunct Scholar at the Fraser Institute and Associate Professor, Economics Department, Holy Cross College, Worcester, Massachusetts. A member of the British Columbia Association of Professional Economists, the Canadian Economic Association, and the Canadian Association for Business Economics, he has worked in various research capacities for the National Bureau of Economic Research, the Tax Foundation, and *Business Week*. He has published numerous popular and scholarly articles on economics, is a regular contributor to *British Columbia Report Magazine* and writes a syndicated column for Sterling newspapers. An economic commentator on national television and radio, he lectures widely on public policy issues to university students, service, professional, and religious organizations. He is the editor of the Fraser Institute books *Zoning: Its Costs and Relevance* (1980), *Rent Control: Myths and Realities* (1981), *Discrimination, Affirmative Action and Equal Opportunity* (1982), *Taxation: An International Perspective* (1984), *Theology, Third World Development, and Economic Justice* (1985), *Morality of the Market: Religious and Economic Perspectives* (1985), *Reaction: The New Combines Investigation Act* (1986), *Religion, Economics and Social Thought* (1986), *Economics and the Environment: A Reconciliation* (1989), and *Economic Freedom* (1991). He is the author of *Defending the Undefendable* (1976), *Amending the Combines Investigation Act* (1982), *Focus on Economics and the Canadian Bishops* (1983), *Focus on Employment Equity: A Critique of the Abella Royal Commission on Equality* (1985), *The U.S. Bishops and Their*

Critics: An Economic and Ethical Perspective (1986), and *Lexicon of Economic Thought* (1988).

Anthony Campbell

Anthony Campbell received a B.A. in economics and history at Queen's University and studied law at the University of Toronto. He joined Canada's foreign service in 1967 and has since been a professional federal public servant. He worked in Canada's diplomatic missions in Guyana (1968) and Spain (1969-72), and in the Economic Bureau of the Department of External Affairs (1972-74), where he specialized in international environmental issues. He was then assigned to economic policy issues: as executive director of the Food Prices Review Board (1974), as secretary of the Anti-Inflation Board (1975), and as director general of Policy Coordination in the Department of Consumer and Corporate Affairs (1976). In 1979 he became director general of International Affairs in the Department of Fisheries and Oceans. From 1984 to 1989, he served in several capacities in the field of regulatory affairs (Treasury Board, Ministerial Task Force of Program Review, and the Privy Council Office) before becoming assistant deputy minister of the Office of Privatization and Regulatory Affairs (1986-89). He is now vice-principal of the Canadian Centre for Management Development.

Colin A. Carter

Professor of Agricultural Economics at the University of California (Davis), Colin Carter received a Ph.D. from the University of California (Berkeley) in 1980. From 1980 to 1986, he was a member of the Department of Agricultural Economics and Farm Management at the University of Manitoba. He has won a number of research and teaching awards including the American Agricultural Economics Association Annual Award for Quality of Research Discovery, and the Canadian Agricultural Economics and Farm Management Society Annual Award for Outstanding Journal Article. From 1986 to 1989, he was a distinguished research scholar with the Kellog Foundation.

John Chant

A Simon Fraser University professor who specializes in monetary economics, John Chant served as research director of the Financial Markets Group at the Economic Council of Canada, producing the study *Efficiency and Regulation* which had an important impact on the Bank Act of 1980. He is the author of several books including *The Allocative Effects of Inflation* and *The Market for Financial Services*. One of the foremost experts in Canada on the regulation of financial institutions, Dr. Chant has served as a consultant to the Bank of

Canada, the Commission of Inquiry into Residential Tenancies, and the Royal Commission on the Economic Union and Development Prospects of Canada. Most recently he has been advising the Government of Indonesia with respect to the regulation of its baking system.

Thomas J. Courchene

The director of the new School of Policy Studies at Queen's University, Thomas Courchene received a Ph.D. from Princeton University in 1967. From 1965 to 1988, he was a professor of economics at the University of Western Ontario, spending the fall of 1986 as a visiting professor at Ecole nationale d'administration publique (Montreal), and then held the John P. Robarts Chair in Canadian Studies at York University in 1987-88. He is the author of well over 100 books and articles on Canadian policy issues including *Social Policy in the 1990s: Agenda for Reform* (C.D. Howe Institute), a four-volume series on Canadian monetary policy for the C.D. Howe Institute, *Equalization Payments: Past, Present and Future* (Ontario Economic Council), *Economic Management and the Division of Powers* (Macdonald Royal Commission), and *What Does Ontario Want?* (1988 Robarts Lecture, York University). Dr. Courchene was chairman of the Ontario Economic Council from 1982 to 1985, has been a senior fellow of the C.D. Howe Institute since 1980, is a member of the Economic Council of Canada, and is a Fellow of the Royal Society of Canada. At Queen's he also holds the Stauffer-Dunning Chair and is a member of the Department of Economics, the School of Public Administration, and the Faculty of Law. His ongoing research is in financial deregulation and the political economy of Canada's regions.

Steven Globerman

Steven Globerman holds a Ph.D. in economics and is currently professor of economics at Simon Fraser University and Adjunct Scholar at the Fraser Institute. He has served on the Faculty of Commerce and Business Administration at the University of British Columbia, the Faculty of Administrative Studies at York University, and the Faculty of Business Administration at Simon Fraser University. He has consulted for government agencies and private sector organizations and has published over 50 journal articles and 15 books and monographs on various aspects of economics and public policy.

Herbert Grubel

Herbert Grubel is a professor at Simon Fraser University in the Department of Economics, specializing in international trade and finance. Born in Germany in 1934, he was educated at Rutgers University and at Yale where he received a Ph.D. in economics in 1962. During 1970-71, he was a senior policy analyst for the U.S. Treasury Department in Washington, D.C., and in 1974-75 he was a visiting research fellow at Nuffield College, Oxford. He has held academic posts at Stanford University, the University of Chicago, the University of Pennsylvania, the University of Nairobi, the Australian National University, the University of Cape Town, the Institute of Southeast Asian Studies, and the Kiel Institute of World Economics. Professor Grubel has been the recipient of research grants from the National Science Foundation and the Canada Council. He is a member of the Fraser Institute Editorial Advisory Board. His publications include 14 books and over 100 scholarly articles in journals and books.

Kurt K. Klein

Professor of economics at the University of Lethbridge, Kurt Klein received a Ph.D. from Purdue University in agricultural economics. He was a visiting professor at the University of British Columbia (1986-87) and Hokkaigakuen University in Sapporo, Japan (1988) and was a research economist with Agriculture Canada before joining the University of Lethbridge in 1981. He has published widely in the fields of agricultural policy, bioeconomic research, and systems models of agricultural production, and is a contributor and co-editor of *The Economics of Agricultural Research in Canada* and *Canadian Agricultural Trade: Disputes, Actions and Prospects*, both published by the University of Calgary Press. Twice he was awarded the Most Outstanding Article Award in the *Canadian Journal of Agricultural Economics*. He has also owned and operated a mixed-enterprise farm in Saskatchewan during the 1960s.

Ashish Lall

A research economist with the Royal Commission on National Passenger Transportation, Ashish Lall received a B.A. from Delhi University and M.A.s from both the Delhi School of Economics and Carleton University. He is a Ph.D. candidate in the Department of Economics at Carleton University. His dissertation is on Canadian railway cost functions.

George Lermer

Dean of the Faculty of Management of the University of Lethbridge, George Lermer received a B.Sc. from Massachusetts Institute of Technology and an M.A. and Ph.D. from McGill University. From 1962 to 1974, he taught at various Canadian universities including Concordia University and the University of Waterloo. He was senior economist at the Economic Council of Canada (1974-76), studying the regulation of financial institutions and markets and contributing to "Efficiency and Regulation," in preparation for the revision of The Bank Act. As director of the Resources Branch, Bureau of Competition Policy, Consumer Affairs Canada (1976-81), he specialized in the enforcement of the Combines Investigation Act in the agriculture and energy industries. In 1980 he was seconded to the Privy Council of Canada, Federal-Provincial Office of the Task Force for the Renewal of Federalism. He has extensive experience as a consulting economist with government departments and private clients. He has advised clients on trade practices, competition policy, industrial structure, and economic regulation, especially of agriculture. The author and editor of several books and numerous articles, his most recent publication is *AECL—An Evaluation of a Crown Corporation as a Strategist in a Global Entrepreneurial Industry* (Economic Council of Canada).

R.M. Al Loyns

Professor at the Department of Agricultural Economics and Farm Management, University of Manitoba, Al Loyns received a Ph.D. from the University of California (Berkeley) in 1968. His past experience includes: research economist with the Prices and Incomes Commission, Ottawa; research co-ordinator, Food Prices Review Board, Ottawa; and assistant deputy minister, Policy Analysis Group, Department of Consumer and Corporate Affairs, Ottawa. He maintains interest in consumer and competition matters while researching and teaching in the area of regulation of the agriculture and food industry.

Denton Marks

An associate professor in the Department of Economics at the University of Wisconsin (Whitewater), Dr. Marks received his M.P.A. (public affairs) and his M.A. and Ph.D. in economics from Princeton University. He has also been on the faculties of the University of British Columbia and Simon Fraser University. His special interests are economics and public policy analysis including labour market theory and policy, income maintenance and replacement policy, housing policy (especially rent regulation), and economic analysis of the political process. He has written several monographs and research papers in these areas; his research has appeared in a variety of publications including *Journal of Urban Economics*, *Land Economics*, *Urban Studies*, *Canadian Journal of Economics*, *Policy Sciences*, and *Monthly Labor Review*. He has worked at the U.S. Department of Health, Education, and Welfare; and he has served as a consultant to Employment and Immigration Canada, Health and Welfare Canada, and the Ontario Commission of Inquiry into Residential Tenancies.

Donald G. McFetridge

Professor of economics at Carleton University, Donald McFetridge received a B.Comm. from the University of Saskatchewan, an M.Sc. from London School of Economics and Political Science, and a Ph.D. from the University of Toronto. He has taught at the University of Western Ontario, McGill University, and Qing Hua University in China and has been a research fellow at Harvard. He has published numerous books and articles on industrial organization and public policy issues as well as served on the research staffs of two Royal Commissions and advised corporations and government departments. His current research is on national systems of technological innovation and the diffusion of new technologies. Among his more recent publications are *Trade Liberalization and the Multinations* (Economic Council of Canada) and "The Economics of the Conserver Society," co-authored with John Chant and Douglas Smith, in *Economics and the Environment: A Reconciliation* (Fraser Institute).

John P. Palmer

Professor Palmer has taught economics at the University of Western Ontario since 1971. His teaching and research specialties include the study of regulated markets, and he has published numerous books and academic journal articles about transportation regulation. Some of his more recent work extends his earlier analyses to other aspects of legal institutions. In 1979 he initiated the Economics and Law Workshops at the University of Western Ontario. Palmer has been the director of the Centre for the Economic Analysis of Property Rights since 1980. In that capacity he has co-ordinated and carried out research on various economic issues involving legal entitlements, including copyrights, patents, parenthood rights, and the legal rights of individuals owning operating authorities in regulated industries. Since 1984, Palmer has also directed the Economics Institute for Journalists, which provides intensive courses in economics for working journalists. He received a B.A. in economics from Carleton College in 1965, attended the Chicago Theological Seminary for two years, and received a Ph.D. in economics from Iowa State University in 1971.

Eric E. Peters

An economist for the Development Branch of Agriculture Canada in Winnipeg, Eric Peters is completing an M.Sc. at the Department of Agricultural Economics and Farm Management, University of Manitoba.

Richard Schwindt

An associate professor of economics and business administration at Simon Fraser University, Richard Schwindt received a Ph.D. from the University of California (Berkeley) where he specialized in industrial organization and the economics of regulation. His research interests lie in the industrial organization and regulation of renewable resource industries, specifically the fisheries, forestry, and agriculture. He has authored and co-authored several monographs and articles in these areas. Professor Schwindt also maintains an active interest in Canadian anti-trust policy and has served as an advisor to both public and private sector parties in a number of proceedings.

Lawrence B. Smith

Professor of economics at the University of Toronto, Lawrence Smith received a B.Comm. from the University of Toronto in 1962 and a Ph.D. from Harvard in 1966. Formerly the director of economics and the associate chairman at the Department of Political Economy, University of Toronto, he is a member of the executives of the Canadian Economics Association and the American Real Estate and Urban Economics Association. Professor Smith's writings in the areas of housing, rent control, mortgage markets, monetary theory, and monetary policy have appeared in the *Journal of Political Economy*, the *American Economic Review*, and the *Journal of Economic Literature*. He has served as a consultant to several government agencies and departments, including the Canada Mortgage and Housing Corporation and the Ontario Ministry of Housing, and to numerous private organizations, including the Committee for Concern, Fair Rental Policy Organization of Ontario, Salomon Brothers Inc., and the Canadian Institute of Public Real Estate Companies. He has also been deputy chairman of the Federal Task Force on the Canada Mortgage and Housing Corporation.

W.T. Stanbury

W.T. Stanbury is UPS Foundation Professor of Regulation and Competition Policy at the Faculty of Commerce and Business Administration, University of British Columbia. He received a B.Comm. from U.B.C. and an M.A. and Ph.D. in economics from the University of California (Berkeley). At U.B.C. he teaches courses on business strategy, business-government relations, and Canadian competition law. His research is wide ranging—from the problems of native peoples to competition policy, government regulation, and the growth of government in Canada. In 1976 and 1977 Dr. Stanbury was a consultant and researcher for the Royal Commission on Corporate Concentration. From June 1978 to November 1979, he was director of the Regulation Reference for the

Economic Council of Canada, and then became director of research for the Regulation Reference until August 1980. From November 1977 to August 1982, he was director, Regulation and Government Intervention Program, Institute for Research on Public Policy. From September 1982 to December 1984, he was senior program advisor for that institute. He has also been a consultant to the Bureau of Competition Policy of the federal Department of Consumer and Corporate Affairs, the Law Reform Commission of Canada, the CRTC, the Federal Treasury Board, MacMillan Bloedel Ltd., CNCP Telecommunications (now Unitel Communications), Cominco Ltd., the Macdonald Commission, the B.C. Ministry of Forests, and the federal Office of Privatization and Regulatory Affairs. He is the author or co-author of more than 200 publications, with articles on regulation and competition policy appearing in *Antitrust Bulletin, Canadian Business Law Journal, Osgoode Hall Law Journal, Canadian Public Policy, Canadian Competition Policy Record, Canadian Public Administration,* and *Canadian Journal of Economics.* In 1989 he was awarded a U.B.C. Killam Research prize for 1989-90 and 1990-91, and was also awarded the Professor Jacob Biely Faculty Research Prize in competition with scholars across U.B.C. His latest book, *Rent Regulation: The Ontario Experience,* is co-authored with John D. Todd.

Michael Walker

Michael Walker is an economist, journalist, broadcaster, consultant, university lecturer, and public speaker. As an economist, he has authored or edited 22 books on economic topics. His articles on technical economic subjects have appeared in professional journals in Canada and the United States, including *Canadian Journal of Economics, The Journal of Finance, Canadian Tax Journal,* and *Health Management Quarterly.* As a journalist, he has written some 450 articles which have appeared in some 60 newspapers, including the *Globe and Mail, The Wall Street Journal, Vancouver Sun, Chicago Tribune, Reader's Digest, Detroit News,* and *Western Star*—the latter being the newspaper in his birthplace, Corner Brook, Newfoundland. He has been a regular columnist in the *Vancouver Province, Toronto Sun, Ottawa Citizen,* and *Financial Post.* As a broadcaster, he has written and delivered 1,800 radio broadcasts on economic topics and appeared on radio and television programs in Canada, the U.S., and Latin America. As a consultant, he has provided advice to private groups and governments in the U.S., Australia, New Zealand, Venezuela, Jamaica, Mexico, Panama, Hong Kong, Bermuda, and Canada. He has lectured to some 700 audiences at universities and in other venues on five continents. Since 1974, Dr. Walker has directed the activities of the Fraser Institute. Before that he taught at the University of Western Ontario and Carleton University and was employed at the Bank of Canada and the federal Department of Finance.

He has served as a director of a number of firms and other enterprises, including Mackenzie & Feimann Limited, Sydney Research Inc., the Canadian Club, and Collingwood Private School. He is a member of the International Trade Advisory Committee to the Government of Canada and the Statistics Canada Advisory Committee on Service Sector Statistics.

G. Campbell Watkins

President of DataMetrics Limited, an economic consulting firm based in Calgary, Dr. Watkins is also adjunct professor of economics at the University of Calgary. His involvement in economic research and policy spans a range of positions including chief economist at the Oil and Gas Conservation Board (1965-69), associate economist at the Royal Bank of Canada (1970-71), director of economic studies at the Gas Arctic Group (1971-72), and petroleum advisor to the Tanzanian Minister of Energy (1987). The past president of the Economics Society of Alberta, he is now president of the International Association for Energy Economics. Dr. Watkins contributed to three earlier Fraser Institute books, *Oil in the Seventies* (1977); *Reaction: The National Energy Program* (1981); and *Petro Markets: Probing the Economics of Continental Energy* (1989).

William G. Watson

An associate professor of economics at McGill University since 1977, William Watson is currently on leave as a visiting associate at the Americas Society in New York. He received a B.A. from McGill and an M.A., M.Phil., and Ph.D. in economics from Yale University. He has served on the board of advisors for the C.D. Howe Institute in Toronto and for the John Deutsch Institute for Economic Policy at Queen's University, and on the board of directors for the Cormier Centre for International Economics at Bishop's University. He has published two books, *A Primer on the Economics of Industrial Policy* (Ontario Economic Council) and *National Pastimes: The Economics of Canadian Leisure* (Fraser Institute). He writes a twice-weekly column for *The Financial Post* and his articles have appeared in *Canadian Journal of Economics*, *Canadian Public Policy*, *Policy Options*, and *Journal of Comparative Economics*. In 1989 he won the National Magazine Award, Gold Medal for Humour.

Chapter 1

Taming the Regulatory Tiger: Revealing the Best Kept Secret in Ottawa

Anthony Campbell

The public policy of regulation richly deserves thorough and informed public debate at this time. Having been involved in the efforts to control regulation since late 1983, I am glad to have this opportunity to reflect on what has and has not been accomplished over those six years. This essay, therefore, is an informal "insider's" report on government efforts to "tame the regulatory tiger."

I often prepare a speech or essay by going to a dictionary or book of quotations to crank up my thinking process by looking up the key words of the theme I have been assigned. This is almost always a mistake. First, because I usually get totally absorbed in reference books and waste a lot of time. And second, because I often try to fit my comments around whatever I find in the reference book and this usually produces an awkward and distorted draft which eventually has to be discarded.

Ignoring the experience of years, I began preparing this presentation by looking up the word "tiger." I found that it is a most appropriate symbol for regulation. A tiger is, with the lion, the most powerful of carnivorous animals. It can be majestic in appearance, but at other times is quite ugly and frightening. It weighs about 200 kilos—exactly the total weight of the Revised Consolidation of Regulations of 1978 and the Revised Statutes of Canada 1985. Its productive life is about 20 years, and it is conceived and usually operates in the dark. The major difference between a regulatory program and a tiger is that tigers always die when they are no longer useful!

By the time this essay will appear, I will have left the field (should I say jungle?) of regulatory reform. After six sometimes frustrating, sometimes satisfying, but nearly always fascinating years in the business of trying to tame the regulatory tiger, this is (to change the metaphor) my "swan song."

Even if I were not about to move on, this would be a good time to look backward at what has been accomplished in economic regulatory policy in recent years and then peer into the present and future challenges in this area. It is timely to put emphasis on the future—the question of where do we go from here—because there are many who consider regulatory reform to be a political fad, something akin to the Charleston or the hula hoop, whose time has come and gone.

I think that it is very important to take issue with that view. The single biggest message that I can discern since the regulatory reform movement emerged some twenty years ago is that the nature and exercise of regulatory authority in the post-Guttenberg, post-industrial age must be subjected to intensive rethinking and redirection, not just on a one-time basis, but continuously, if we are to keep this most important of the governing instruments relevant and in harmony with Canada's ongoing economic and political needs.

Ongoing regulatory reform, revitalization, and adaptation is not a matter of choice, it is a matter of necessity. It is certainly not a matter of ideology, but a reality of public administration which all governments, from Albania to Zimbabwe, must face up to. If this is correct and if, as I believe, the emergence of regulatory affairs is the most important recent development in the field of public administration, then it follows that we are nowhere close to the end of its useful life cycle. If anything, we are only at the beginning and it is important regularly to reinvigorate the ongoing pursuit of what we in Ottawa call "smarter regulation."

Here, then, is a view from inside the tiger cage of the past, present, and future of regulatory reform in Canada. Although I estimate the regulatory reform movement to have begun in about 1968-69, it did not have a noticeable impact as far as Canada was concerned until the mid-1970s. Even then, its impact was limited to only a few thinkers—in contrast to the U.S. where it had already resulted in far reaching major decisions and, more importantly, a very fundamental shift in the way people viewed government's use of its coercive legal powers.

One of the interesting questions for historians of this movement to explore should be why the Americans grappled with the issues so much ahead of Canadians. Why were we so slow to pick up the new intellectual currents? Had we by the 1970s become mere "branch plant thinkers"? And why, generally speaking, were our institutions comparatively resistant to the winds of adaptation and change? Are we still slow adapters or have we learned anything from our experience? Are Canadian "interest groups" more strongly entrenched than their American counterparts?

In short, why was it possible for the excellent work of the Economic Council of Canada, which detailed the social and economic costs of so much of Canada's ill conceived economic and social regulation, to be totally ignored for so long and why did it take until 1984 for Canada's federal government to get down to serious regulatory reform? Why for that matter have most provinces and municipalities not got down to it even yet—a case in point is the disappointing progress in ongoing negotiations to reduce interprovincial barriers to trade. In low moments, my response is to mutter those opening words of our national anthem—"Oh Canada!"

Whatever the answer to these questions, the fact is the federal government took a dramatic change of direction in 1984, first under the Turner and then more decisively under the Mulroney administrations and since then has quietly but steadily turned in one of the more impressive regulatory reform performances in the world. Indeed, Canada has since outpaced even the U.S. in many important respects, and it is no exaggeration to suggest that the Bush administration's regulatory policy actually adheres quite closely to Canada's own pragmatic regulatory policy. Similarly, recent policy announcements by the U.K., New Zealand, and other governments seem to have copied from Canada's innovative work in this area.

Before looking a bit more closely at what has happened in the federal tiger's cage since 1984, let me explain that, if there is a touch of braggadocio in what follows, I hope you will understand that we have a lot of difficulty transmitting the message of Ottawa's regulatory reform accomplishments to the public. This is partly because of the media's resistance to undramatic news. But it may also have been that our good old Canadian penchant for 'aw shucks' modesty muffled our message so much that even experts in academia seem not to have heard about it. For example, *The Age Of Regulatory Reform* (Oxford Clarendon Press), a recent book that scanned developments around the globe contained not one but two articles on Canada's experience by two of our most knowledgeable experts and neither mentioned a word about most of what I am about to tell you.

There are many ways to measure accomplishment. For example, one can measure against an absolute ideal, or by relative progress from a defined starting point. Using these two standards, Ottawa's accomplishments would probably rate a C and B, respectively, in its regulatory reform performance since 1984. In government, however, we usually measure our success against what was possible. By that measure, I think the federal government is entitled to an A+.

By the way, to avoid any impression of partisanship by this professional public servant, who believes strongly in a non-partisan public service, I would like to emphasize that the A+ grade for the federal government's performance would include some of the preliminary experiments and analysis done by the

Trudeau/Turner governments as well as the pivotal leadership provided by Lloyd Axworthy while Minister of Transport in early 1984. The bottom line, however, is that while the Mulroney government came to power in the fall of 1984 with only a few cautious words about regulatory reform or deregulation in its campaign platform, it proceeded to launch the most comprehensive and coherent regulatory reform initiative of any government elsewhere in Canada or the world. The government coming second on my list would be the Jimmy Carter administration (1976-80), followed until the last few months by New Zealand. The Reagan administration, contrary to public image, was more like most governments over the years—long on rhetoric and short on action. As for Margaret Thatcher, her intentions have no doubt been good. But the British have had very little experience with some types of economic regulation because of their traditions and penchant for Crown monopolies. Thus, as their privatization policies result in many new untried and, in my view, unstable regulatory regimes, the ironical possibility is that Margaret Thatcher could go down as having introduced more new and unworkable regulation than any other prime minister in British history!

Rather than going over every detail of Canada's gold medal performance, I would like to summarize the case by listing a whole series of "firsts"—16 of them—that individually and cumulatively illustrate the innovative and far-reaching importance of the federal regulatory reform record since 1984.

1. The first government to establish and publish a formal list of all of its regulatory programs as distinct from the traditional lumping of regulatory activities under expenditure programs. Only in 1984 did we learn that the federal government runs 145 regulatory related programs.

2. The first government to initiate a top to bottom review of all its regulatory programs to identify needed reforms. This was conducted by the Ministerial Task Force on Program Review in 1985 against 11 criteria (including economic criteria). The review involved a joint private-public sector team, itself an innovative regulatory reform technique, and it generated suggested reforms to two-thirds of federal programs.

3. The first government in the world to adopt a meaningful and comprehensive regulatory reform strategy calling for change in every dimension of government regulatory activity.

4. The first government to promise (and actually carry out the promise) to report to the public on its performance against the goals of the strategy.

5. The first government to define and enunciate a formal regulatory policy that departed from knee-jerk deregulatory rhetoric by emphasizing the principles of "smarter regulation." These pragmatic but meaningful principles have since been adopted by other governments, including the present Bush administration.

6.   The first government to establish performance standards for regulators. The Citizens Code of Regulatory Fairness issued in 1986 gave ministers and the public a unique set of criteria for holding regulators accountable not only for the substance but also the management of their regulatory responsibilities. The significance of this "first" is illustrated by the fact that the Scowen Commission in Quebec and committees in the Ontario and, I am told, Manitoba legislatures have all recommended that the federal code be adopted by their provincial governments. So far, none have done so.

7.   The first government to appoint a minister with explicit generic responsibility for regulatory affairs at the cabinet table.

8.   The first government to recognize formally the critical role of sound regulatory management in achieving regulatory objectives. No matter how good a regulatory program design may be, its value is zero if it is not properly managed.

9.   The first government to introduce compulsory approved annual regulatory planning. The U.S. and Canada introduced regulatory "agendas" in the early 1980s but these covered indeterminate periods of time and in Canada's case were voluntary and therefore incomplete. The U.S. has since copied Canada's annual plan.

10.   The first parliamentary government to require full regulatory impact analysis for decision-making by ministers.

11.   The first parliamentary government to establish positive cost-benefit criteria for all regulatory decision-making.

12.   The first and still the only government to publish the regulatory impact analysis underlying cabinet's regulatory decisions.

13.   The first government to establish a cabinet committee with explicit responsibility for regulatory policy and thus to extend normal cabinet approval procedures used for "big" policy decision-making to cover all subordinate legislation decisions. This replaced the traditional rubber stamp procedures typically (and still) used by most governments in the world based on the mistaken belief that new regulations and amendments are "routine" decisions.

14.   The first government to establish a central agency function for the overall management of the regulation development process as well as for co-ordination, research, and review concerning generic or "horizontal" regulatory policy issues.

15.   The first government to recognize "regulatory affairs" as a distinct public policy sector and to establish administrative structures and allocate resources to upgrade public service management expertise in this area. As educators, you may be interested to know that there has been a

flowering of training and development activities in the federal administration directed toward the goal of "smarter regulation." These include activities in the Canadian Centre for Management Development, the Department of Justice (Compliance and Regulatory Remedies Project), the Solicitor General's Department (Federal Law Enforcement Under Review or FLEUR Project), as well as experimental training programs developed in the Office of Privatization and Regulatory Affairs.

16. The first *parliamentary* government (the Americans were first) to adopt the principle of publishing regulatory initiatives to encourage public access to and direct participation in the regulatory process. It is fascinating to look at a copy of the weekly *Canada Gazette*, part I, to see the results of this innovation. In addition to the exact words of each proposed regulatory change, you will find a "RIAS"—a Regulatory Impact Analysis Statement—which explains what the change is intended to do, why it is being proposed, and with what expected impact.

All of these innovations were directed at taming the regulatory tiger. They were not the stuff of headlines and heated public debate. But they were peaceful and orderly public management improvements that were intended to and have succeeded in fostering better government—and, dare we say, even "good" government at the federal level.

Chapter 2

Is There a Theory of Deregulation?

Donald G. McFetridge and Ashish Lall

1. Introduction

The purpose of this paper is to examine what implications some recent examples of deregulation in the United States and Canada have for the theory of regulation. Specifically, the question is whether the traditional public interest theory of regulation or the more recent interest group theories would have predicted either the occurrence or the outcome of deregulation in transportation, energy, telecommunications, and financial services sectors.

The paper begins with a brief description of the major examples of deregulation, taken here to involve the virtual elimination of price, entry, and exit controls, which have occurred in Canada. More detailed descriptions appear in other papers of this volume. The description is followed by an analysis of the respective assumptions and predictions of the alternative theories of economic regulation. Finally, we explore whether the major examples of deregulation are consistent with either of the two contending theories.

2. Deregulation in Canada

2.1 Energy

The Western Accord of 1985 eliminated federal regulation of the price of natural gas sold in interprovincial trade. About 80 percent of all reserves in the producing provinces are under long-term contract primarily to TransCanada PipeLines. The remaining gas can be sold directly to users at a negotiated price. The number of contracts between gas producers and gas consumers has increased from 24 in 1986 to 354 in May 1988. These direct sales compete with and displace gas provided under long-term contract (system gas).

The Alberta government has attempted to discourage direct sales by refusing to issue removal permits in some cases and by changing its royalty calculations in others. The National Energy Board has also limited direct sales by forbidding self-displacement (replacing system purchases with direct purchases) by gas distributors. This restriction was removed in November 1989.

2.2 Finance

As of July 1988 all restrictions on the ownership of securities dealers have been eliminated. Legislation which will grant chartered banks fiduciary powers has been proposed. It is also proposed that chartered banks be allowed to own insurance companies, although restrictions would remain on their ability to act as insurance agents.

2.3 Telecommunications

In this industry regulatory change has occurred through decisions of the CRTC rather than through legislation. CNCP Telecommunications was allowed to interconnect with Bell in 1979 and B.C. Tel in 1981 in order to provide competing private line and data transmission services. The ability of the CRTC to order interconnection with Alberta Government Telephones, which was challenged by the province of Alberta in 1982, was upheld by the Supreme Court in August 1989.

The ability of the CRTC to exempt certain competitors from price regulation has been challenged successfully in the courts. In September 1986 CNCP applied to CRTC for exemption from price regulation since CNCP had a small segment of the telecommunications market and did not have a monopoly in any individual sub-market. The application was supported by the Consumer's Association of Canada and the Bureau of Competition Policy. On September 27, 1987, the CRTC lifted the regulatory burden on CNCP since it was convinced that there was sufficient competition to ensure a loss in business if prices were raised by CNCP. On October 13, 1988, in *Telecommunications Workers Union v. CRTC and CNCP*, the Federal Court of Appeal set aside the CRTC decision and referred it back for reconsideration. The court ruled that the CRTC's jurisdiction did not include the authority to relieve a firm from the requirement to file for toll approval. CNCP intends to take this issue before the Supreme Court.

2.4 Transportation

The federal law deregulating interprovincial trucking, the Motor Vehicle Transportation Act, came into effect on January 1, 1988. The "public necessity and convenience" test that had been used to restrict entry was replaced by a "fitness" test that directed authorities to grant a licence to any applicant who satisfied basic insurance and safety requirements. Public hearings were no longer required unless there was evidence of public detriment. The new law reversed the onus under the old one in that those opposing the licence were now required to show detriment; previously, the applicant was responsible to show that the new service was required and would not damage incumbents.

In Ontario the Minister of Transport and the Ontario Highway Transport Board both sought the ultimate authority to issue licences. The Minister had advocated a more liberal entry policy than the Board (requiring opponents of entry to show *serious* detriment). Judicial decisions in 1988 gave ultimate authority to the Board and rejected the Minister's interpretation of entry requirements.

The National Transportation Act also came into effect in January 1988. It increased competition among railways by providing for confidential contracts with shippers, by increasing the scope for interswitching (i.e., increasing the number of consumers with access to a competing railway), and by eliminating provisions of the Railway Act which encouraged joint rate-making.

With respect to airlines, the National Transportation Act eliminated entry restrictions (except in northern Canada) and the regulation of fares, flight schedules, and equipment. Exit restrictions were liberalized (120 days notice is required), and confidential contracts with shippers were allowed. Only fare increases on "monopoly" routes can still be appealed.

3. The Public Interest Theory of Regulation

The public interest theory holds that regulation exists to correct market failures. Regulation thus increases societal wealth. The sources of market failure which regulation is said to remedy include natural monopoly, asymmetric information, and externalities.

The regulation of natural monopoly was historically thought to allow the realization of the economies of large scale production while avoiding the "deadweight" loss associated with simple monopoly pricing. Critics of the natural monopoly rationale have pointed out first that the "deadweight" loss associated with simple monopoly pricing can and presumably would be avoided without regulation by a regime of multipart tariffs (non-linear pricing). Second, as Demsetz (1968) argued, that distributive concerns can be satisfied by auctioning off the monopoly right.

Goldberg (1976) salvaged a role for regulation with the argument that, even with franchise bidding for monopoly rights, the contract between the franchisee and consumers (or state) would bear a close resemblance to existing regulatory regimes. Regulatory control over pricing, entry, and exit is seen by Goldberg and Williamson (both 1976) as a means by which the government, acting on behalf consumers, can induce producers to make long-lived investments in specialized assets. Baldwin (1989) has examined cases in which this "regulatory contract" fails because parliamentary governments, acting as both contractors and adjudicators, cannot constrain their opportunism. The result is the replacement of regulation with government enterprise.

With respect to other forms of market failure, it is generally accepted that there are potential efficiency gains to be derived from setting entry-restricting minimum quality standards in markets characterized by asymmetric information (Leland, 1979) and from restricting the number of users of common property resources. Entry standards or restrictions need not be imposed by the government, but the latter is likely to have scale and/or credibility advantages.

4. The Special Interest Theory of Regulation

In the special interest theory, regulation is a means by which special interest groups use the political process to extract wealth from other groups in society. Apart from the redistribution itself, these transfers involve a "deadweight" loss and are therefore collectively wealth-reducing.

Stigler (1971) formalized the special interest theory as an economic theory of regulation. He argued that particular industries or occupational groups can use the state's coercive power to facilitate and sustain an increase in their prices or fees and thus increase wealth at the expense of customers.

Since these transfers involve a deadweight loss, they would be rejected in a direct vote by an informed electorate unless the beneficiaries constituted a majority and no less burdensome means of transfer were available. In a representative democracy, however, voting is an expression of preferences on a variety of issues. Voters rationally choose to remain uninformed on issues not perceived as material to them. As a consequence, policies benefiting a minority at a small cost to individual members of the majority may not evoke substantial opposition.

Political parties fashion a majority coalition of interest groups seeking to extract wealth from the public at large via regulatory or other means. Political parties thus serve the entrepreneurial function of promising regulatory benefits in the form of entry control, restrictions on the supply of substitutes, and facilitation of joint price determination in return for the interest group's votes and financial support. The industries that obtain regulatory benefits are those that can deliver votes and financial support and whose customers cannot.

Peltzman (1976) elaborated Stigler's theory. Political parties again "sell" regulatory benefits to industry and occupational groups in the form of higher prices and profits in return for votes and campaign contributions. As the price set by a regulated industry increases, however, it benefits more consumers to inform themselves and to campaign and/or vote against the proponents of the regulatory regime in question. As a consequence, the regulatory advantages an industry or occupational group is able to extract fall short of full monopolization.

Peltzman's model implies that regulation of either otherwise monopolistic or otherwise competitive industries will command greater political support than will regulation of oligopolies. Regulation of the polar cases promises either a big increase in profits or a big decrease in prices while regulation of oligopoly promises only marginal changes in prices and profits.

The model also has the comparative static implications that regulators will require increased profits resulting from either demand increases or cost decreases to be "shared" with consumers in the form of price reductions. Regulated industries will, according to the model, also be allowed to buffer the effects of cost increases or demand decreases on profits by raising prices. Taken together, these propositions imply that regulation amplifies the effect of cost changes and attenuates the effect of demand changes on prices.

A refinement to the special interest theory was suggested by Posner (1971) who observed that regulation often serves to benefit one group of customers at the expense of another. The regulated industry becomes a conduit, though not necessarily a disinterested one, through which resources are transferred from the "taxed" group to the "subsidized" group. Regulation is thus an alternative to direct taxation and subsidization. Regulation as public finance is further considered in section 5.

Becker (1983, 1985) embedded the special interest theory of regulation in a general theory of rent-seeking. For him, wealth transfers are the result of political interplay of contending interest groups. The groups that are more efficient at producing political pressure benefit at the expense of the less efficient. Interest group efficiency depends on the ability to organize, deliver political support, and influence public opinion.

In Becker's model regulation is but one of the means by which wealth may be transferred. Moreover, a regulated industry may be the beneficiary or the source of a wealth transfer or merely a conduit. Becker's key insight is that the greater the deadweight loss associated with a wealth transfer, the less likely it is to occur. This limits the size and nature of transfers and implies that regulatory regimes may contain the seeds of their own destruction. He obtained his insight by recognizing that an interest group will spend up to its anticipated wealth loss to forestall taxation and up to its anticipated wealth gain to secure subsidization.

The wealth loss of the taxed group is equal to the tax revenue derived from it *plus* the deadweight loss resulting from tax-induced changes in behaviour. The wealth gain to the subsidized group is the tax revenue transferred *less* the deadweight loss resulting from subsidy-induced changes in behaviour. Thus, given equal political effectiveness, the taxed group will prevail over the group seeking subsidization. Put another way, groups seeking subsidization must be more politically effective than tax paying groups if they are to succeed.

By the same reasoning, wealth transfers which either increase allocative efficiency (correct market failures) or entail small deadweight losses (inelastic supplies and/or demands) are more likely to occur than transfers that induce large deadweight losses. Moreover, holding political effectiveness constant, there is a mutual interest in choosing the efficient method of taxation. That is, the more efficient the taxation method, the smaller the wealth loss of the taxed group for any given subsidy. The same may be (but is not always) true of efficient subsidization. The implication is that if regulation is used to transfer wealth then it must be the most efficient (smallest deadweight loss) method of making the transfer.

Becker concedes that the most efficient mode of transfer may not be adopted if political effectiveness depends on the mode of transfer. "Hidden" regulatory taxes (in the form of above-cost prices) may evoke less opposition from the taxed group than more visible taxes. A subsidy-seeking group may prefer a "hidden" tax that requires less lobbying to obtain over a more visible tax, even though the latter has a smaller excess burden.

While existing regulatory regimes need not be efficient in the narrow sense of minimizing the deadweight loss associated with a given redistribution, efficiency of a broader sort is implied. Existing regulatory regimes must be regarded as efficient in the sense of maximizing political support. As Trebilcock et al. (1982) argue, the support-maximizing redistributive instrument will have the characteristic of providing highly concentrated benefits to marginal voters while imposing costs on infra-marginal voters or dispersed costs on other marginal voters. The preferred instrument will also be one which allows for the exploitation of the poorly informed by exaggerating its benefits and understating its costs. Given equivalent instruments in these respects, political competition militates in favour of the one with the lower deadweight loss.

A problem with the special interest theory and the public interest theory is their vagueness about what political support is and how it is maximized. Indeed, these theories leave the political sector virtually unspecified (Posner, 1974; Romer and Rosenthal, 1987). Political parties, legislatures, and regulatory agencies are treated as interchangeable. They are assumed to maximize support but the means by which this occurs remain unstated. What might constitute support or contribute to political effectiveness is not discussed. Although the special interest theory turns on coalition formation and political entrepreneurship, neither is modelled. Similarly, the public interest theory does not indicate how the political system determines the public interest. As the discussion in section 8 will indicate, the failure to model a political sector reduces the ability of these models to explain the incidence and timing of deregulation.

5. Regulation as Public Finance

The public finance approach draws from both the public interest and the special interest theories of regulation. It recognizes that regulation is one of a number of policy instruments available to governments for taxation and subsidization. As such, regulation may benefit any or all workers, owners of other factors, or a group of customers at the expense of another group of customers. Public finance regulation may serve the special (minority) interest or the general (majority) interest. It may increase or reduce deadweight losses.

Examples of regulatory tax-subsidy systems include the subsidization of rail passenger and grain movement with freight profits (McManus, 1979), the subsidization of local telephone service with long distance profits (Breslau and Smith, 1982; Globerman and Stanbury, 1986) and the subsidization of the maritime and prairie air services with transcontinental profits (Baldwin, 1975). Legislation governing intercity bus transportation in Quebec explicitly requires that the ability of existing carriers to cross-subsidize low density routes be taken into account when the licensing of new carriers is considered.

Posner (1971) argues that regulatory cross-subsidization is most likely to prevail in industries providing infrastructure services, such as utilities and common carriers. Such services have the useful property of being difficult to resell, thus allowing government to restrict the benefits of cross-subsidization to a target group of users. Posner also suggests that infrastructure industries are subject to regulatory cross-subsidization because of "political" decisions that their services should be widely available.

Globerman (1986) describes the web of cross-subsidization that exists in the telecommunications industry in Canada. As noted above, long distance revenues are used to subsidize local rates. In addition, local business subscribers subsidize local residential subscribers and intraprovincial long distance callers subsidize rural subscribers (at least in Saskatchewan and Manitoba).

The situation in telecommunications illustrates that the system of regulatory transfers can be complex and the ultimate beneficiaries are not always readily identifiable. Where, for example, is the ultimate incidence of the higher rates paid by local business subscribers? The problems likely to be encountered in identifying the ultimate beneficiaries of regulatory transfers also make it difficult to test the special interest theory of regulation.

Regulatory cross-subsidization has also been used as an industrial and regional development tool. One example of this is Canada's National Oil Policy. Baldwin (1982) shows that this policy was motivated fundamentally by a desire of the federal government to increase exports of western Canadian crude oil to the United States. In return for access to the U.S., Canada was obliged to commit itself to not replacing exported crude with (cheaper) imported foreign crude in domestic use. As a consequence, Ontario refineries were required to run domestic crude. Competition from offshore products which continued to "leak" into Ontario reduced refining and distribution margins in Ontario. The major petroleum refiners benefited from the NOP to the extent that it raised the price at which they could sell their western Canadian crude and were hurt by the NOP to the extent that it reduced their Ontario refining and distribution margins. Baldwin calculates that Imperial and Gulf were net beneficiaries of the policy while the benefit for Shell was marginal (pp. 91-92). The NOP increased royalty income and drilling and related activity in western Canada. The cost was borne by Ontario consumers. The industry served as a conduit receiving benefits just sufficient to induce the marginal national major to participate in the scheme.

A second example is due to Acheson (1989) who analyzes the terms and conditions of the Canada-United States auto pact. The pact restricted the right to import U.S.-built cars into Canada duty free to bona fide Canadian producers who met Canadian content provisions. The U.S., in contrast, allowed duty-free importation of Canadian-built cars by any U.S. resident. The producers used their exclusive right to duty-free importation to maintain higher prices for cars in Canada than in the U.S. for the first ten years of the pact. The pact also provided for an expansion of vehicle assembly operations in Canada. The emphasis on a relatively low wage and labour-intensive component of automobile production reflected a Canadian concern with jobs and job creation as opposed to income per capita.

The automobile producers were induced to enter the auto pact by the guarantee of higher profits on Canadian production. The producers, in turn, induced U.S. labour to agree to the expansion of employment in Canada by increasing the wage rates of their U.S. workers relative to their Canadian employees. Thus, the apparent Canadian desire for a bigger automobile industry was realized in return for higher profits to the (U.S.) companies and higher wages to U.S. labour.

These examples serve to emphasize that the raising and spending of revenue by governments can involve a variety of policy instruments of which the type of economic regulation being discussed here is just one. Moreover, the incidence of benefits is not necessarily confined to one group ("big oil" or "big labour") and dispersed interests (such as potential auto workers) can be and probably often are among the beneficiaries.

Examples of the use of regulation for industrial policy purposes continue to arise. A recent one involves the amendments to the Patent Act. The amendments effectively lengthen the patent term on pharmaceuticals for patentees performing R&D in Canada. In this case the subsidy is the additional profit earned over the longer period of monopoly. The tax is the excess of the monopoly price over the more competitive price that would have prevailed had the period of exclusivity not been extended.

6. Provinces as Interest Groups

The type of interest groups contemplated in the theories discussed in the preceding sections are occupations or industries. Acheson (1989) concludes that the principal Canadian beneficiaries of the auto pact were potential auto workers rather than existing union members. The cross-subsidy in this case was to increase employment rather than real wages. It is difficult to envisage either existing union members choosing more employment over higher real wages or potential auto workers as an effective interest group.

Acheson sees the auto pact as yet another example of public regulatory and other policies designed to reduce real wages at the margin so as to increase employment. This "taste for employment" continues to motivate both federal and provincial regulatory policies. Provincial economic interests have also accelerated the pace of deregulation in some cases (airlines, finance, and energy) and retarded it in others (telecommunications).

With respect to airlines, Schultz and Alexandroff (1985) conclude:

> It would be inaccurate to claim that the intergovernmental conflicts over air policy that emerged in the last decade were the sole cause of the decision to deregulate the Canadian airline industry significantly. Other factors clearly played a role, especially the U.S. deregulation beginning in 1978 and the subsequent "haemorrhaging" of Canadian traffic to U.S. border points such as Burlington, Vermont; Buffalo, New York; and Bellingham, Washington. In addition, partisan and personal motives on the part of then Minister of Transport Lloyd Axworthy were doubtless instrumental. It is our contention, however, that no other single reason played as important a role as that of intergovernmental conflict. To the extent that airline deregulation represented "an idea whose time has come" the decade of conflicts and the numerous setbacks for the federal government, as well as many stalemates, were crucial to federal acceptance, and willingness to act, on that fact (p. 60).

For these authors, the end came for airline regulation when provinces began to see air service as an instrument of economic development policy and their respective interests came into conflict both with other provinces and with the federal government.

Provincial economic development interests are also the driving force behind financial deregulation in Canada. Much of the impetus for deregulation came from Quebec which was, in turn, attempting to slow the relative decline of both the Montreal Stock Exchange and Montreal as a financial centre (McNish, 1989). Further pressure against federal restrictions on concentrated and cross-ownership of financial institutions has also come from Quebec which is attempting to insulate major Quebec-based companies from ownership changes and possible exit from the province (Courchene, 1990).

The opposite situation prevails in telecommunications where the three prairie provinces have successfully resisted attempts to increase competition in long distance services (Globerman and Stanbury, 1986). While it could be the case that the provinces are merely fronts for local special interest groups, it is also possible that they reflect the general interest of their respective jurisdictions.

7. Theories of Regulation as Theories of Deregulation

7.1 Predictions Regarding the Incidence of Deregulation

The public interest theory predicts that deregulation would occur if the market imperfection which necessitated regulation in the first place were to disappear. An example would be a change in technology which eliminated a natural monopoly. The public interest theory also predicts that deregulation would occur if it were discovered that a regulatory regime that had been perceived to be in the public interest either never had been or no longer was. It may turn out that, in the light of experience, the cost of the regulatory apparatus is or has become greater than the loss resulting from the market imperfection it was designed to correct (Posner, 1974). Thus, it may become apparent only with experience that entry restrictions are a relatively costly way to enforce airline safety standards. A variant of this explanation is that assertions by various parties regarding the public interest in regulation are revealed to be self-serving only with experience.

Another possibility which touches on the special interest theory is that the regulatory process may be co-opted (captured) over time by the industry or occupational group it was designed to control so that regulation which was initially in the public interest is no longer so.

New information plays a crucial role in the public interest theory of deregulation. Deregulation occurs because of information that the market no longer requires it or that the regulatory process is more costly than anticipated or that the regulators are pursuing objectives at variance with those that had been intended.

The Stigler-Peltzman version of the special interest theory suggests a number of factors which may give rise to deregulation. First, a reduction in the cost consumers must incur in order to inform themselves regarding the effect of regulation on them. For example, price comparisons between regulated and non-regulated jurisdictions can assist consumers in estimating the effect of regulation on the prices they pay. Second, increasing substitutability between regulated and non-regulated products should reduce the profitability and hence the incentive to lobby for regulation-induced price increases. Substitution may occur between regulated and unregulated industries or between regulated and unregulated jurisdictions. Third, a change in industry structure can reduce either the incentive or the ability to lobby for regulation. An increase in the number of firms in an industry or a convergence of their respective interests may increase the incentive to free ride and make it more costly to organize in support of politicians promising regulatory benefits (Stigler, 1974).

Becker's generalization of the special interest theory predicts that the incidence of rent-seeking, of which regulation is but one form, is reduced if (a) the taxed group becomes politically more effective; (b) the subsidized group becomes politically less effective; or (c) the deadweight loss associated with the transfer increases.

Political effectiveness again depends on interest group size and composition and on the cost of gathering information regarding the consequences of regulation. The deadweight loss associated with a wealth transfer increases with the ability of individuals to substitute in favour of the subsidized activity or away from the taxed activity. The extent of substitution may increase over time either because investment horizons are long (involving long-lived, specialized assets) or because the invention of substitutes which either escape tax or qualify for (more) subsidy is encouraged. Substitution may be discouraged by further regulation. This too is costly.

Increased substitutability erodes the tax base and/or dissipates the subsidy, thereby discouraging regulatory and other forms of wealth transfer. If substitutability increases over time, regulation will become increasingly difficult to sustain and deregulation may follow.

7.2 Is there a Bias against Deregulation?

A number of authors maintain that the tendency of regulated industries is not toward deregulation but toward the entrenchment of regulation. There are two types of arguments. The first is that regulation increases the political constituency in favour of continued regulation. The second is that, given the political influence of contending interest groups, the incentive is greater to seek regulation than deregulation.

Noll and Owen (1983) argue that, over time, the beneficiaries of regulation will grow (hence in political influence), while groups that lose will contract. In other words, as some exit the taxed activity, others will enter the subsidized activity. The community with a vested interest in regulation is further expanded if there are unintended beneficiaries from regulation.

This argument is not compelling for a number of reasons. First, while exit from the taxed activity implies that there are fewer voters engaged in that activity, it also erodes the tax base. Similarly, entry into the subsidized activity implies more voters with an interest in it but with a reduced interest per voter.

Second, exit from the taxed activity and entry to the subsidized activity need not change the political balance. The lobby for subsidy includes both current and potential beneficiaries while the lobby against taxation would not derive strength from current marginal (low rent or no rent) participants in the taxed activity. Potential entry and exit are thus already reflected in the pre-exit and pre-entry political effectiveness of the contending interest groups. There will, of course, be unintended beneficiaries from regulation. There will also be unintended losers. There is no reason to believe that the unintended effects of regulation should increase the effectiveness of the subsidized relative to the taxed interest group.

Noll and Owen also argue that once regulation is in place its characteristics and consequences are known while the consequences of deregulation are a matter of conjecture. While the assertions of all contending interest groups are likely to be discounted by the average voter or legislator as self-interested, the assertions of regulated firms being, in a sense, "on the inside" may be more plausible and more persuasive than the arguments of outsiders (i.e., those without industry expertise). Of course, those groups seeking new regulation must also overcome an imperfect information problem. It is quite possible that imperfect information burdens any attempt to change the status quo whether this involves regulation or deregulation.

Given interest group structure, substitutability, and information, McCormick et al. (1984) offer two reasons why the incentive to regulate is greater than the incentive to deregulate. The first is that the cost of seeking regulation may be as much as the present value of the anticipated wealth transfer involved, and if this cost is sunk it is not recoverable in the event of deregulation. These authors reason that, because the amount of the transfer has effectively been lost to the economy, no one gains from deregulation and thus it receives little political support. This argument is false. As Cherkes et al. (1986) point out, the gain to consumers from eliminating monopoly power is the same whether the cost of obtaining the monopoly is sunk or not. More generally, the incentive of the taxed group to oppose the continuation of a tax is the same whether the initial cost of seeking or opposing the tax is sunk or not.

The second argument of McCormick et al. is that, if regulation increases the marginal cost of production, both the increase in consumer surplus and the increase in total surplus resulting from deregulation (i.e., expanding output) are smaller than the initial losses in consumers and total surplus due to regulation. Under these circumstances consumers have less incentive to lobby for deregulation than to oppose regulation when it is proposed. If they fail to stop the introduction of regulation they are even less likely to obtain its removal. Lott and Reynolds (1989) point out that this argument is false if deregulation results in the decline of marginal cost to its initial value. The latter scenario appears the more probable (see section 9).

8. Evidence Regarding Factors Contributing to Deregulation

The theories of regulation discussed in sections 3 to 5 suggest that deregulation should be associated with the presence of new information, increased substitutability, and changes in interest group characteristics. New information plays a role in all theories. For the public interest theory, information that regulation no longer serves the public interest or never has is decisive. For the special interest theory, new information changes relative political effectiveness. In particular, the emergence of a comparable unregulated market may provide the taxed group with better information regarding the magnitude of the regulatory tax burden it is bearing. Armed with this new information, members of the taxed group may find it less costly to organize their opposition.

The demonstration effect of unregulated markets has been cited as playing an important role in a number of instances. Bailey et al. (1985) cite the importance of the unregulated intrastate air carriers in California and Texas in demonstrating the costs of interstate air transport regulation in the United States. Robyn (1987) notes that the fare reductions resulting from airline deregulation helped to convince opponents of interstate trucking regulation in the U.S. that efforts to eliminate it would be worthwhile. The demonstration effect of the U.S. experience has played a role in Canadian deregulation of air transportation and trucking (Schultz and Alexandroff 1985; Ludwick and Associates, 1987). Note, however, that deregulation of financial services in Canada has led, not followed, the U.S., and the regulation of long distance telecommunications in Canada seems not much influenced by the spectacular deregulation that has occurred in the U.S.

The role of new information is also stressed by political scientists studying deregulation. In their examination of the factors leading to the deregulation of the U.S. airline, trucking, and telecommunications industries, Derthick and Quirk (1985), Robyn (1987), and Quirk (1988) emphasize the changes in intellectual climate and political entrepreneurship in both the legislative and executive branches.

The implication of the view that "ideas matter" is that regulation is intended to serve the general interest rather than special interests. The problem is that politicians and voters are often mistaken as to what policies serve the general interest. It follows that economic studies demonstrating that regulation has benefited the few at the expense of the many and that it has resulted in large deadweight losses along the way constitute new information which may lead to a change in government policy.

There is no question that the intellectual climate of opinion regarding regulation has changed. In his 1964 presidential address to the American Economics Association, George Stigler characterized the approach of the economics profession to regulation as one of simply assuming that regulation reduced the inefficiencies endemic in markets (reprinted in Stigler, 1965). Stigler's admonition to demonstrate rather than assume the consequences of regulation is somewhat ironic for it implies that at least some regulation is the result of a mistaken attempt to serve the public interest rather than knowingly serve special interests, as his 1971 theory suggests.

Increased substitutability should act to discourage special interest and public finance regulation by eroding the regulatory tax base, increasing the deadweight loss associated with a given wealth transfer, and providing the taxed group an incentive to oppose the transfer. It may also contribute to the dissipation of the subsidy, thus reducing the initial incentive to seek it.

Increased substitutability has figured in a number of recent incidents of deregulation in Canada and the United States. McManus (1979) argues that truck competition eliminated the tax base available for the cross-subsidization of rail passenger service and grain movement, ultimately leading to the deregulation of railways in Canada. Peltzman (1989) makes a similar argument with respect to U.S. railways. Others point out, however, that railway deregulation in the U.S. lagged the exhaustion of the regulatory tax base by many years (Noll, 1989).

Schultz and Alexandroff (1985) and Ludwick and Associates (1987) find that the loss of passengers to U.S. carriers contributed to the deregulation of Canadian airlines. Substitution of this nature was not a factor in U.S. airline deregulation. While the regulatory tax base appears to have remained intact, some argue that attempts by the airlines to engross a larger portion of the excess profits made possible by regulation dissipated these profits and eliminated the incentive to lobby for continued regulation (Becker, 1985; Peltzman, 1989). Others dispute the assertion that significant dissipation occurred or that support for regulation waned within the airline industry (Levine, 1989). Substitution away from the regulated product also contributed to the deregulation of brokerage commissions on the New York Stock Exchange (Jarrell, 1982) and to the elimination of regulatory ceilings on bank deposit rates in the U.S. (Hammond and Knott, 1988; Peltzman, 1989).

The absence of significant cross-border substitution may have been one of the factors retarding deregulation of telecommunications in Canada in the face of a massive U.S. deregulation. Globerman (1988) reports that diversion of Canadian traffic to lower cost U.S. long distance carriers has been minimal.

Little evidence is available on the role played by changes in the structure of interest groups in bringing about deregulation. The deregulation or, more properly, the elimination of regulatory sanctions for collective commission setting by brokers on the New York Stock Exchange (NYSE) was, according to Jarrell (1982), due in part to the emergence of a strong contending interest group in the form of institutional traders. The institutional traders changed the political balance and increased the elasticity of demand for the NYSE's services by trading on other exchanges. These actions also split the ranks of the NYSE members on the basis of willingness to compete for institutional business and reduced their political effectiveness.

Changes in interest group structure are not cited in other cases of deregulation. Indeed, in some cases commentators have noted explicitly that deregulation has occurred without any change in the structure of the contending interest groups. For instance, trucking deregulation occurred in the U.S. without any erosion of the regulatory tax base and any measurable change in the ability of the trucking lobby to deliver votes and financial support. Robyn's account emphasizes the role of ideas, to wit, the idea that deregulation could reduce trucking costs and the role of political and bureaucratic entrepreneurship, specifically the determination of the Carter administration to be seen as doing something about inflation.

To summarize this highly impressionistic survey, new information and demonstration effects have contributed to deregulation in some cases. The erosion of the regulatory tax base as a result of substitution away from the regulated product has frequently played a role as has the dissipation of surplus by the regulated industry. Changes in interest group structure have not been important.

While this is not a remotely definitive test of the special interest group theory, it must nevertheless be concluded that the theory does not do particularly well in explaining the major incidents of deregulation which have occurred in the U.S. These have generally occurred without a discernible change in interest group structure. New information and demonstration effects have mattered but these are consistent with either a public interest or special interest explanation.

Increased substitutability, the erosion of the regulatory tax base, and the dissipation of surplus have been important and these are consistent with a special interest explanation. Peltzman (1989) concludes that these factors were present in five of the seven incidents of deregulation he examined. He regards this as confirming the importance of the special interest theory.

Others have pointed out that, while these factors may have been present at the time of deregulation, they were also present for various lengths of time prior to deregulation. The theory does not do well with respect to timing. The concentration of the major U.S. deregulations in the 1970s suggests that both common as well as industry-specific factors were at work. Among those common factors that have been suggested are the increased complexity of regulation due to the volatility of interest rates and of energy and other prices. This volatility was in part a consequence of the inflation experienced during the 1970s. This, together with the political opportunity presented by being seen to "solve" the inflation problem, may explain the timing of major U.S. deregulations.

It is also important to note that while the erosion of the regulatory tax base eliminates the opportunity for regulatory wealth transfers, it does not reflect whether these transfers served the general interest or special interests. When the opportunity for cross-subsidization disappears so, ultimately, does cross-subsidization.

9. The Theories of Regulation and the Consequences of Deregulation

Another source of evidence on the balance of general and special interests underlying a regulatory regime is the price, profit, and product quality consequences of its elimination. Who has gained from deregulation? The best evidence on the consequences of deregulation comes from the U.S. airline, motor carrier, brokerage, and telecommunications industries. The consequences of U.S. airline deregulation are assessed by Moore (1986) as "mainly beneficial" with some fare rebalancing (relative fares rising on low density routes) and some losses to airline employees. Morris and Winston (1986) conclude that "deregulation has led to a yearly welfare gain to travellers and carriers of roughly $8 billion 1977 dollars without generating any substantial losses to specific groups in society" (p. 51). The magnitude of this gain and the apparent absence of large losses to any particular group lend some support to the view expressed by Levine (1987, 1989) that airline regulation was simply a mistake, a failure to understand where the general interest lay rather than a result of capture by special interests.

With respect to motor carrier deregulation, the evidence is that over $5 billion dollars worth of operating authorities (licences) were rendered almost valueless (Felton and Anderson, 1989). In addition, average length of haul and average load size increased and unit costs fell (McMullen and Stanley, 1988). Rose (1985) provides further evidence that the loosening of regulatory restrictions by the Interstate Commerce Commission (ICC) prior to the passage of the Motor Carrier Act reduced trucking company monopoly profits. The effects of deregulation on trucking company share prices were fully capitalized prior to passage of the Motor Carrier Act (Rose, 1985; Schipper, Thompson, and Weil, 1987).

The evidence here is fairly clear. Regulation involved a large transfer to trucking companies and significant deadweight losses. It would be an excellent illustration of the special interest theory were it not for the truckers' inability to restrain either the ICC or congress from deregulating.

Deregulation of brokerage fees on the New York Stock Exchange resulted in a reduction in the value of NYSE seats and a decline in aggregate broker profits. The anticipated profitability of national publicly traded brokerage firms increased. This case is characterized by the emergence of a contending interest group (large fund managers), a divergence of interest within the brokerage community (national versus New York brokers), and an increased ability to substitute (trade at other exchanges). Of the examples of deregulation which have been examined in detail this is the most compatible with the special interest theory.

MacDonald (1989) provides a comprehensive analysis of the consequences of railway deregulation for agricultural shippers in the United States. The general decline in freight rates for grain and the rapid spread of unit-train and multiple-car shipments lead him to reject the hypothesis that regulation benefited all agricultural shippers in favour of the hypothesis that regulation benefited small agricultural shippers at the expense of large ones in areas where the railways were sheltered from intermodal (barge) competition. It is not clear from MacDonald's discussion whether regulation also served to increase railway profits.

Other studies of railway deregulation in the U.S. (Grimm and Smith, 1986) and in Canada (Tansz, 1988) conclude that railway deregulation has resulted in lower rates and better service. MacDonald reasons that these lower rates are probably a result of efficiency improvements rather than reductions in monopoly profit.

With respect to telecommunications, Perl (1990) concludes that deregulation facilitated a rebalancing of long distance and local telephone rates resulting in annual welfare gains in the amount of $3.8-$4.2 billion while maintaining the universality of the service.

This cursory review of the evidence yields the following tentative conclusions. First, the effect of deregulation has been salutary in the sense that it has resulted in welfare gains from both the restoration of cost-based pricing and from real cost savings. Second, deregulation has resulted in wealth transfers among producers, among consumers, and between producers and consumers. Cross-subsidization appears to have been a prominent feature of telecommunications regulation and perhaps railway regulation. The other regimes do not appear to have been serving any public interest or public finance purpose at the time of deregulation. Whether they had ever been intended to do so cannot be determined from this evidence.

10. Conclusion: Is there a Canadian Theory of Deregulation?

The public and special interest theories of regulation have rightly been criticized for their vagueness regarding transactions in political markets. In the simplest terms the political decision process is still a black box. Moreover, as Noll (1987) and others have concluded, empirical work in this area lags theory. As it stands, the evidence on deregulation supports an eclectic theory of deregulation embracing both the public and special interest theories. The two are part of a continuum. Regulation is used to effect wealth transfers. These transfers may benefit highly concentrated special interest groups, such as taxicab owners. They may also benefit larger groups, such as residential telephone subscribers, potential auto workers, or the residents of Alberta. Some regulatory regimes would be approved by a majority in a direct vote. Others would not. Some are difficult to categorize.

In seeking regulatory benefits, special interests cloak their arguments in the public interest. A consequence of this is that ideas matter and that there is political opportunity in introducing new ones or repackaging old ones. This may account for the problem the public special interest theories have in explaining the timing of deregulation. It is not only necessary for the regulatory tax base to be eroded, for example, but also for this to be seen as the case. The two events may be widely separated in time.

In a Canadian context future deregulation is likely to be associated with several factors. First, the demonstration and, more importantly, diversion effects principally from less regulated U.S. industries. Second, the erosion of the regulatory tax base through domestic interindustry substitution and the dissipation of subsidies together with the complexity of the additional regulation necessary to prevent this will continue to be factors. And finally, the industrial development aspirations of provincial governments and the extent to which they are compatible with existing regulatory regimes will also play a role.

References

Acheson, K. (1989), "Power Steering the Canadian Automotive Industry," *Journal of Economic Behaviour and Organization* 11, pp. 337-51.

Bailey, E., D. Graham and D. Kaplan (1985), *Deregulating the Airlines* (Cambridge: MIT Press).

Baldwin, J. (1975), *The Regulatory Agency and the Public Corporation* (Cambridge: Ballinger).

Baldwin, J. (1982), "Federal Regulation and Public Policy in the Canadian Petroleum Industry: 1958-1975,"*Journal of Business Administration* vol. 13, no. 1-2, pp. 57-98.

Baldwin, J. (1989), *Regulatory Failure and Renewal: The Evolution of the Natural Monopoly Contract* (Ottawa: Economic Council of Canada).

Becker, G. (1983), "A Theory of Competition Among Pressure Groups for Political Influence,"*The Quarterly Journal of Economics* 98 (August), pp. 371-400.

Becker, G. (1985). "Public Policies, Pressure Groups and Deadweight Costs,"*Journal of Public Economics* 28, pp. 329-47.

Blais, A., J.M. Cousineau and K. McRoberts (1989), "The Determinants of Minimum Wage Rates,"*Public Choice* 62, pp. 15-24.

Breslau, J. and J. Smith (1982), "Efficiency, Equity and Regulation: An Optimal Pricing Model for Bell Canada," *Canadian Journal of Economics* 15 (November), pp. 634-48.

Cherkes, M., J. Friedman and A. Spivak (1986), "The Disinterest in Deregulation: A Comment," *American Economic Review* 76 (June), pp. 559-63.

Courchene, T. (1990), *Quebec Inc.: Foreign Takeovers, Competition/Merger Policy and Universal Banking* (Kingston: School of Policy Studies, Queen's University).

Demsetz, H. (1968), "Why Regulate Utilities?" *Journal of Law and Economics* 11 (April), pp. 55-66.

Derthick, M. and P. Quirk (1985), *The Politics of Deregulation* (Washington: Brookings).

Felton, J. and D. Anderson (1989), *Regulation and Deregulation of the Motor Carrier Industry* (Ames, Iowa: Iowa State University Press).

Globerman, S. (1986), "Economic Factors in Telecommunications Policy and Regulation" in W.T. Stanbury ed. *Telecommunications Policy and*

Regulation: The Impact of Competition and Technological Change (Montreal: Institute for Research on Public Policy), pp. 1-80.

Globerman, S. (1988), *Telecommunications in Canada* (Vancouver: The Fraser Institute).

Globerman, S. and W. Stanbury (1986), "Changing the Telephone Pricing Structure: Allocative, Distributional and Political Considerations," *Canadian Public Policy* 12 (March), pp. 214-26.

Goldberg, V. (1976), "Regulation and Administered Contracts," *The Bell Journal of Economics* 7 (Autumn), pp. 426-48.

Grimm, C. and K. Smith (1986), "The Impact of Rail Regulatory Reform on Rates, Service Quality and Management Performance: A Shipper Perspective," *The Logistics and Transportation Review* 22 (March), pp. 57-68..

Hammond, T. and J. Knott (1988), "The Deregulation Snowball: Explaining Deregulation in the Financial Industry," *Journal of Politics* 50 (February), pp. 3-29.

Jarrell, G. (1984), "Change at the Exchange: The Causes and Effects of Deregulation," *Journal of Law and Economics* 27 (October), pp. 273-312.

Kalt, J. and Zupan (1984), "Capture and Ideology in the Economic Theory of Politics," *American Economic Review* 74, pp. 279-300.

Leland, H. (1979), "Quacks, Lemons and Licensing: A Theory of Minimum Quality Standards," *Journal of Political Economy* 87, pp. 1328-46.

Levine, M. (1987), "Airline Competition in Deregulated Markets: Theory, Firm Strategy and Public Policy," *Yale Journal on Regulation* (Spring), pp. 393-494.

Levine, M. (1989), "Comments and Discussion," *Brookings Papers on Economic Activity: Microeconomics 1989*, pp. 42-48.

Lott, J. and M. Reynolds (1989), "Production Costs and Deregulation," *Public Choice* 61, pp. 183-86.

Ludwick, E. and Associates (1987), "The Canadian Transportation Industry in a Deregulated and Free Trade Environment" (Halifax: Institute for Research on Public Policy Series on Trade in Services).

MacDonald, J. (1989), "Railroad Deregulation, Innovation, and Competition: Effects of the Staggers Act on Grain Transportation," *Journal of Law and Economics* 32 (April), pp. 63-93.

McCormick, R., W. Shugart and R. Tollison (1984), "The Disinterest in Deregulation,"*American Economic Review* 74 (December), pp. 1075-79.

McManus, J. (1979), "On the New National Transportation Policy After Ten Years," *The Logistics and Transportation Review* vol. 15, no. 1, pp. 209-30.

McMullen, B. and L. Stanley (1988), "The Impact of Deregulation on the Production Structure of the Motor Carrier Industry," *Economic Inquiry* 26 (April), pp. 299-316.

McNish, J. (1989), "Parizeau Embodied in Quebec Reforms," *Globe and Mail Report on Business* (March 21), p. B1, B4.

Moore, T. (1986), "U.S. Airline Deregulation: Its Effects on Passengers, Capital and Labor," *Journal of Law and Economics* (April), pp. 1-28.

Morris, S. and C. Winston (1986), *The Economic Effects of Airline Deregulation* (Washington: Brookings).

Noll, R. and B. Owen (1983), *The Political Economic of Deregulation* (Washington: American Enterprise Institute).

Noll, R. (1987), "Economic Perspectives on the Politics of Regulation," Discussion Paper No. 137 (Stanford, California: Workshop on Applied Microeconomics, Department of Economics, Stanford University).

Noll, R. (1989), "Comments and Discussion," *Brookings Papers on Economic Activity: Microeconomics 1989* (Washington, D.C.: Brookings) pp. 48-58.

Olsen, M. (1982), *The Rise and Decline of Nations* (New Haven: Yale University Press).

Peltzman, S. (1976), "Toward a More General Theory of Regulation," *Journal of Law and Economics* 19 (August), pp. 211-40.

Peltzman, S. (1984), "Constituent Interest and Congressional Voting," *Journal of Law and Economics* 27 (April), pp. 181-210.

Peltzman, S. (1989), "The Economic Theory of Regulation after a Decade of Deregulation," *Brookings Papers on Economic Activity: Microeconomics 1989* (Washington, D.C.: Brookings) pp. 1-41.

Perl, L. (1990), "Changes in U.S. Telecommunications Regulation: A Quantitative Evaluation" (paper presented to "Telecommunications in Canada," a *Financial Post* Conference, Toronto).

Posner, R. (1971), "Taxation by Regulation," *Bell Journal of Economics and Management Science* 2 (Spring), pp. 22-50.

Posner, R. (1974), "Theories of Economic Regulation," *Bell Journal of Economics and Management Sciences* (Autumn), pp. 335-58.

Quirk, P. (1988), "In Defense of the Politics of Ideas," *The Journal of Politics* 50 (February), pp. 31-34.

Robyn, D. (1987), *Breaking the Special Interests* (Chicago: University of Chicago Press).

Romer, T. and H. Rosenthal (1987), "Modern Political Economy and the Study of Regulation," in E. Bailey ed. *Public Regulation* (Cambridge, Mass.: MIT Press).

Rose, N. (1985), "The Incidence of Regulatory Rents in the Motor Carrier Industry," *Rand Journal of Economics* 516 (Autumn), pp. 299-318.

Schultz, R. and A. Alexandroff (1985), *Economic Regulation and the Federal System* (Toronto: University of Toronto Press).

Stanbury, W.T. (1987), "Direct Regulation and Its Reform: A Canadian Perspective," *Brigham Young University Law Review* vol. 1987, no. 2, pp. 467-539.

Schipper, K., R. Thompson and R. Weil (1987), "Disentangling Interrelated Effects of Regulatory Changes on Shareholder Wealth: The Case of Motor Carrier Deregulation," *Journal of Law and Economics* (April), pp. 67-100.

Stigler, G. (1965), "The Economist and the State," *American Economic Review* (March).

Stigler, G. (1971), "The Theory of Economic Regulation," *Bell Journal of Economics and Management Science* 2 (Spring), pp. 3-21.

Stigler, G. (1974), "Free Riders and Collective Action: An Appendix to Theories of Economic Regulation," *Bell Journal of Economics and Management Science* 5 (Autumn), pp. 359-65.

Tansz, A. (1988), "Shippers Like Deregulated Railways," *Transportation Business* (October), p. 10.

Trebilcock, M. et al. (1982), *The Choice of Governing Instrument* (Ottawa: Economic Council of Canada).

Williamson, O. (1976), "Franchise Bidding for Natural Monopolies: In General and with Respect to CATV," *Bell Journal of Economics and Management Science* 7 (Spring), pp. 73-104.

Discussion of the McFetridge Paper

John Baldwin

McFetridge had a very difficult task set for him. He was asked to describe and distinguish various models of regulation in order to evaluate whether there is a good "general" theory of regulation; to provide the means by which we could discriminate among the several theories that he chose to evaluate; to evaluate the success of the profession in doing so; to ask how the deregulation literature extends our ability to distinguish among the various theories; and to ask how the Canadian regulatory experience adds to our knowledge. McFetridge's task was especially daunting because he was restricted to writing a paper of thirty pages or less.

I enjoyed reading McFetridge's paper, because he summarized many of the models especially well and also because he left me with a number of issues to think about. Economists have a difficult task in analyzing the regulatory process. We don't have, as McFetridge recognizes, a sufficiently large number of cases to allow us to test a variety of models. In many instances, therefore, our attempts to investigate what is happening behind the scenes of the regulatory process and to test a general theory of regulation must deal with few observations. Despite this, I think progress is possible, even if we sometimes have to adopt the political scientists' approach of sorting through many events in order to isolate alleged causes and effects, an effort that generally turns into a taxonomy which fails to explain regulatory outcomes deductively from a general theory.

With the above caveats stated, let me turn now to McFetridge's attempts to draw distinctions between the various theories—the public interest theory, the special interest or capture theory, and what he calls the public finance theory.

First, I have difficulty distinguishing between the capture theory and McFetridge's public finance theory. These theories place only a slightly different emphasis on the role of various special interest groups. But I don't think McFetridge would disagree with that. I tend to agree with him that his adduced evidence of deregulation is often perfectly capable of supporting a pure public interest theory on the one hand or one among many variations of capture theories on the other. But that is also the case when looking at theories explaining the establishment of regulation. It is often difficult to distinguish between the two classes of models of the political process. Evidence for a capture theory often comes from the observation of differential prices and the appearance of cross-subsidization of one group by another. But in a model where natural monopolies and economies of scale exist, differential prices that lead to cross-subsidization can also turn out to be optimal in welfare economic theory. In such cases, and there are many, what at first blush appears to be evidence for a capture theory can also be justified by a public interest argument. Whether we look at the origins of regulation or deregulation, it is difficult for the profession to distinguish between the capture theory and the public interest theory.

Second, I have some difficulty with analytical approaches that attempt to explain the origins of regulation or deregulation based on a single event. The process of regulation and deregulation in every industry has evolved over an extended time. For instance, from my analysis of the Canadian airline industry, I observed various periods of regulatory or deregulatory change that date back to the mid-1960s. Therefore, when economists try to apply a theory to a particular industry, they have to look at a great number of such distinct events. Some events may seem to conform with one theory, while others conform with another, despite the apparent stability of the affected stakeholder groups' political status. Since the turn of the century, the Canadian railway industry has experienced at least seventeen different major events that either led to a major increase in regulation or a significant decrease in regulation.

Despite the difficulties in trying to discriminate among alternative models of regulatory political behaviour, the economic analysis of these events is superior to the standard political science approach. A political scientist will claim that the public expressions of public and private interests—ideology—are all that matter to the political process. We do not have to accept that ideology is exogenously determined. We can ask whether or not changes in the regulatory environment that seem to be associated with a change in ideology can be placed within a standard context of changes in objectives, changes in costs of instruments, and to some extent changes in the circumstances of different interest groups.

Let me turn to one major difficulty I have with McFetridge's conclusions. He feels that there are substantial problems with the set of theories economists draw upon to structure their understanding of regulatory markets. Two conflicting economic theories—the public interest theory and the capture theory—fail to encompass relevant non-industry related influences, such as the role of ideas and political entrepreneurship. McFetridge recognizes that the capture theory is weak because it appears that very few people gain at the penultimate or ultimate step of deregulation, which convinces him that this theory is probably an incomplete model of the regulatory process. But identification of a public interest model in any particular event is equally elusive. One has to look back in time and examine the evolution of regulation to draw a conclusion. For example, the U.S. literature on the airline industry amply illustrates the regulatory authority's control loss over an extended period. Gradually, prices that were above cost levels, initially used to transfer benefits among groups (combining the interest group and public finance motives), were eroded by competition for franchise rights, with the evolution of substitutes. Eventually, support for regulation disappeared as its benefits eroded for all constituencies. Either private interest had in some sense captured and exhausted the available public benefits, or the regulatory process had failed to maintain itself. But one could argue equally well that a public interest model of regulation simply went awry. The public interest model that guided regulatory managers had failed to reach its objective, and so they finally gave up on the effort. In this particular example it is difficult to distinguish between a public interest theory and a private interest theory.

Finally, one point in McFetridge's concluding section gives me difficulty. It is the notion that regional groups have different impacts on regulation in Canada than in the United States. No doubt the provinces are actors in the regulatory game in this country; however, states and regions are also actors in the United States, but in a different way because of a different legislative system. Certainly, the history of airline and telecommunication regulations showed that the states via their local representatives lobbied for various policies to be followed at a national level. I do not think it is true that we have a stronger public finance motive in this country.

Discussion of the McFetridge Paper

William G. Watson

To place this paper in the literature, it is a Canadian version of the sort of thing Sam Peltzman has done in the *Brookings Papers* (Peltzman, 1989). It is also more than that, since it presents a somewhat different typology of regulation, but it addresses the same question in positive economics as Peltzman does, namely, what explains which industries get deregulated and which don't? I'm not sure the paper succeeds in answering this question—I'm not sure Peltzman's does, either—but I very much enjoyed the attempt and I learned a lot from it. This is the sort of study that might easily—or at least profitably—be turned into a book. At every turn, the reader hankers after more and more institutional and political detail. I would love to read a book-length version of this story, though I can understand why McFetridge might not wish to produce it.

As suggested, the problem at hand is a positive one. We have seen the deregulation of transport, energy, telecommunications, and, in part, financial services. The questions the paper asks are: Why now? Why all at the same time? And why these industries and not others? Of course, there's a corollary question that normally doesn't get asked, and in fact doesn't get asked here: Why has deregulation failed in the many other industries in which it *hasn't* occurred? John Baldwin complained about the small number of data points we have in this area. I disagree. We have a very large number of data points: we have virtually the entire economy. Lots of people, certainly lots of Fraser Institute people, have been urging deregulation in many other areas of the economy and haven't succeeded, and, of course, we have had massive new regulation in still other areas. This is information any study of deregulation should take into account. I do understand why it is tempting to focus on areas where we have seen deregulation succeed, but, in a sense, these four industries where deregulation has occurred must be seen as pathological cases.

To the person on the street, the answer to the positive questions that have been posed is very simple: this is the age of Thatcher and Reagan—and, in this country, their imperfect clone, Mulroney. In the popular view, political vogue is what has produced deregulation, while what has produced political vogue is ideology. In short, ideas count and the ideas that count these days are right-wing, pro-market, anti-interventionist, and deregulationist.

To state the argument this baldly is, of course, to suggest it is not true. I was cleaning up my office the other day, something done every ten years whether it needs it or not, and came across a cover story from *Fortune* for May, 1981, titled "Mrs. Thatcher: Why She May Yet Succeed." Widely regarded as a failure in early 1981, Mrs. Thatcher obviously has succeeded masterfully since. But the lesson is that events appearing inevitable in retrospect certainly need not appear inevitable at the time.[1] That a sweeping ideological revolution was such a close-run thing suggests that, in fact, it wasn't all that sweeping to begin with.

My view is that there has been a slight change in what might be termed "the intellectual climate." In 1985 it did not seem possible to talk about the privatization of Air Canada as a realistic possibility. By 1989, the deed was done. We now even have a minister of the Crown willing to talk about privatizing the post office. Many of us have proposed this at conferences such as this, but now the minister is talking about it in public without appearing to have suffered for it, though I suppose we will find out at the next election just how successful his talks have been. The important point is that there are options that now can be stated in public that were politically very risky to mention just a few years ago.

On the other hand, if we put our faith in the general public's conversion to relatively sophisticated economic good sense, our faith is misplaced. The massive new regulation of the labour market that took place in the 1980s, in the form of employment equity and equal pay for work of equal value, is on a scale and of a ferocity that would do the late Ayatollah proud. In my own province, the economics taught in high schools is essentially Naderism. The curriculum is devoted mainly to explaining why the political system must regulate the behaviour of large corporations, which never are to be trusted. Perhaps the high schools are inevitably 20 years behind the intellectual vanguard. Perhaps this means that in 2005 they will be using texts published by the Fraser Institute. But before then, hordes of Naderized young people will be participating in the political system. This does not augur well for a grass-roots deregulationist movement. Most proposals for environmental regulation are precisely that, environmental *regulation*.

What Dick Lipsey has called the "Great Free Trade Debate" of 1987 and 1988 indicates that there is still a good deal of economics education needed in this country. As things stand, the most convincing corollary to the proposition

---

1   As an aside, I say thank God for Argentina. Without its attack on the Falklands we probably would not have had Thatcherism through the 1980s. The "Reagan-Foot Era" has nothing like the same ring. Nor would it have had the same effect on social policies in the West.

that ideas are important is that dumb ideas remain most important of all. As Lipsey himself has said, the dialectics are skewed against good sense. Somebody will say something in one sentence that is completely stupid but it takes several minutes of explanation to make clear exactly why it is stupid, by which time a commercial has intervened or the audience's attention span has expired. But most of us here are in this business and we know how difficult it can be to get these ideas across.

It seems to me that what the intellectual climate does is to establish what the clear non-starters are. There are areas of the economy, back-room areas, hidden-away areas, where the work of experts, including economists, clearly is consequential, perhaps even decisive.[2] On the other hand, what politicians are most afraid of is to have one of these arcane policy areas suddenly become the object of extensive scrutiny by the media. I suspect this explains the snail's pace of financial deregulation at the federal level. No Minister wants a technically sensible policy initiative to blow up in his or her face, with the result that he is ridiculed on "The Journal" or elsewhere. To take another concrete example, in the age of computer electronics, local metering of telephone service is probably a sensible idea. But while it might take several minutes to explain why a sensible local metering scheme could be set up, it takes only a few seconds to get peoples' backs up about it.

So I am not wholly convinced, as I believe is the case for McFetridge, as far as stories about changes in ideology or the intellectual climate are concerned. At most, such changes may alter the burden of proof, so that defenders of regulation must be more adroit in their defence. And they may broaden the range of questions that can be asked. But while there is a feeling in the country now that new and more fundamental questions can be asked, it is not clear by any means that the deregulationists have won the day. Events in the labour market are not the only evidence of this. As mentioned, the virtually universal response to our born-again[3] concern for the environment is that the government should engage in the most brutish forms of direct regulation of industrial processes.

To take the question down to the industry level, the message I get from McFetridge's paper, and I think it is Peltzman's message as well, is that what has had the most to do with the deregulation that has taken place in these industries are specific changes in their technologies and other objective circumstances. I find this argument very persuasive, if also very discouraging for

---

2 Monetary policy is clearly an example, though perhaps an example that proves the rule, since it is conducted by an unelected official.

3 Does no one out there remember the 1970s?

free-marketeers. In fact, I'm not so hard on the tax-elasticity argument as he is. That rents get competed down to zero strikes me as a perfectly satisfactory explanation for the withering away of rent-seeking.[4] The seeking no longer occurs because the rent is no longer there to be sought. I agree there is not much predictive power in this line of thinking. To achieve predictive power would require us to foretell in which areas of the economy, and at what pace, technological change will succeed in destroying rents, and if we knew that, we would be silly to keep doing economics. But it does "explain" *ex post facto* very well indeed, and in the industries in question, it does seem to have been important.

An alternative hypothesis, very much in the Becker tradition, is that the relative importance of interest groups will change over time. McFetridge argues that in fact the league table of interest groups does not change very much, or at least changes very slowly in comparison to the rate at which other things change. That probably is true; on the other hand, many of the policy changes he has examined have taken place very slowly. In several cases in the U.S. it has taken 30 or 40 years to get industries out of their regulatory clothing.

There are also, of course, purely random elements in the deregulation movement. Had the Teamsters not developed the habit of dressing their political enemies in cement and depositing them into rivers, or had not allied themselves politically with the only U.S. president ever to resign from office, deregulation of trucking might not have been so popular politically. There is also no way to capture something like the generation-long Kennedy-Teamster vendetta. It is no accident, comrade, that Edward Kennedy chaired the congressional committee that oversaw deregulation of trucking. In a world of infinite examples of regulation and deregulation, such details would cancel out across industries. But where only four or five industries are being studied, they can be discouragingly important.

A third possible influence on deregulation—and, many think, a potential antidote to excessive regulation—is changes in the way public decisions are made. I was happy to learn from Tony Campbell that more information about possible economic costs is now required within the bureaucracy from anyone who proposes a regulatory change. It will be interesting to see over the next decade or two whether this requirement in fact discourages the proliferation of regulation. I'm not convinced that it will.

I disagree with McFetridge on one technical point. It is unclear to me that there is any systematic connection between his various theories of regulation and the voter support that might attach to any given example of regulation. If

---

4   Rather than unsatisfactorily perfect, i.e., tautological, as he seems to think it.

public interest regulation involves a true Pareto improvement, then it should get unanimous approval at the ballot box, though, of course, we hardly ever vote on these things. Neither do we insist on the redistribution that normally is required in order to change a potential Pareto improvement into an actual Pareto improvement. So, in theory, a policy could receive the support of only one member of society and still constitute a potential Pareto improvement and thus be motivated by public interest concerns. By contrast, many capture-theory policies could receive much wider public support, even majority support, though obviously not unanimous support. Since not much use is made of these distinctions in McFetridge's paper, however, this is more a quibble than anything else.

In sum, I like this kind of analysis. The metaphor it suggests is of putting regulatory clothing on an industry. The public interest suit may fit when the regulations first go on, but as the industry develops over time, the suit may start to impose some uncomfortable constraints. The regulatory clothing that may satisfy public interest demands in one era may cause problems later on. I think this is a natural domain for the contemporary economic historian and I hope we will have more such work in future.

On the other hand, it is difficult work. I wrote a similar piece of analysis on the free trade debate in which I tried to explain why the Mulroney government opted for free trade (Watson, 1987). Were there changes in the objective circumstances of the economy that pointed in that direction? Were there ideological changes or changes in the influence of interest groups? My conclusion was that you could not rule out the possibility that the decision was a political mistake. You couldn't explain it as a sensible political decision. So if the opposition hadn't been headed by an inept leader, the deal might well have not gone through. But while difficult, this kind of politico-economic analysis strikes me as very important. We should always be talking about what is actually going on.

References

Peltzman, Sam (1989) "The Economic Theory of Regulation after a Decade of Deregulation," *Brookings Papers on Economic Activity: Microeconomics 1989*, (Washington, D.C.: Brookings Institution), pp. 1-41.

Watson, William G. (1987), "Canada-U.S. Free Trade: Why Now?" *Analyse de Politique—Canadian Public Policy* XIII, 3, pp. 337-49.

Chapter 3

Crumbling Pillars:
Creative Destruction or Cavalier Demolition?

Thomas J. Courchene

An examination of national financial structures can illuminate the economic strategies of these governments and the political conflicts that accompany economic adjustment. The particular arrangements of national financial systems limit both the marketplace options of firms and the administrative choices of government. That is, financial markets in each country are one element that delimits the ways in which business and the state can interact. The structure of those markets at once influences a government's capacity to exert industrial leadership and the nature of the political conflicts that arise from its economic objectives ...by following the money flows in the market economy and dissecting the institutions that structure that flow, we can learn a great deal about the uses to which the society's resources are put, by whom, and how control is obtained and exerted (John Zysman, 1983, pp. 16-17).

My contention is that a prime but too little spoken about function of government is the organization of financial power within its boundaries. My further contention is that we are currently in the country going through a sea change. Why? Because a couple of years ago Ottawa and the provinces suddenly changed all the rules about the distribution and management of financial power. In fact, I believe that what we did then under the guise of deregulation of financial institutions is without precedent or analogy in the contemporary world...All that is creating a new pattern of distribution of financial or money power which, by the way, is why Ottawa, the ultimate guarantor of power in our political system, is finding it so difficult to come up with new ground rules for financial institutions. Its deregulation process started a kind of realignment of the San Andreas Fault within our financial power system. It is not easy to lay an appropriate grid of roads and avenues until the tremors have subsided and one can gain a clearer view of the new landscape. In the meantime, you try to roll with the punches as best you can and avoid being crushed by the collapsing pillars (André Saumier, 1990, p. 44).

1. Introduction

My assigned role is to focus on developments and issues in the Canadian financial sector. The most appropriate approach to this topic is one that commingles analysis with recent history. The story might begin as far back as the Royal Commission on Banking and Finance in 1964 and the ensuing 1967 Bank Act. It would surely include the 1980 Bank Act and the resulting influx of schedule B banks. In rough chronological order (but not exhaustively) the historical survey would then touch upon the Ontario Securities Commission Report (The Dey Report), the Crown/Seaway/Greymac debacle and resulting reports by Robert Wyman on the role of the Canada Deposit Insurance Corporation (CDIC) and by Stefan Dupré on the Ontario environment, the federal Green Paper, the Northland/CCB (Canadian Commercial Bank) fiasco and ensuing investigation by Justice Estey, the House of Commons' (Blenkarn) Reports, the Senate (Murray) Reports, the federal Blue Paper, the chartered bank take-over of the securities industry, and, most recently, the financial institution provisions of the Canada-U.S. Free Trade Agreement (FTA). To this series of events one must add the intriguing developments at the provincial level (principally the comprehensive initiatives implemented by Quebec's Associate Finance Minister, Pierre Fortier) as well as the never ending parade of financial institution conferences. Moreover, this process is far from over: the Economic Council of Canada is about to release a major study on the financial sector and all players are awaiting Ottawa's new regulations on ownership and powers, at which point the whole process will begin anew—House of Commons and Senate hearings and reports, provincial counter-initiatives and, of course, a new round of financial conferences, many of which are already scheduled. This historical survey would then need to be layered with the underlying policy issues—efficiency, solvency, self-dealing, consumer protection including deposit insurance, ownership, concentration, corporate governance, and the perennial chestnut—federal-provincial jurisdictional and co-ordination issues.

While such a paper obviously deserves to be written, it is, as already hinted, not how I have chosen to approach the topic. In part, this is because I probably cannot approach many of these issues with the required degree of objectivity for a survey essay. For example, in recent papers (1988, 1989) I have already cast my vote in favour of commercial links and in favour of the benefits that can flow from multiple jurisdictions, both of which probably put me offside the analytical mainstream, not to mention the powerful banking lobby. More importantly, I am passing on this approach because a careful evaluation of the pros and cons of the various issues will have very little to do with how financial deregulation will eventually sort itself out. Phrased differently, the forces impinging on financial deregulation cannot easily be accommodated or ameliorated by a rational, internal redesign of the financial sector. For decades, most of the English-speaking world plus Japan had in place some version of Glass-Steagall—the separation of market intermediaries and financial intermediaries. Yet within less than one year the Canadian chartered banks gobbled up over 80 percent of the assets of the Canadian securities industry. If this "one-pillar" model made sense in 1987 and 1988, why not in 1977 or 1947?

More positively, in what follows I shall attempt to document aspects of two powerful forces that are being brought to bear on the redesign of the Canadian financial environment. The first of these is admittedly straightforward—the developments in global finance that led, inevitably, to the integration of the four pillars. The second, only beginning to emerge as a significant force, is far more controversial and, while also driven by globalization, has more to do with concerns arising from the real/commercial side of the economy, namely the initiatives toward universal banking as an overall industrial strategy. Sandwiched between these two sections will be a return to the mainstream, i.e., an assessment, albeit subjective, of some of the bread-and-butter issues relating to financial deregulation.

The philosophy underlying the ensuing analysis reflects the two initial quotes: the structure of the financial sector has implications that transcend the important but more narrow concerns of what might constitute an internally consistent approach to the design of the financial environment. "Financial determinism" may be a strong phrase, but it conveys the basic point that how we restructure our financial sector will reflect the way our citizens, businesses, and governments decide to confront the global economy. No doubt, the impetus for Canadian financial reform now has its roots in the globalization of finance, although it was no doubt triggered initially by the spate of financial institution failures. Once opened, however, this Pandora's box cannot be shut until Canadians sort out how we shall address the forces of integration and restructuring on the commercial side of the economy. These are not only tough issues analytically, they are explosive politically—are the so-called "heritage" firms, such as Stelco, CPR, Bell Canada Enterprises, and Falconbridge, now open to foreign take-overs? The recent swipe at CPR by the Americans has already generated a substantial groundswell of opinion favourable to ensuring that such firms somehow remain in Canadian hands. Unwittingly perhaps, Canadian financial reform is progressively finding itself square in the middle of this "who shall own Canada?" issue, especially since the universal bank route as a means of preserving and enhancing domestic ownership of commercial firms is well on its way to being implemented by the province of Quebec. What may ultimately be at stake in financial deregulation is nothing less than the most significant rethinking of overall industrial strategy since John A. Macdonald's National Policy.

2. The Integration of the Pillars

A: The Pressures for Reform

The Internationalization of Finance

Underlying the ongoing pressures toward more uniform financial regulation across the various national markets is what I shall refer to as the "internationalization" of finance, following de Vries and Caprio (1986). Actually, the term may be somewhat misleading since it could well refer to the overall process whereby national markets are progressively becoming integrated into one international market. I have in mind here something less grandiose, but none the less equally significant, namely the gradual post-war development whereby financial institutions established branches or subsidiaries outside their home countries.

Recent data indicate that there are over 700 foreign banks in the U.S., roughly 550 in the U.K. and from 150 to 400 in countries such as Germany, Switzerland, and France. As a result of the 1980 Bank Act, there are now upwards of 60 schedule B banks in Canada.

The presence of these foreign banks implies that domestic policy authorities and regulatory agencies quickly apprize financial developments and innovations elsewhere in the global system, thereby exerting pressure for more uniform laws and regulations across all jurisdictions. To be sure, this internationalization of finance was not sufficient, of and by itself, to generate uniform national regulatory regimes, as post-war financial history amply demonstrates. None the less, the presence of offshore banking does become a critical catalyst in this regard when the combination of technological advances and global shocks, elaborated below, thrust the global system toward intensified competition and innovation.

There is a second and related aspect of this internationalization of finance that exerts pressure on policy-makers. Increasingly, Canadian governments and large corporate borrowers have been accessing foreign merchant bankers or securities firms for their new issues. Domestic regulatory authorities could always turn a blind eye toward these developments so long as domestic financial players could be assured, through protection or regulation, of a captive domestic market for a substantial subset of these activities. However, the global market-place has now evolved to the point where it is becoming increasingly difficult, and indeed increasingly meaningless, to distinguish between financial transactions that are "foreign" and those that are "domestic." Thus, the pressure on policy-makers intensifies because the sheer mobility of financial services tends to undermine any moves in the direction of keeping markets "captive."

The Mushrooming of the Euro-market

Roughly paralleling, although conceptually distinct from, the internationalization of finance, was the emergence of the Euro-market—the offshore or extra-national market, initially in U.S. dollar financial instruments but increasingly in yen, marks, and other currencies. Lecturers in international finance typically impress their students by ascribing the origins of the Euro-market to the cold war: central banks in Russia and Eastern Europe preferred to leave their dollar balances on deposit with their correspondents in France and Britain rather than in accounts in the United States. Thus, the Moscow Norodny Bank of London is frequently given the honour of creating the first Euro-dollar deposit. (It is probably the case that Canadian banks could claim to have been in the vanguard, if the definition of a Euro-dollar deposit encompassed *any* U.S. dollar deposit outside the United States. Initially, however, Euro-dollars meant U.S. dollar deposits in Europe). In any event, the growth of the Euro-market was driven in large measure by payment imbalances—in rough chronological order, Soviet-bloc money, U.S. deficits associated with Vietnam, the petro-dollar recycling of the 1970s, and more recently, the payment imbalances of the West and the debt burden of the Third World. However, it was the "extra-national" or "supra-national" and, therefore, unregulated feature that lent this market its competitive and innovative qualities. Thus, the fact that U.S. banks emerged as dominant Euro-market players can be traced in large measure to the very restrictive American laws and regulations (e.g., the McFadden Act preventing interstate banking, Glass-Steagall preventing the integration of commercial and investment banking, and provisions like Regulation Q that limited interest rate levels on deposits) which literally drove them offshore in order to acquire freedom to manoeuvre. Indeed, London's current role as a premier, perhaps the premier, world financial centre owes a great deal to the restrictive regulatory regime in the U.S. Had the U.S. financial system been more open, London would not likely have developed its current global financial status.

There is a certain irony in all this. While restrictive U.S. regulations propelled the Euro-market, the immense growth and success of the Euro-market and the rising dominance of non-U.S. financial institutions in this market are now undermining the ability of American legislators to maintain these domestic restrictions. As later sections of this paper will contend, the Americans will probably soon undergo sweeping deregulation, regardless of the fact that Congress currently appears intent on holding the line. In effect, the U.S. is becoming "Canadianized" to the extent that in terms of global finance it too is a small open economy and, hence, ultimately a "price-taker" with respect to financial activities in the rest of the world.

Euro-market Integration
It has become customary in Canada to refer to the "four pillars" of finance—banking, insurance, trusts, and underwriting (securities). The cornerstone of much of post-war Canadian financial policy, both federal and provincial, has been to maintain this separation—in terms of both function and ownership—across the pillars. To be sure, reality was increasingly offside with respect to this conception. Over the recent years the rise of financial conglomerates and the deregulatory process embarked upon by Quebec have served to facilitate integration across the pillars.

In terms of the Euro-market, however, financial integration (i.e., one pillar) has long been the rule rather than the exception. In the United States Glass-Steagall prevents Citicorp from becoming a full service broker but, internationally, Citicorp can probably lay claim to being a member of more stock exchanges than any other financial institution. In Canada the Royal Bank was until recently limited to banking. Internationally, it has operated across all pillars. Orion Royal, its merchant banking arm, acquired Kitcatt and Aitken as its entry into London's Big Bang (although since then the Royal Bank has scaled back its European operations). And thanks to the recent financial deregulation in Australia, the Royal Bank's presence there now embraces all four pillars and even beyond since it is involved in hire-purchase.

Overall, then, the internationalization of finance and the mushrooming of the Euro-market led to the situation where many of the world's largest banks had considerably more ability to manoeuvre internationally than they did in their home jurisdictions. At the best of times, this makes for an uneasy co-existence between the Euro-market and national financial markets. But the last decade or so does not qualify as the "best of times." Enter the spate of global shocks.

The Energy Shocks
The two energy shocks of the 1970s resulted in a dramatic shift in wealth and income from the oil consuming countries to OPEC. The resulting payment

imbalances were of such a magnitude that the international financial markets necessarily played a crucial role in the recycling of these petro-dollars. For the world's banks, however, this turned out to be a mixed blessing. On the positive side of the ledger, the OPEC nations were partial to short-term bank deposits, which in turn led to a substantially enhanced role for banks and, relatedly, a dramatic escalation in syndicated loans which was the other side of the intermediation process. Without question, this represented the high watermark in terms of the role of commercial banking in post-war international finance. However, the negative side of the ledger was closely related, although delayed by several years: the exuberance associated with syndicated loans led to inappropriate risk exposure to Third World borrowers and, in Canada at least, to the oil patch. When oil and commodity prices tumbled, the banks found themselves in rather dire straits.

The Balance of Payments (Macro) Shocks

Of and by themselves, plunging oil and commodity prices would have created sufficient problems for the banks. However, the resulting macro or balance-of-payments adjustments, embodying massive payments deficits for the U.S. and equally massive aggregative surpluses for countries such as Japan and Germany, further complicated matters for the banks. It was not just the mere shift in the balance-of-payments surplus that impacted on the banks. Rather, the portfolio preferences of these new surplus nations differed markedly from those of the OPEC nations—emphasis shifted away from short-term bank deposits and toward treasury bonds (i.e., away from bank intermediation and toward capital markets). Also contributing to this trend was the restructuring of corporate balance sheets which reduced the excessive reliance on bank loans (incurred during the inflation and interest-rate cycle of the early 1980s) by recapitalizing balance sheets.

In its own right, this inflation cycle was an integral part of the macro shock impact on international finance. The resulting volatility in interest rates and exchange rates (or rather the desire to minimize the implications of this volatility) was instrumental in the development of interest-rate swaps, currency swaps, and financial futures markets. This served to enhance the substitutability between fixed and floating rate instruments and across currencies and, as such, represented yet another factor favouring investment banking over commercial banking. Now that reference has been made to the development of sophisticated instrumentation, it is instructive to focus more generally on the role of technology in global finance.

The Technology Revolution

The financial services area is at the leading edge of many aspects of the revolution in computer and telecommunications technology. When one considers that over the past 25 years computational and telecommunication costs have been reduced per year by a staggering 25 percent and 15 percent, respectively (de Vries and Caprio, 1986), it is hardly surprising that these developments should have altered dramatically the nature of world financial markets. In analytical terms, the resulting explosion in financial architecture and instrumentation can, following Stevenson (1987, p. 39), be classified into three conceptually distinct types:

- innovations that embody *transfer of risk* (e.g., the "bought deal" transfers price risk from the equity issuer to the intermediary, "futures" transfer risk temporally, note-issuance facilities transfer credit risks, and interest rate and currency swaps transfer interest rate and currency risks);
- innovations that *enhance liquidity* (note-issuance facilities fall into this category as does securitization, to be dealt with later);
- innovations that *enhance access to markets* (interest rate and currency swaps certainly widen access to markets and the range of innovations referred to above all increases access to capital markets relative to traditional channels like bank borrowing).

Among the implications that derive from the juxtaposition of internationalization of finance on the one hand and the technological revolution on the other is that markets have become so interlinked that one can meaningfully speak of a round-the-clock global marketplace. The major trading books pass from New York (Toronto) to Tokyo, then to London and back to New York (Toronto). Moreover, if conditions in, say, Australia present a window of opportunity in terms of available investment funds, these funds can be accessed quickly in any currency and in either fixed or floating rates. This combination of global outreach and 24-hour trading has redefined what it means to be a significant player on the world's financial stage. Ability to access funds from the four corners of the globe is not sufficient; increasingly it is necessary to provide liquidity, i.e., to acquire the ability to trade in the local securities of the world's three key time-zone markets—London, New York, and Tokyo. Not surprisingly, this is exerting substantial pressures on national regulators, typically in the form of reciprocal arrangements, to accommodate this global outreach. More generally, by facilitating risk transfer, by enhancing liquidity, and by increasing the number of national markets and currencies that comprise the global marketplace, technology-driven instrumentation represents yet another factor favouring investment banking relative to commercial banking.

To this point the implicit argument has been, and will largely continue to be, that developments on the international finance front were placing the chartered banks in a position where it was becoming increasingly critical that they get domestic access to investment banking functions. However, the message emanating from the brief focus on technology is, in part at least, that investment banking is increasingly a highly capital-intensive activity. Apart from the capital required to become a global player, the trend for investment dealers to act as principal and not merely as agent (as typified by the "bought deal," for example) is also capital consuming. This created a special set of problems for the Canadian securities industry, since the industry's *aggregate* capital prior to deregulation was scarcely more than one billion dollars—a value well below that of several of the world's major firms. Thus, in terms of the Canadian financial environment, international developments were generating pressures for striking down Glass-Steagall from both the demand and supply sides.

Disintermediation
The combination of the above factors paved the way for the highest quality borrowers to turn to capital markets rather than bank credit as the source for their funding—a move away from intermediated credit and toward direct credit. The economics underlying this shift were that many of the high-quality borrowers were now able to access capital on terms better than those available to the international financial institutions. To a considerable degree this reflected the tarnished credit ratings of many of the world's premier financial institutions. For example, in 1980 nine North American banks had AAA ratings. By 1986, there was only one top-rated bank. Why borrow through an intermediary when your credit rating is higher than that of the intermediary? Phrased differently, the comparative advantage in servicing high-grade corporate borrowers shifted from commercial bank credit to the international securities markets.

The reaction of the world's major banks to this included two initiatives. First, they joined the march toward direct financing in the sense of becoming major issuers and purchasers of securities as well as arrangers and managers of these new securities issues. Table 1 presents data relating to the magnitude of these developments. Euro-bank loans fell by more than a factor of four over the 1981-85 period—from $96.5 billion to $21.6 billion U.S.—while international bond and note issues increased by a similar factor—from $44 billion to $162.8 billion U.S. As panel B of table 1 indicates, the banks have replaced these loans by adding securities to their asset portfolios (line B-1). Even more interesting, the banks have become very important issuers of securities, so much so that in 1985 their total issues ($43.0 billion U.S. from panel B-2) exceeded their gross syndicated lending ($21.6 billion U.S. from panel A-2).

The banks also reacted to these trends in a second, more aggressive, manner by assuming a prominent role in the development of a sophisticated range of financial innovations which, on the one hand, facilitated direct finance across a much wider array of financial instruments and currencies and, on the other hand, served to shift the banks' income sources away from interest income and

Table 1
The International Credit and Capital Markets
($ Billion U.S.)

	1981	1982	1983	1984	1985
A: New Issues in International Markets					
1. International bonds and notes	44.0	71.1	72.1	108.1	162.8
2. Syndicated Euro-bank loans	96.5	100.5	51.8	36.6	21.6
B: Bank Holdings and Issues of Securities					
1. Holdings of bonds and securities (new and existing)	46.7	59.2	76.7	99.5	157.7
2. Securities issued by banks	6.6	11.0	11.9	23.1	43.0

Source: Bank for International Settlements, *Recent Innovations in International Banking*, *April 1986*, Basle: Board for International Settlements, tables 5.1, 5.4, and 5.5.

toward fee income, reflecting the new reality. Thus, much of the banks' increased borrowing activity, as reflected in panel B of table 1, is best explained in terms of enabling the banks to pursue these new activities. In the current jargon, the banks became progressively engaged in pursuing fee-generating or off-balance-sheet activities rather than their traditional fare of interest-earning or balance-sheet items.

The underlying message here is that, in the international markets, the world's major banks accommodated to the move toward direct finance rather well. Indeed, once the trends became obvious, in many cases they became leaders rather than followers. This is hardly surprising since in the international environment most of these commercial banks are, in reality, also merchant bankers, i.e., investment bankers. The story was much different in terms of domestic markets, particularly for countries like Canada and the U.S. where Glass-Steagall variants held sway. Banks found it much more difficult, regulation-wise, to "follow their customers" as the latter joined the generalized march toward direct finance. Prior to detailing the resulting deregulatory initiatives, it is convenient to focus in turn on three further factors that hastened regulatory action—the rise of "real-side" bankers, securitization, and the Japanese ascendancy.

In-House (Corporate) Banking

It is becoming increasingly apparent that the global marketplace is essentially a vast and sophisticated information, co-ordination, and telecomputational network. From this perspective, it is hardly surprising that Reuters, for example, is emerging as a significant player on the scene, among other ways, by taking a leading role in moving trading off the exchange floor and facilitating electronic trading with the use of non-geographic trading screens. Similarly, it should come as no surprise that IBM, AT&T, and, in Canada, Bell Enterprises are embracing aspects of banking. This concept of the international financial service markets may also help explain why commercial giants like General Electric and British Petroleum have become global financial players. It is easier for commercial giants to acquire the traditional bankers' skills, such as covering risk and matching assets and liabilities, than for national financial firms to develop or approximate what these companies already have—a computation, information, and co-ordination system capable of accessing and distributing funds and services across continents.

Some of these corporate or "in-house" banks have been "in the neighbourhood" for years. Ford and General Motors have long had well-established credit companies. But the new trend is toward financing the sales of other corporations. As Rosenblum and Siegel (1985, p. 2) note:[1]

> Many of the captive finance companies of these manufacturers who originally financed only the sale of their parent's products have evolved to provide credit, if not to all owners, then to a wide clientele involved in purchasing goods other than their parents'. For example, by 1981 financing of General Electric Products accounted for less than 5 per cent of GECC's [General Electric Credit Corporation] financing volume, and over 90 per cent of Borg-Warner Acceptance Corporation's income and assets resulted from financing other companies' products. Similarly, Westinghouse credit extended about 1 per cent of its credit to finance Westinghouse products.

British Petroleum's activities in international financial markets are certainly not typical, but they may be the way of the future as far as global multinationals are concerned:

> Last year [1985] BP raised an aggregate of $990 million in the Euro-bond markets with ten public issues denominated in dollars, sterling, yen and New Zealand dollars and one private placement. Often deals involved more than one swap, producing considerable savings. With an AA credit rating, BP is able to raise funds in the capital markets at levels substantially below the Libor rate. Simply by warehousing those funds in a variety of

---

1   The following quotes are adopted from McFetridge's chapter.

investments for a return of, say, Libor, the oil company is able to make a profit.

The range of activities which comes under the aegis of BP Finance International is impressive: standard treasury operations, including forex [foreign exchange] trading, which totals around $100 billion annually, the funding of 70 companies associated with BP world-wide, a capital markets group to define new funding products. It also has BP's long-term interest rate swap and trading books, an M&A [mergers and acquisitions] group and a business finance group looking after leasing and property credit (Crabbe, 1986, p. 32).

Finally, any discussion of the movement by commercial enterprises into the financial arena has to devote some time to Sears Roebuck. Sears is already an integrated financial supermarket. But it is now challenging the financial institutions at their own game—plastic money. As Stevenson (1986, p. 50) notes:

Sears, Roebuck is already America's bigger issuer of plastic with 60M card-carrying customers. Now it will send its cardholders 25M discover cards, allowing them to get cash from a network of 5,000 ATMs as well as to use more sophisticated savings accounts. Discover threatens the banks because it is the first card in America issued by a retailer to be used outside its own stores.

These initiatives pose a dual problem for the banks. First, the corporate banks are playing an increasingly important role in the global marketplace. Second, the U.S. banks are experiencing a declining market share at home, which erodes the base on which their international activities are based. For example, in the ten years preceding 1986, the U.S. commercial banks' share of total short-term credit for manufacturing companies with more than $1 billion in assets fell from 40 percent of the market to 26 percent (Wood, 1987, p. 26). Small wonder, then, that the national financial authorities are under tremendous deregulatory pressure.

Securitization
Securitization (defined here as pooling various sorts of loans—car, house, and credit-card—and issuing marketable securities collateralized by these pools) represents a further complicating factor. At one level, securitization represents but another innovation in financial technology. But this innovation has a peculiar twist: it leads to blurring the distinction between financial instruments since in the limit there is very little difference between a securitized loan and a security. In turn, this also leads to blurring the distinction between banks and securities dealers. In the larger context, it makes the striking down of Glass-Steagall less of a revolutionary step since the banks are now into some aspects of underwriting via the securitization route.

Securitization is different from most of the earlier examples in financial technology in yet another dimension. Some of the largest players are typically not even viewed as financial institutions in the traditional sense of the term. GMAC has recently been referred to as being engaged in "securitizing the American dream," because of its securitization of both home and car loans. Indeed, in 1986 GMAC took a $276 million offering of car-loan-backed securities to the Euro-market, the first securitized deal in the Euro-market. And more recently GMAC has, perhaps not surprisingly, begun securitizing leveraged buy-out (LBO) debt. So far, GMAC falls back on an investment banker to aid with the underwriting and distribution. However, General Electric Credit Corporation has gone the next step and acquired its own investment dealer, Kidder Peabody, one reason for which was to facilitate securitization. For their part, the banks appear to be falling behind, partly for regulatory reasons. The Fed has no problems with banks' securitizing assets, but if they also guarantee these assets, the Fed will not allow the banks to take these assets off their books for capital adequacy purposes. Non-bank issuers like GMAC are not so constrained, adding further fuel to the pressures for reform.

The Japanese Ascendancy

A decade or two ago the list of the world's largest bankers read more or less like a "Who's Who" of North American banking. Not so today. There are no U.S. banks in the top 25, measured by value of deposits: Citicorp ranks 28th while Canada's Royal Bank is no longer in the top 50. The Japanese have taken over. All top 10 banks are Japanese, as are 17 of the top 25. Four of the remaining eight are French while West Germany and Britain have two each. While Japanese ascendancy is obviously related to the combination of the high Japanese savings rate (and Japan's resulting balance-of-payments surplus) and the surging value of the yen, it is none the less the case that the waning American influence in world financial markets has added further impetus to U.S. deregulation. Among the recent proposals has been one for the creation of five to ten domestic "superbanks," where the working definition of a super-bank is a financial institution with assets roughly double those of Citicorp. An integral part of this proposal (referred to as the Gould proposal and at one point endorsed by Fed Chairman Alan Greenspan) would be the elimination of Glass-Steagall, the allowance of interstate banking, and the elimination of barriers to the flow of commercial capital into the financial sector.

More generally, the emergence of Japanese financial power sends some critical signals to national regulators: the domestic regulatory environment may be a determining factor in terms of the ability of a nation's financial institutions to maintain a meaningful presence in global finance. Phrased somewhat differently, markets have become global rather than national and regulators must correspondingly rethink the rules of the game.

With this as backdrop, I now turn briefly to the manner in which Canada is altering its rules of the game.

B: Canadian Financial Deregulation

The Green Paper

The story line to this point is rather straightforward: the accumulated pressures emanating from developments in global finance were pointing to allowing chartered banks entrance in the securities field, i.e., to combining commercial and investment banking. Some domestic factors were also pointing in the same direction. Several of the important schedule B banks were concentrating their efforts more in the investment banking area than in commercial banking. Since their parents were frequently world-class investment bankers, this was exerting competitive pressure on the schedule A's and the Canadian securities industry. The point has already been made that Canadian firms were woefully undercapitalized. From the early 1970s onward, the Ontario policy (which effectively drove the Canadian securities industry policy) was to carve out certain captive or protected markets to be served by Canadian-owned firms. While for many years this proved to be a comfortable and profitable niche, the emerging internationalization of finance and the inherent fungibility of money and ideas implied that these barriers would soon be overwhelmed by the global tide—or much worse, from Ontario's vantage point, the local players would move to a more amenable regulatory clime.

Ottawa's initial response was the so-called "Green Paper" (*The Regulation of Canadian Financial Institutions*, 1985). In many ways this was a very creative document, although one would never gather as much from the ensuing public debate. Prior to addressing this debate, it is important to outline the Green Paper's main provisions, albeit highly stylized: First, its provisions applied only to non-banks. This is way offside vis-à-vis the above analysis, but it reflected the ongoing reality which was that the statutes for non-banks (essentially trust and insurance companies) had not been revised for several decades whereas the Bank Act is reviewed and reworked roughly every decade. Implicit, if not explicit, in the Green Paper was the commitment to update chartered bank regulations in line with the Green Paper proposals *after* the proposed modernization of the non-bank statutes. Second, the longstanding concerns of the non-banks to increase their powers (not hitherto documented in this paper, an obvious defect in terms of not pursuing the format outlined in the opening paragraphs) was accommodated, but *not* by increasing their powers, per se. Rather, they were allowed, via a holding company, to acquire a "schedule C bank" through which they would then be able to enhance their commercial lending activities. Third, this holding company would be federally regulated, the implications of which are spelled out later. Fourth, these holding companies (which, significantly, could be formed by either non-bank financial institutions or the corporate sector) would be allowed to acquire market intermediaries (i.e., securities firms), subject to agreement by the provincial regulatory authorities.

Analytically, the Green Paper was essentially a blueprint for how financial and corporate Canada could get into banking (with, as already noted, the proviso that the powers relating to banks would be elaborated at a later date). This recognized the global movement toward the integration of the pillars. However, the Green Paper scheme preserved the separation of the functions: the integration was to occur at the *ownership* level, via the federally regulated holding company. Moreover, and very significantly in terms of recent developments, the philosophy underlying the Green Paper was that *who* owned banks was *irrelevant*, as long as there was a federally regulated financial holding company between the owners and the schedule C bank.

Almost immediately, however, the Green Paper ran aground. The banks were obviously offside partly on principle but more so on timing. The non-banks were also unhappy—they wanted greater asset-side powers (greater commercial lending potential) without the necessity of creating a holding company and establishing a schedule C bank. Most importantly, however, the provinces were incensed. The Green Paper was viewed as a federal power grab—the holding company would be federally regulated and any downstream holdings, particularly of securities firms, would likely end up directly or indirectly under federal supervision and, ultimately, regulation. The end result set in motion a legislative free-for-all at the provincial level which is still ongoing. This is a bit disconcerting, even to those of us who are ardent decentralists, because there was much in the Green Paper that, suitably doctored, could (and still might) serve as a rapprochement not only between Ottawa and the provinces but also between Canadian and global financial communities.

Opening Up the Securities Industry

Even before the appearance of the Green Paper, the Ontario Securities Commission and the Province of Ontario recognized the inevitability of introducing greater competition into the securities markets. Spurred on, perhaps, by London's "Big Bang" and the Green Papers' willingness to allow federally chartered financial holding companies to acquire securities firms, Ontario proposed in the middle of 1986 what was for it a bold initiative—up to 30 percent of a securities firm could be owned by non-securities-industry interests. A month or so later the proposed percentage was increased to 49 percent. This piecemeal approach was effectively scuttled when the Bank of Nova Scotia, taking advantage of a loophole in the Bank Act and the very open regulatory environment in Quebec, established a securities firm in Montreal in the fall of 1986. Almost immediately, Ontario reacted by removing all constraints on the ownership of securities firms. This initiative coincided with the appearance of the federal "Blue Paper" (*New Directions For the Financial Sector*, Hockin, 1986) which, among other items, struck down our version of Glass-Steagall and allowed banks to enter the securities sector.[2] As noted above, within roughly one year of full implementation, the banks have acquired roughly 80 percent of the securities industry's assets. (This share will presumably decline somewhat as foreign firms establish a presence in Canada. Relative to domestic firms, foreign entry was delayed one year.)

There are aspects of this dramatic policy shift that probably merit further study, such as whether opening up the industry to American firms in the midst of the free trade negotiations weakened Canada's eventual bargaining position with respect to reciprocal financial access. None the less, external forces made it imperative that we integrate financial and market intermediaries, and the manner we went about it essentially guaranteed that the sector would remain Canadian controlled—for those that worry about these matters. Put a bit more bluntly, the banks got what they wanted.

The Federal Blue Paper

Apart from the provision that any federally chartered financial institution could incorporate a securities firm or acquire an existing firm, the Blue Paper was essentially a reversal of the Green Paper. The latter was all about who could own a bank and how. The Blue Paper was really about who else besides the banks could integrate across the pillars. The quick answer is anybody that is owned like a bank (i.e., widely held), so that mutual life companies and credit unions also qualified. Relatedly, whereas the Green Paper was basically silent on ownership and commercial links (i.e., the commercial sector owning the financial sector), these issues were front and centre in the Blue Paper.[3] Moreover, whereas the Green Paper maintained the existing powers of non-banks and allowed them to engage in greater commercial lending only via the schedule C bank route, the Blue Paper proposed conferring bank-type lending powers on the non-banks. Essentially, therefore, the philosophy underlying the Blue Paper is that all financial institutions are in effect banks, and (apart from

---

2 While the Blue Paper has not seen the legislative light of day, the provision relating to integrating financial and market intermediaries has been implemented.

3 Although frequently related in practice, majority (narrowly held) ownership and commercial links are conceptually distinct. In the case of the Canada Trust-Imasco relationship, Canada Trust is both narrowly held and commercially linked. If Bell Canada's purchase of Montreal Trust is allowed to proceed, Montreal Trust might not be viewed as narrowly held (because Bell Canada is widely held), but it would still be commercially linked. If I were to purchase a trust company, it would be narrowly held but not commercially linked.

grandfathering the status quo for narrowly held and commercially linked financial institutions provided they have 35 percent of their shares publicly traded) to take advantage of any *new* cross-pillar activities, these institutions would have to be owned like banks. As was the case with the opening up of the securities industry, the Blue Paper, particularly in relation to the Green Paper, represented a major victory for the banks.

To this point, the story line has been that developments in global finance effectively forced the hand of Canadian regulatory authorities in terms of (a) allowing ownership integration between financial intermediaries and market intermediaries and (b) more generally, allowing ownership integration across all pillars, at least for widely held institutions. What is clearly not pre-ordained by international factors, however, is the precise manner in which the policy authorities attempt to achieve this integration. This is evident from the concerns relating to ownership and commercial links. In other words, given the broad outlines of financial deregulation, Canada is layering this process with a set of internal values reflecting historical, cultural, and jurisdictional concerns. This search for "internal consistency," as it were, in one's financial environment, is a near impossible task as the next section attempts to demonstrate. The final section of the paper argues that pursuing reform solely in terms of the financial sector's perceived needs is likely to be overwhelmed by a much broader set of emerging issues, namely the overall industrial policy issues in an integrating world.

There is, however, a bit of unfinished business that needs to be addressed. If global factors forced Canada to deregulate, why have the Americans and the Japanese not also struck down their versions of Glass-Steagall? I do not have a full answer to this, but the following section develops some thoughts.

Glass-Steagall: U.S. and Japanese Experience

One obvious approach is to argue that the demand-side pressures are indeed as strong in these countries as in Canada. Commercial banks in the U.S. and Japan are lobbying strenuously to acquire full investment banking powers domestically. The difference, the argument would go, resides in the relative strength of the existing investment dealers. The Canadian securities industry was so weak, relative to their foreign counterparts and to the chartered banks, that it was destined for complete overhaul in any event. The choice then was whether it would fall under the control of foreign or domestic financial intermediaries. This is clearly not the case for the Japanese and American investment dealers.

There is another possible answer in terms of the United States. Congress is literally shell-shocked by the extent of insolvency problems among the S and L's. The recent bail-out legislation is estimated to be in the order of $1,000 per capita. Glass-Steagall issues cannot rise to the fore with problems of this severity elsewhere in the system. My best guess is that, after some cooling off period, Congress will enact measures to mitigate the impact of Glass-Steagall (e.g., the proposed Gould report referred to earlier).

These possibilities aside, there is another way of viewing the issue, namely that for an important subset of U.S. banks Glass-Steagall is effectively history. Citicorp (1986, p. 31) points out that the effect of Glass-Steagall binds on only $265 billion of the $5,800 billion total of domestic securities transactions. In large measure, this ability to manoeuvre reflects an earlier Federal Reserve ruling allowing three banks (Citicorp, J.P. Morgan, and Bankers Trust) to underwrite and deal in municipal revenue bonds, mortgage-backed securities, and commercial paper. In mid-1987 the Fed gave approval to six banks (Chemical New York, Chase Manhattan, Citicorp, Bankers Trust, Manufacturers Hanover, and Security Pacific) to underwrite and deal in a new type of security called consumer-receivable-related securities. (These new securities are collaterized debts such as car-purchase loans to individuals and personal credit-card accounts.) And in January 1989 the Fed allowed five commercial banks (the above except Chemical New York) to set up subsidiaries and underwrite corporate debt securities, subject to a few provisos. The point is that while Glass-Steagall is still in place, progressively it is honoured more in breach than in observance.

On the surface, the Japanese system appears to have evolved little from its traditional compartmentalized financial system which incorporated Glass-Steagall prohibitions as well as a raft of other barriers within the financial intermediary sector. However, what has been occurring is a coming together of the financial pillars into more or less closely knit groupings. Moreover, most of these financial groupings are linked to existing industrial groupings. In other words, the system is evolving in the direction of universal banking. As *The Economist* (March 25, 1989, p. 92) notes:

> The outlines of several new Japanese universal banks can already be seen among the existing industrial groups. Three are heirs to bank-centred prewar *zaibatsu* that the occupying Americans never really managed to break up, the Mitsubishi, Mitsui and Sumitomo groups. Three more, the Fuyo, DKB and Sanwa groups, are postwar versions put together by the large clients of national commercial banks, often piecing together bits of medium-sized prewar *zaibatsu* that were broken up, such as the Yasuda group. A seventh is a grouping of regional financial institutions led by the Tokai Bank from the industrial city of Nagoya.
>
> There is also an eighth, which is arguably most advanced, that based on Industrial Bank of Japan. With its banking, securities and other financial business in America and Europe, it is already a universal bank everywhere but in Japan.

Table 2 presents the structure of only one of the eight—the Sumitomo Group. The remaining groups are similar except that some also include firms in the consumer lending area. *The Economist*'s closing observation serves as an appropriate conclusion:

> These links will provide a head start to a ready-made supply of business relationships, bringing pension-fund mandates and mergers and acquisitions advice, for example. That will make large areas of Japanese business even more difficult for rivals to compete in and give the new universal banks tremendous defensive strength in what promises to be cut-throat com- petition as the financial system is reorganised into the 1990s.

Table 2
Japanese Universal Banking:
The Sumitomo Group

Sector	Ranking in Sector	Relation to the Group
Banking		
Sumitomo Bank	No. 2 city bank	Strong
Sumitomo Trust	No. 2 trust bank	Strong
Kansai Bank	Middling ex-mutual bank	Medium
Mie Bank	Small regional bank	Medium
Insurance		
Sumitomo Marine & Fire	No. 4 non-life co.	Strong
Sumitomo Life	No. 3 life insurer	Strong
Leasing		
Sumisho Lease	Small leasing co.	Medium
SB General Leasing	Middling leasing co.	Medium
Securities		
Daiwa Securities	No. 2 securities co.	Medium
Meiko Securities	Middling securities co.	Strong
Property		
Sumitomo Realty & Development	No. 3 property developer	Strong

Source: *The Economist* (March 25, 1989), p. 92.

3. Canadian Financial Deregulation: Redesign From Within[4]

Ideally, this section would come to grips with the whole range of complex and controversial issues alluded to in the opening paragraphs of this paper. Having already signalled my intention not to address these issues in any appropriate degree of detail, I shall limit what follows to a few observations, almost all of which are very subjective. My overall impression is that the federal regulators' approach was (and perhaps still is) to bring the Canadian system broadly in line with the global prerequisites first, then to fine-tune the regulatory process in terms of their perception of how the Canadian financial system "should" operate. As the heading indicates, I am labelling this as "redesign from within" by which I mean redesign in terms of some normative characteristics that ought to apply to the financial sector largely in isolation from what is happening elsewhere in the system.

Thus, my view of the Blue Paper is that it was an attempt to convert all non-bank financial institutions into banks. This was to be accomplished in two ways. First, grant roughly full banking powers to the non-banks; second, impose bank-type-ownership on the entire system. The overall rationale for this approach embodied a number of arguments. First, finance is conceptually separate from commerce and ought to remain so—hence the 10 percent ownership limit and the general prohibition against the commingling of commerce and finance in any new financial initiatives. Second, and relatedly, the legitimate concerns with respect to solvency, consumer protection, and self-dealing were deemed to be best addressed by these ownership and commercial link prohibitions. My view is that Ottawa backed itself into this position because it refused to bite the bullet in terms of any meaningful reform of deposit insurance and because it believed that enhanced corporate governance along, say, the Senate Report (1986) lines were simply inadequate. Therefore, prohibiting majority ownership and/or commercial links became an indirect way to limit some aspects of self-dealing. Third, in the time frame of the Blue Paper, the corridors of power were literally invaded by the spectre of concentration—not so much market concentration but economic concentration which would escalate if narrowly held commercial conglomerates were able to branch out into the financial sphere. This was yet another rationale for bank-type ownership restrictions. Finally, but not exhaustively, the federal government probably believed in an

---

4   This section deals with the emergence of universal banking and draws in part from a recent School of Policy Studies roundtable. In this context it is a pleasure to acknowledge the insights of all participants, and in particular Tom Kierans and André Saumier. I would also like to acknowledge the informative discussions with John Prato of Queen's.

integrating global financial system, control over Canadian financial developments ought to rest more with the central government. By dramatically increasing the powers of the non-banks, the presumed intent was to lure these non-banks into federal charters since, for those institutions that qualified as banks in terms of ownership, the Blue Paper approach offered a remarkably open and deregulated system.

To say that this approach misfired is surely an understatement. Most of the goals sought by Ottawa are now further from realization than they were when the Blue Paper first appeared. Canadians, by "voting" with their dollars, simply did not share Ottawa's views that longstanding institutions, like Montreal Trust, Royal Trust, Canada Trust, London Life, Great West Life, etc., were somehow tainted by either or both majority ownership and commercial links and, thereby, for the good of the transacting public, ought to be forced to undergo wholesale reorganization in order to take advantage of a more open regulatory environment. More to the point, neither did provincial governments—in particular, Quebec. Indeed, whereas mutual life companies were obvious beneficiaries under the Blue Paper (because they were deemed to be widely held), Quebec launched into a financial reform that allowed downstream holding companies for insurance firms and encouraged demutualization and joint venturing. One result was a charter flight from Ottawa to Quebec.

At the time of writing, we are still awaiting the next round of federal proposals. My view is that Ottawa has little choice (short of a court challenge which it likely would win) but to seek a compromise in terms of the ownership/commercial links issue. Unfortunately, this is difficult to accomplish without violating "internal consistency" because Ottawa has already committed itself to full banking powers for non-banks. My preference is for reform along the lines of the Senate Report which allowed commercial links provided a 35 percent equity was publicly traded but did not grant full banking powers to non-banks. Not surprisingly, another potential solution to Ottawa's dilemma has recently appeared on the policy scene, namely abolishing the 10 percent ownership rule for chartered banks and raising it to, say, 25 or 35 percent.

I want to make two final comments in the context of Canadian financial deregulation. Both are in the form of norms or precepts that ought to serve as guiding principles, but were never embraced by Ottawa. The first is in an era of rapid innovation and globalization of the financial sector, any action or innovation ought to be viewed as acceptable unless it can be demonstrated to be contrary to the public interest. The implication of this for public policy is that the "burden of proof" with respect to the public interest should lie with those that defend the status quo, not with the innovators.

The second precept is at the centre of most of Ottawa's problems, namely that Canadian firms ought to be treated *roughly* on par with foreign firms. Short of identical international regulatory regimes, fully equal treatment is impossible. This is especially the case when it comes to negotiations relating to bilateral or multilateral reciprocal access or treatment. Inevitably, some Canadian firms will not be able to manoeuvre domestically to the same degree that identically situated foreign firms can. "National Treatment," the cornerstone of the FTA, will probably not even guarantee this. Therefore, the issue boils down to ensuring that the unavoidable degree of discrimination is viewed as acceptable to Canadians. My perspective with respect to this precept is that Ottawa went well beyond any reasonable level of general acceptability and, as such, this foreign preference quickly became the Achilles heel of the federal government's entire policy. Because this is such a critical aspect of the federal government's overall approach it is worth detailing a few examples.

Consider first the two take-overs of regional banks—the Hong Kong and Shanghai Bank take-over of the Bank of British Columbia and the Lloyd's Bank take-over of Continental. I will only focus on the former. I am not questioning the final result: it may well be that a Pacific Rim take-over of a Vancouver-based bank is fully appropriate in terms of the underlying geo-economics or even geopolitics, particularly if the alternative was a central Canadian acquisition. The principle at stake, however, is quite different. The major chartered banks were not interested in the take-over. Because of the Blue Paper, existing schedule B banks were, in effect, next in line where Canadian-based firms such as Royal Trust or the Power Corporation group, whether or not they were interested, were excluded automatically because of their commercial links. To put it mildly, this is an intriguing situation. One of the most foreign-dominated (in terms of ownership) countries in the world is forced to look abroad for a purchaser because potential Canadian buyers run afoul of the "internally consistent" conception of how our financial system ought to operate. In terms of the solvency/depositor protection goals driving much of this policy, the implications are somewhat bizarre: effectively the Government of Canada is expressing greater confidence in whoever is the ultimate regulator of the Hong Kong and Shanghai Bank than in our ability to monitor any Power Financial or Royal Trust take-over of the Bank of British Columbia. From a political standpoint, I may well be making too much of this, since there was no evidence of any public outcry with respect to this preferential treatment of foreigners.

This was not the case for later take-overs, however. What catapulted this issue onto the policy centre stage was an attempted take-over of the Commerce Group in Quebec by Bell Canada Enterprises (henceforth BCE). Consistent with the Blue Paper philosophy, Ottawa said "no" since BCE was commercially linked and the target company was federally chartered. As a result, the Commerce Group was bought out by Dutch financial interests, a jurisdiction where there are no provisions relating to either ownership levels or commercial links.

It does not take much imagination to realize that under this approach to policy, most of our large trust companies and narrowly held insurance companies are eventually either going to fall under control of the major chartered banks or foreign interests. The policy leaves no middle ground for acquisition by Canada's financial conglomerates.

The issue has come to a head with Montreal Trust. With the backing of Quebec, BCE has purchased Montreal Trust. To my knowledge, the federal government has not attempted to block the take-over. In any event, Ottawa is caught between a rock and a hard place. Does the federal government say no to the take-over, in favour of another foreign suitor who will likely be unconstrained by the commercial links concern that may rule out BCE? More than anything else, it is this implicit preference for foreigners over Canadians that has effectively reduced the Blue Paper to the back burner.

And there are more problems on the horizon. Under the Free Trade Agreement, American schedule B banks have acquired a preferred position vis-à-vis other schedule B banks. As I interpret the recent Basel propositions relating to capital adequacy, acceptance of these regulations will essentially remove the distinction between schedule A and B banks. In turn, this will imply that the Americans will effectively have the ability to operate a closely held (narrowly held) schedule A bank, an option not currently open to Canadians. Not surprisingly, the Europeans are taking a dim view of the special privileges granted to U.S. schedule B banks, even to the point of suggesting recently that unless this discriminatory treatment is eliminated the ability of Canadian chartered banks to manoeuvre under Europe 1992 will be substantially curtailed (Lascelles, 1989).

To conclude this section, one is literally forced to comment on the incredible about-face on Ottawa's part in granting American Express, on election day (November 21, 1988), a schedule B charter. Granting a schedule B charter to the Amex Bank of Canada does not sit well with the Bank Act nor with the Blue Paper. From a recent paper prepared by the Library of Parliament (Thomas and Zafiriou, 1989, p. 3):

> The *Bank Act* requires that the applicant for a foreign-owned schedule B bank must be a "foreign bank." "A Guide For Foreign Banks" issued by the Office of the Superintendent of Financial Institutions sets out two guidelines to help determine such status. One is that "the applicant should be considered a bank by the regulatory authorities in its home jurisdiction." The second is that "the applicant should generally be in the business of lending and borrowing money, with the latter including the acceptance of deposits transferable by order." As Amex does not operate as a regulated bank in the U.S., it does not meet the first of the two

criteria. It is also doubtful that it meets the second, unless we define the sale of travellers cheques as a deposit-taking activity.

From the Canadian Bankers Association (CBA) perspective, the problem does not end with the fact that an Amex schedule B bank is offside the Bank Act: it also runs afoul of the Blue Paper. This is so because Amex would be permitted to continue, via subsidiaries, commercial operations in Canada, such as travel management and direct mail merchandising which are not permitted to Canadian commercial banks. Obviously, it is difficult for Ottawa to attempt to pressure the provinces to maintain a separation of commercial and financial business when the federal government has been caught red-handed violating its own principles.

Complicating all of this may have been the realization on Ottawa's part that failure to grant a schedule B licence would be tantamount to inviting Amex to charter provincially. Again, from the Thomas and Zafiriou paper (1989, p. 7):

> Amex [could] get the equivalent of a banking license in the guise of a provincially chartered trust company. There is nothing in the legislation of any province that would deny a commercially linked investor entry into the financial services industry simply on the basis of its commercial links. The normal principal requirement is the capacity of the applicant to support a financial subsidiary in Canada—a point not at issue in the case of Amex. Indeed, Quebec has already indicated that it would be prepared to grant Amex a trust company license should the federal government deny it a banking license. In that event Amex would have essentially all the powers that can be had through a federally chartered bank with the main difference that it would be subject to provincial rather than federal regulation.

The authors conclude that

> For the government the problem seems to be how to apply that policy [prohibition of commercial links] in a world where the neat separation between finance and commerce is the exception rather than the rule, particularly where that world includes all 10 Canadian provinces.

In its forthcoming position paper, Ottawa could, of course, hold tight on its ownership/commercial links policy and attempt, via the courts perhaps, to bring the provinces in line. I recognize that a majority of Canadians may well prefer this route, especially after the recent Supreme Court ruling on telecommunications. In my view, however, this would be counter-productive. For one thing, the existing commercial links are already too extensive: the resulting rollbacks or restructuring would be incredibly disruptive both in terms of financial markets and federal-provincial relations. For another, the end result would be inevitable—these institutions would eventually come under the control of the big five chartered banks (unless we allowed foreigners to buy them). This would substantially concentrate Canadian financial markets. Hence my earlier suggestion for a compromise along the lines of the two Senate Reports. There is, however, a further reason. Commercial links, that is, the ownership of the financial sector by the commercial sector, are quickly becoming yesterday's issue. The emerging issue is "financial links," the ownership of the real sector by the financial. Federal financial policy and, until recently, overall Canadian policy as well, was premised on the assumption that the financial sector could not buy the real sector. However, Quebec is now actively pursuing a policy that encourages financial links. Intriguingly, this policy has little to do with how one would, in isolation, redesign the financial sector. Rather, it is an attempt to rethink and restructure overall industrial policy in an integrating global economy. And on the political level, it is intimately bound with the issue of who will own Canadian industry in the new global economic order.

Presumably this is what André Saumier had in mind (in this chapter's second introductory quote) when he referred to the realignment of the financial sector equivalent of the San Andreas Fault. The challenge is no longer one of designing an optimal financial system (however defined) but whether or not Canadian financial deregulation or reregulation can avoid being overwhelmed by these more general industrial policy concerns. The remainder of the paper is devoted to this emerging issue, beginning with a brief analytical overview of "financial determinism," the relationship between financial and industrial policy.

4. Quebec Inc.: Towards Universal Banking

Universal Banking and Industrial Policy

In a recent analytical perspective on the relationship between financial structure, industrial policy, and government intervention, Berkeley's John Zysman (1983) posits three alternative finance-driven models (summarized in table 3):

1. A capital-markets, competitive-pricing prototype, in which the longer-term source of corporate finance is supplied competitively by the capital markets. The United States conforms to this model.
2. A state-dominated, credit-based financial system, in which the longer-term sources of corporate finance tend to take the form of credit rather than equity and in which both the price and allocation of capital are monitored closely by the state. France and Japan are his examples.
3. A bank-dominated, credit-based financial system. West Germany is the obvious example.

Table 3
Financial Systems and the Adjustment Process

Country	Financial System	Predicted Adjustment	Actual Adjustment
France	credit-based,	state-led	state-led
Japan	price-administered		
West Germany	credit-based, institution- dominated	tripartite- negotiated	tripartite- negotiated
Great Britain	capital market-	company-	unclear (Britain)
United States	based	led	company-led (U.S.)

Source: Zysman (1983), tables 6.1 and 6.2.

Zysman's thesis is that the structure of the financial system matters in several important ways.[5] First, there is a substantial difference in the nature of financial instruments in market-based and credit-based systems. In particular, in market-based systems the longer-term financing of the corporate sector is generally accomplished through capital markets. In credit-based systems, financing of the business sector takes place largely through loan markets. Second, there are equally significant differences in the structure of the financial sectors. Typically under credit-based systems, financial intermediaries are also very active as "market intermediaries" or, more correctly, as providers of long-term corporate finance. Third, there are dramatic differences at the level of director-ships. In Canada, upper-level management of the commercial and industrial sectors generally dominate the banks' boards of directors and high-ranking bankers have rather severe limits on their ability to assume directorships of real-side corporations. The German situation stands in stark contrast:

> Of the 400 top companies in Germany, 318 have bankers on their supervisory boards. There are 570 bank executives on the boards of these 318 large companies: an average of 2 bankers on each board. The domination of the big three [banks] is displayed once again in this area. The banking industry controls 145 of the 1480

---

5   As an introductory aside, the differences outlined below have presumably narrowed in light of the developments outlined in the first part of this paper, e.g., the blurring of the distinction between instruments and even between types of institutions as a result, respectively, of technology driven instrument sophistication and the erosion of Glass-Steagall.

seats on the 100 largest companies [and] the big three took 68 per cent of these seats and 15 seats as board chairmen (Richard Medley, cited in Zysman, op. cit., p. 264).

Fourth, and perhaps most important in terms of what follows, the nature of the financial sector significantly affects the economic process and government's role within this process. In the capital-based model, where prices are determined in competitive markets, economic adjustment is essentially company-led. This is in stark contrast to the situation in the state-dominated, credit-based systems, where

> credit extended by institutions becomes a linchpin in the system of industrial finance and government is drawn in to bolster the system and to make administrative choices about allocation...The borderline between public and private blurs, not simply because of political arrangements, but because of the very structure of financial markets (pp. 71-72).

Adjustment in this case is characterized as state-led (as table 3 indicates). In the third category, also a credit-based system, a limited number of financial institutions dominate the system without themselves being dependent on state assistance:

> Government does not have the apparatus to dictate allocative choices to the financial institutions and consequently it has no independent instruments in the financial system within which to influence companies. Banks, however, can serve as policy allies for government on terms negotiated between government and finance (ibid., p. 72).

Zysman labels the adjustment process in this case as "negotiated."

Zysman does not attempt to locate Canada in terms of his schema. On the one hand, it is clear that Canada, like the U.S., has a capital-markets-based system, although with the erosion of Glass-Steagall, the banks of virtually all countries are acquiring, in the *financial* arena, powers similar to those of universal banks. (Moreover, there is a move afoot to reduce the *industrial* reach of the German universal banks: The second European banking directive, proposed by the EEC Commission, would limit a bank's equity stake in companies to 15 percent.) On the other hand, this capital-markets-based approach rests much less comfortably with the prevailing Canadian attitudes toward government than with those associated with the American creed. One might even speculate that it was this financial-structure barrier to active intervention in credit allocation that led Canadians to be far more active in terms of commercial Crown corporations. In any event, these observations with respect to alternative financial structure cannot, of and by themselves, have much to do with the ongoing financial deregulation, since they existed in other deregulation periods, e.g., 1967 and 1980. To have an influence now, something else must be afoot.

The Take-over Wave

That "something else" is the foreign take-over wave arising from global integration and intensified in Canada's case by the Free Trade Agreement. Following Kierans (1990), I shall assume that from a global standpoint Canada's assets are undervalued and that the emerging foreign take-over wave is likely to be more of a secular than a cyclical phenomenon. Analytically, what this probably means is that Canadians would, under a scenario of "unconstrained" integration both of the global and FTA varieties, continue to own 10 percent or so of joint Canadian/U.S. assets, but increasingly this 10 percent will be spread more evenly across the two countries. To the extent that this is the case, the obvious implication is that many of the Canadian commercial "stars" (CPR, Stelco, Dofasco, Falconbridge, etc.) will likely be targets for foreign take-overs. Some already are.

It is not obvious how all this would wash out in terms of economics. But the politics are rather clear, as the concern about the potential CPR take-over has already made very evident. A significant number of Canadians, perhaps a majority, would argue for maintaining Canadian control of these "heritage" firms. Short of a FIRA-type prohibition or nationalization, both highly unlikely, there is only one way to maintain control, namely to utilize the existing capital pools to keep them in Canadian hands. But of necessity this means allowing the financial sector to buy into the commercial sector, i.e., universal banking. Enter Quebec Inc.

Quebec's "Mammoth" Corporations

In early 1989 Quebec Financial Institutions Minister Pierre Fortier announced to the Canadian Club of Montreal that his goal was to foster the development of "mammoth" corporations—corporations where financial and commercial interests would work side by side and where one of the roles of these mammoths would be to keep ownership and head offices of commercial "stars" in Quebec:

> It is also clear that if we wish to retain a substantial degree of control over our commercial and industrial companies, our financial institutions will have to be involved in takeovers of these companies, either individually or jointly. Accordingly, we have to start promoting the development of industrial, commercial and financial conglomerates which, by pooling of their resources, will provide Quebec with the means to act both here at home and abroad (Fortier, 1989).

Almost immediately, both the Caisse de dépôt and the Mouvement Desjardins announced that they could be counted on in this endeavour. And each is armed with nearly $40 billion in assets. The Quebec Mutual Life companies are obviously onside as well, and together bring tens of billions of additional assets: already Laurentian has offered to take a sizeable slice of Domtar. The National Bank is likely onside, to a degree at least, although since it is federally regulated it is limited in any share participation. But every 5 percent counts. Clearly onside as well is the Solidarity Fund of Quebec labour, the assets of which are growing by tens of millions monthly. And then there is the Quebec Stock Savings Plan for individual participation by Quebecers. Where large private Quebec-based holdings stand on this issue is not so clear, but given appropriate circumstances they might be counted on as well.

All told, therefore, we are talking about a war chest of $200 billion or so. Actually, it is more like a juggernaut since once it starts moving it will not long remain within Quebec borders (as Fortier suggested in the earlier quotation).

To this point, Quebec Inc. might appear like a frontal charge on the traditional canons of Canadian financial and industrial policy. It may well develop into this, but in its origins in the Lesage Government with the creation of the pension fund arm (Caisse de dépôt) and in its evolution over the last decade or so (where successive Quebec governments have enhanced the powers of indigenous financial institutions such as the mutuals and the caisses populaires), it should probably be characterized as a defensive (pro-Quebec) strategy rather than something directed against the rest of Canada. No doubt the flight of capital from the province in the late 1970s contributed to the manner in which the policy developed. And in the current environment, there is no doubt that the take-over of Consolidated Bathurst by Stone Containers of Chicago helped trigger the "mammoth" corporation strategy. However, if and when this juggernaut begins to roll it will certainly take on an "offensive" posture—drawing funds on Canadian and international markets to enhance Quebec ownership.

Prior to focusing on the implications of Quebec Inc. for Canadian financial deregulation, it is important to link this strategy to the Zysman analysis. The most significant feature of the Quebec Inc. participants is that they are effectively *take-over proof*. They are either government-run pension funds or credit unions or mutuals or widely-held banks. Following Saumier (1989), this means that they are probably much more amenable to government or "societal" wishes than would be the case if they were owner- rather than management-driven institutions. Moreover, whereas the power of family wealth typically dissipates after a generation or two, the dynastic power of a bureaucratic structure stays forever (ibid.).

However, where Quebec Inc. really differs from universal banking is that under one interpretation of the Quebec model at least, Fortier is essentially calling on these institutions to help forge the province's industrial policy, i.e., the province is effectively privatizing important aspects of industrial policy. These observations make Quebec Inc. conceptually distinct from the German universal bank model where the banks operate at more arms' length from the government. Indeed, there are aspects of Zysman's second model in operation here. Hence the label "Quebec Inc."—intended as a proxy for some combination of the Japanese and West German models.

Thus far, nothing in the above description of Quebec Inc. suggests that the model makes sense in terms of the underlying economics. It is relatively easy to generate scenarios where investments based on non-economic criteria (and ownership considerations probably fall into this category) in an open-economy environment can lead to disaster. Note that in the parenthetical comment in the previous sentence I used the word "probably." This is so because without a head office in Quebec there is little prospect that French will be the working head-office language, which in turn restricts the range of opportunities for québécois, let alone the potential for profitable interaction with the emerging Quebec entrepreneurial class. In this sense, language acquires overtones of being an economic as well as a socio-cultural issue, as I have argued elsewhere (1989a), and ownership is an effective means of achieving this end. But not the only way. For example, in the recent privatization of Air Canada, one of the provisions of the deal was that the head office was to remain in Montreal: Ottawa is part of Quebec, Inc.!

Implications for Financial Deregulation

These "distinct society" concerns aside, the question at hand is whether financial deregulation can avoid getting caught up in, or even overwhelmed by, this general industrial strategy issue. While on the surface this may appear to be yet another area where Quebec is attempting to force Ottawa's hand (and to some extent, of course, it is), it is important to recognize that Quebec Inc. is really a response to a challenge that impinges on all of Canada, namely how Ottawa should or could respond to the likely foreign take-over wave.

The range of responses is, in principle at least, extremely broad. First, Ottawa could insist that so-called heritage firms remain under Canadian control. Since the value of such firms clearly exceeds the investment threshold under the FTA for the application of FIRA, a resurrection of FIRA with teeth is certainly consistent with the letter of the agreement, although not with the spirit nor with the global trend toward integration and the freeing up of investment flows. More importantly, perhaps, this approach will not sit well with the existing shareholders of these heritage firms because the mere existence of a take-over attempt is a signal that their company is more valuable in the hands of others than in the hands of the present management. At the very least this will trigger action in terms of shedding selected assets or subsidiaries. Personally, I do not view this prohibition strategy as a viable approach, although in terms of the issue at hand it will facilitate the prohibition of "financial links."

The second approach is at the other end of the spectrum, namely let the take-overs proceed. There would be some obvious limits. Most countries protect their "sensitive" sectors and Canada would do the same. Even here, however, it is important to distinguish between ownership and regulation. Canada will presumably always regulate telecommunications and this regulation should, in principle at least, be independent of who owns the individual companies. For example, B.C. Tel (regulated federally) and Quebec Tel (regulated provincially) are majority owned by GTE of New York. (Presumably, as a result of the recent Supreme Court decision, both will now fall under federal regulation.) More generally, this approach avoids the subjectivity and interventionist mentality of the above "protectionist" model. Why, for example, should CPR be designated as a "heritage" company when Ottawa is in the process of privatizing or dismantling Via? There is another point to make in terms of this market approach: if there is a $2 billion foreign take-over then Canadian individuals or institutions must have $2 billion to reinvest. How these assets are likely to be redeployed must be assessed before passing judgement on this model. It should not come as a surprise that the mainstream of the economics profession would likely prefer this "efficiency" model to the earlier "political" approach. But here too the financial deregulators can largely ignore the universal banking model.

The problem is that (a) neither the "efficiency" nor the "political" polar model is likely to be acceptable and (b) there is no consistent middle-of-the way approach. Recognizing this, Kierans (1990) suggests for consideration a policy that would allow some of the real-side "stars" to be bought out, offset by a concerted effort on the government's part to encourage Canadian ownership of small and medium-sized firms. He posits that this may well be good economics as well since growth, employment and innovation are more likely to be associated with smaller dynamic firms than with large conglomerates. Among his concerns with his own proposal is whether the enhancement of Canadian ownership at the level of the medium-sized corporation is sufficient, politically, to offset the symbolism of losing "heritage firms."

The above three approaches (and one could add more) are alternative policy responses to a potential wave of foreign take-overs. However, none of them fares very well when the foreign surge is layered with Quebec Inc. Consider the so-called "efficiency" model. Suppose that in response to an American take-over bid for some Canadian flagship company, Quebec Inc. (utilizing largely financial-institution-based capital) makes a counter offer. To make this somewhat more realistic, suppose Quebec Inc. topped the Stone Containers offer for Consolidated Bathurst. What would, or indeed could, Ottawa say? Surely it would not object in strictly political terms. Even with anti-Quebec sentiment running at high levels in this Meech Lake era, English Canadians would presumably support the Quebec initiative. And, setting aside a constitutional challenge, it is not obvious that Ottawa could prevent it on regulatory grounds. However, if Quebec Inc. were to succeed, then the floodgates would open.

At this juncture, the reader is no doubt concerned that conjecture is passing for reality, let alone analysis. He/she is entirely correct. I have bought into the Kierans (1990) assertion that the foreign take-over wave will become an ongoing feature in a globalizing and post-FTA world. I have also bought into the assumption that politically, Ottawa cannot stand idly by in the face of any such take-over wave. Finally, I have accepted Quebec Inc. as an emerging reality. Rather than attempting to iterate or intuit incrementally where all of this might lead, I shall indulge in even more conjecture and move directly to focus on the characteristics of one polar variant.

Under this scenario, Quebec Inc. would impinge an overall Canadian policy in at least two ways. First, Quebec Inc. will counter foreign take-overs. Initially, at least, this aspect will go down well politically and will engender among many quarters in the rest of Canada a desire to emulate Quebec Inc. Second, Quebec Inc. will begin to manoeuvre on the domestic front. My hunch is that the first target has to be Bell Canada Enterprises, given that it now controls Montreal Trust. CPR may be the obvious next target. Both of these would presumably lose priority in the case of a take-over of BAT, since Imasco's holdings including Canada Trust would be up for grabs, as it were. Clearly, this will not be easily accepted in the rest of Canada, but the English Canadian response will be divided between (a) demands that Ottawa restrain Quebec, (b) considerable ambivalence if the alternative is a foreign take-over of these firms, as noted earlier, and (c) arguments on the part of provincial governments and other interests that they too would like to deploy their indigenous financial/pension fund leverage as an element of an industrial strategy.

One possible outcome is that coalition of nationalist sentiment on the one hand and Quebec Inc. on the other would lead Ottawa to embrace universal banking. What this means is that the substantial assets of the banking sector can be unleashed to acquire commercial enterprises. It may well be that the banks would not be tempted to purchase the Falconbridges of the country, but there is an important subset of commercial Canada that would clearly pique the banks' immediate interests, e.g., telecomputational firms and leasing firms to mention just two. While the thrust of the earlier take-over discussion ran in terms of flagship companies (largely because of their symbolism), it may well be that following Kierans, an influx of capital into medium-sized leading-edge industries may be more critical to our competitive future and this may well be where a generalization of Quebec Inc. would direct its interests.

Only a year ago the notion that Canada might take steps toward universal banking would have been viewed as far-fetched. During my several months working closely with Finance officials leading up to the Blue Paper there was plenty of discussion of commercial links, pro and con, but I do not recall a single occasion where the possibility of financial links received any substantive attention. Earlier, as a scribe for the Senate (Murray) Reports (1985, 1986), the prohibition of financial links was simply asserted without any accompanying rationalization because none was assumed to be needed.

On reflection, this degree of antagonism toward universal banking is passing strange for a country so dominated by foreign investment, so concerned about concentrations of asset power in the hands of powerful "families," and so sympathetic to government intervention in the economy on the one hand *and* possessing such powerful chartered banks on the other. That the prospect of marrying these to counter our age-old concerns with respect to foreign owner-ship and branch plants has never surfaced as a policy issue is puzzling, and, apart from the fact that it represents a buying into the Anglo-American tradition, it must also reflect a deep-seated industrial philosophy on the part of Canadians relating to the separation of the financial and commercial sectors.

In order to illustrate how this philosophy has been embodied in the Bank Act, consider the proposals relating to the acquisition by banks of approved financial subsidiaries. The Blue Paper proposes that a bank can have up to a 10 percent equity share in an approved subsidiary. As long as this asset satisfies certain other criteria it will be treated for capital purposes like a loan, i.e., it can be levered at, say, 20 to 1. However, if the bank goes above 10 percent then the *entire* value (not just the portion above 10 percent) of the asset must be subtracted from its capital base (one to one, or zero leverage) in determining overall capital adequacy standards. And this provision relates only to "ap-proved" acquisitions (i.e., not commercial acquisitions). Presumably this has to be rationalized in terms of industrial policy considerations since it makes little sense in terms of solvency or portfolio diversification criteria. A bank in the West can lever itself 20 to 1, or whatever the ratio is, in terms of non-geo-graphically diversified loans, but if it were to attempt to acquire, say, 15 percent in an approved subsidiary that might have an offsetting cyclical pattern in terms of risk, it would be required to have *more* not less capital to engage in this initiative.[6] This general issue will come to the fore as part of Quebec Inc. and

---

6   A recent paper by Gilbert (1988) addresses this issue. Although the standard deviation on the return on equity is lowest for banks, in comparison with other

currently is being thrust on the policy agenda by the Quebec-based insurance companies. Their argument is that in terms of underlying solvency concerns, it simply does not make sense that the leverage ratio should fall from, say, 15 to 1 to a ratio of 1 to 1 when the 10 percent equity threshold is reached. They point out, quite correctly in my view, that there are plenty of ratios between the extremes of 15 to 1 and 1 to 1 and that state-of-the-art regulation focusing on market values of assets surely could assess risk exposure on an ongoing basis. It is a bit ironic that a financial institution could normally extend this amount of loan finance to the corporation levered at 15 to 1. There is, of course, a sleeper in the Quebec insurance company proposals. Many of them want the approved subsidiaries to include real-side companies.

The underlying message is, therefore, that financial policy is already intimately bound up with a conception of industrial policy. The expressed federal preference for prohibiting commercial links and favouring widely-held institutions will, if implemented, inevitably imply that at a minimum, the non-mutual insurance companies and the narrowly held trust companies will eventually end up in the hands of the chartered banks or, perhaps, foreigners. At this point the five big chartered banks will be in virtual control of all of Canadian finance (as noted above, they already have the securities sector) and will be ideally situated to then argue that the obvious next step is to allow them to move into the commercial sector, for many of the reasons outlined earlier in the paper.

My personal view is that this last scenario, desirable as it may be from the standpoint of both the banks' and the federal government, will not come to pass. First, as noted above, regardless of what Ottawa may deem desirable in terms of ownership, a prohibition of "commercial links" will not sell politically. Nor will an attempt to prevent Quebec's policy of "financial links," particularly under a Mulroney government. Moreover, without taking a position on foreign ownership, the fact remains that if Canadians want to ensure that Canadian control of domiciled companies does not erode substantially under integration, there is no alternative but to free up financial institution and pension-fund capital. While it is true that under certain circumstances a universal banking model may be prone to government manipulation, it is, none the less, fundamentally a market approach and, as long as the border is open, it will be driven by market precepts.

---

industries, the profit rates of banks are not positively correlated with the profits of firms in many industries that, under existing proposals, they may be allowed to enter. Thus, banks could diversify their risk by entering many non-banking industries even if the profits of firms in those industries are more variable than those of banks.

Thus, the real challenge for financial deregulators is not how to redesign the financial sector in accordance with some "ideal" financial precepts but rather how to prevent financial deregulation from becoming subsumed in the growing concern about who shall own Canada. If the foreign merger/take-over wave is for real, I doubt that financial regulators will be able to avoid moving toward some version of universal banking.

References

Citicorp/Citibank (1986), *Banking on Investment* (New York: Citicorp Investor Relations).

Courchene, Thomas J. (1988), "Re-regulating the Canadian Financial Sector: The Ownership Controversy" in R.S. Khemani, D.M. Shapiro, and W.T. Stanbury (eds.) *Mergers, Corporate Concentration and Power in Canada* (Halifax: Institute for Research in Public Policy), pp. 521-82.

Courchene, Thomas J. (1989), "Dissent" in Economic Council of Canada, *A New Frontier: Globalization and Canada's Financial Markets* (Ottawa: Ministry of Supply and Services Canada), pp. 55-56.

Courchene, Thomas J. (1989a), *What Does Ontario Want?* (Toronto: Robarts Centre for Canadian Studies, York University).

Crabbe, Matthew (1986), "Inside the New In-House Banks," *Euromoney* (February), pp. 24-41.

de Vries, Rimmer and Gerald Caprio (1986), *World Financial Markets* (New York: Morgan Guaranty Trust).

Department of Finance (1985), *The Regulation of Canadian Financial Institutions* (Ottawa: Ministry of Supply and Services Canada). This is generally referred to as the Green Paper.

The Economist (1989), "Japan's Centres of the Universals" (March 25-31), p. 92.

Fortier, Pierre (1989), "Reform of Financial Institutions: Where are We and Where are We Going?," Address to Canadian Club in Montreal (February 13).

Gilbert, R. Alton (1988), "A Comparison of Proposals to Restructure the U.S. Financial System," *Federal Reserve Bank of St. Louis Review* (July-August), pp. 58-75.

Hockin, Thomas (1986), *New Directions for the Financial Sector*. Tabled in the House of Commons (December 18). This is typically referred to as the Blue Paper.

Kierans, Thomas (1990), "The Takeover Wave" in Thomas J. Courchene (ed.) *Quebec Inc: Takeovers, Competition Policy and Universal Banking* (Kingston: School of Policy Studies, Queen's University).

Lascelles, David (1989), "European Study Slams Canada's Banking Rules," *The Financial Post* (August 17), p. 8.

McFetridge, Don (1987), "The Effects of Concentrated Ownership and Cross-Ownership on the Stability and Efficiency of the Financial System" in R.S. Khemani, D.M. Shapiro, and W.T. Stanbury (eds.) *Mergers, Corporate Concentration and Power in Canada* (Halifax: Institute for Research in Public Policy), pp. 333-74.

Rosenblum, H. and D. Siegel (1985), "Competition in Financial Services: The Impact of Non-Bank Entry" in *Proceedings of a Conference on Bank Structure and Competition* (Chicago: Federal Reserve Bank of Chicago).

Saumier, André (1989), "Musings on Quebec, Inc." in Thomas J. Courchene (ed.) *Quebec Inc: Takeovers, Competition Policy and Universal Banking*, pp. 43-47.

Senate of Canada (1985), *Deposit Insurance*, 10th Report of the Standing Senate Committee on Banking, Trade and Commerce (Ottawa: Ministry of Supply and Services Canada).

Senate of Canada (1986), *Towards a More Competitive Financial Environment*, 16th Report of the Standing Senate Committee on Banking, Trade and Commerce (Ottawa: Ministry of Supply and Services Canada).

Stevenson, Merril (1986), "The Consumer is Sovereign: A Survey of International Banking," *The Economist* (March 22), pp. 1-68.

Stevenson, Merril (1987), "Survey on International Banking," *The Economist* (March 21), pp. 1-70.

Thomas, Terrence and Basil Zafiriou (1989), "The Proposed Amex Bank of Canada," Research Branch, Library of Parliament (Ottawa: Library of Parliament).

Zysman, John (1983), *Government, Markets and Growth: Financial Systems and the Politics of Industrial Change* (Ithaca: Cornell University Press).

Discussion of the Courchene Paper

John Chant

Before turning to Courchene's paper, I want to make a couple of preliminary points about the beginnings of deregulation in Canada. The financial sector was one of the leaders in this process. The Porter Commission provided the foundations for the very substantial liberalizing steps that were taken in the Bank Act of 1967. Later, there were our efforts at the Economic Council where George Lermer, our editor and host, put together the solution to allowing foreign banks to come into Canada through a two-tiered arrangement, so that we could determine in a controlled way whether entry of foreign banks would be beneficial to the financial system. The process of deregulation in the financial sector has had a long, if somewhat erratic, history.

Like Tony Campbell, I have two talks. First, as the time for the Conference came nearer and nearer and I had not yet received Courchene's paper, I decided to try to predict what he would say and respond to it. Courchene wrote a very good paper and my comments were superb! When the paper arrived two days before the Conference, I had a dilemma: should I peek at it, find I was right, and deliver the first talk? I peeked at it and found it was not the expected paper.

I had expected Courchene to deal with the regulation of the financial system as advertised. Instead he provides a broad, sweeping, insightful overview of what he describes as nothing less than the need for the most significant rethinking of an overall industrial policy since John A. Macdonald's national policy. Courchene asserts that so much is at stake in overall industrial policy that the forces impinging on financial deregulation cannot be easily accommodated or ameliorated by a rational internal redesign of the financial system. I am not sure whether he's being predictive or prescriptive. I hope he is not being prescriptive, and I also hope that if it is a prediction, it is wrong.

According to Courchene, the rational internal redesign of the financial system may be impossible because its regulation has become inextricably tied up with grand national issues. I will argue that the mixing together of grand national issues with the mundane issues of financial regulation can only be to the detriment of both. The failure to separate these two issues may lead to disastrous results in both cases. We have reached the crisis that Courchene describes because we do not remind ourselves adequately of the basis for financial regulation. Ownership policy, the link that Courchene identifies between national industrial policy and financial regulation, need not and should not be an integral part of our financial market policy.

What is the basis for financial market policy? When I first started writing and teaching, I had a long list of justifications for financial market policy. Fortunately, George Lermer eliminated the maintenance of Canadian ownership as one of them. But I have now reached a very small list. Assuming that we have a system of law that protects and provides sanctions against fraud and misrepresentation, there really are just two issues that motivate the regulation of financial institutions. One is the protection of certain groups of customers— unsophisticated investors. This can be justified by either the economics of transaction costs or by depositor protection being an integral part of our system of property rights. The other argument is the assurance of a stable payment system. Both arguments support some form of regulation of deposit taking institutions, and the former supports the regulation of things like insurance companies, but not necessarily in the form of regulation that we have today.

At present, depositor protection and the stability of the payments system are solved primarily through deposit insurance. But financial regulation is much more sweeping than this. We have upstream ownership provisions that govern who owns financial institutions. We have downstream ownership provisions that govern what financial institutions themselves can own. We have not quite two hundred pounds of the Bank Act, but it is a pretty weighty document.

Deposit insurance itself is not the complete answer and is not even a good answer in its present form. The deposit insurer, like any insurer, must control the terms of its insurance and the risks that it accepts. But in Canada we have turned this all around. When setting up deposit insurance, the federal government, faced with the threat of Ontario having its own deposit insurance, seized control of deposit insurance while leaving many of the insured institutions under provincial supervision. In effect, the deposit insurer insured institutions that operated under terms set by others.

So far, I have said little about regulation. With deposit insurance, the primary purpose of regulation is to protect the deposit insurer. We should not be complacent about our system of regulation: it cannot be depended on to meet this responsibility. It faltered badly with the Canadian Commercial Bank, the Northland Bank, and the Greymac scandal. It also produced the Dome Debacle and the Third World debt problem. It is not too different in principle from the system of regulation that precipitated the savings and loan crisis in the United States.

Can we have a system of regulation that will effectively limit the risks of the deposit insurer? I think it can be done only by discarding most of the present system. We must isolate those parts of the financial system that will be insured or guaranteed; limit the investments that financial institutions hold against these claims to safe assets; constrain the deposit insurer from guaranteeing any other claims; and educate the public to the nature and limits of the government's guarantee. It must be firmly stated that the government has no obligations for any other claims of financial institutions. Every one of these principles has been violated under the present system of regulation or in its administration.

This scheme may be a rather Utopian view of regulation, and will be dismissed by many as impractical. This scheme is not new to me and has long historical roots. It has, almost unbelievably, the support of both Milton Friedman and James Tobin—both Nobel prize winners, one the advisor to Republican presidents and the other to Democratic presidents.

What do these narrow issues of financial regulation have to do with the grand themes of industrial policy invoked by Courchene? He asserts that issues of financial regulation cannot be kept separate from those of national industrial policy.

But failure to untangle the two issues can have very costly consequences for both. The policies that I have described make restrictions on ownership of financial institutions a non-issue for the purposes of financial regulation. Anyone can own the insured part of a bank because there are severe restrictions on what the bank can do. This policy also makes what insured banks can own a non-issue because their assets are tightly constrained. This proposal creates a clear quid pro quo: institutions that offer insured deposits must accept severe restrictions on the assets that they hold. Contrary to the criticisms levied against it, it does not eliminate lending from financial institutions to the private sector. It creates a narrow set of financial institutions that offer insured deposits. Other financial institutions do not need to be restricted in this way as long as they do not offer insured deposits. They may be regulated, but not guaranteed, by government in much the same as banks were before deposit insurance.

Ideally, the government should prevent itself from guaranteeing uninsured deposits or rescuing institutions in any way. Regulators have the responsibility to monitor financial institutions and to close them down once they become insolvent as shown by the value of their liabilities exceeding the *market* value of their assets. The government must find some way to resist undertaking any rescues, given the past performance of regulators and deposit insurers who inevitably succumb to protecting uninsured depositors. In the case of the Bank of B.C. the deposit insurance corporation paid out $200 million dollars and still left something for the equity holders!

Through following these steps, we can deal with the mundane issue of policy for regulating financial institutions by itself. After that, we can turn to the grand issues, which Courchene deals with in his paper, that are well beyond the scope of those of us who focus on financial markets.

Courchene does go beyond his grand theme and discusses some matters of narrow financial policy. Like many others, he underestimates the magnitude of the problems we face and supports ill-considered measures. He expressed support for the Senate proposal that tightly held financial institutions must divest themselves of 35 percent of their equity if they wish to grow beyond a certain size. This proposal only muddles things because it puts ownership policy back at the centre of financial market policy. But even as a financial market policy, it has many problems. First, at one extreme, the requirement for 35 percent equity may just lead to another group that will be protected against the failure of financial institutions. If an institution fails, these outside shareholders will claim that they were not responsible, and indeed could not be responsible for management, and will point to precedents like the rescue of the shareholders of Bank of B.C.

In terms of influencing corporate governance, the 35 percent rule is no more than a palliative. Its purpose is presumably to make these shareholders conscious of the risk created by management, so that they will pay a price for their equity that reflects the risks that financial institutions adopt. But if a bank maintains an 8-percent ratio between its capital and borrowing and if 35 percent of equity must be owned by outsiders, this ownership that supposedly damps the controlling interest's tastes for risk will account for only 2.8 percent of the firm's total funds. Even a large risk premium on such a small share of total funds will fail to provide any significant disincentive against the risk taking by the financial institution.

I will finish by coming back to Courchene's grand theme. I am very worried about one problem that arises for the combination of universal banking with major commercial interests. As major banks and other major financial institutions fall into industrial hands, we may find that there will be very strong pressures against the deregulation movement. Suddenly the fact that there are a small number of cohesive and powerful groupings that have an influence in finance and commercial activities will provide a strong reason for getting the economy back under regulatory control. It will provide an excuse for an intrusion of politicians and the government into the economy, reversing the successes of the deregulation movement that we came here to discuss.

Discussion of the Courchene Paper

George Lermer

At the outset, I should explain that I was assigned as a commentator on Courchene's paper because I wrote a paper for the Economic Council of Canada on self-dealing and conflicts of interest in financial institutions. They chose not to publish it and I always look for an outlet for my work. This is it. Another reason is that I spent some two years in the early 1970s studying, with John Chant, the regulation of deposit-taking institutions for the Economic Council. That association makes me prone to agree with Chant and that means perforce to disagree with much of what Courchene describes and prescribes. In particular, I agree that with no deposit insurance, disclosure is the only regulation anyone requires and that would also eliminate the geopolitical concerns so well described by Courchene. But, unfortunately, we have deposit insurance, so no responsible insurer is going to take the position of complete deregulation but for disclosure. We are stuck with the problem. Chant's solution is to restrict the scope of deposit insurance, and severely restrict the assets of those institutions whose liabilities are government insured. By contrast, Courchene suggests that deposit insurance cannot be reigned in and that financial regulation must be concerned with the full gamut of financial institutions.

Reading Courchene's paper reminded me of the way I felt about financial regulation when I first got involved with the Economic Council and John Chant in the early 1970s. What struck me as strange then was that we have so much regulation in just that part of the economy which is the most malleable, fungible, flexible, efficient, well-informed, where substitutes are available everywhere, and where there are no rents. One can't think of any other area of the economy where this is equally true by comparison. In financial markets there are few sunk-costs except for investments in reputation, and skills are transferable between institutions, geographical regions, and industry. Everything is in place for the market to operate efficiently. None the less, financial markets are a traditional area of regulation. It struck me then, and again today, that we may not have a complete answer in a theory that posits regulation to be a means to appropriate rents. In financial markets it is hard to find any rents. One of the interesting points made by Courchene creates some difficulty for interest group models of regulation; it is that nations sometimes seem to regulate against their own firms' interests. I am thinking of the American regulatory structure preserving London as a banking centre. No one in the U.S. seems to notice or do much about it. The other thing I learned from Courchene's paper, and you may think this is a strange quip to make though it's made with a serious intent, is that until I read the paper, I had no idea that B.C. Tel was owned by GTE. Frankly I don't care that I didn't know. I think that is the deepest thing I can say about Courchene's paper. I just don't care. I offer that flippantly but the fact is of course that the public's point of view about ownership of financial institutions is, as Chant states and Courchene accepts as inevitable, a real concern and a real threat to the development of an effective regulatory scheme.

As of the early 1970s, I think that a lot of economists, including myself, didn't think that ownership of financial institutions mattered. I think it may matter now. I appreciate Chant's comments about some of the regulatory schemes that were dreamed up in those days, you might call them hair brained or, more charitably, political necessities. The ownership issue in the 1970s was examined from the point of view of traditional industrial organization theory. It was an artificial entry barrier, plain and simple. Ownership restrictions were not then examined from the viewpoint of the role of experimentation with organizational structures, and the discipline that the take-over market brings to bear on an institution's management, that is, from an agency theory point of view. I would attach far more significance to the latter aspect of the ownership issue today, and it follows from that perspective that publicly enforced protection for the managers of banks and other financial institutions is to be avoided whatever the sacrifice in other political objectives.

Herein lies the merits and demerits of Courchene's paper. First, I should acknowledge that this is a super paper. I was thrilled and surprised when I first read it because he better than anyone else maps some of the political future facing us. It is unfortunate that Courchene is probably right because I would prefer settling on a model for the regulation of financial institutions. Courchene tells us that the snail's pace of regulatory reform of the present enormously expensive and unsatisfactory scheme is going to be submerged in grander issues. I was more casual about the timetable for reform before I read about how the boards of directors of some of Alberta's banks regulated their institutions and let, for instance, the C.E.O. sit in California and run things by telephone. Anyone who reads the Estey Report on the Commercial Bank failure will read a bizarre story, and because I am forced as a taxpayer to be the insurer of these institutions, I'm not pleased with the present circumstances. The common or corporate law is not providing enough protection to the deposit insurer. If I wasn't the insurer, of course, I wouldn't care. So I am bothered by financial regulation becoming consumed in the heat of a political agenda that is fired by concern for an industrial policy and not the effective means of regulating insured financial institutions.

My concern about Courchene's paper is rooted in a view of what economists can and cannot do in the public arena. We are supposed to provide structure to economic and political issues, which is why we look for models to help us. Without structure, you get beat at the table. Lawyers and politicians out-talk economists every time. If I don't have a well-structured fundamental model to rely upon, I often find myself eventually becoming convinced by the rhetoric of alleged practicality. Unfortunately, structure is a difficult thing to bring to bear on industrial policy. To illustrate this problem, here is a list of policy targets extracted from Courchene's paper: industrial policy, nationalism, federal-provincial relations, Quebec-Ontario elites (which I think is an underestimated issue in our political life, especially the conflict between those two groups), and, eventually, financial regulation and security of institutions. The latter issue gets the short straw. I think Courchene's story is all true. He points out that politics, rather than any technical question, has been slowing down our getting some semblance of rationality in the financial regulatory structure. There is one good thing coming from the jurisdictional disputes, however, and that is jurisdictional competition. And the Free Trade Agreement is pertinent here. Between those two things, we will probably see the end of ownership controls on banks and, in accordance with Courchene's paper, some kind of universal banking. This may happen for possibly nationalistic reasons—to avoid the foreign acquisition of certain Canadian owned firms. Whether that is good or bad, I don't know. But, politically, Courchene's point is that there is going to be a political outcry if some of our major heritage firms, like Canadian Pacific, are going to become foreign owned. For somebody who spent most of a summer examining whether Li Ky Shing's son is a Canadian for purposes of several applicable pieces of legislation and the rigmarole that goes along with these nationalistic regulations, I truly hope this sort of thing is done away with. I have some confidence in the old Kindleberger approach to ownership and national and local advantage, which Courchene fails to mention, to the effect that there are some on-the-spot advantages to people that they can use to reasonably good effect, for instance, better lobbying powers with local governments, better knowledge of their markets, etc., and I would hope there is enough of a barrier to foreign entry in those real advantages to modify the political concern. Unfortunately, the feature of Canadian banks that, according to Courchene, makes them attractive to politicians is that they must be widely held institutions, that is, bank management is safe from bank investors. This protects government and financial elites, but whether it protects the deposit insurer and ultimately the taxpayer is quite another matter. Though I am confident that a real-financial conglomerate regulated by the market would correct any tendency to pour good depositor money after a bad investment made by a real segment of the conglomerate, especially if deposit insurance did not apply, I am terrified of the consequences for the taxpayers should Quebec or Canada Inc. have access to deposits when a prestige laden "leading" firm within the group is in difficulty.

Traditional restrictions on ownership are an outmoded means of regulating financial institutions. If they bar foreigners, they have no purpose but to provide protection for nationals. If they restrict real sector firms from owning financial institutions, they artificially single out one segment of the financial service industry for special treatment without affecting others. There is no clear case for making this distinction between real and financial activities because it is simple for a real sector firm to go by the financial barrier and walk through another door, that is, they can do the same financial business under some other title. Moreover, if ownership limits are enforced, management is artificially protected from competition. Thus, a barrier is erected against new firms and new management teams entering that segment of the industry in which ownership restrictions apply. I'm not going to predict the social costs of such restrictions. But the weakening of existing ownership restrictions, combined with general availability of government-sponsored deposit insurance, requires some other method of regulation and especially some means of monitoring self-dealing.

After reviewing all the U.S. and Canadian literature on self-dealing, it always seems to be around during the final phases of financial institutions collapse, though it is rarely the cause of the problem. There are many other factors at play. I have definite concerns about the advisability therefore of relying upon auditors and armies of people going in and regulating directly by examining financial transactions and assets in detail, because there have been armies of teams regulating in the U.S. and they very rarely catch anything. This is an awkward fact for accountants, I suppose. But if expensive direct regulation cannot safeguard the solvency of financial institutions other less direct regulatory models must be put in place.

The model from the Department of Finance's Green Paper fails in this regard, not because it banned self-dealing, which it did, but because it defined affiliation and control too broadly. This model for regulating financial markets had many virtues because it allowed for corporate and institutional structures that would help accountants report and lawyers litigate, yet it was, despite its appearance to the contrary, a functionally based regulatory scheme. As it allowed a real-financial organization to operate in all the pillars of the financial market, it was a good idea. On the other hand, it also meant that anyone who is connected through about a 15 percent ownership to a subsidiary of one of these real-financial conglomerates couldn't make a loan to the other part of the conglomerate. The Green Paper's model would have led to huge office buildings full of people trying to keep things clean. Is that loan dirty or is that loan clean, or is that investment dirty or clean? It portended a horrendous compliance problem for financial-real conglomerates. I just can't imagine how it would have worked. It probably would have meant that a lot of real and financial interests would have remained outside a joint real-financial conglomerate in order to avoid having their flexibility limited. So I think it failed on that ground. If we must have ownership restrictions, the rationale for which I don't understand, and I think such restrictions are dangerous to the efficiency of financial markets, I prefer the Senate Standing Committee's to the Department of Finance's model. The Standing Committee favoured ownership restrictions but not for institutions holding under 10 billion dollars in assets. Since no Canadian institution exceeds the 10 billion dollar mark, it leaves everybody out so long as that 10 billion moves up at least at the rate of inflation. So the proposal was a pretty good political cut-off, eliminating ownership restrictions on all existing financial institutions while mollifying the fearful by placing a ceiling on the size to which institutions free of ownership restrictions might grow.

Current restrictions on the assets of financial institutions extend to limiting financial institutions from the holding of shares of public corporations and those real assets not auxiliary to carrying on a financial business. The issue of real and financial separation was also a big issue in the 1970s. To argue that it was a meaningless issue was virtually to be branded in Ottawa as irresponsible, but it was then and remains today difficult to identify why it ought to provoke concern. Frankly, I don't think it is a concern from the deposit insurer's perspective. There is no reason to treat the holding of real assets differently from the holding of financial assets. Regulations limit the type of assets that can be held and the share of each type within a firm's asset portfolio. Regulations also prohibit over-exposure to a single debtor by restricting the share of assets assigned to any single debtor. Similar restrictions, motivated by a desire to ensure prudence, can be extended to "real" assets and the holding of equities.

I conclude that ownership restrictions can be rejected as a means of reducing the abuse of conflicts of interest and lowering the frequency of self-dealing. Rules on ownership should be used for the purpose of discouraging concentrations of power and only the very largest firms should be forced to be widely held. I would back away from the latter position, but as a practical matter it is politically necessary. Separation of financial institutions by function is anti-competitive and unnecessary. It is true that conflicts of interest will exist for those within firms that operate in two or more pillars of the financial market, but these conflicts do not threaten the solvency of financial institutions. Our best protection against conflicts is to be sought through disclosure regulations and the control of legal liability that is facilitated by disclosure rules. Self-dealing should be tightly regulated in owner-controlled firms and restricted also for conglomerates owning and operating both real and financial subsidiaries. But the Department of Finance's model went too far in how it defined self-dealing as it would virtually have eliminated such dealings.

I am less convinced than ever, and here I might disagree a little with Chant, about the arguments for the necessity of government mandated deposit insurance. I am not too concerned with the instability of the payments system that is the alleged result of bank failures in the absence of deposit insurance. People seem to require and continue to deal with financial institutions in the most unstable of circumstances. Banks have survived the collapse of several Canadian financial institutions, and would again in the future. There is little empirical evidence of the so-called "contagion" effect by which the failure of one institution leads to a run on other financial institutions.

But I realize that technical regulations are critical here because there is no chance that deposit insurance will be relaxed and thereby reduce the regulatory burden. So the agenda for analysis of financial markets cannot be deregulation, it must be the efficient regulation of the market on behalf of the state that has chosen to become the deposit insurer. Like Chant, I am not sure we are coming to a reasonably efficient system and I am worried that we are not getting there because the issues that Courchene raised in his paper fill the political agenda for those in governmental circles concerned with financial regulation. And that is a scary thought.

Chapter 4

Deregulation of Telecommunications: An Assessment

Steven Globerman

Introduction

The broad purpose of this paper is to evaluate the economic case for a faster and more comprehensive deregulation of the Canadian telecommunications industry than has been undertaken to date. Movement towards deregulation in Canada has been halting in comparison to the U.S. experience and other countries, including Japan, New Zealand, and the United Kingdom.[1] The deliberate pace of deregulation in Canada ostensibly reflects a concern among policy-makers that important public policy objectives would be sacrificed if a faster pace was adopted. At the same time, strong arguments can be made that the existing regulatory structure imposes significant direct and indirect costs on the Canadian economy and that these costs will grow over time.[2]

Much of the current debate in Canada is about the liberalization of restrictions on interexchange competition which primarily encompasses Message Toll Service (MTS). By contrast, there has been relatively little discussion to date about deregulating local exchange service, although with the emergence and growth of cellular radio, this latter issue may grow in importance. The principal concern has been with whether more common carriers should be able to provide basic long distance (MTS) service. Another major issue that has received less attention is whether to continue comprehensive regulation of tariffs and service

---

1   For an extensive discussion of the deregulation experience of the EEC countries, see DIW (1988). For a description of the U.S. experience, see Chessler (1988), pp. 16-23.

2   These costs are discussed in Globerman (1986), pp. 1-80.

offerings by authorized carriers. Both the above describe dimensions of regulatory policy, i.e., of the regulation of structure and conduct, and both will be assessed in this paper.

By way of background, the second section of this paper offers a brief review of the current regulatory environment for telecommunications in Canada. In the third section, the theoretical arguments for and against deregulation are briefly identified and discussed. The fourth section of the paper summarizes and evaluates empirical evidence on the performance of the telecommunications industry under regulation, while the fifth section assesses the impacts of past deregulation in Canada and elsewhere. The sixth and final section of the paper offers an assessment of deregulation of the industry. A focus of the concluding section is whether observed impacts of past deregulation can be extrapolated to conclusions about the likely effects of further deregulation.

The Current Regulatory Environment

The Canadian telecommunications industry is currently dominated by two national systems: Telecom Canada and CNCP Telecommunications (now Unitel).[3] Both of these systems merge into the overseas network that is operated by Teleglobe Canada. Telecom Canada is an association of the largest telephone companies operating in each province and Telesat Canada, the domestic satellite carrier. Currently, Telecom Canada members operate two of the three Canada-wide microwave networks that form the backbone of Canada's telecommunications network.[4] Unitel operates the third microwave network; however, Unitel is restricted to providing private line service, meaning that the voice traffic it carries cannot be connected to the switched telephone network operated by Telecom Canada. Both Unitel and Telecom Canada members can carry written messages, e.g., telex, computer data, facsimile, and television broadcast signals on their network.[5]

---

3   The following description of the Canadian telecommunications industry is taken from Globerman (1988a).

4   Telecom Canada members include: Alberta Government Telephone, Bell Canada, British Columbia Telephone, Island Telephone, Manitoba Telephone, Maritime Tel and Tel, New Brunswick Telephone, Newfoundland Telephone, Sask Tel and Telesat.

5   In April 1989 Canadian Pacific Ltd. and Rogers Communications Inc. announced their plan to form a "strategic alliance" that would compete in the Canadian long distance telecommunications industry. Rogers will buy 40 percent of Montreal-based CP's CNCP Telecommunications unit. The companies also announced a plan for CNCP to apply to Canadian regulators for authority to offer switched long distance service. See "Canadian Firms to Set Up Long-Distance Phone Unit" (1989), the *Wall Street Journal* (Europe), April 21-22, p. 30.

There are approximately 100 telephone companies operating in Canada without Telecom Canada affiliation, the vast majority of which operate in Ontario and Quebec. These companies are by and large local carriers. There are also hundreds of radio common carriers and two cellular telephone networks. Radio common carriers provide telecommunications service to the Canadian public in the form of radio paging (as do the telephone companies). In addition, radio common carriers provide services in remote areas not served by wireline carriers. Most radio common carriers are community-oriented enterprises serving a relatively restricted geographical area. Cellular radio services are provided by two rival networks. One is operated by each of the terrestrial common carriers within its provincial jurisdiction(s). The other is operated by Cantel of which Rogers Communications Inc. is the major shareholder.

Canadian telecommunication common carriers are regulated either by the federal regulatory agency (CRTC), a provincial government public utility board, or a municipal board. Table 1 provides a list of major telecommunications companies and their respective regulatory agencies.

The point to be emphasized here is that all facilities-based common carriers offering inter or intraprovincial switched long distance or local telephone service are regulated by one or another agency, with the two largest (Bell Canada and B.C. Tel) being regulated by the CRTC. The two cellular networks, i.e., Cantel and the set of companies operated by the Telecom Canada companies, are regulated by the CRTC. In summary, all basic long distance and local telephone traffic carried on public networks is subject to regulation.[6] The applicable regulations encompass conditions of entry, review, and approval of tariffs for purposes of comprehensive rate-of-return analysis, and approval of new service offerings.

Currently, in the CRTC's jurisdiction, there are two terrestrial carriers (Telecom Canada and Unitel) authorized to provide Type I private network services, e.g., private lines or other bulk lines. These services are private in the sense that the carriers' facilities are used to transmit messages among a set of telephone stations for a single customer or group of customers.[7] However, only

---

6   The Telecom Canada consortium of companies is not directly regulated.

7   Where provincial PUCs are the relevant regulators, Unitel may not be allowed to offer even private line service, since interconnection to the common carriers' switchboards is not allowed. This is the case in Alberta, where CNCP launched a lawsuit demanding interconnection to Alberta Government Telephones' local switching network. In its landmark decision in August 1989, the Supreme Court of Canada ruled that Ottawa can impose a single set of rules over the three provincially owned telephone companies in the prairie provinces and the four investor-owned utilities in the Maritimes; however, the Supreme Court sided with provincially owned Alberta Government Telephones in finding that it is currently exempt from federal regulation because federal laws have not stripped the company of its Crown

Telecom Canada can own and operate facilities to provide public switched telephone messaging, i.e., service whereby customers can call any subscriber on the network through either toll or local calling. CNCP challenged this restriction, although the restriction was upheld by the CRTC.[8] A new CRTC hearing of Unitel's application for the right to provide public switched long distance message service will take place in spring 1991.

There are ostensibly no entry restrictions on leasing common carrier facilities for purposes of reselling capacity or sharing capacity among a set of users, as long as the applications qualify as value added services or private line services. Value added activities, as distinguished from the basic service, involve a significant alteration or modification of the basic voice message. In fact, the definition of value added is unclear even to members of the industry, and ambiguity is inevitable in an environment where potential suppliers are continuously identifying new services that might be offered in a reselling capacity.[9]

The uncertainty surrounding the definition of value added services might itself be an implicit regulatory barrier to entry into reselling and sharing telecommunications services. Another is the distinction between Type I and Type II carriers. Canadian regulatory policy effectively prohibits the ownership and operation of transmission facilities by non-basic carriers. The former have transmission facilities while the latter do not. Type I carriage encompasses the provision of basic switched public network local and long distance service, while Type II carriage encompasses the use of Type I facilities for resale and sharing of services other than basic switched public network local and long distance service. If resale as a non-facilities-based carrier is riskier and/or less profitable than resale as a facilities-based carrier, the Type I/Type II distinction could be another indirect barrier into a nominally competitive sector of the industry.

---

immunity. Legal experts say that the decision creates a void under which Alberta Government Telephones is currently not regulated either by the federal or provincial governments. See Surtees (1989).

8   See CRTC Decision 85-19, "Interexchange Competition and Related Issues." The CRTC does allow cellular and private mobile radio systems to interconnect to the public network for calls initiated or terminated on cellular or mobile terminals.

9   One recent illustration of the inevitable contention that arises in the existing environment involves Call-Net, a reseller providing discount private line long distance service to customers in Toronto and Montreal. Call-Net argued that it was providing value added services in a private line context. Initially, the regulator ordered Bell Canada to disconnect Call-Net's lines over which it provided resale services. After Call-Net's appeal to Cabinet, the CRTC announced its intention to review its policies towards reselling and sharing of private line services. See Barnes (1989). Subsequently, reselling and sharing of private line services was approved by CRTC.

Table 1
Major Canadian Telecommunications Carriers and Their Regulatory Agencies

Carrier	Regulatory Agency
Newfoundland Telephone	Newfoundland Board of Commissioners of Public Utilities
Terra Nova Telecommunications	CRTC
Island Telephone	Public Utilities Commission of P.E.I.
Maritime Telephone	N.S. Board of Commissioners of Public Utilities
New Brunswick Telephone	N.B. Board of Commissioners of Public Utilities
Bell Canada	CRTC
Quebec-Telephone	Regie des services publics du Quebec
Telebec	Regie des services publics du Quebec
Northern Telephone	Ontario Telephone Service Commission
Thunder Bay Telecommunications	Ontario Telephone Service Commission
Manitoba Telephone System	Manitoba Public Utilities Board
Saskatchewan Telecommunications	Saskatchewan Public Utilities Commission
Alberta Government Telephones	Alberta Public Utilities Board
Edmonton Telephones	City of Edmonton
British Columbia Telephone	CRTC
Prince Rupert	City of Prince Rupert and B.C. Utilities Commission
B.C. Rail	Not regulated by an agency
Northwestel	CRTC
Telesat Canada	CRTC
CNCP Telecommunications	CRTC
Teleglobe Canada	CRTC

Note: The constitutionality of continued provincial review of telephone companies is uncertain in the three prairie provinces as explained in footnote 7. It is unconstitutional in the case of the four Maritime telcos. Since the time of writing, AGT was privatized and is now regulated by the CRTC. The Maritime telcos are also regulated by the CRTC.

Source: Globerman (1988), p. 8.

One important area in which regulatory restrictions have been substantially relaxed is interconnection. Historically, attachment and maintenance of the hardware that facilitated the pick-up and delivery of electronic signals from and to the network was the exclusive privilege of the carriers. Federal and provincial "interconnect" decisions since 1979 have allowed private ownership of telephone equipment and other subscriber apparatus as well as satellite Earth stations. The precise rules governing interconnection are quite complex given provincial regulation of specific Telecom Canada members. A few provinces still have restrictions on the use of subscriber-owned network addressing equipment.

One other feature of the broad telecommunications regulatory environment might be mentioned; namely, non-carrier provided local systems and public non-voice systems can be interconnected to the facilities of federally regulated carriers. In practice, this allows private intra-exchange networks and intracity public data networks to connect to the public communications network. One practical and potentially important implication of this regulatory (CRTC) condition is that cable TV companies can interconnect with the public telephone network. This is potentially important to the extent that cable TV companies ultimately expand the range of services they carry over fibre optic cable that they are planning to install in new or rebuilt cable systems. Some of the services offered may compete directly with the telephone companies. Indeed, one can imagine local cable companies interconnecting subscribers operating addressable switches to the public network, thereby effectively creating a rival network to Telecom Canada's.[10]

Figure 1 presents an overview of the major telecommunications services and the major participants. It serves as a basis for summarizing the current regulatory environment. Public switched telephone services are provided under monopoly conditions by Telecom Canada member companies and independent telephone companies. In most regions of the country, private lines for voice, data, and program transmission are available from Telecom Canada and independent telephone companies—Unitel and B.C. Rail in British Columbia. Telesat Canada provides satellite-based private line services directly to business customers. Overseas leased circuits are available by interconnection to Teleglobe facilities at its gateway switches in Vancouver, Toronto, and Montreal.

With respect to the provision of data services, the environment is similar to that for voice, with the exception that Unitel operates a public switched data service (Infonet) in competition with Telecom Canada's switched data service

---

10 Presumably Unitel would provide the fibre optic backbone long distance facility. The ability of cable systems to compete directly with the telephone companies will be considered in a later section.

Figure 1
Overview of Telecommunications Services

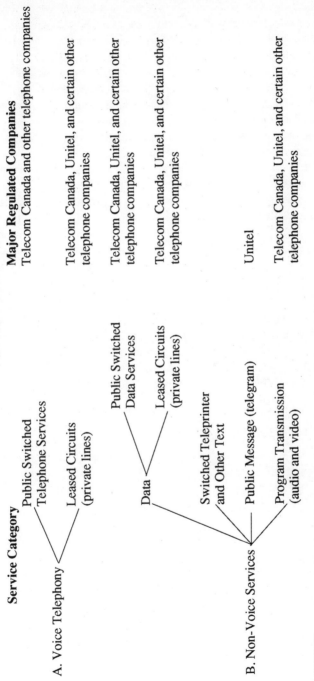

Service Category		Major Regulated Companies
A. Voice Telephony	Public Switched Telephone Services	Telecom Canada and other telephone companies
	Leased Circuits (private lines)	Telecom Canada, Unitel, and certain other telephone companies
B. Non-Voice Services	Data — Public Switched Data Services	Telecom Canada, Unitel, and certain other telephone companies
	Data — Leased Circuits (private lines)	Telecom Canada, Unitel, and certain other telephone companies
	Switched Teleprinter and Other Text	
	Public Message (telegram)	Unitel
	Program Transmission (audio and video)	Telecom Canada, Unitel, and certain other telephone companies

Source: Globerman (1988a), p. 16.

(INet). Other non-voice services are similar in structure to data with the exception of telegram service (a virtually extinct service in which Unitel holds a joyless monopoly) and program transmission in which Telesat rents transmission capacity to Canadian broadcasters.

In summary, the Canadian telecommunications industry is regulated in a fairly comprehensive manner. No competition is allowed in the provision of public switched voice telephone service which comprises upwards of 90 percent of all traffic on the telephone network. There is only limited competition in the leasing of private lines for voice and/or data use. There are numerous value added computer networks, but they are not allowed to function as switched networks; i.e., they connect to the Telecom Canada switching nodes. There are a limited number of resellers of telephone service, notwithstanding the ostensible liberalization of competition in this area. In comparison to the U.S. system especially, the Canadian system is closed to new entry in most sectors, and carriers are subject to more comprehensive review of proposed changes in tariff structure and new service offerings in a rate-of-return environment.[11]

Theories of Regulation Applied to Telecommunications

In order to assess empirical evidence on the deregulation experience, it is important to have some theoretical construct within which to evaluate the available evidence. In the absence of a theoretical framework, it is difficult to establish the type of evidence that is relevant to the investigation, as well as whether the available evidence is a reliable indicator of the impacts of different regulatory regimes.

Overview of the Regulation Literature

An extensive literature, focusing on the determinants of regulatory regimes, ranges from historical case studies through econometric studies. Rather than reviewing that literature, we focus here on specific points of controversy that distinguish the major competing theories.

---

11 In the United States, AT&T is the only long distance carrier still subject to regulatory review by the FCC. In 1989 the FCC formally abandoned rate-of-return regulation with respect to AT&T in favour of implementing ceiling prices. The price cap plan allows AT&T to raise rates 3 percentage points less than the rate of inflation in three categories of service: residential and small business; 800 calls; and other business services, mainly for large customers. AT&T can raise or lower rates up to 5 percent for individual services within these categories by giving 14 days notice to the FCC, which will presume the changes to be lawful. The burden of proof then would be on challengers. See "FCC Clears Way for AT&T to Use Price Cap Plan," *Washington Post*, June 28, 1989, p. 1.

The overriding controversy divides on how allocative and distributional consequences will differ with direct regulation and absent regulation. One broad school of thought maintains that regulation contributes to an improvement in social welfare, either because it corrects for market failures of one sort or another or because it contributes to a "fairer" social distribution of resources. This argument can be traced back to early "consumer protection" theories of public utility regulation. The consumer protection theory stressed the natural monopoly characteristics of regulated activities and posited the benefits to consumers achievable by regulating the prices charged by natural monopolists.[12]

With an accumulation of evidence that many regulated activities did not have conventional natural monopoly characteristics, a related efficiency argument emerged which stressed the role of transaction costs as a motive for regulation.[13] In this model, suppliers of utility-type services are required to make major sunk-cost investments which exposes them to risks of opportunistic behaviour on the part of consumers. For example, consumers may demand to renegotiate lower utility rates. Conversely, if consumers absorb the sunk costs, they are potentially subject to hold-up by suppliers. The point here is that when there are large sunk costs associated with an activity, there is the potential for post-contractual opportunism.[14] If this potential is not mitigated, the required investments may not be made in the first place. In this framework, the regulator might be seen as an impartial referee to guarantee the supplier a monopoly franchise through which capital investments can be recovered, while guaranteeing the consumer protection against "unreasonable" profits being earned by the supplier.

The transactions cost model of regulation rests upon the sunk-cost characteristics of an industry. Ultimately, large sunk costs act as a barrier to contestability. Therefore, in the final analysis, the transactions cost model converges to a broader natural monopoly model. The key empirical issue hinges upon ease of entry to and exit from the industry. Where entry and exit are relatively easy, there are no substantive efficiency gains that should be expected from regulation. Where entry and exit are costly and require relatively long periods of time, regulation has the *potential* to improve efficiency.

---

12 A review of the broad "theories of regulation" literature can be found in Crew and Rowley (1988), pp. 49-67.

13 The seminal article defining natural monopoly in a multi-product context is found in Baumol (1982). Discussions of transactions costs in relationship to regulation can be found in Williamson (1979), pp. 73-104, and Goldberg (1976), pp. 426-48. For a historical examination of transaction cost-based motivations for implementing regulation or public ownership, see Baldwin (1989).

14 For a discussion of post-contractual opportunism, see Klein, Crawford, and Alchian (1978), pp. 297-326.

An alternative view of regulation is offered by models of "rent-seeking" that stress the role regulation plays in redistributing income.[15] In these models, producers and consumers compete for protection and subsidies in "political" markets. Early versions of these models emphasized the inefficiencies associated with political rent-seeking. The inefficiencies derive ultimately from the characteristic of benefits from government intervention being highly concentrated in the population with the associated costs being broadly dispersed.[16] In this circumstance, beneficiaries ordinarily have strong incentives to lobby for specific policies which promise favourable redistributions of wealth, while "losers" have weak incentives to lobby against those same policies. The result is a systematic tendency for excessive amounts of government intervention from a social welfare perspective.

More recent models of rent-seeking behaviour highlight the characteristic that different groups do not entirely win or lose the competition for political influence which contrasts with earlier models embodying "all-or-nothing" outcomes.[17] As a result, a broad array of outcomes is possible from rent-seeking behaviour, including the correction of conventional market failures. Furthermore, competition among pressure groups will favour more efficient methods of government intervention. While rent-seeking in the aggregate ordinarily imposes deadweight efficiency costs on society, these costs may be smaller than has been suggested in earlier public choice literature.[18]

Becker's model of competition among pressure groups suggests that while there will be some "tyranny of the status quo" associated ultimately with inelasticities of supply and demand for specific resources, political protection against changes in the private sector is likely to be incomplete and temporary.[19] Thus, deregulation can be an expected outcome of rent-seeking behaviour, particularly as the marginal deadweight costs of protection rise. In sum, the consequences of government intervention, including direct regulation, will depend upon similar characteristics affecting the efficiency of private markets,

---

15 The seminal article here is Posner (1974), pp. 335-58.

16 See Downs (1957).

17 A seminal article presenting this broader general equilibrium theory of competition among pressure groups is Becker (1983), pp. 371-400.

18 Evaluating the efficiency consequences of government intervention is further complicated to the extent that intentional subsidies are included in the definition of public sector "output." See Becker (1983), p. 387.

19 The propensity for regulation to delay reactions to changes in demand and cost conditions is emphasized in Noll and Owen (1983). They suggest the reason is that outside interests are motivated to provide more evidence and analysis in support of a regulation conferring actual benefits than in support of a proposal conferring only anticipated benefits. Regulation is therefore seen as a process that can be used by incumbents to resist change.

e.g., barriers to entry associated with participating in political markets, asymmetries in the distribution of information, externalities, and so forth.

Numerous researchers have identified specific inefficiencies of regulation as an instrument of government intervention. For one thing, the bureaucrat as regulator does not compete for political support and therefore may enjoy more discretion than the typical politician does to pursue his or her own personal agenda for the industry. For another, impacted information is likely to be a characteristic of the regulation process. For example, Bell Canada is likely to have much better information about the expected value of a long distance franchise than will an outsider to the industry such as IBM. This suggests that the variability of the expected outcome of the "political bidding" process is lower for Bell Canada than for IBM, *ceteris paribus*. Using a mean-variance framework to characterize risk, one can show that Bell Canada might be willing to spend more on keeping IBM out of the long distance sector than IBM is willing to spend to get into the sector, notwithstanding that net social output might increase with IBM's entry.[20] In other words, consumers may be unaware or misinformed about opportunities under a deregulated regime, since these opportunities would emerge only with deregulation.

Regulation of Telecommunications

Any single theory of regulation drawn from the literature and applied to the telecommunications industry would encounter some "inconvenient" empirical challenges. For example, the interest group theory of direct regulation would seemingly not predict the current status whereby toll calls are effectively "taxed" to provide undifferentiated subsidies for local subscribers. This is because toll calling is fairly concentrated, primarily among business subscribers, while local subscription is diffused throughout virtually the entire population.

Wenders suggests that, in fact, the underlying logic of the interest group model fails to apply in the case of telecommunications because local subscribers are well informed at relatively low cost about changes in local rates and need relatively little organizational effort to affect the political process through their access to elected representatives.[21] However, it might also be argued that local subscribers are well represented by lobby groups and, furthermore, that specific provincial governments have been particularly effective lobbyists for

---

20 This example is hypothetical as there is a more direct barrier to IBM's entry as a Type I carrier. Namely, foreign-owned companies cannot operate in Canada as Type I carriers. Baldwin (1989) notes that legislative conditions surrounding the ability of the government to pre-empt private property rights also condition the efficiency of alternative instruments of government intervention.

21 See Wenders (1987).

the current rate structure. In addition, intensive users of long distance service may pass most of the costs on to consumers, in which case the final incidence of higher longer distance rates may be best thought of as being widely diffused.

In short, it is difficult to dismiss out-of-hand the relevance of interest group models to telecommunications regulation; there are arguments both for and against public interest models. For example, many observers argue that the industry is in numerous respects a natural monopoly. Others argue that regulation is required to sustain "socially desirable" cross-subsidies or to impart some stability to a "risk-averse" Canadian populace. Counter-arguments are offered to the effect that comprehensive regulation is not necessitated by natural monopoly and that there exist more efficient methods of cross-subsidies.[22]

It is not the objective of this paper to discriminate among various normative models of the determinants of regulation or to seek reconciliation of the various theories within the broader framework suggested by Becker. Rather, the objective is to present and evaluate positive evidence on the economic impacts of telecommunications regulation and deregulation, with a view towards assessing the potential net economic benefits (or costs) of further deregulation of the industry.

Examination of telecommunications regulatory processes underscores the importance of income redistribution as an objective of regulation. Noteworthy is the underlying diversity of subsidy "targets." For example, in some countries industrial policy objectives have been imposed upon the national carrier. These objectives are often related to promoting the growth of local telecommunications equipment suppliers. Closely related to industrial policy objectives is employment policy, particularly the preservation of higher-paying technical jobs in the industry. In other cases, regulation has sought to subsidize the extension of low-cost telecommunications services to less-developed or remote geographic regions, or to otherwise perceived disadvantaged social groups.[23] Occasional references are made to the need for government to prevent "excessive" duplication of telephone networks or to the goal of reducing telecommunications prices; however, in recent years, income distribution has emerged as a dominant target for regulators of telecommunications.

---

22 These arguments can be found, among other sources, in W.T. Stanbury's Discussion paper following this chapter.

23 For example, telecommunications regulation has been identified as an aspect of labour market policy in countries such as Austria, Italy, Holland, Norway, and Spain. The use of regulation as an instrument to promote local equipment suppliers has been noted in some of these same countries, as well as in France and Germany. See DIW (1988). The extension of regional subsidies as a motive for regulation is present in European countries such as Germany, Italy, Norway, and Spain, as well as in Canada.

The extent to which "socially desirable" transfers take place, as well as the extent to which they are efficiently effected, are ultimately empirical questions. Observation of the mechanics of regulation in different countries does not encourage a sanguine outlook on either issue. Generally, regulatory objectives are informal, complicated, and often conflicting.[24] Furthermore, regulators usually operate with far fewer resources than the established common carriers. Nevertheless, efficiency considerations are clearly not ignored by the regulatory process. In an increasing number of countries, the adverse impact on efficiency of cross-subsidies in the tariff structure has been identified by regulators. This awareness has followed from increased international competition and consequent "demonstration effects" from countries where significant deregulation has been implemented.[25]

In Canada, as in many other countries, these efficiency costs have not been seen as sufficiently large to encourage a faster abandonment of telecommunications regulations as an instrument for redistributing income. Partly, this complacency derives from a widely held view that the telecommunications network remains a natural monopoly, so that the real costs of providing telecommunications services are minimized by having a single carrier (or at most, two carriers) supplying network services.[26] It also reflects the perspective that the telecommunications regulatory system has not adversely affected, at least to date, the provision of telecommunications services in Canada. As one respected researcher has remarked of the Canadian telecommunications industry, "We possess a nationally integrated system that, in terms of availability, reliability, range of services and costs, is reputed to have few equals. Although there may be some disagreement over the criteria and evidence for this claim, it is one that is generally acknowledged, most notably by the governments who seek changes in the regulatory system."[27]

No one to my knowledge has argued that regulation is costless or that socially undesirable transfers of income do not take place; however, there remains a great deal of controversy surrounding the precise impacts of regulation on resource allocation within the industry, with only somewhat less controversy surrounding the ultimate distributional consequences of deregulation. These latter issues are the primary focus of the next two sections of this paper.

---

24 See DIW (1988).
25 Large business subscribers usually cross-subsidize residential subscribers. Increased international competition reduces the ability of regulators to impose implicit taxes on domestically based companies.
26 For a statement of this position in the Canadian context, see Quayle (1989), pp. 145-58.
27 See Schultz (1984), p. 43.

Performance Under Regulation

The telecommunications industry has been the subject of intense empirical examination. While some disagreement surrounds the precise impacts of regulation, a reasonable degree of consensus joins telecommunications economists on the general performance of the industry under regulation.

The performance of the industry can be evaluated along the standard two dimensions of efficiency and equity. Efficiency, in turn, can be thought of in both allocative and technical terms. Allocative efficiency exists when no conceivable reallocation of resources across different sectors of the economy will encourage an increase in real output. Technical efficiency exists when any chosen basket of output is produced at lowest possible cost.

Technical efficiency at any point in time is associated with the capture of extant economies of scale and scope, while technical efficiency over time is associated with technological change in the industry. The "optimal" rate of technological change is difficult to identify. In principle, it is the rate at which the marginal social returns to further technological change equal the associated marginal social costs. In practice, analysts evaluate dynamic efficiency by seeking to determine if firms have exploited all apparent opportunities to adopt and implement new technology.

Allocative Efficiency

Most economists agree that there are substantial allocative inefficiencies associated with the existing regulated telephone pricing structure. In particular, the welfare losses are caused by the overpricing of long distance service and the underpricing of residential access. The impact of regulated pricing cross-subsidies is illustrated in figure 2. The first panel shows that the overpricing of long distance service leads to a foregone "welfare" triangle (ABC) whose area depends upon the elasticity of demand. The welfare triangle is defined by the excess of price (PL_D) over marginal cost (MCL_D) over the relevant range of output ($QL_DQ^1_{LD}$). The second panel shows that the underpricing of local access leads to a welfare triangle loss (DEF) defined as the excess of marginal cost (MC_L) over price (P_L) over the range of output ($Q_LQ^1_L$). Given that long distance demand is much more price elastic than demand for local access, the primary welfare effects of mispricing telephone services are associated with the overpricing of long distance.[28]

---

28 For a review of available evidence on the demand for long distance service, see Globerman (1989a). Surveys of demand patterns for local telephony can be found in Taylor (1980) and Coopers and Lybrand Consulting Group, vols. I and II, October 1985 and February 1986.

Figure 2
Allocative Consequences of Telephone Pricing Cross-Subsidy

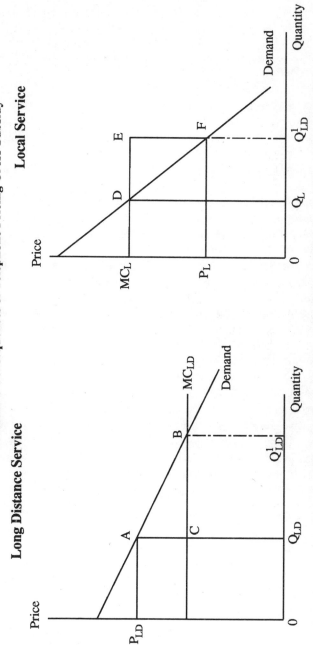

Long Distance Service

Local Service

For convenience, demand curves are assumed to be linear and marginal cost is assumed to be constant.

Using data for the United States as a guideline, Globerman offers a crude estimate of the welfare losses from telephone pricing cross-subsidies in Canada of around $2 billion per year using 1984 prices.[29] The order of magnitude of this estimate roughly agrees with the estimate of a more recent study that found that a 40 percent across the board toll rate reduction would have provided a net gain in consumer surplus of over $0.6 billion per year in Canada in 1982.[30] This social welfare loss far outweighs any plausible estimates of possible benefits from network externalities derived from an increased number of subscribers on the telephone network.

When evaluating the allocative consequences of regulated prices, one considers also whether existing cross-subsidies are instruments to accomplish broader social objectives. In the latter case, it would be inappropriate (as Becker suggests) to classify as waste the allocative costs due to departures from efficient pricing without acknowledging the social benefits. Indeed, it has been suggested that the regulator could implement Ramsey-type prices thereby giving more weight to the allocative efficiency objective.[31] That the regulator could, in theory, duplicate efficient prices does not, of course, by itself imply that such duplication would avoid undesirable consequences, although such consequences have been claimed by opponents of deregulation.

The primary concern is that deregulation will lead to fewer subscribers to the network which would attenuate the universality of telephone service. A close examination of this threat finds that for plausible increases in local access charges, the drop-off problem would be minimal.[32] It is true, however, that efficient telecommunications prices would, at least in the short run, increase the overall telephone bills of most residential and small business subscribers, while lowering the overall telephone bills of large business subscribers. The ostensible redistribution of income from the many to the few might be seen as socially undesirable; however, this conclusion would ignore several considerations. One is that a substantial portion, perhaps all, of the savings realized by large business subscribers would, over time, be passed on to consumers in the form of lower prices. Another is that the repricing of telephone services will not necessarily be closely related to resulting changes in the distribution of income. This follows because household income accounts for only 2 to 10 percent of the observed variation in toll and local usage. Other demographic

---

29 See Globerman (1986). It is likely that the annual losses would be somewhat lower in constant dollar terms at the present time given the substantial reductions that have taken place in long distance rates in the past few years. These rate declines are likely larger than decreases in the marginal cost of long distance service that have also occurred in recent years.

30 See Peat Marwick (1984), pp. vi-17.

31 See, for example, Selwyn and Townsend (1988).

32 See Wenders (1987).

factors, such as size of household, age of household, and location are far more important to explaining toll usage patterns.[33]

In principle, it is certainly true that the regulator could implement Ramsey prices and achieve allocative efficiency by fiat. Indeed, several studies argue that this would maximize the allocative gains from "rate rebalancing," since it would not result in foregone economies of scale associated with spreading any given amount of calling over several competitors.[34] In practice, however, it would appear that the regulator is concerned with perpetuating a relatively complex redistribution of income that is not clearly correlated with income levels. In the view of some observers, a complex and largely obscure redistribution of income is what is to be expected from the regulatory process because of imperfect information, lags in decision making, imprecise tools of analysis, and, more generally, diseconomies to centralized pricing.[35]

Technical Efficiency

The debate about the "optimal" structure of telecommunications chiefly addresses the conditions necessary to exploit extant economies of scale and scope. Whatever its motivation, to the extent that regulation renders a natural monopoly sustainable, it could contribute to improved technical efficiency.

In principle, a set of production conditions can lead to unsustainable market prices for a natural monopoly.[36] As a practical matter, these conditions are sufficiently restrictive so as to have little policy relevance. Far more relevant are the cross-subsidies flowing from the industry's pricing structure. Telecom Canada has long argued that the subsidy from toll to local, in particular, invites "uneconomic" entry, i.e., entry by higher cost carriers, which, in turn, fragments economies of scale and scope in the network. In this context, it is regulation itself that creates a sustainability problem. An extension of this argument is that barriers to industry entry are required if cross-subsidies are to be maintained together with a technically efficient industry structure. A corollary is that the elimination of rate rebalancing can presumably proceed more efficiently under the monopoly structure than under competition, since the benefits of economies of scale and scope can be exploited.[37]

---

33 See Faulhaber (1987), p. 162.
34 See Peat Marwick (1984) and Peat Marwick (1988).
35 See, for example, Johnson (1982). Some observers argue that the experience of the FCC in trying to make regulated prices correspond more closely to cost demonstrates the infeasibility of regulatory efforts to identify the economic costs of specific services. See Noll (1989), pp. 11-48.
36 For one discussion, see Panzar and Willig (1977), pp. 1-22.
37 See Peat Marwick (1988).

Several potential problems limit this "constrained" natural monopoly argument on behalf of regulation. Most importantly, evidence on the magnitude of economies of scale and scope is inconclusive at best. Specifically, most econometric studies find some evidence of economies of scale in the aggregate telecommunications services cost function; however, the evidence is of very weak economies of scope, and no reliable evidence supports the existence of product specific economies of scale.[38] Engineering studies tend to provide stronger support for the existence of substantial economies of scale and scope in both switching and transmission technologies with the magnitudes of these economies increasing as a function of evolving technology, especially fibre optics transmission.[39] However, engineering studies are subject to a host of potential biases.

In my opinion, a more important caveat to the policy relevance of extant economies of scale and scope in the industry is the likelihood that the rate of technological change will be a much more important determinant of industry performance in the long run. It is for their technological performance that regulated common carriers have been especially criticized. Specifically, rate-of-return regulation discourages dynamic efficiency for a host of reasons, including the absence of residual claimant rights on the part of the service supplier to any efficiency gains associated with innovation.

The technological performance of regulated telecommunications carriers is itself affected by several regulatory constraints, including the rates at which "superior" production techniques are implemented and superior new products are introduced to the market. Since there is no absolute standard of technological efficiency against which to compare the performance of the regulated carriers, the available evidence tends to be impressionistic rather than definitive. Nevertheless, taken as a whole the pattern of evidence is persuasive to the effect that the major North American telephone companies have exhibited great technological virtuosity notwithstanding comprehensive rate-of-return regulation. The caveat to this conclusion is that the exploitation of technology was vigorous and aggressive from the purely technical point of view, but remarkably pedestrian from a market point of view.[40]

This particular story is told with special reference to AT&T. The pre-divestiture era is described as the golden age of technology for the Bell System. Bell Labs practically founded the field of solid-state physics. The transistor which, in turn, became the basis of the digital-electronics revolution grew out of this effort. Similarly, the Bell System successfully deployed direct distance dialling (DDD) nationwide, as well as the sophisticated cable and radio transmission

---

38 For a review of this literature, see Globerman (1988a).
39 See, for example, Coopers and Lybrand Consulting Group (1988).
40 See Faulhaber (1987), p. 14.

systems needed to carry the resulting traffic. But this concentration on improving service through technological progress did not extend to a concern about sales. The Bell System allowed small firms to provide the specialized services that AT&T management felt were not fundamental to operating the core network.

This perspective on the Bell System is captured in Temin's seminal history of the AT&T divestiture:

> As service organizations, the operating companies had been used to asking customers what their service needs were and then specifying a system to satisfy them. There was no question of offering options: The Bell System knew best. If marketing was unhappy, they were told to go back and explain to the customer why he should be happy. There was hardly any feedback from customers to design. There was certainly no tradition that the customer was always right. However, the system was a technological success story.[41]

An issue here, of course, is whether the emphasis on engineering technology at the expense of marketing innovation was inherently promoted by regulation, per se, or whether it followed primarily from the organizational structure and managerial background of AT&T pre-divestiture. Some insight into this issue is provided by the post-divestiture experience of AT&T. After divestiture, AT&T gave the line of business heads effective control over the functions needed to serve their markets, along with responsibility for their effective deployment. In the past, there were tri-company committees and a General Departments organization trying to figure out what the company's priorities should be. In the new corporate structure, authority for decision making was moved closer to the customer.

The R&D functions performed by Bell Labs remained the major exception to this rule. Matrix management, initially employed in the market-segmented units of the operating companies in 1978, survived in the new AT&T in 1983. But even in the renamed AT&T Bell Labs, operations were realigned and decision-making authority was modified to give the line of business heads the major influence over the lab's priorities and projects. In this type of organization, the head of each line of business is assigned a measure of authority over the researchers in Bell Labs that are working in areas related to his or her line of business.[42]

The greater attention paid to marketing considerations pursuant to deregulation is also an important characteristic of the subscriber equipment interconnection industry which will be detailed in a later section of this paper. The main

---

41 See Temin (1987), p. 143.
42 Ibid., pp. 327-28.

point to be made here is that product variety expanded dramatically with the liberalization of restrictions on subscriber-owned apparatus.[43]

The Experience Outside of North America

While the regulatory structure outside of North America differs from country to country (and also differs from the North American experience), certain parallels in performance can be identified. Most notably, cross-subsidies are a prevalent feature of the pricing structure, and the resulting mark-ups, contrary to Ramsey rules, are ordinarily highest on more price-elastic demand curves. While some European telecommunication firms have been relatively slow to implement new technology such as digital switching and fibre optics, others have been remarkably quick to implement specific innovations such as cellular telephones. As a general statement, Western European carriers have supplied a captive national market with a limited range of technically rather conservative customer premises equipment that were only saleable there.[44] But before one generalizes about the weaknesses of captive suppliers it should be noted that the family of domestic suppliers to Nippon Telephone and Telegraph (NTT) are acknowledged to develop some of the best products available in the industry.[45]

Performance Under Deregulation

More direct potential approaches to evaluating the impacts of deregulation involve comparing the performance of given suppliers of telecommunication services before and after deregulation, and/or comparing the performance of different suppliers operating under alternative regulatory regimes.

Performance Under Different Regulatory Regimes

Given the wide range of regulatory regimes across countries as well as across individual states and provinces, there is rich potential for examining the implications of deregulation through the judicious use of cross-section studies. This methodology, however, is affected by the simultaneous effect of other non-regulatory factors that influence performance. These include telephone calling patterns, exchange rate changes, and so on. Moreover, given the complex differences in the characteristics of national common carriers, including state versus private ownership, integration versus non-integration with the

---

43 See Globerman (1988b), pp. 55-58. While not as comprehensively documented as in the AT&T case, there is anecdotal evidence that the Bell Canada-Northern Telecom linkage emphasized technological breakthroughs rather than responsiveness to changing market demands. See Globerman (1980), pp. 977-98.

44 See DIW (1988).

45 See Harris (1989), pp. 113-31.

postal service and so forth, it is difficult to identify the precise effects of specific regulatory policies.

These difficulties are illustrated by the international comparison of "typical" annual telephone bills summarized in figure 3. In order to control for the influence of fluctuating exchange rates, the chosen measure of performance is the average number of hours of work needed to pay a typical telephone bill. Figure 3 illustrates that notwithstanding divergences in regulatory policies over time across the sample countries, there has been a substantial convergence in the relative costs of telephone service over the period 1973 to 1988. Apparently, relative productivity increases in the provision of telephone service over this period were ubiquitous and dominated the influence of country specific differences in regulatory policies. What is particularly striking in these data is the relative deterioration in the performance of the United States from 1975 to 1988, notwithstanding that deregulation proceeded faster and more extensively in the United States than elsewhere.

One explanation of this anomaly is that the data in figure 3 are ultimately based on a calling "basket" for a representative country, in this case West Germany. To the extent that the West German basket is unrepresentative of the baskets for other countries, the cost comparisons will be distorted. In this case, the choice of the basket probably biases upward the relative U.S. costs because one consequence associated with the U.S. experience is a decline in the ratio of long distance to local rates. All other things the same, long distance calling should have increased relative to local calling in the United States. The use of a U.S. basket instead of a West German one should therefore prove to be more favourable to U.S. performance. In other words, international comparisons, where the basket of calls is a function of the structure of tariffs, will be sensitive to the index chosen as a base. Comparisons are complicated further by differences in calling patterns flowing from such factors as the geography of a country, the mix of residential and business subscribers, and so forth. Relative changes in this mix between countries over time will, independently of tariff changes, affect aggregate cost comparisons among these countries.

Non-regulatory related influences on relative performance would likely be modest for comparisons between the United States and Canada because of similarities in demographics, real income levels, and related factors. We have some confidence, therefore, in the estimates of the unit cost positions of two Canadian and four U.S. intercity networks (in terms of the Canadian dollar) as a function of standardized long distance volume as provided in figures 4 and 5. The comparisons presented in figures 4 and 5 are from accounting data for 1986.[46] The researchers responsible for figures 4 and 5 argue that the data

---

46 A full description of the methodology underlying these figures is provided in Coopers and Lybrand Consulting Group (1988). The two Canadian networks are

document the existence of economies of scale over the range of output produced by North American long distance carriers. They also suggest that Canadian network costs are lower than those of the U.S. networks primarily due to differences in the route configurations in the two countries, i.e., a single east-west route in Canada versus a complex grid in the U.S. In addition, if network access charges are removed from the U.S. data, the industry cost curve shifts down, becoming almost a direct extension of the Canadian curve.[47]

While the output-adjusted costs of the Canadian and U.S. long distance telephone networks may be comparable, prices to consumers are significantly different. In particular, overall telecommunication costs to businesses in Canada are significantly higher than those in the United States where the services are based on a "market basket" comprising local, toll, and WATS components.[48] Except for low mileage bands, costs of message toll service are also much higher in Canada. For example, a three-minute call (customer-dialled, business day) over a distance of 1,500 miles in Canada would be more than double a similar call over AT&T lines. At the same time, local rates in Canada are substantially lower than in the U.S.

If the data in figures 4 and 5 are taken at face value, a suggestive story follows about the impact of deregulation on the telecommunications industry taken in conjunction with telephone prices in the two countries. Specifically, the data suggest that while deregulation is associated with a closer convergence of prices to costs, technical efficiency may be relatively insensitive to the specific regulatory regime. This hypothesis is not implausible in an industry such as telecommunications where costs will be heavily influenced by technological change, where regulators are sensitive to suppliers' choice of technology, and where technology diffuses fairly rapidly across different suppliers. Yet it may be that technological change in the past was relatively stable and that with a recent significant acceleration in the rate of technological change in the industry, the consequences of regulatory bureaucracy will become more apparent in future international comparisons.[49] Already, telecommunications managers in a range of industries, including financial services, have recently argued that adoption rates for new technology in Canada are beginning to

---

Telecom Canada and CNCP. The U.S. networks are AT&T, MCI, Sprint, and Western Union. Figure 4 provides estimates of units costs expressed in Canadian dollars. Figure 5 estimates costs in local currency terms and excludes access charges for the U.S. networks.

47 Ibid., p. E7.

48 See D.A. Ford and Associates Ltd. (1986).

49 For some evidence that economies of scale rather than technological change has been the most significant historical source or productivity growth in the industry, see Kiss and Lefebvre (1984).

Figure 3
International Comparison of Typical Annual Telephone Bills*

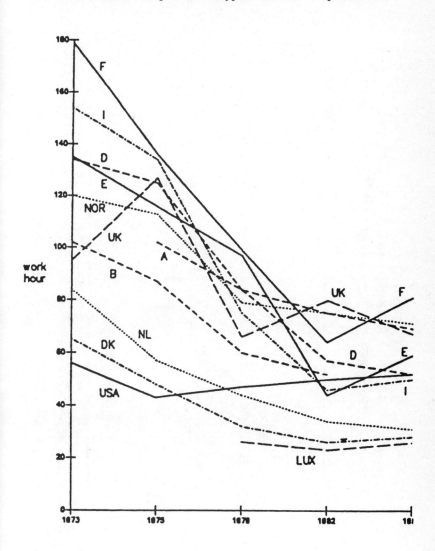

*based on number of working hours required to pay for the basket of charges

Source: DIW (1988), p. 45.

Figure 4

Competitive Cost Position of Canadian and U.S. Intercity Networks
From Financial Results—Canadian Currency

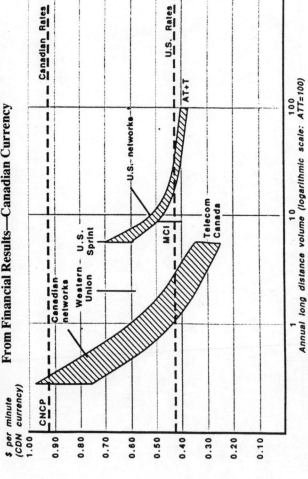

* The cost data for U.S. networks includes access charges

Source: Coopers and Lybrand (1988), *The Effect of Changing Technology on the Structure of Costs for the Provision of Public Long Distance Telephone Service* (Ottawa: Supply and Services Canada), p. E-14. Reprinted with permission.

Figure 5

Competitive Cost Position of Canadian and U.S. Intercity Networks
From Financial Results—Local Currencies

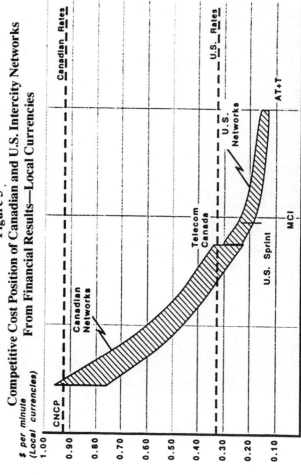

Source: Coopers and Lybrand (1988), *The Effect of Changing Technology on the Structure of Costs for the Provision of Public Long Distance Telephone Service* (Ottawa: Supply and Services Canada), p. E-16. Reprinted with permission.

noticeably lag rates in the United States. Examples include the ubiquity of fibre optic transmission lines and high capacity data lines.[50]

Indices of relative costs are in any event only partial measures of dynamic efficiency. The introduction of new products and services is another, along with the modification of existing products to better suit the tastes and preferences of consumers. Unfortunately, data required to document relative diffusion rates for new products and services are often unavailable. Instead, the researcher usually has to consider partial and anecdotal information about the availability of new products and services in different parts of the world. Certainly, one would anticipate a greater range of new services in more deregulated environments, *ceteris paribus*, and casual evidence suggests that this is the case. On the other hand, one can point to examples of countries such as Singapore where a monopoly carrier is acknowledged to provide state-of-the-art telephone services in an international context. To be sure, the latter example has more to do with Singapore's industrial policy (and associated public subsidies to the industry) than with the state of competition in Singapore's domestic telephone industry.

One might also argue that Singapore's monopoly domestic carrier is actually in vibrant competition with other international carriers for the role of telecommunications node in the Asia-Pacific region. In this context, the Singapore experience might be seen as support for the hypothesis that competition promotes the diffusion of new products and services. However, one must prudently acknowledge that it is difficult to assign weights to the impact of differences in regulatory regimes on technological diffusion given the present state of information.

This latter observation is underscored by patterns of technological diffusion among European post, telephone, and telecommunication services (PTTs). Notwithstanding a range of alternative institutional arrangements, there is no clear pattern of dominant technological leaders and followers. For example, the relatively unregulated British Telecom network is considered to be using a high proportion of modern technology compared to many other PTTs. At the same time, the highly regulated French telephone network is considered to be one of the most modern in the world. As another example, the Norwegian telephone system was one of the first in western Europe to establish a domestic satellite system. It also has the highest rate of diffusion of mobile communications in

---

50 See, for example, Hogg and Horhota (1989). In the Canadian context, the deployment of new technology as embodied in physical equipment might also be affected by Department of Communications' policies with respect to rights-of-way, spectrum use, equipment certification, and the like. These policies are outside the ambit of policies associated with direct regulation by the CRTC.

the world. At the same time, it has been one of the last to abandon manually operated telephone exchanges.[51]

Evidently, rankings of technical efficiency will be influenced by how one measures such efficiency, as well as by a host of factors such as relative input prices that are not necessarily related to differences in regulatory structure.

Performance Impacts of Deregulation

As noted above, another approach to identifying the effects of deregulation is to compare the performance of specific carriers or a specific set of carriers before and after a change in the regulatory regime. This "time series" approach may have an inherent advantage over the "cross-section" approach in that it may be more plausible, *ceteris paribus*, to invoke assumptions in the former case.

The most obvious case for such a time series study is the U.S. telecommunications industry, as deregulation of the industry in the U.S. arguably took place earlier and in a more comprehensive manner than in other developed countries. However, an obvious problem is how to date and quantify the nature and extent of deregulation. On this point, some might argue that competition in the long distance sector became a relevant influence on the performance of AT&T only with the advent of equal access. Others might argue that the initial decision to allow MCI interconnection with AT&T for purposes of providing private line service should have provoked notable responses from AT&T.[52]

Not surprisingly, there have been quite a large number of investigations of the performance of the U.S. telephone industry in the post-divestiture environment. In fact, several major studies were commissioned by the CRTC as part of the Federal-Provincial-Territorial Task Force examination into the Canadian telecommunications industry. Given the potential importance of these studies to the issues that concern this paper, it is useful here to review part of the available literature in some detail.

One comprehensive review of the U.S. experience, undertaken by Selwyn and Townsend, concludes that many of the substantive changes that took place in the U.S. industry were either unrelated to competition or incidental to competition.[53] For example, toll price reductions reflected regulatory action with respect to reductions over time in the non-traffic sensitive cost recovery responsibility imposed upon long distance service and the rate reductions

---

51 See DIW (1988).

52 At least one researcher argues that due to the gradual advent of competition in the U.S. telephone industry, it is extremely difficult to state a date at which the industry became competitive, let alone sufficiently competitive as to affect the behaviour of the established firms. See Chessler (1988).

53 See Selwyn and Townsend (1988).

imposed upon AT&T under conventional rate-of-return regulation. Selwyn and Townsend acknowledge that regulatory decisions to move long distance and local prices closer to their respective costs might have been in response to the prior commitment to open up the long distance market to competitive entry. One might extrapolate that had AT&T's prices been deregulated sooner, a more rapid "rate rebalancing" would have taken place under market force influences than in fact took place under political influences. The latter supposition is supported by the observed correlation between the overall level of toll rates and the applicable level of competition. Specifically, interstate interlata rates are generally lowest, followed by intrastate interlata rates, followed by intrastate intralata rates.[54]

More specific evidence of the changing patterns of public network telephone rates for the United States is provided in table 2. The data in table 2 show that the annual average price decrease in the more deregulated interstate MTS markets exceeded the annual average price decrease in the intrastate MTS markets by a considerable margin in the 1982-87 period, whereas decreases in the latter exceeded decreases in the former in the 1972-82 period. The pattern for WATS rates is quite comparable over the two time periods. One might conclude that in the more heavily regulated (intrastate) long distance markets, the convergence between prices and costs is proceeding more slowly than in the essentially unregulated interstate market.

Selwyn and Townsend also acknowledge that at the interexchange (IX) level, new pricing and packaging arrangements have proliferated rapidly as a consequence of competition, as carriers have sought to segment the market and appeal to specific customer groups. These pricing and packaging arrangements have generally involved such strategies as bulk discounts and combinations or unbundling of existing service capabilities, as opposed to any new technical features. At the same time, the presence of competition in the IX long distance market in the United States has not directly affected the development of new services or the general availability of service options on the local exchange level.[55]

On a more technical level, the entry of competing interstate common carriers into the market for switched and dedicated IX transport services has resulted in the introduction of several new physical serving arrangements that combine switched and dedicated facilities which, in turn, facilitate the offering of numerous different service packages. These packages differ primarily with respect to their pricing. The equal access conversion requirements of the AT&T divestiture settlement also helped compel local carriers to modernize their exchange networks, improving both the quality of long distance connections to

---

54 Ibid., p. 16.
55 Ibid.

non-AT&T carriers and the basic central office facilities used in the provision of local service generally.

In sum, Selwyn and Townsend's analysis highlights the major impact that deregulation in the United States has had on the range of private line and switched network services. They find that competition has apparently stimulated a noteworthy effort on the part of carriers to expand the range of competitively priced services tailored to the calling characteristics of distinct user groups. While there were some concerns expressed in the early stages of the post-divestiture period about delays in service ordering, billing errors, confusion about tariff structures, and quality of the services offered by other common carriers (OCCs), these concerns have by now largely dissipated. For example, U.S. Sprint's fibre-optic network is now apparently the "cutting edge" of communications technology.[56] Moreover, fears of significant "drop-offs" from the network have been largely unfounded. Indeed, local telephone subscription has been increasing both in absolute terms and in terms of penetration. Some rural states have, in fact, shown small decreases in penetration rates, but these effects are more attributable to recession in local industry than to changing telephone service prices.[57]

Another comprehensive analysis of the U.S. experience with deregulation argues that measures of real costs per unit of output in the industry—per telephone, per telephone call, or per unit of aggregate output—all increased in the 1980s, whether their long-term trends had been declining (as had costs per call) or rising (as had the other two measures).[58] These results are summarized in table 3. Moreover, measures of output per labour hour in the 1980s were noticeably lower than the long-term averages, while total factor productivity in the industry was also below its long-term average (see table 4).

While Chessler is unable to tie the below-average productivity performance directly to the AT&T divestiture or other manifestations of competition, the results are heavily influenced by major cost increases recorded by the industry in 1984.[59] Chessler acknowledges that this jump in costs may be associated with network reconfiguration and other divestiture-related expenses, although the latter should presumably be amortized. He also notes that the rapid introduction of new products and services in the 1980s undoubtedly biased upwards conventional price indices for the industry, since these new services were primarily directed towards large price-sensitive businesses. Moreover, the

---

56 See "People Aren't Laughing At U.S. Sprint Any More," *Business Week*, July 31, 1989, p. 82.

57 Selwyn and Townsend (1988), p. 42.

58 See Chessler (1988).

59 Constant dollar expenses per unit of output increased by almost 20 percent in 1984. The largest increase prior to that year was 5.33 percent in 1982. See Chessler (1988), p. 55.

Table 2
Annual Rate of Change in Real Telephone Rates
1972-87 (Percentage)

Period	Interstate MTS	Interstate WATS	Interstate MTS	Interstate WATS	Local Residential	Local Business
1972-82	-3.5	-5.4	-3.9	-3.6	-2.9	-2.8
1982-87	-6.8	-5.8	-1.6	-3.9	+4.2	+3.9

Source: Crandall (1989), p. 54.

Table 3
Average Annual Changes in Expenses Per Telephone and Per Call
(GNP Deflator, 1982 = 100)

Average Percentage Change Expenses Per Telephone		Average Percentage Change Expenses Per Call		Average Percentage Change Per Unit of BLS Output	
Years	% Change	Years	% Change	Years	% Change
(1951-80)	0.138	(1951-80)	-0.273	(1952-80)	-2.900
(1951-83)	0.192	(1951-83)	-0.234	(1952-83)	-2.564
(1981-86)	1.886	(1981-86)	0.529	(1981-86)	2.262
(1984-86)	3.038	(1984-86)	0.906	(1984-86)	3.841

Source: Chessler (1988), p. 52 and p. 56.

Table 4

Communications: Indexes of Real Output, Inputs and Productivity Ratios

(1977 = 100)

Annual Percent Change, Selected Years

Year	Output and Inputs				Productivity Ratios			
	Real Output	Labour Input	Capital Input	Total Factor Input	Total Factor Productivity	Output Per Unit Labour	Output Per Unit Capital	Capital-Labour Ratio
1948/1986	6.4	1.0	6.0	2.5	3.8	5.4	0.3	5.0
1948/1965	6.6	0.0	6.2	1.0	5.6	6.6	0.4	6.2
1965/1973	8.2	3.4	6.7	4.7	3.4	4.7	1.4	3.2
1973/1979	6.2	1.9	5.9	3.7	2.4	4.3	0.2	4.0
1979/1986	4.0	-0.1	5.0	2.6	1.3	4.1	-1.0	5.1

Source: Chessler (1988), p. 109.

proliferation of options available to subscribers suggests a greater opportunity to substitute lower-cost for higher-cost options, thereby accentuating the upward bias of "fixed-weight" output baskets.

Other explanations for increases in costs and prices in the 1980s include accounting and depreciation changes mandated by the Federal Communications Commission (FCC), the cost of providing equal access, and the substitution of technology-embodying capital for labour. This latter factor may be especially relevant given the fact that Chessler uses gross rather than net capital as the input series in his productivity index. This may seriously overstate the growth of recent capital inputs and, hence, understate the growth in productivity. Higher quality service and the installation of (temporary) excess capacity may also be relevant factors. It is suggestive that Bell Canada reported substantial productivity increases over the mid-1980s. Since the Bell Canada and AT&T productivity experiences were comparable over most of the post-war period, the divergence in the post-divestiture period suggests that AT&T (and rival carriers) were initiating changes in anticipation of a radically altered competitive environment.

Chessler also goes to great lengths to argue that any improvements in AT&T's performance in the post-divestiture period is primarily the result of opportunities created by exogenous technological change. Moreover, many of the manpower reductions undertaken by AT&T took place in the company's computer division. It is unclear why either observation mitigates against concluding that AT&T was responding in conventional ways to competitive pressures. Chessler also discounts the many new services introduced by AT&T as being primarily "disguised bulk discounts," notwithstanding that finer pricing options for subscribers can clearly be welfare enhancing.

Thomas argues that the concentration of market share in the long distance sector, despite the radical structural changes to the industry, suggests a fundamental absence of competitiveness.[60] He acknowledges that there has been almost a four-fold increase in the number of IX carriers (mostly resellers) providing long distance service in the United States in the post-divestiture period. Yet, AT&T's current share of the interlata market is approximately 70 percent, whereas its share of the interexchange market in the mid-1970s was around 83 percent. Furthermore, each of the seven regional Bell holding companies (or independent carriers) continues to carry close to 100 percent of the intralata traffic in its area, even in those states where intralata competition is allowed.

The persistence of a relatively high market share for AT&T is consistent with the existence of a contestable market for telecommunications sources because of lags in consumer responses to changes in market opportunities. In

---

60 See Thomas (1988).

particular, one would not expect residential subscribers to respond quickly to the initiatives of competitive IX carriers given that most residential subscribers make few long distance telephone calls. It is instructive therefore that AT&T's share of interstate business traffic dropped from 91.6 percent in 1979 to around 59 percent in 1987.[61] Furthermore, non-predatory competitive responses by AT&T may well account for part of the explanation of its persistent high market share, especially as AT&T continues to enjoy higher ratings than its major rivals for service quality and technical performance according to business subscribers.[62]

With the most liberalized telecommunications institutions in Europe, the performance of Britain's telecommunications industry is also of particular interest. The United Kingdom is unique in Europe in permitting an alternative carrier of basic network services to compete with the established national carrier. In addition, deregulation of the customer premises equipment (CPE) and value added network services (VANS) segments of the industry has been more extensive than in other European countries.[63]

While competitive threats to the established carrier, British Telecom (BT), have been relatively limited, to date BT has responded in a predictable manner. Specifically, it has moved prices substantially closer to costs with long distance tariffs on dense traffic routes falling particularly sharply, while tariffs for local calls and line rentals have risen. It might be noted that BT had more flexibility to move its tariffs away from a route-averaged basis than did AT&T. The pricing behaviour of BT with respect to route densities therefore suggests that competition can probably be counted on to drive prices closer to costs on a more disaggregated basis than can regulated competition, either because route price averaging is a durable intended form of cross-subsidy or because of regulatory inertia.[64]

BT's productivity growth averaged about 3 percent per annum for the first three years after the entry of its network competitor and accelerated to over 4 percent for the next two years. This was an improvement over the 2 percent per annum averaged in 17 years before liberalization, but comparable rates were achieved during the latter for short periods of time. Hence, it may be too soon

---

61 Ibid., p. 199.

62 Ibid., pp. 112-13.

63 The following summary of the British experience with telecommunications deregulation is taken largely from Foreman-Peck and Manning (1988), pp. 257-78.

64 Under the British Telecommunications Act of 1984, BT can raise prices for particular groups of services up to a price cap without requiring regulatory approval; however, the Office of Telecommunications (OFTEL) retains the responsibility to "promote" consumer interests in respect of prices. In this regard, OFTEL has warned BT that its rate rebalancing has gone far enough for the present. Ibid., p. 266.

to conclude whether competition has stimulated measurable long-run increases in BT's cost efficiency.

Similar to the AT&T experience, the presence of network competition has apparently stimulated BT to be more "customer-oriented." Quality of service has improved in recent years; and the range of services offered by BT has expanded. BT has also apparently become more diligent in seeking out lower cost sources of capital equipment.[65] Also, like the U.S. experience, new service options have proliferated, particularly for large business customers. BT has reformed its organizational structure to give more focus to the customer. One apparent difference from the AT&T experience is that BT has reduced its real R&D expenditures in recent years.

Part of the difficulty in inferring the consequences of deregulation from the network services experience is that there has been a very short history of competition, and the competition that has taken place has been relatively "controlled"; i.e., it has been competition managed by the regulator.[66] The telecommunications equipment sector offers the deregulation analyst a longer and less constrained experience with deregulation.

The U.S. and Canadian experience with interconnection of telephone equipment is longer than the European experience, so our brief review concentrates on the former.[67] Over time, restrictions on subscriber ownership of equipment were progressively relaxed so that, in most North American jurisdictions, there are effectively no prohibitions against ownership by either residential or business subscribers. Until 1956, in the United States the local telephone companies enjoyed an uncontested monopoly in the rental of subscriber equipment. Reflecting this situation, Bell System equipment accounted for 85 percent of all subscriber equipment in place at that time. Bell System equipment, in turn, was manufactured by Western Electric, the Bell System's domestic equipment manufacturing arm. Liberalization of the Canadian regime can be dated to 1980 for the federally regulated carriers and post-1982 for other provincial carriers.

It is extremely difficult to piece together a comprehensive picture of changes in the structure, behaviour, and performance of the terminal equipment industry pursuant to the liberalization of regulatory restrictions on interconnection primarily due to a lack of consistent time series data. Nevertheless, it is clear that new competition was slow to erode the Bell System's dominant

---

65 Ibid., p. 272.

66 Thus, NTT has not been allowed to de-average its long distance rates or raise its local rates. At the same time, authorities maintain a sizeable difference between NTT's rates and those of rival carriers. Not surprisingly, the latter are gaining a large share of new business in Japan. See Harris (1989).

67 For a chronology of deregulation of the equipment sector of the industry in the United States and Canada, see Globerman (1988b), pp. 48-57.

position over the 1960s and 1970s. For example, in 1969 PBX and Key Telephone System sales made by interconnect companies in Bell System territories accounted for less than one-half of 1 percent of all sales in those territories. By 1974, this percentage had risen to 3.7. Nevertheless, prices of PBXs and Key Telephones declined over the period, as did profit margins at AT&T. There was also a significant expansion in the range of product choice available to consumers.[68] Brock notes that by the end of 1973, customers had a choice of 39 Key Telephone System models available from 28 different manufacturers.[69]

Western Electric's share of the aggregate market continued to decline over the 1970s. One estimate placed Western Electric's share of the total market for Key Systems and small PBXs at 67 percent in 1974; by 1979, it was down to 58 percent. For large PBXs, the 80 percent share of the market in 1974 had declined to 67 percent by 1979. For conventional telephone sets, the corresponding shares were 72 percent and 62 percent, respectively.[70] Western Electric's market share continued to decline in the 1980s. For example, in 1984 AT&T accounted for only around 19 percent of all new PBX lines shipped.

More important, perhaps, is the observation that in the midst of liberalization, average real (and in some cases nominal) prices of terminal equipment declined. For example, since 1983, the average price per line for PBXs has dropped around 20 percent. Since 1981, the average cost to end-users for key telephone systems has been reduced by more than 50 percent. The average price of standard telephone instruments has remained flat or declined slightly over recent years despite the frequent addition of new features. In the case of specialty and "decorator" telephones, prices have steadily fallen.[71]

To be sure, technological change has made an important contribution toward lowering the costs of terminal equipment and expanding the range of features that can be economically offered at any given set of prices. In particular, the falling costs and increasing power of microchips has been a major factor enhancing the ability of telecommunications equipment suppliers to offer improved and cheaper subscriber equipment. Nevertheless, evidence clearly suggests that competition has played an important role in stimulating producers to take advantage of available technology and to pass a large portion of available benefits on to consumers. Such evidence includes observations that an increasing percentage of equipment was supplied from lower-cost offshore sources,

---

68 Ibid., p. 51.

69 See Brock (1981).

70 See A Report By the Majority Staff of the Subcommittee on Telecommunications, Consumer Protection and Finance, U.S. House of Representatives (Washington, D.C.: Government Printing Office), November 1981.

71 See Cormier (1985).

including AT&T equipment, and that profit margins at Western Electric dropped significantly over time.

The Canadian experience after interconnection is similar to the U.S. experience. Specifically, independent equipment manufacturers were able to capture a significant share of the market in the post-interconnection period. Also, where interconnection was permitted, the range of product choice increased dramatically. Evidence also suggests that technology was introduced at a more rapid rate. New Key Telephone Systems and PBXs are software driven with new additions, called generics, regularly introduced by the manufacturer. The interconnect companies introduced these new generics months ahead of the telephone companies.

In summary, the North American experience with deregulation of the terminal equipment sector of the telecommunications industry strongly suggests that consumers benefited from a faster adoption of new technology by equipment suppliers as manifested in lower prices and improved product features. An expanded range of product choices is also an identifiable feature of the interconnection experience. The interconnection experience also suggests that the beneficial effects of competition are experienced with a time lag. This is a potentially relevant caveat to those expecting "instant gratification" from the AT&T divestiture.

Taken as a whole, the available, albeit fragmented, evidence suggests that the introduction of competition into various sectors of the telecommunications industry has, on balance, encouraged a greater convergence between prices and costs, i.e., allocative efficiency, a proliferation of new products and services, and a faster adoption of new cost-saving technologies, i.e., dynamic efficiencies. Perhaps equally noteworthy, there is little evidence of the dire consequences that some observers of the industry cautioned would be the result of deregulation, in particular large drop-offs of subscribers from the network with a reduction in the magnitude of cross-subsidization and adverse cost trends associated with the sacrifice of network economies of scale and scope.

Assessing the Merits of Future Deregulation

The important issue for policy-makers, particularly Canadian policy-makers, is whether this relatively favourable perspective is strong enough to encourage a faster and more extensive deregulation of currently regulated sectors of the industry, most particularly switched network services. One can certainly reverse the burden of proof so that the relevant question is whether deregulation has net social costs; however, the two questions are essentially duals of each other. If deregulation promises net social benefits, continued regulation in an opportunity cost sense promises net social costs.

Policies toward deregulation have two broad features: (1) who should be allowed to compete in an activity? and (2) how should firms be allowed to compete? While these two issues are, of course, closely related, as a procedural matter, structural issues normally are considered separately from pricing issues. Thus, at one extreme, a sector might be completely opened to all potential entrants with the existing Combines Act used as the tool to "police" anti-competitive behaviour. At the other extreme, entry might be allowed for specific competitors with the behaviour of firms in the industry regulated as it is currently done. In between are a range of intermediate solutions, e.g., controlled entry with a significant relaxation of regulatory restraints on pricing, service offerings, and so on.

The "Natural Monopoly Concern"

As noted above, one continuing reservation about deregulating long distance and local services is that the existing network is a natural monopoly. Hence, deregulation would merely provide an opportunity for the network supplier to extract monopoly rents at the expense of consumers. A potential answer to this concern is to liberalize entry conditions to test whether these sectors are, in fact, natural monopolies. Two rejoinders are usually offered in response to undertaking entry-based tests of cost conditions: (1) given the existing pattern of cross-subsidies in the industry, "inefficient entry" will take place; and (2) incumbent common carriers will engage in predation and foreclosure so as to perpetuate their monopoly positions.

Several observations seem relevant in this regard. One is that using the telephone pricing structure as an instrument for cross-subsidies is likely to impose higher deadweight costs than other potential instruments. As noted earlier, telephone usage patterns are not necessarily closely tied to income or other demographic factors usually relevant to subsidy policy. Nor is it clear that the existing subsidy pattern encourages the expansion of "favoured" activities; e.g., rural development. It can as easily be argued that subsidized local services have spawned a host of telephone "pests" who impose external costs on other network users.[72] If the regulator has clearly identified individuals or groups whose access to telephone service would be threatened by a convergence between prices and costs of different telephone services, or whose usage rates would be seriously constrained by real income effects, there are innumerable "lifeline" rate programs and direct income assistance programs that might be put in place.[73] In short, one might argue that entry should be delayed pending

---

72 For a more extensive discussion of the distributive effects of existing pricing cross-subsidies, see Globerman and Stanbury (1986), pp. 214-26. Direct marketing by telephone is, in my mind, one such access diseconomy.

73 For a discussion of such programs, see Johnson (1988). Note that lifeline rate

rate rebalancing, but it is not credible to argue that regulatory barriers to entry should be maintained in the long run in order to support existing cross-subsidies.

Nor is it credible to argue that easing entry barriers is irrelevant, since incumbent carriers would merely predate potential competitors out of existence. Similar arguments were made in the case of easing restrictions on subscriber ownership of telephone equipment. While concerns were raised from time to time about predatory cross-subsidies in the Bell System, the evidence is that a host of new competitors entered the telecommunications equipment and interconnect markets and won a durable and large share of AT&T's business. In fact, a theoretical argument can be made that if a sector of the industry is contestable, a firm participating in that sector as well as in a monopolized sector has no incentive to engage in predatory cross-subsidization unless there are regulatory imperfections. Specifically, if the firm has confidence that all costs incurred in predating will be moved into the rate-base and if the allowable rate-of-return exceeds the cost-of-capital, a regulation induced incentive to predate may be created.[74] Of course, this potential should be addressed directly by improving the regulatory process, rather than by preventing entry into contestable markets.

The issue of foreclosure may be of more relevance to the extent that competition in one sector of the industry depends upon access to "monopoly" facilities in another sector of the industry. In the telephone industry, the local exchange is seen as a monopoly bottleneck to competition in other more contestable sectors of the industry. Whether a monopolist would have anti-competitive incentives to diversify into competitive segments of the industry is a dubious proposition.[75] In any event, access is an issue that can be addressed, at least in theory, by competition policy authorities or by a regulator.

In summary, the caveats against using market-based tests of natural monopoly, i.e., allowing competitive entry, are at best temporary and at worst specious. However, if one or more segments of the industry are structurally "incontestable," one might hesitate to recommend eliminating all regulatory restrictions on pricing. We will turn to the issue of behavioural restrictions below. First, we briefly reconsider the evidence on the industry as a natural monopoly.

---

programs and income assistance programs might be targeted at different groups of individuals.

74 See Brock and Evans (1983), pp. 41-60, and Globerman (1985), pp. 319-33.

75 The proposition here is that monopoly rents can presumably be extracted at the source, i.e., at the local exchange. It might be noted that bypass of the local exchange is an increasingly economical proposition, at least for large subscribers. On this point, it has been noted that since divestiture took place, half of the new capacity in local facilities has been constructed by entities other than local telephone companies. See Noll (1989), p. 33.

As noted above, the available empirical evidence supports a claim that there are economies of scale in the provision of network services, but it stops short of demonstrating persuasively that there are both economies of scale and scope. Moreover, no reliable evidence establishes the existence of product economies of scale. Nevertheless, most observers of the industry argue that local exchange services are probably marked by extensive economies of scale that render the local sector a natural monopoly in the traditional sense of the term.[76] There is much less agreement about cost conditions for long distance services.

As argued earlier, static measures of cost conditions are an incomplete test of natural monopoly. Specifically, technological change may be a more import- ant competitive factor in the long run than the positions of existing firms on a given cost surface. This is arguably an increasingly relevant and important caveat given the growth in demand for "customized" network services, espe- cially on the part of business subscribers. This suggests that potential entry could serve as a viable competitive discipline in the long run even if extant carriers enjoy large scale economies. In the Canadian context, the issue of natural monopoly in the long distance sector would be moot in any case if the prohibition against foreign carriage of Canadian-originated and -destined traf- fic was abandoned. Specifically, it is relatively economical for resellers to channel Canadian-originated traffic into the U.S. to be carried on a U.S. discount service and then to be re-routed back into Canada.

In any case, comprehensive rate-of-return regulation is not a necessary concomitant of natural monopoly. If policy-makers are concerned about mo- nopoly prices being charged, it is arguably more effective to have "rate caps" while allowing the carrier to lower prices at will and share in some of the gains in efficiency that presumably underlie price reductions.[77]

Certainly, if price caps were put in place, the local exchange carrier in particular might have a stronger incentive to extract monopoly rents in more competitive sectors; i.e., foreclosure would be more of an issue. Structural divestment along the AT&T lines is one, albeit radical, solution to this problem. Other structural solutions, e.g., requiring the local carrier to operate separate subsidiaries or not allowing the local carrier to participate in specific activities under any conditions, are arguably either cosmetic or inefficient solutions to the monopoly bottleneck problem. Without proposing a specific approach to

---

76 Interestingly, researchers argue that local telephone markets were reasonably contestable in the early stages of the industry. For example, there are numerous instances where, after a Bell exchange acquired a competing independent exchange and raised prices, another competing independent exchange quickly appeared. See Bornholz and Evans (1983), p. 34.

77 For a discussion of some potential problems associated with the use of rate caps, see Noll (1989). Indeed, Noll questions whether rate caps will be a sustainable policy instrument given the potential for company profits to fluctuate substantially.

the problem, an implication of the foregoing analysis is that regulators should focus on insuring that competitive suppliers have "fair and reasonable" access to bottleneck facilities and abandon comprehensive rate-of-return regulation.

Changes in Underlying Cost and Demand Conditions and Deregulation

Notwithstanding certain theoretical objections to completely deregulating the Canadian telecommunications industry at the present time, it might well be argued that underlying cost and demand conditions in the industry are changing systematically and having the effect of increasing the net social costs of continuing regulation. Once again, this topic is too broad to discuss in any comprehensive way in this paper. Hence, we will merely identify several relevant changes. One is the growing potential for large users to bypass the telephone network in order to avoid subsidizing other users. Such bypass activity can result in allocative and technical inefficiencies.[78] A second is growing price sensitivity on the part of business subscribers, in part tied to the Canada-U.S. Free Trade Agreement. Indeed, the Free Trade Agreement may not only encourage Canadian firms to look for lower cost alternatives to the public network, it may also stimulate the U.S. government to take actions against Canadian government restrictions preventing competition in inter-exchange carriage.[79] A third is the emergence of rival technologies to the telephone network, including cellular telephone, switched fibre optic cable, and very small aperture satellite telecommunications which may make it possible for complete end-to-end network services to be provided by new carriers.

These new technologies not only enhance the ultimate contestability of the switched public network, they also promise substantial benefits to consumers in the form of new services and lower costs. Opening up entry into all sectors of the telecommunications industry, as well as into the cable industry and into other potential rival technologies (e.g., broadcasting and cellular radio) to the telecommunications industry, should stimulate efforts on the part of entrepreneurs to find ways to offset any competitive disadvantages entrants into an emerging communications industry might face vis-à-vis established carriers. If Canadian policy-makers continue to balkanize the communications industry through regulation, it could discourage innovative efforts on the part of Canadian communications firms to enter the industry by establishing rival systems

---

78 For a more comprehensive discussion of this point, see Globerman and Stanbury (1986). The need to monitor bypass activity also provides an additional source of deadweight costs. Indeed, some observers suggest that the costs of trying to maintain regulation in the face of ongoing technological change will be prohibitive. See, for example, Willig (1986), pp. 78-116.

79 For a discussion of these points, see Steven Globerman (1989b), pp. 319-28.

and/or by exploiting emerging economies of scope created by digital and wide band fibre optics technologies. The resulting costs to the Canadian economy are likely to be quite substantial.

Concluding Comments

Reasonable people may disagree about the net social benefits of comprehensive deregulation of the Canadian telecommunications industry at the present time. They may also disagree about whether rate rebalancing requires competitive entry; however, it is difficult to gainsay a conclusion that efficiency costs associated with the existing cross-subsidies in the telephone pricing system are substantial and that the social desirability of the cross-subsidies are at best dubious. It is also arguable that competitive entry stimulates dynamic efficiency gains that would not be realized through regulatory efforts to emulate competition, and that these dynamic efficiency gains are growing over time.

An existing barrier to comprehensive deregulation of the industry is the limited contestability (at present) of the local exchange network. In fact, allowing entry into this segment of the industry may hasten the date at which this sector of the industry becomes workably competitive from substitutes such as cellular and cable. A minimalist approach towards regulating the industry for the foreseeable future might involve the imposition of price caps on the local exchange carrier along with equal access requirements.

The long distance sector is arguably contestable at the present time with declining costs of switching and transmission equipment. There would certainly be little argument on this point if restrictions on reselling and sharing of switched long distance services were eliminated, along with restrictions on double border crossings of telephone calls. The only behavioural regulation that might be justifiable under emerging competitive conditions in this sector is a price cap on the dominant carrier.

References

Baldwin, John R. (1989), *Regulatory Failure and Renewal: The Evolution of the Natural Monopoly Contract* (Ottawa: Ministry of Supply and Services).

Barnes, Angela (1989), "Call-Net Brass Pleased at CRTC Re-examination," *Globe and Mail*, January 12, B6.

Baumol, William (1982), "Cost-Based Tests of a Natural Monopoly," *American Economics Review*.

Becker, Gary S. (1983), "A Theory of Competition Among Pressure Groups For Political Influence," *The Quarterly Journal of Economics* XCVIII, 3 (August), pp. 371-400.

Bornholz, Robert and David S. Evans (1983), "The Early History of Competition in the Telephone Industry," in David S. Evans (ed.) *Breaking Up Bell: Essays on Industrial Organization and Regulation* (New York: North Holland).

Brock, Gerald W. (1981), *The Telecommunications Industry: The Dynamics of Market Structure* (Cambridge, Mass.: Harvard University Press).

Brock, William A. and David S. Evans (1983), "Predation: A Critique of the Government's Case in U.S. v. AT&T," in David S. Evans (ed.) *Breaking Up Bell: Essays on Industrial Organization and Regulation* (New York: North Holland), pp. 41-60.

Chessler, David (1988), *The Effect of Toll Competition on Prices, Costs and Productivity of the Telephone in the United States* (Ottawa: Supply and Services Canada).

Coopers and Lybrand Consulting Group (1988), *The Effect of Changing Technology on the Structure of Costs for the Provision of Public Long Distance Telephone Service* (Ottawa: Supply and Services Canada).

Coopers and Lybrand Consulting Group, "Survey of Local Telephone Pricing and Usage Issues Among Consumers in Ontario," prepared for the Ontario Government, Ministry of Transportation and Communications, mimeo, vols. I and II, October 1985 and February 1986.

Cormier, Anne, ed., (1985), *The Fifth Interconnect Industry Survey* (Potomac, Maryland: Phillips Publishing, Inc.).

Crandall Robert W. (1989), "Fragmentation of the Telephone Network" in Paula R. Newberg (ed.) *New Directions in Telecommunications Policy* 1 (Durham: Duke University Press).

Crew, Michael A. and Charles K. Rowley (1988), "Toward a Public Choice Theory of Monopoly Regulation," *Public Choice* 57, pp. 49-67.

D.A. Ford and Associates Ltd. (1986), "The Impact of International Competition on the Canadian Telecommunications Industry and Its Users," (Ottawa, August), mimeo.

DIW (Deutsches Institut für Wirtschaftsforschung) (1988), "The Spectrum of Alternative Market Configurations in European Telecommunications," Part 1 (Berlin: mimeo).

Downs, Anthony (1957), *An Economic Theory of Democracy* (New York: Harper and Row).

Faulhaber, Gerald R. (1987), *Telecommunications in Turmoil* (Cambridge, Mass.: Ballinger).

Foreman-Peck, James and Dorothy Manning (1988), "Telecommunications in the United Kingdom," in DIW, "The Spectrum of Alternative Market Configurations in European Telecommunications," Part 1 (Berlin: mimeo), pp. 257-78.

Goldberg, Victor (1976), "Regulation and Administered Contracts," *Bell Journal of Economics* 7 (Autumn), pp. 426-48.

Globerman, Steven (1989a), *Elasticities of Demand For Long-Distance Telephone* (Ottawa: Canadian Radio-Television and Telecommunications Commission).

Globerman, Steven (1989b), "The Canadian-U.S. Free Trade Agreement and the Telecommunications Industry," *Telecommunications Policy*, Vol. 13, No. 4, pp. 319-28.

Globerman, Steven (1988a), *Telecommunications in Canada* (Vancouver: The Fraser Institute).

Globerman, Steven (1988b), *The Impacts of Trade Liberalization on Imperfectly Competitive Industries: A Review of Theory and Evidence*, Discussion Paper no. 341, (Ottawa: Economic Council of Canada).

Globerman, Steven (1986), "Economic Factors in Telecommunications Policy and Regulation," in W.T. Stanbury (ed.) *Telecommunications Policy and Regulation* (Montreal: The Institute For Research on Public Policy), pp. 1-80.

Globerman, Steven (1985), "Predatory Pricing and Foreclosure Issues in Telecommunications," *Telecommunications Policy* 12, 4 (December), pp. 319-33.

Globerman, Steven (1980), "Markets, Hierarchies and Innovation," *Journal of Economic Issues* xiv, 4, pp. 977-98.

Globerman, Steven and William T. Stanbury (1986), "Changing the Telephone Pricing Structure: Allocative, Distributional and Political Considerations," *Canadian Public Policy* xii (March), pp. 214-26.

Harris, Robert G. (1989), "Telecommunications Policy in Japan: Lessons for the U.S.," *California Management Review* (Spring), pp. 113-31.

Hogg, Philip and George Horhota (1989), "Competition the Route to Efficiency in Balkanized Telecommunications," *Globe and Mail* (July 2), B2.

Johnson, Leland J. (1988), *Telephone Assistance Programs For Low-Income Households: A Preliminary Assessment* (Santa Monica: The Rand Corporation).

Johnson, Leland J. (1982), "Competition and Cross-Subsidization in the Telephone Industry" (Santa Monica: The Rand Corporation), mimeo.

Kiss, Ferenc and Bernard Lefebvre (1984), "Comparative Analysis and Econometric Forecasting of Factor Inputs and Productivity: Some Empirical Results in Canadian Telecommunications," Paper prepared for The Fourth International Symposium on Forecasting, London, England, July 8-11.

Klein, Benjamin, Robert Crawford, and Armen Alchian (1978), "Vertical Integration Appropriable Rents and the Competitive Contracting Process," *Journal of Law and Economics* 21 (October), pp. 297-326.

Noll, Robert and Bruce Owen (1983), *The Political Economy of Deregulation* (Washington, D.C.: American Enterprise Institute).

Noll, Roger (1989), "Telecommunications Regulation in the 1990s," in Paula R. Newberg (ed.) *New Directions in Telecommunications Policy* 1 (Durham: Duke University Press), pp. 11-48.

Panzar, John and Robert Willig (1977), "Free Entry and the Sustainability of Natural Monopoly," *Bell Journal of Economics* (Spring), pp. 1-22.

Peat Marwick (1988), *The Financial Impacts of Competition in Public Long Distance Telephone Services on Canada's Telephone Companies*, Consulting Report 7, Federal-Provincial-Territorial Task Force on Telecommunications (Ottawa: Ministry of Supply and Services Canada).

Peat Marwick (1984), "Impacts of Competition in Message Toll Telephone Services," Study carried out for the Department of Communications and Provincial Governments, Toronto (September 28), mimeo, pp. vi-17.

Posner, Richard (1974), "Theories of Economic Regulation," *Bell Journal of Economics and Management* 5 (Autumn), pp. 335-58.

Quayle, Michael J. (1989), "Canadian Telecommunications: Technological Change, Structural Regulation and Entry," *Telecommunications Policy* 13, 3 (June), pp. 145-58.

Schultz, Richard (1984), "Partners in a Game Without Masters: Reconstructing the Telecommunications Regulatory System," in Robert Buchan, et al., (eds.) *Telecommunications Regulation and the Constitution* (Montreal: The Institute For Research on Public Policy).

Selwyn, Lee L. and David N. Townsend (1988), *A Study of Selected Impacts of Competition in the Long Distance Telephone Industry*, CRTC Consulting Report 2, prepared for Federal-Provincial-Territorial Task Force on Telecommunications (Ottawa: Supply and Services Canada, December).

Surtees, Lawrence (1989), "Ottawa regulates phones, court says," *Globe and Mail*, August 15, pp. B1 and B4.

Taylor, Lester (1980), *Telecommunications Demand: A Survey and Critique* (Cambridge, Mass.: Ballinger).

Temin, Peter with Louis Galambos (1987), *The Fall of the Bell System* (Cambridge, England: Cambridge University Press).

Thomas, Brownlee (1988), *A Profile of the U.S. Experience With Competition in Public Long-Distance Telephone Service* (Ottawa: Supply and Services Canada).

Wenders, John (1987), *The Economics of Telecommunications: Theory and Policy* (Cambridge, Mass.: Ballinger).

Willig, Robert (1986), "The Changing Economic Environment in Telecommunications: Technological Change and Deregulation" in *Proceedings from the Telecommunications Deregulation Forum*, Tucson, Arizona (June 5-6), pp. 78-116.

Williamson, O.E. (1979), "Franchise Bidding For Natural Monopoly—In General and With Respect to CATV," *Bell Journal of Economics*, pp. 73-104.

Discussion of the Globerman Paper

W.T. Stanbury

Introduction

Professor Globerman's paper is a thoughtful, balanced, and concise assessment of the *economics* of regulation and deregulation of telecommunications in Canada. Therefore, rather than discuss possible refinements to such issues as the nature and significance of natural monopoly in the production of long distance services (Porter, 1987), or whether David Chessler (1988) has properly measured increases in productivity in the telecommunications sector in the U.S., I propose to offer some comments on the *politics* of deregulating telecommunications in Canada. The reasons are simple. First, Globerman has chosen to devote little space to such matters. Second, and much more importantly, the decision to modify a regulatory regime, or to go so far as to deregulate it, is a profoundly political one (Derthick and Quirk, 1985). While economic forces (including changes in technology) are creating pressures for less regulation and more reliance on market forces, political considerations—whether we like it or not—remain paramount. Therefore, my comments are designed to complement Professor Globerman's admirable paper.

Aspects of the Politics of Regulatory Reform in Telecommunications

Regulatory decisions—despite the technical or legal rhetoric—are fundamentally political decisions involving a trade-off between basic values (or norms) of which economic efficiency is only one. In Canada, regulatory decisions in telecommunications—to a surprising degree—revolve around changes in income distribution (Stanbury, 1986). Decisions that involve substantial deregulation challenge the fundamental nature of direct regulation as a political institution. That is why the path toward deregulation is always difficult.

Does The Economic Theory of Regulation Hold in the Case of Telecommunications?

The well-known interest group theory of direct regulation[1] would not predict the outcome we observe in telephone regulation in Canada. Regulators "tax"

---

1   See Stigler (1971) and Peltzman (1976, 1989).

monopoly toll outputs whose consumption is relatively concentrated to provide an undifferentiated subsidy for virtually every household in the form of lower rates for local service.[2] Indeed, the economic theory of regulation is couched in terms of the ability of concentrated interests to exert political pressure to create or redirect economic regulation in ways that will benefit such interests at the expense of more widely-diffused interests. Examples that support this theory include supply management marketing boards, transportation regulation, the regulation of electricity and natural gas distribution, and most kinds of occupational regulation (Stanbury and Lermer, 1983).

Why is telecommunications different? Three facts seem to be very important. First, all consumer-voters are affected by changes in telephone rates (over 98 percent penetration rate in Canada and over 93 percent in the U.S.), although some households make very little use of long distance service. Second, the flat monthly rate nature of charges for local service means consumers are more sensitive to price increases. Further, there is no practicable substitute for local telephone service. Third, relatively little organizational effort is needed for telecommunications consumers to affect the direct election process (Wenders, 1987, pp. 154-55).

The economic theory of regulation is "wrong" in the case of telecommunications because it assumed that it would be too costly for the widely-dispersed beneficiaries of regulation-induced cross-subsidies to organize to exert political pressure which, in turn, is felt by the regulators (Wenders, 1987, p. 156).

Regulation as a Political Instrument

The economic disadvantages of direct regulation of a potentially structurally competitive industry are well known. There are, however, substantial advantages which accrue largely to the regulators themselves, their political masters, and to members of certain groups whose interests are the most politically salient to the first two groups. For example, most of the beneficiaries of the policy of high long distance and low local rates are middle-class households who are both

---

2 More precisely, the large mark-up on toll calls is used to cover most of the fixed common costs of access to the network. Local revenues do cover local variable costs and make a contribution to access costs. In 1988, for example, Bell Canada had a net revenue surplus of $1779 million from monopoly toll calls and one of $650 million from monopoly local calls using the Phase III methodology developed in the CRTC's Cost Inquiry. However the fixed common costs of "Access" amounted to $2487 million. Hence the "mark-up" on monopoly toll calls recovered over 70 percent of the costs of "access" (Filing by Bell Canada with the CRTC, September 29, 1989). While allocative efficiency would dictate that access costs should be recovered from local users (because their price elasticity of demand is nearly zero) from a distributional point of view, it is arbitrary as to how such fixed common costs are recovered. Therefore, the term "cross-subsidy" is being used rather loosely in this context.

more numerous, better organized, and more vocal than the poor in whose name the policy is allegedly justified.

Direct regulation can provide the illusion of control by regulators and, when they desire it, by the cabinet through the appeal process. The point is that regulators can control some things (prices/rates, entry, and exit), but they can only do so by being unable to control others, e.g., costs, X-inefficiency, capital intensity, service quality, and the rate of innovation.[3] The CRTC genuinely, but mistakenly, believes it can by direct regulation obtain all of the benefits of entry/competition (which it acknowledges), but that it can do so "without tears," to use Hudson Janisch's evocative phrase. It proposes to undertake rate rebalancing prior to any decision regarding competition in MTS/WATS markets.[4] At the same time, the CRTC and its supporters can point to a number of decisions in which competition has been favoured as evidence of their enlightened approach to regulatory reform.[5] While these decisions have been beneficial, their significance is not as great in terms of efficiency gains as easy entry and wide-ranging competition in MTS/WATS markets would be.

Direct regulation can slow down the pace of economic change in an industry—thereby giving the appearance of predictability and orderliness. Canadians distrust markets and competitive process generally and favour political modes of decision making because they believe they are more responsive to popular control and will result in more orderly and predictable change. Regulation is used as a vehicle to slow the pace of economic change (Owen and Braeutigam, 1978) for Canadians are a cautious and risk-averse people. Politicians are hardly unwilling to resist what appears to be the public's desire for regulatory control over many activities—including telecommunications.

Direct regulation can provide a useful governing instrument for politicians to retain power. This is done by using price and entry controls to redistribute income to groups likely to be grateful at the polls. The techniques are cross-subsidization, "taxation by regulation," and price discrimination. Success in these endeavours requires the political masters to craft the necessary legislation, signal their preferences through policy pronouncements, pick "sensitive" regulators, and/or provide feedback through their decisions in political appeals.

As a means of social control of private firms, direct regulation is attractive to a nation that believes in protecting the status quo,[6] and is more interested in distributional matters than allocative efficiency. In other words, direct regula-

---

3   This point is now recognized by the Federal Communications Commission (1989) which is adopting price cap regulation in place of the traditional rate base rate-of-return approach that still prevails in Canada.

4   See CRTC Telecom Decision 88-14.

5   See Janisch and Romaniuk (1985, 1989) and Romaniuk and Janisch (1986).

6   This is illustrated in the recent policy proposals of the federal Department of Communications (1987, 1988).

tion suits Canada's political and economic culture. Moreover, under Canada's unique version of federalism, direct regulation has been balkanized in such a way as to ensure the triumph of local (distributional) concerns over national interests (allocative efficiency, economic growth, and technological innovation).[7] This may, however, change in light of the Supreme Court of Canada's decision in the Alberta Government Telephone case in August 1989:

> The ramifications of the Supreme Court's decision to uphold the earlier judgment go well beyond AGT. The federal government today has exclusive jurisdiction over the seven provincially based telecommunications companies, as well as Bell and B.C. Tel. It alone has the authority to regulate not only rates and services, but most importantly the terms governing long-distance competition and the attachment of customer-owned equipment. The only limitation is that the three Prairie phone companies are in regulatory limbo. Until the immunity is lifted, they're not subject to any government's supervision (Schultz, 1989b, p. 36).

Progress has been slow, however, in implementing the legislative changes necessary for the federal government to assert its authority. While Minister of Communications Marcel Masse introduced amendments to the Railway Act stripping the prairie telcos of their Crown immunity from federal regulation on October 19, 1989,[8] they had not been enacted sixteen months later.[9]

---

7 "When compared with other federal states, the central government has been strikingly deferential to provincial interests, especially in the 1980s...The federal government has not sought national authority with any degree of vigour, but is coyly holding back in the hope of not defending the provinces" (Janisch and Romaniuk, 1989, pp. 25, 26). The ownership of their regional telco by Alberta, Saskatchewan, and Manitoba has reinforced the provincialization of interests. This has not been offset by the federal government's assertion of a strong national interest. As for the provinces, Schultz (1989b, p. 36) notes, "For their part, the pretensions of the provinces have known no bounds. At one point they collectively asserted the right to control all the telecommunications systems except the space segment. Encouraged by federal uncertainty, they've refused to accept that there's an overriding national dimension and the need for national standards and policies governing telecommunications. Ottawa until recently has been far too accommodating in its proposals, which, if accepted by the provinces, would have entrenched existing barriers."

8 See *Globe and Mail*, October 20, 1989, pp. B1, B4; *Financial Post*, October 20, 1989, p. 3.

9 In September 1990, 60 percent of Alberta Government Telephones, renamed Telus Corp., was sold for $951 million, largely to Alberta residents (*Globe and Mail*, September 12, 1990, p. B1). As a result, Telus became subject to federal regulatory jurisdiction. Further, it is expected that Manitoba Tel will come under federal jurisdiction in the fall of 1991 pursuant to a federal-provincial agreement.

Finally, direct regulation—like a bad surgeon—has the advantage of "burying its mistakes." Politicians (and regulators) can take advantage of the fact that most people are far less sensitive to opportunity losses than reductions in their present or accustomed economic position (e.g., cash losses). That is one reason why the "costs" of allowing competition in MTS/WATS markets is seen as an increase in local rates which is merely a redistribution of income. The large losses in terms of allocative efficiency due to the present price structure are hidden and diffused. Hence they are ignored. Moreover, the complexity of direct regulation obscures its effects from most Canadians.

Effect of Entry and Competition in MTS/WATS Markets

The proponents of the status quo (e.g., Consumers' Association of Canada [CAC], National Anti-Poverty Organization [NAPO], prairie and maritime provinces) believe that entry and competition in interexchange (IX) markets (notably MTS/WATS) will result, before very long, in large reductions in these long distance rates. Hence it will "kill the goose that lays the golden eggs" and local rates will have to rise.[10] Because the distribution of toll calls is highly skewed among households (as well as among businesses), about three-quarters of all households, it is argued, will not benefit from rate rebalancing.[11]

The benefits of competition in MTS/WATS markets, in distributional terms, are seen to be highly concentrated in the hands of a small fraction of households and a tiny fraction of business users, primarily large firms. These groups are seen as "rich and undeserving" in popular mythology (demonology?). The popular view, reinforced by regulators and politicians, is that high long distance rates embody a substantial excise or sales tax that is desirable for several reasons: demand is inelastic; big business is (believed to be) highly profitable and can afford to pay the tax (it is assumed to fall on shareholders); long distance telephone calls are a "luxury" good like single-malt scotch whisky—a suitable target for a high tax rate; and the tax is quite well-hidden.

The potential losers in distributional terms if entry into MTS/WATS markets also results in rate rebalancing (households whose total telephone bill increases) are many and widely dispersed in the population. Normally, this makes a policy change easier, i.e., interests that receive concentrated benefits almost always defeat groups with diffused interests. Telecommunications is different, however, as noted above. Moreover, federal and provincial cabinet ministers in

---

10 This is also Bell Canada's position which has been articulated repeatedly in the newspapers, e.g., *Globe and Mail*, April 21, 1989, p. B2; *Financial Post*, February 14, 1990, p. 29; March 23, 1990, p. 44; *Globe and Mail*, May 7, 1990, p. B23.

11 Recall the discussion in CRTC Telecom Decision 85-19 (CRTC, 1985) and Stanbury (1986) which describes CAC's position. See the data reported in Federal-Provincial-Territorial Task Force on Telecommunications (1988).

April 1987 strongly committed themselves to "universal access to basic telephone service at affordable prices" which is the code phrase for having the price of long distance calls cover a high fraction (now 70 percent) of the fixed common costs associated with access charges. Further, the potential losers are well represented by CAC, NAPO, and particularly by the prairie provinces which fear the adverse effects of the loss of settlements from toll calls revenue on their Crown-owned telcos. CAC, in particular, has couched their opposition to rate rebalancing in terms of protecting the poor, neglecting to point out that only a tiny fraction of those adversely affected are below the poverty line. CAC will also ignore the large gains in efficiency attributable to rate rebalancing following entry.[12]

Opportunity Costs Are Not Recognized

The gains from entry/competition and rate rebalancing in terms of allocative efficiency are large, but they would be widely diffused throughout the nation entering the GNP through the lower price of long distance telecommunications which reduces input costs generally and eventually (under competition) results in lower output prices (Janisch and Schultz, 1989). Correspondingly, the failure of the CRTC to allow entry/competition results in large opportunity losses rather than obvious cash costs (Stanbury, 1990). However, opportunity losses are less salient to individual consumers, and particularly to politicians, than are sharp reductions in current wealth or the loss of an accustomed position (Leone, 1986, pp. 114-18). Unless these losses can be made "real" to CAC, NAPO, and the politicians, the implicit price of the present method of redistribution will never be acknowledged—let alone become the basis of trade-offs toward more competition and lower toll rates.

Need to Solve the Distribution Problem

Despite the vast public choice literature, economists often greatly underrate how distributional issues dominate debates over public policy. It will be impossible for Unitel Communications (formerly CNCP Telecommunications) or any other firm to obtain entry and competition in MTS/WATS unless they can find a way to overcome the politically most significant adverse effects of competition.

> It serves no purpose to argue that more competition will lead to greater economic efficiency, while at the same time ignoring the economic rights issue [to low-priced local service] or arguing that

---

12 Recall that Globerman (1986, p. 41) estimates the deadweight welfare loss attributable to the present inefficient price structure to be some $2 billion annually. More generally, see Globerman and Stanbury (1986).

the problem will somehow take care of itself. It is equally unproductive to insist that a potential increase in economic efficiency should be avoided if it in any way diminishes some economic right that the public now takes for granted (Zajac, 1981, p. 104).

It is evident that any application to enter MTS/WATS markets in Canada immediately raises the rate rebalancing issue. For example, Pierre Pontbriand, spokesman for the CRTC, in response to the announcement that CNCP (now Unitel) would be making another application to enter MTS/WATS markets, stated that

There could be a number of benefits to competition. But the price of local calls would have to be rebalanced in some way, and [the new group] would have to ensure that people still have access to local service [at low rates].[13]

Bell Canada's Linda Gervais stated that entry by CNCP "would not be in the best interest of the customer. People would end up paying more for general telephone service." She went on to say, "Our long-distance rates have come down 25 percent in the past two years. Local rates have not risen. There is no big advantage in moving from a monopoly to a duopoly."[14] To reinforce this point, Bell subsequently sought more reductions in both public and private line long distance rates without raising local rates. These actions make entry less attractive and convey the impression that it is unnecessary. Bell argues that Canadians can "get all the benefits of competition" under a regulated monopoly.

The proponents of change must offer practicable means to protect the most disadvantaged, but not the middle class.[15] In general, they must destroy the idea that the telephone rate structure should be used to redistribute income to the poorest households or to middle-class households that make few long distance calls.[16] This would appear to require

- the presentation of hard evidence of the large real economic costs of failing to allow competition and rate rebalancing;

---

13 Alexander Bruce, "Dialling for megadollars," Financial Times, April 24, 1989, p. 13. The application was delayed until May 1990.

14 Ibid. Note that in nominal terms, local rates have increased slightly in the previous few years.

15 In telecommunications policy making in Canada, Rawlsian criteria seem to hold. See Stanbury (1986).

16 On the distribution of long distance calls among households (and business) see Federal-Provincial-Territorial Task Force on Telecommunications (1988). Columnist Diane Francis goes so far as to argue that "business and long-distance rate subsidies for local rates are excessive, unnecessary and damaging to business [in Canada]. It is equivalent to asking business to pay the costs of maintaining highways and airports and letting the public ride for free."

- a move to tripartite pricing (for local exchange service, recovery of access costs, long distance service) that will make the public aware of the alternative ways of recovering the fixed, common costs of access; and
- a fairly detailed practicable plan to protect the most disadvantaged, e.g., a small tax on all bills to create an "affordable service fund" to subsidize the poorest (or otherwise "most deserving" customers; "budget services," "telestamps"; lifeline rates; targeted, overt subsidies, etc.[17]

The purpose of the next section is to provide advice on how to advance the case for entry and competition in MTS/WATS markets followed by extensive rate rebalancing.

A Positive Program for Obtaining Competition in MTS/WATS Markets

If competition is to be introduced into MTS/WATS markets (where it is most needed given the size of the distortions created by the present pricing policy), it will be necessary to challenge the central objective of federal (and provincial) telecommunications policy: universal access to the network based on low ("affordable") flat monthly rates for local service financed in large part (70 percent) by large mark-ups on public switched toll service. The bases of arguments to do this successfully might include the following:

1. Canada has had for some time the highest telephone penetration in the world (98.5 percent, up from 50 percent in 1947). In other words, it's time to declare victory and move on to more important things like assisting Canada's international competitiveness and improving allocative efficiency.

2. Local rates in Canada are low by international standards and even lower as a fraction of average household income. So only a small fraction of households will be hurt much if local rates were doubled. (Further, it may not be necessary to double local rates, and, if it is, the increase could be spread over several years.)

3. The price elasticity of demand for local service is very low, about -0.01. This means that even with much higher local rates very few people will drop off the network. However, even if few drop off, low-income households will find it harder to pay their telephone bills. There is a good

---

17 Zajac (1981, p. 102) points out that "until 1969, telephone service for low income families in the State of New York was subsidized directly out of tax revenue. Persons on welfare who were judged by their case worker to have a need for telephone service were given an allowance of $15.00 per month to obtain it." More generally, see the review of different approaches in the U.S. by Schultz (1989a).

case for helping them by using targeted subsidies (see Schultz, 1989a). It is essential that the poor be helped, and the onus be shifted to the middle class to show why society should incur such large costs in terms of allocative efficiency to keep their local rates constant or falling in real terms.

4. On average, Canadian households spend as much every month on toll calls as they do for local service.[18] While the present estimates indicate that more households will "lose" than "win" in terms of their total telephone bill after extensive rebalancing of local and long distance rates, much of the indirect benefits of rebalancing will accrue to households through the process of competition.[19] Moreover, the volume of long distance calls is rising rapidly and will increase with lower rates.

5. Canada is one of the few countries that compounds the distortions created by high toll/low local rates by making no use of local measured service. It appears that Bell Canada fumbled the proposed experiment and no telco has shown any initiative in trying to develop local measured service (LMS) in Canada. (In Australia, for example, local service is priced at about 21 cents per local call regardless of its duration—hardly optimal, but moving in the right direction. In the U.S., in about half the states, some form of LMS is used.)[20]

6. The present CRTC policy of keeping local rates low by having them cover a much smaller fraction of fixed common costs (access charges) than toll calls is both inefficient and highly questionable in terms of horizontal equity. Every household, rich or poor, receives the same benefit every month. No wonder Alfred Kahn has called such cross-subsidies "mindless and unfocused." With over 98 percent of households in Canada having a telephone, it amounts to a 'demogrant.' It is like paying the Family Allowance to all adults whether they have children or not or whether they are married or not. It is, to say the least, a grossly inefficient subsidy—unless its real purpose is to redistribute income within the middle class from toll users to non-toll users. If so, no one has ever explained why this should be done.

---

18 In 1988, for example, Bell Canada's total revenue from monopoly toll service was $2758 million versus $1761 million from monopoly local services (Filing by Bell Canada with the CRTC, September 29, 1989). Of course, business accounts for a large fraction of all long distance revenues.

19 Price elasticity estimates based on small changes are unlikely to be accurate when large changes in price (say, from 25 to 50 percent) are effected. The usage by the presently low volume toll users will probably increase more than expected as they learn the benefits of cheap toll calls.

20 See the papers in Schultz and Barnes (1984).

Yet these cross-subsidies are hard to identify in terms of amount, beneficiaries, and those who pay for them.[21] They defy accountability both in practice and principle. Moreover, "consumers would be better off with no regulation and no subsidies" (Cornell et al., 1981, p. 46).

The current view of the opponents of rate rebalancing is that it is the heaviest users of long distance services ("big business") that are being "taxed" to keep monthly local rates low. This is probably wrong. It is the big users that have the greatest incentive and opportunity for bypass in one form or another (e.g., creating private networks).[22] They have already forced the regulated telcos to bring toll rates down much closer to costs through various bulk services. The result is that it is smaller toll users, both business and residential, that are paying the fixed common costs of access. The advocates of continued high cross-subsidies will have to come up with a new story.

It is both more efficient and more equitable to help low-income households with the burden of higher local rates through the use of targeted subsidies.[23] The U.S. experience indicates that competition in interexchange markets which results in extensive rate rebalancing need not threaten universal service, and that targeted subsidies work.

> Rebalancing in the United States has not undermined universal service; if anything it has strengthened the resolve and commitment to the principle. Rebalancing has ended universal subsidization of those who demonstrably do not need subsidies and permitted a much more focused approach on those who are truly in need. Indeed, it has encouraged and permitted a richer program of subsidization than was previously available. Low-income subscribership has grown in the United States precisely because of the efforts of regulators, telecommunications companies and low-income and other consumer advocates to develop and implement programs that serve low-income needs rather than simply

---

21 There is a welter of cross-subsidies in telephone service: from MTS/WATS to local service (more properly to cover access costs), from high density to low density toll routes, from urban to rural customers, and from high volume to low volume users of local service both of whom pay the same monthly fee.

22 An example of Canada-Canada bypass was reported in the *Financial Post*, March 10-12, 1990, pp. 1, 12. An example of bypass for overseas calls is reported in the *Financial Post*, April 10, 1990, p. 3.

23 It is difficult to reconcile targeted subsidies and the general principle of non-discrimination by public utilities. However, the Railway Act prohibits "unjust discrimination" and if there is widespread agreement as to which subscribers are deserving of assistance, the discrimination may easily be held to be "just" and therefore legal.

entrenching, on the backs of the poor, "one of the best consumer bargains"—low cost local telephone service (Schultz, 1989a, p. 73).

Finally, Zajac (1981, p. 98) suggests that "the attainment of economic efficiency is...itself a form of economic justice." Why? Because, "if there is some beneficial exchange of resources that will benefit some without hurting others, it clearly seems unjust to prevent that exchange from taking place." There is a fundamental and inescapable dilemma: "Society can guarantee its citizens economic rights only at the risk of sacrificing economic efficiency" (Ibid., p. 99).

7. It would probably be useful to ridicule the very low rates presently charged for local service and also to turn the spotlight on our high MTS/WATS rates as compared with the U.S. For how many items in the consumer's budget is it possible to say that price has fallen substantially in real terms over the past several decades? For example, Bell Canada's local rates rose only marginally in nominal terms from 1983 to 1989 while the price of intra-Bell toll calls fell by 26 percent and the price of longer distance calls fell by 31 percent.

Moreover, absolute monthly rates are low (typically $8 to $15 per month). This is the price of 1.2 to 2.1 movie admissions. Janisch (1989) is right when he says that local rates should be measured in "Garths" or "Drabs" in honour of the former price leader in the local movie theatre business. (I wonder if this means we can also expect 10-second commercials before we are connected to the person we have just dialled?) It needs to be emphasized only four, three-minute Canada-U.S. calls spanning 3000 kilometres now cost as much as one month's unlimited local calling. Fourteen cans of beer or a 12.5 ounce bottle of Drambuie in Ontario costs about the same as one month of local service in Toronto. Columnist Diane Francis—an advocate of competition in public long distance services—argues that "the bottom line is, if residential rate subsidies were reduced in line with U.S. rates—Canadian [local] rates would then be $17 a month—the hike could be spread over several years and be the equivalent to the cost of a Big Mac and fries. Big deal."[24]

The CRTC's concern (and that of CAC, NAPO, and the prairie provinces) with the few thousands of households likely to drop off the network if local rates were doubled must be shown to be a very costly obsession. The high deadweight losses associated with the present policy must be hung like an albatross around the necks of the opponents of competition and rate rebalancing.

---

24 *Financial Post*, May 9, 1990, p. 3.

8.   The advocates of entry, competition, and the efficient pricing of telecommunications service (a new holy trinity?) need to redefine the central issues in the public debate as has occurred after competition was introduced into IX markets in the U.S. Schultz (1989a, pp. 43-44) explains what happened in the U.S.

> To the extent that universal service has been a political issue over most of the past decade, the question has been defined in terms of the potential negative impact of price changes on residential customers. Events of the past five years clearly have forced a redefinition of the issue. The universal service issue is currently being redefined to focus on low-income residential customers. The question is no longer "What will the adverse impact be on residential customers from increases in, and a restructuring of, local rates?" Instead, the issue today is "how can low-income customers be kept on the system?" In addition, and most significantly, with an appreciation that penetration is strongly linked with income, the new question is "how can non-subscribing low-income families and individuals be offered the opportunity to subscribe to telephone service?" This fine-tuning and rephrasing of the issue of universal service is undoubtedly the greatest consequence of the restructuring of telecommunications pricing in the United States over the past decade.

Concluding Remarks

Lest we lose perspective, we need to try to imagine how today's discussion about introducing competition into public long distance telephone markets will look a decade from now. I am confident that a few years after extensive deregulation, we will look back and wonder what all the fear and fuss was about. Think of airlines, rail, trucking, etc., in the U.S., Canada, and elsewhere (see Button and Swann, 1989). Alternatively, we should ask what Mikhail Gorbachev would think of the CRTC's views in Decision 85-19.[25] Canada too

---

25 In Decision 85-19 the CRTC (1985) appears to have established a set of conditions that no entrant could possibly meet with respect to entry into MTS/WATS. The entrant must be able to "guarantee" it will be able to offer universal service within 10 years so that the benefits of competition are widely diffused and not confined to large scale users or users in major cities. The entrant must offer substantial discounts from prevailing prices (20 to 30 percent). The entrant, even though it will be operating in competition with a telco, must prove that it will earn what the regulator calls a "reasonable rate of return" while meeting all other criteria. The entrant must not offer a lower quality of service because existing telcos might wish to match the new lower price and lower quality offering and the telcos "would be likely to seek to be

needs *perestroika*. We have too long been constrained by the *nomenklatura* of protectionist senior officials in the Department of Communications and the CRTC. We must challenge the politicians' practice of using the telephone system to redistribute income to confer largely undifferentiated subsidies on many households at the expense of large (but hidden) losses in allocative efficiency. Planners' and politicians' sovereignty must be replaced by consumers' (not just residential subscribers) sovereignty reflected in competitive markets. Unitel Communications (1990, p. 8) argues forcefully that competition in MTS/WATS markets will enlarge the total market and increase the revenues of the telephone companies. Hence with the payments Unitel will make to the telcos to cover access charges, long distance rates can be reduced and Canadians can have the benefits of competition "without any threat to universal service at affordable rates."

We must adopt a more efficient division of labour in which market forces are used to allocate our scarce resources, and government uses taxes and transfers to alter the distribution of income in the names of "equity" or "social justice," or even "the Canadian identity."

---

permitted to provide a lower quality of service on routes not subject to competition." The entrant must pay a level of contribution comparable to Bell or B.C. Tel. The entrant must not have any adverse effect on the revenues of telcos that operate outside federal jurisdiction. Entry must not result in substantially increased regulatory intervention. Generally, see the discussion in Stanbury (1986, 1990).

References

Button, Kenneth and Dennis Swann, eds. (1989), *The Age of Regulatory Reform* (Oxford: Clarendon Press).

Chessler, David and Associates (1988), *The Effect of Toll Competition on Prices, Costs and Productivity of the Telephone Industry in the United States* (Ottawa: Federal-Provincial-Territorial Task Force on Telecommunications).

Cornell, Nina et al. (1981), "Social Objectives and Competition in Common Carrier Communications: Incompatible or Inseparable?" in H.M. Trebing (ed.) *Energy and Communications in Transition* (East Lansing: Michigan State University), pp. 43-74.

CRTC (1985), Interexchange Competition and Related Issues, Telecom Decision 85-19, August 29.

Department of Communications (1987), "A Policy Framework for Telecommunications in Canada" (Ottawa: DOC, July), mimeo.

Department of Communications (1988), "Proposed Guidelines for Type I Telecommunications Carriers" (Ottawa: Communications Canada, January), mimeo.

Derthick, Martha and Paul J. Quirk (1985), *The Politics of Deregulation* (Washington, D.C.: Brookings Institution).

Federal Communications Commission (1989), "In the Matter of Policy and Rules Concerning Rates for Dominant Carriers, Report and Order and Second Further Notice of Proposed Rulemaking," Released April 17, FCC 89-91, Docket no. 87-313.

Federal-Provincial-Territorial Task Force on Telecommunications (1988), *Competition in Public Long Distance Telephone Service in Canada* (Ottawa: Ministry of Supply and Services Canada, December).

Globerman, Steven (1986), "Economic Factors in Telecommunications Policy and Regulation" in W.T. Stanbury (ed.) *Telecommunications Policy and Regulation* (Montreal: The Institute for Research on Public Policy), pp. 1-80.

Globerman, Steven and W.T. Stanbury (1986), "Changing the Telephone Pricing Structure: Allocative, Distributional and Political Considerations," *Canadian Public Policy* 12, 1, pp. 214-26.

Janisch, H.N. (1989), "Telecom 2000—A Glance at Future Trends in Canadian Telecommunications Regulation" (Speech to the Canadian Bar

Association, Media and Communications Section, Vancouver, August 20-23), mimeo.

Janisch, H.N. and B.S. Romaniuk (1985), "The Quest for Regulatory Forbearance in Telecommunications," *Ottawa Law Review* 17, 3, pp. 455-89.

Janisch, H.N. and B.S. Romaniuk (1989), "The Canadian Telecommunications Industry: A Study in Caution" (Revised version of a paper presented at the Conference on Pacific Basin Telecommunications, Hosei University, Tokyo, Japan, October 29-31, 1988), mimeo.

Janisch, H.N. and R.J. Schultz (1989), *Exploiting the Information Revolution: Telecommunications Issues and Options for Canada* (Toronto: Royal Bank of Canada, October).

Leone, Robert A. (1986), *Who Profits: Winners and Losers and Government Regulation* (New York: Basic Books).

Owen, B.M. and R. Braeutigam (1978), *The Regulation Game* (Cambridge, Mass.: Ballinger).

Peltzman, Sam (1976), "Toward a More General Theory of Regulation," *Journal of Law and Economics* 19, 2, pp. 211-39.

Peltzman, Sam (1989), "The Economic Theory of Regulation After a Decade of Deregulation" in M.N. Baily and C. Winston (eds.) *Brookings Papers on Economic Activity: Microeconomics* (Washington, D.C.: The Brookings Institution), pp. 1-41.

Porter, Michael E. (1987), *Competition in the Long Distance Telecommunication Market: An Industry Structure Analysis* (Cambridge, Mass.: Monitor Company Inc., June).

Posner, R.A. (1971), "Taxation by Regulation," *Bell Journal of Economics and Management Science* 2 (Spring), pp. 22-50.

Romaniuk, B.S. and H.N. Janisch (1986), "Competition in Telecommunications: Who Polices the Transition?" *Ottawa Law Review* 18, 3, pp. 561-661.

Schultz, Richard (1989a), *United States Telecommunications Pricing Changes and Social Welfare: Causes, Consequences and Policy Alternatives* (Report prepared for the Regulatory Affairs Branch, Bureau of Competition Policy, Department of Consumer and Corporate Affairs, Ottawa, February).

Schultz, Richard (1989b), "Is Ottawa Willing to Untangle the Telecommunications Snarl?" *Financial Times*, August 28, p. 36.

Schultz, Richard J. and Peter Barnes, eds. (1984), *Local Telephone Pricing: Is There a Better Way?* (Montreal: Centre for the Study of Regulated Industries, McGill University).

Stanbury, W.T. (1986), "Decision Making in Telecommunications: The Interplay of Distributional and Efficiency Considerations" in W.T. Stanbury (ed.) *Telecommunications Policy and Regulation* (Montreal: The Institute for Research on Public Policy), pp. 481-516.

Stanbury, W.T. (1987), "Direct Regulation and Its Reform: A Canadian Perspective," *Brigham Young University Review* 2, pp. 467-539.

Stanbury, W.T. (1990), "The Case for Competition in Public Long Distance Telephone Service in Canada," *Evidence of Unitel Communications Inc. Public Long Distance Service Application*, Part 9, Vol. III, August.

Stanbury, W.T. and George Lermer (1983), "Regulation and the Redistribution of Income and Wealth," *Canadian Public Administration* 26, 3, pp. 378-401.

Stigler, G.J. (1971), "The Theory of Economic Regulation," *Bell Journal of Economics and Management Science* 2, 1 (Spring), pp. 3-21.

Unitel Communications Inc. (1990), *Application to Provide Public Long Distance Telephone Service* (Toronto: Unitel, May 16).

Wenders, J.T. (1987), *The Economics of Telecommunications: Theory and Policy* (Cambridge, Mass.: Ballinger).

Zajac, Edward E. (1981), "Is Telephone Service an Economic Right?" in H.M. Trebing (ed.) *Energy and Communications in Transition (East Lansing: Institute of Public Utilities, Michigan State University), pp. 94-109.*

Discussion of the Globerman Paper

William G. Watson

Globerman's paper is essentially a normative discussion of whether Canada should entertain further deregulation of telecommunication in addition to the relatively modest changes that already have taken place. But since that is not my area of expertise, I focus very generally on how deregulation of telecommunications might fit into a positive theory of deregulation. On the normative side, I am persuaded that more deregulation would help in Canada, but I was persuaded of that before I read the paper, which only reinforced my belief.

I want to turn first to this problem of inside and outside questions. There is an inside-Ottawa policy loop that likes to deal with these problems independently of public opinion and seems quite unhappy when they become outside questions. For instance, I'm sure the CRTC's interconnect decision of 1979 resulted from its having been embarrassed into action because of a clear international demonstration effect. Whenever Canadians visited the U.S. they see a full panoply of phone equipment on sale, often at prices less than the monthly rental charge for similar equipment in Canada.

Despite all indications to the contrary, the CRTC probably does have some political sensibilities, so the same sort of embarrassment may be beginning to work in consumers' favour in the area of pay-TV and basic cable. There is clearly the potential for a TV-taxpayers' revolt in this country. More Canadians realize that they pay three to four times the U.S. rate for a much narrower package of channels, many of which people don't watch.[1] As in the interconnect decision, this knowledge is going to seep into public consciousness.

This raises the problem of conjecture, which Don McFetridge also addressed. What occurred to me as I went through these two telecommunications papers (Globerman's and McFetridge's) is that conjecture never seems to be a problem for regulationists. Despite my comments on McFetridge's paper, the burden of proof may not really have changed. People are always very leery about the likely effects of deregulation, and yet we set up complicated new regulatory regimes in many areas apparently without the slightest thought about the many difficulties they may cause. I think Bill Stanbury's comments may have given us the reasons why.

---

1 I watch "Newsworld" avidly, but by all reports am one of only several thousand Canadians who do.

A second general point I want to make concerns the evolutionary approach to regulation. These industries are not natural monopolies now, but technology has changed a great deal over the last ten or fifteen years. I wonder if there wasn't a time when they were natural monopolies. Again, it may simply be a question of the regulatory regime no longer fitting the industry it was designed to clothe. Most people who propose regulation of one kind or another really are not duplicitous but sincerely believe that what they propose will be good for society at large. And in fact, at the time the regulations are introduced, they may be correct. It certainly can be argued that this was the case for much telecommunication regulation. The existing regulatory regime may well have been appropriate to an early generation of technology. But technological change may have rendered it inappropriate and may have created the opportunity for rent-seeking. Similarly, the TV regulation we have now may well have made sense with 1950s technology, which relied mainly on signals that were more or less classic public goods. It probably does not make sense, however, now that the technology exists to deliver TV signals as essentially private goods. As a result, 1950s-style regulation is more constrictive and redistributive now, with inappropriate technology, than it was then, when technology was more appropriate.

Another example of an industry outgrowing useful regulation is pay-TV. As Tony Campbell indicated, by the time the CRTC finished its eleven- or twelve-year deliberation about whether or not to introduce pay-TV, the VCR had made the technology largely obsolete, at least for the delivery of movies. It is interesting from the economist's perspective that the main rationale for the continued regulation of telecommunication seems to be redistributional. It is also interesting that the current redistribution apparently is toward the local user, presumably the most diffuse consumer category. Why, in light of this, does regulation persist? There are a couple of rather compelling political considerations as to why it should. First, the most intensive users of long distance are businesses, and business still is not very popular. Second, it *is* the phone company we are talking about here. Anybody who was a fan of Lily Tomlin in the 1970s understands that the phone company is immensely unpopular. I realize this is not very sophisticated political analysis, but I bet this is the real reason politicians are reluctant to step forward and direct the CRTC to push deregulation. Any politician that did so would risk being ground up by public opinion.

On more detailed points: figure 3 in the paper, which is quite interesting, looks at the working-hour cost of the average phone bill. I wanted to see some indication about what was going on in the U.K., where the pattern seemed to be very much stop-go in the 1970s.[2] In connection with figure 3 there is a

---

2 Apparently this was the pattern for just about everything in the U.K. in the 1970s.

discussion of the convergence of rates across countries, but I would like some indication of what the standard deviation of rates is at both the beginning and end of the period because, although every country's rates had gone down, it wasn't clear to me that the dispersion of rates had changed.

Globerman mentions a plethora of papers commissioned by various Canadian governmental agencies on the effects of deregulation in the U.S. It would be fascinating, in a public-choice context, to know which agencies commissioned which papers, and whether there was any pattern by agency as to the conclusions reached by the various papers. I agree with the paper's conclusion that U.S. deregulation has not had many harmful side effects, yet Canadian agencies apparently succeed in finding people who argue that it has had many such side effects. This is an interesting and instructive fact in and of itself.

There was a comment toward the end of the paper to the effect that there may be increased political pressure for deregulation in Canada because of the FTA and concomitant increased worry about price competitiveness in Canadian industry. That may well be true as a description of the arguments people are making, but, of course, it is an argument about absolute advantage. If all industries are equally burdened by high long distance charges, then there is no effect on comparative advantage. Here is a case where economists are torn between telling the truth and doing good. It's not easy to stop people who are making the right argument for the wrong reason, but I expect in the long run it is for the best.

Finally, on the price cap. I've read a number of articles that finish up by decrying the costs of detailed regulation and then argue that what is needed instead, if we must have regulation, is a price cap. This argument shouldn't be accepted without challenge. Regulation Q in the U.S. financial sector was introduced as a price cap that nobody thought would ever bind. Eventually it did bind and there is every evidence that the damage it did was immense. So I would like to see a much more detailed normative analysis of the likely effects of price caps and, in fact, would not be surprised if such an analysis concluded that it would be best to abandon all forms of price regulation.

Chapter 5

Truck and Rail Shipping: The Deregulation Evolution

John P. Palmer

> ...no good theoretical link has been forged between the structure
> of [an] industry and the degree to which competitive pricing
> prevails, because no good explanation has been provided for how
> present and potential rivals are kept from competing without
> some governmentally provided restrictions on competitive
> activities.[1]

Introduction

With the growth of air shipping throughout the global trading community, it
must seem a bit passé studying the old stand-bys: railway and truck freight.
Nevertheless, these two industries have continued to grow during the past two
decades, and they continue to play a central role in Canada's economy. Their
gross revenues have consistently amounted to more than 3 percent of Gross
Domestic Product, and their value added has always been in the neighbourhood
of 1/2 to 2 percent of GDP.[2]

While these percentages may seem to indicate that the industries are small,
they can perhaps be put into perspective by considering some minimal welfare
effects of deregulation in the industries. Suppose that deregulation were able
to improve efficiency in these industries by an amount equal to only 1/2 of 1
percent, i.e., by about $40 million per year. Such a welfare-enhancing policy
change would on average confer on each Canadian resident an amount of

---

1 Demsetz (1974), pp. 166-67.
2 See Palmer (1988).

money not quite enabling them to buy one additional Big Mac each year in perpetuity.

This amount may seem small to those who are not familiar with the calculations of Harbergerian triangles. It is, however, quite large in comparison with many welfare calculations, and it would represent a one-time wealth increase of approximately $1.3 billion, discounting a $40 million annual return at a real interest rate of 3 percent.

This rough calculation is presented not so much to indicate the feasible gains from deregulation. Rather, it is presented simply to indicate that truck and rail freight continue to be important in the economy. And given the importance of these industries to the Canadian economy, it behooves us to continue to consider potential welfare gains from further deregulation and potential welfare losses from reregulation.

Deregulation in the 1960s and 1970s

Canada

The evolution of transportation deregulation began over two decades ago, in 1967, with the National Transportation Act, which effectively deregulated most of the rates charged by the railways. Prior to the passing of the 1967 act, the MacPherson Commission had recognized that the railways were being required by law to operate at or near a loss by the infamous Crow Rates, which pegged the transport rates for grain and flour for export at levels well below cost. Employing a well-practised political strategy, the act did not abandon the Crow Rates; instead it encouraged a regime of cross-subsidization. It maintained the old Crow Rates but allowed the railways broad latitude within which they were free to set rates for carrying other items.[3]

The policy of cross-subsidization formalized in the 1967 National Transportation Act was consistent with many political economy theories of regulation. It provided highly visible benefits to several clearly identifiable groups while at the same time taxing other diffuse groups by a small, less-visible amount. The act had the eager support of farm owners in the Prairies because it meant that artificially high economic rents for their land would be maintainable. It also had some support from the railways because it provided them with some modicum of relief from the onerous Crow Rates. The only people hurt were those with non-grain interests, but the pain was spread rather broadly and thinly, so as to be hardly noticeable.

Nevertheless, the policy of cross-subsidization was doomed from the beginning. The necessary conditions for a successful policy of cross-subsidization

---

3   For a history of transportation policy in Canada, see Heaver and Nelsen (1977) and Purdy (1972).

did not exist and could not easily be legislated into existence.[4] In particular, most regulation of the trucking industry fell within the jurisdiction of the provinces, and the provincial attempts to regulate interprovincial trucking were quite varied. As a result, the railways faced increasing competition from the for-hire trucking industry. This competition reduced their latitude for charging high enough rates to compensate for the losses generated by grain shipping. In the face of the persistent inflation of the 1970s and early 1980s and the reduced ability to cross-subsidize, it is not surprising that the regime of the 1967 National Transportation Act was a long-term economic failure despite whatever short-term political successes it may have had. But despite this failure, it set in motion the two decades of deregulation by increasing the pricing freedom of the railways for carrying non-grain products.

In the trucking industry, the authority and responsibility for creating and enforcing regulations was established in the landmark Canadian Supreme Court cases of *Winner et al.* (1952).[5] This decision gave the federal government the right to regulate all interprovincial and international trucking operations. In response, Parliament passed the Motor Vehicle Act of 1954, which gave the provinces the right to regulate all trucking, whether inter or intraprovincial, so long as the same regulatory standards were imposed for both types of trucking. Needless to say, the panoply of provincial regulations wreaked havoc with interprovincial trucking, adding considerably to the regulatory costs faced by interprovincial truckers.

Once again, the National Transportation Act of 1967 came to the rescue. Part III of this act transferred regulatory control of interprovincial trucking from the provinces to the Canadian Transport Commission. However, the control of the CTC over published rates was limited. Trucking firms had considerable discretion in their rate setting for interprovincial shipments.

Meanwhile, the individual provinces regulated intraprovincial trucking quite differently, with Alberta having the least controlling regulations and Manitoba and Saskatchewan having the tightest regulations. In the early 1970s many different studies (mostly based on the same data, however) indicated that the provinces with tighter regulations also had higher freight rates.[6] At the same time, in the U.S., Alfred Kahn published his definitive two-volume treatise, *The Economics of Regulation*.[7] Academics were beginning to question whether the interventionist views of their colleagues from the early and middle twentieth

---

4   A short discussion of these conditions is provided in Palmer (1974), pp. 207-12.

5   *Attorney General for Ontario et al. v. Winner et al.; Winner et al. v. S.M.T. (Eastern) Limited et al.*, confirmed on appeal to Her Majesty's Privy Council, February 22, 1954, *All England Law Reports*, October 21, 1954.

6   Sloss (1970), pp. 327-66; McLachlan (1972), pp. 59-81; Palmer (1973a), pp. 655-64. Another excellent study, using different data, is that by Bonsor (1977).

7   Kahn (1971).

century held much benefit for consumers, especially in the area of trucking regulations.

By the end of the 1970s, great quantities of evidence had been amassed indicating that provincial trucking regulations were hampering the efficient allocation of Canadian resources. Hearings had been held; studies had been accumulated. Nevertheless, the changes were slow in coming. Generally, provincial legislators faced the problem of how to deregulate and not wipe out the large amounts of wealth that had been fostered by the regulations. Operating authorities were exchanging for well over a million dollars on some trucking routes, and it was feared that deregulation would impose unfair (or politically unwise) losses on some individuals. In effect, deregulation was carried out slowly, via alternative institutional arrangements. There was a growth in pseudo-leasing arrangements, freight forwarding, and private trucking, all of which provide effective alternatives for much for-hire trucking. Also, the newly allowed latitude in railway rate setting hindered the monopolies created by provincial licensing boards. The result was that although many of these alternatives were often more costly than unregulated trucking, they also were frequently less costly than regulated trucking, and they flourished.

The United States

The course of regulation was much different in the U.S. To the extent that the agricultural lobby had any political power, it was unable to have below-cost rates legislated for grain and flour shipments. And the threat of competition from trucking was headed off by the expansion of the Interstate Commerce Commission, which regulated both entry and rates in trucking.[8] The ICC had strong control over both industries with the exception of allowing rates to be competed downward along routes also served by unregulated water shipping.

Not only did the regulatory regime confer considerable power on the ICC, but it also obfuscated most attempts to discern the ICC's rate-making goals and strategies. In some cases carriers were not allowed to reduce rates because the ICC wanted to preserve intermodal competitors; in other cases carriers were not allowed to raise rates because the ICC wanted to preserve its concept of what amounted to rate-of-return pricing. The net effect was confusing and confused.

In 1962 President Kennedy sent a transportation message to Congress which was heralded as a harbinger of deregulation. Although the message did not lead to any legislation, it and the surrounding debate set the political stage for deregulation in the next decade.

Many people identify the beginning of transportation deregulation in the U.S. with the ascendancy of Alfred Kahn through the Civil Aeronautics Board

---

8   For a good description of the pre-deregulation ICC era, see Wilson (1970) and Peck (1970).

to the executive offices of President Carter. My own view, though, is not so much one of great men in history as it is one of fortuitous circumstance: rapidly changing fuel prices in the 1970s made rate regulation a dog's breakfast. The result of this regulatory, bureaucratic nightmare was that the ICC began significant deregulation on its own, prior to the ascendancy of Kahn and prior to the enactment of the Motor Carrier Act and the Staggers Act, both in 1980.

This view of the deregulation process in the U.S. is based on several strong empirical assumptions. First, it is assumed that regulatory bureaucrats prefer stability, quietness, and making decisions involving traditional parameters. Second, it is assumed that people with such preferences find bureaucratic jobs through a process of natural selection. Third, it is assumed that once these people find such jobs, the costs of leaving them (lost utility and otherwise) would be larger than for most people. The result of this natural selection process is that the regulation bureaucracy fell into chaos when stability and quietness were shattered by the fuel price shocks to the economy. Deregulation took place over a space of four or five years within the ICC because it was less threatening and easier than continued regulation.

Support for this view is provided by evidence that the stock markets had already capitalized most of the effects of deregulation long before the Motor Vehicle Act of 1980 was even proposed.[9] Fritz Kahn also argues that deregulation was de facto accomplished prior to becoming de jure in 1980.[10]

The thrust of this argument is that formal deregulation followed economic events, but did not lead them. As relative prices changed and as the pace of change quickened, regulation followed.[11] As I have argued elsewhere, "In the end, Darwinian survivalism probably had more to do with deregulation than any of the arguments put forward by well-meaning academics, the author included."[12]

---

9   Although their results are carefully hedged and far from conclusive, see Schipper, Thompson, and Weil (1987), pp. 53-66.

10   Kahn (1979), pp. 5-11.

11   While it is generally the case that political and vested-interest theories of political economy can explain the evolution of regulation and deregulation, as McFetridge and Lall point out in their article in this volume, "Is There a Theory of Regulation?," there are many instances of regulation and deregulation in the transportation industries that do not appear to conform nicely with these theories. The additional theory put forth here seems to help provide an explanation for these events.

12   Palmer (1988), p. 102.

Deregulation in the 1980s

Canada

On November 17, 1983, Royal Assent was given to Bill C-155, the Western Grain Transportation Act. Under the Crow Rate legislation, freight rates for grain and flour shipments designated for export had been pegged a levels equal to only 2 or 3 percent of the value of the grain. At the same time, other rates were:

Product Shipped:	Rates as a percent of value of Shipped Product:
Lumber	38 %
Coal	38 %
Sulphur	23 %
Potash	38 %

Bill C-155 abandoned the Crow Rates, but provided for a gradual transition from the statutory rates to market rates. Rates were allowed to rise by specified amounts over a seven year span. In addition, compensation was provided for the railways during the first year to help make up for the losses imposed upon them under the Crow Rates. In subsequent years the railways received less of a subsidy, but farmers received a subsidy to ease the transition to cost-based grain freight rates. As table 1 shows, by July 1984 grain rates had already shown a 20 percent increase, the maximum increase allowable under the act.

Table 1
Grain Freight Rates, 1983 and 1984

	Statutory Rates To:		July 31, 1984, Rates To:*	
	Thunder Bay:	Vancouver:	Thunder Bay:	Vancouver:
From:				
Winnipeg	3.18		3.83	
Regina	4.40	5.72	5.25	7.02
Calgary	5.72	4.40	7.02	5.15

*All rates are from Statistics Canada, 22-201, and are stated as dollars per metric tonne. Unfortunately, data are not available for subsequent years.

The next major legislation affecting the railways came from the National Transportation Act of 1987 (Bill C-18). This act was part of the deregulation fanfare played by the then Minister of Transportation, Don Mazenkowski, on July 15, 1986. While his proposals dealt primarily with airline deregulation, they also led to some refinements of the regulations governing railway freight movements.

Until 1987, the railways had engaged in what was euphemistically referred to as collective rate-making. Despite the creative choice of phrase, most people recognized it for what it was: government-sanctioned collusion. And despite opposition from railway interests, Bill C-118 did away with collective rate-making.[13]

Other sections of the act also promoted increased competition, both intramodally and intermodally: railways are now allowed to negotiate confidential contracts, a practice that severely increases the costs of policing implicit and explicit cartels; captive shippers are now allowed to negotiate access to other carriers; and, because the rates are slowly becoming more cost-related, the regulations governing railway route abandonment have been eased.

Another prong in the 1986-87 attack on regulation was Bill C-19, the Motor Vehicles Act. This bill did not, indeed could not, deregulate intraprovincial trucking. It did, however, make some gestures toward reducing the regulatory structure surrounding *interprovincial* trucking.[14]

The United States

Although deregulation of the railway and trucking industries had begun de facto in the early 1970s, it reached a head with the passage of the Staggers Act and the Motor Carrier Act in 1980. The Staggers Act granted the U.S. railways the freedom to set their own rates within very broad limitation, a deregulation policy that had already been in effect in Canada for more than a decade. It also banned the use of rate-fixing bureaus and encouraged the use of confidential contract rates, two pro-competitive policies not introduced in Canada until 1987.

The Motor Carrier Act reduced the barriers to entry into interstate trucking and removed the anti-trust exemption from tariff bureaus. Both of these measures were strongly pro-competitive. The lowering of barriers to entry was analogous to, but more definitive than, similar attempts made in 1967 and 1987 in Canada.

The Effects of Deregulation

The effects of deregulation in the United States have been studied at some length. In one of the most thorough and careful studies carried out, James

---

13 One of the most impressive defences of collective rate-making is presented by Heavor (1981).

14 For a thorough discussion of the arguments involved in Bill C-19, see Dawson and Parent (1987), pp. 86-96.

MacDonald shows that the Staggers Act had more of an effect on grain shipments on the Prairies than on those for which unregulated water shipping had long been a viable substitute.[15] He points out that as the railways were allowed to compete more freely with each other and with the newly deregulated trucking industry, they began to offer more discounts for multiple-car and unit train shipments. MacDonald argues that the use of larger and more efficient sized shipments in the post-Staggers era is due in large part to the deregulation that no longer required carriers to set rates that divided up the business among efficient and inefficient carriers alike. Pre-Staggers rate-making often inhibited efficiency by requiring rates high enough to cover the costs of the smaller, less efficient carriers and shipments. Although MacDonald attributes this change primarily to the Staggers Act, he also indicates that the trend in this direction had already begun in the mid-1970s as the ICC relaxed its regulations in many different areas. In other words, although he attributes the effects of deregulation to the Staggers Act, they might just as well have been observed anyway since the ICC was already moving in the direction of similar deregulation.

The direct effects of deregulation on freight rates is quite difficult to determine, especially relative to the ease of discovering rate schedules under a regime of regulation. With rates changing more frequently in response to changes in economic conditions, and with the growing use of confidential negotiated contracts, the data are more costly to acquire and less reliable. MacDonald summarizes an interesting technique for examining the effects of deregulation in the U.S. railway industry. This technique involves examining a time trend of the price spread of a particular product between its point of production and its final delivery point. In the case of grain, prices at midwestern grain elevators were compared with the prices paid for the same products at international ports. If deregulation had the effect of lowering the shipping costs of grain, then one would expect this price spread to have narrowed over time. The studies summarized all showed rising price spreads until Staggers, and then declining spreads when Prairie origins were used. If data were used from origins near competitive water routes, there appeared to be a slow, gradual decline in the price spreads throughout the time period, both before and after the Staggers Act became law.

Applying this same technique to Canadian grain shipments should yield the opposite results. As the Crow Rates were phased out and rail rates increased, one would expect, *ceteris paribus*, that the spread in prices would increase, not decrease. Unfortunately, the data provided in Statistics Canada Catalog 22-201 do not permit even a rough test of this hypothesis.

Rising rail rates for shipping grain in Canada can be expected to have several important effects. First, one would expect the rental value and asset value of

---

15 MacDonald (1989), pp. 63-96.

interior farmland to fall in relative terms. Rising transportation costs would reduce the demand for wheat grown on farms farther from international ports, and hence these farms would become less valuable. Tests of this hypothesis, however, are simply impossible since so many other variables were changing in the mid-1980s that one cannot separate the influences. In particular, subsidies to farmers were put in place to help compensate them for these anticipated losses.

Second, under deregulation, one would expect the railways to concentrate more on the business for which they have a comparative advantage. As I have shown previously,[16] by the end of 1984, the railways had begun to concentrate much more on longer distance hauling from the western and prairie provinces to international ports (see tables 2 and 3). While some of this change may have been due to fuel price changes, it may also have come about because of changing supply and demand conditions internationally, or it may also have been an effect of the de-Crowed grain rates.

Much of the switch in haulage resulted from increased international shipments of B.C. coal. Table 4 shows the amounts loaded of some of the major products shipped by rail during the past decade.

These data reveal little or nothing about the effects of deregulation. It appears that total railway freight shipping has generally increased over the decade, but no definite trends leap out of the table. However, if one compares the amount of wheat loaded in December of each year with the amount of wheat produced in the same calendar year, some results appear which may have been due to regulatory changes. Table 5 presents these data. Notice that the ratio of December wheat loadings to annual production dipped noticeably in 1984 when the grain rates were de-Crowed, and they rose noticeably in 1987 and 1988 at the same time increased competition was being induced by the 1987 National Transportation Act. Of course, the timing of these observations may simply be coincidental or the result of many other possible influences. The relationship is quite dramatic, though, as shown in figure 1.

As I said above, this correlation between December carloadings and changes in regulations could have been due to many other influences. There may have been sharp changes in international demand, international supply, labour conditions, relative storage costs, or other transport costs. Of course, it makes little sense that shippers would reduce their shipments in response to the rising rates in 1984 if they expected the nominal freight rates to rise by another 15 to 20 percent in 1985. It did make sense, however, to hold back on shipments

---

16 Palmer (1988), pp. 56-57.

Table 2
Metric Tonnes Shipped by Origin and Destination, 1977
(In Thousands)

Origin: \ Destination:	NFLD	PEI	NS	NB	QUE	ONT	MAN	SASK	ALTA	BC	NWT	US	Marine (Exports)	Total
NFLD	223.7	0.1	5.4	1.3	10.9	6.3	0.1	0.1	0.1	0.2	0.0	57.5	0.5	306.2
PEI	8.8	1.1	2.2	2.8	44.5	71.6	0.3	0.0	0.0	0.1	0.0	1.9	35.9	169.2
NS	38.2	52.0	4795.1	271.9	201.0	111.8	27.8	3.5	9.2	7.6	0.0	437.3	29.7	5985.1
NB	59.6	64.9	85.2	1531.5	419.5	315.8	5.9	0.6	8.6	10.9	0.1	459.8	913.6	3875.0
QUE	62.0	23.0	262.7	536.4	6584.9	4361.7	278.1	80.0	403.2	290.6	0.2	4336.2	1382.3	18601.3
ONT	100.5	47.3	615.5	636.7	5086.5	26502.0	1023.9	390.8	1503.9	1066.0	2.8	5738.7	2628.4	45343.0
MAN	15.3	1.3	35.9	29.7	376.6	1635.1	2692.7	521.0	298.9	115.2	0.1	520.0	2534.5	8776.3
SASK	7.5	17.2	30.1	47.3	260.0	3091.9	2050.6	791.6	219.5	1365.3	0.0	7170.0	11944.9	26995.9
ALTA	4.4	1.2	42.2	58.0	585.8	1082.4	491.1	892.1	3028.2	2894.4	37.3	4267.2	12487.1	25871.4
BC	20.4	6.5	35.6	68.0	456.5	901.4	353.4	316.3	1904.1	5616.8	2.2	5275.4	8976.6	23933.2
NWT	0.0	0.0	0.0	0.0	0.0	0.6	9.3	0.0	3.9	237.7	0.0	2.7	112.0	366.2
US	8.1	6.4	106.2	125.5	2221.9	4083.3	254.2	204.7	986.9	857.0	25.2	4182.0	0.1	13061.5
Marine	1.0	2.0	44.3	18.0	380.3	1195.1	34.3	21.4	269.2	19.0	0.1	0.0	0.0	1985.6
(Import) Total	549.5	223.0	6060.4	3327.1	16628.4	43359.0	7221.7	3222.1	8635.7	12481.7	68.0	32448.7	41045.6	175270.9

Table 3
Metric Tonnes Shipped by Origin and Destination, 1984
(In Thousands)

Origin: \ Destination:	NFLD	PEI	NS	NB	QUE	ONT	MAN	SASK	ALTA	BC	NWT	US	Marine (Exports)	Total
NFLD	56.5	0.1	5.2	0.7	27.4	36.2	0.0	0.0	0.0	0.0	0.0	22.4	16.1	164.6
PEI	1.5	0.1	0.0	0.1	22.9	87.0	2.7	0.1	0.2	0.0	0.0	0.3	0.1	115.0
NS	42.8	1.6	4086.1	138.4	256.8	96.6	5.6	4.7	14.4	13.1	0.0	325.7	1531.5	6517.3
NB	51.0	74.7	115.4	1389.5	567.5	246.4	26.2	0.3	3.4	4.7	0.0	314.1	543.1	3336.3
QUE	137.0	12.1	264.6	466.7	4872.8	2954.5	239.5	101.5	372.5	301.2	0.2	5888.0	1068.5	16679.1
ONT	136.6	42.3	659.6	613.6	4451.3	19256.7	1035.7	445.8	1751.1	1068.8	3.0	5991.7	2874.4	38330.6
MAN	4.0	17.2	91.7	50.2	424.7	934.7	865.6	426.9	286.9	215.5	0.0	559.7	5121.4	8998.5
SASK	5.7	8.1	68.6	28.2	374.5	3581.6	651.2	506.2	311.0	852.4	0.0	4797.7	21098.6	32283.8
ALTA	9.5	11.1	92.7	76.8	651.6	3122.7	888.7	606.7	1446.7	2977.7	209.3	5911.6	21308.8	37313.9
BC	16.5	3.6	50.3	56.8	887.5	2205.6	307.6	113.7	1620.2	7019.3	9.2	4324.7	19342.1	35957.1
NWT	0.0	0.0	0.0	0.0	0.0	0.1	0.0	0.0	3.9	278.6	0.1	0.0	60.2	342.9
US	0.4	1.3	44.6	120.4	1332.1	3003.4	221.0	363.6	874.7	875.1	0.7	3340.6	590.5	10768.4
Marine	3.5	0.1	36.5	10.0	1005.9	2031.4	74.3	41.0	246.1	116.0	0.9	649.0	0.0	4215.3
(Import) Total	465.0	172.3	5515.3	2951.4	14875.0	37556.9	4318.1	2610.5	6931.1	13723.0	223.4	32125.5	73555.3	195022.8

Note: The differences between the totals reported above and those in table 2 are the result of different data collection processes implemented in the two different surveys.

Sources for tables 2 and 3: Statistics Canada, *Railway Transport* (cat. 52-214) April 1982 and March 1986.

Table 4
Millions of Metric Tonnes Loaded

PRODUCT	1978	1979	1980	1981	1982	1983	1984	1985	1986	1987	1988
Wheat	1.34	1.24	1.38	1.95	2.13	1.84	0.96	1.52	2.22	2.66	1.40
Other grain	0.55	0.72	0.57	0.90	0.69	0.71	0.53	0.67	1.14	0.74	0.68
Coal	1.71	1.28	1.56	2.08	1.97	2.42	2.84	3.38	3.31	3.73	3.85
Potash	0.83	0.82	0.99	0.80	0.68	0.92	0.92	0.90	1.07	1.22	1.06
Iron ore and concrete	4.15	4.60	2.35	3.29	1.64	2.15	3.19	3.33	2.27	3.52	3.29
Pulpwood chips	0.76	0.61	0.72	0.60	0.45	0.57	0.62	0.59	0.70	0.73	0.63
Manufactured and miscellaneous	0.32	0.27	0.24	0.21	0.20	0.15	0.11	0.15	0.13	0.11	0.11
Total frt. loaded	17.51	17.45	16.00	17.52	13.87	16.60	16.93	18.68	19.36	22.57	21.05

* These data are for the month of December only in each year.

Source: Statistics Canada Catalog 52-001. Data for annual carloadings reveal a much less striking pattern.

Table 5
Annual Wheat Production and December Wheat Carloadings*

	1978	1979	1980	1981	1982	1983	1984	1985	1986	1987	1988
Annual Wheat Prodn	21.14	17.18	19.29	24.80	26.74	26.51	21.20	24.25	31.38	25.95	15.65
Wheat loaded	1.34	1.24	1.38	1.95	2.13	1.84	0.96	1.52	2.22	2.66	1.40
(row 1)/(row 2)	.06	.07	.07	.08	.08	.07	.05	.06	.07	.10	.09

* The first two rows are in millions of metric tonnes.

Source for row 1 is Statistics Canada 22-201.

Figure 1
Proportion of Grain Production that was Shipped by Rail

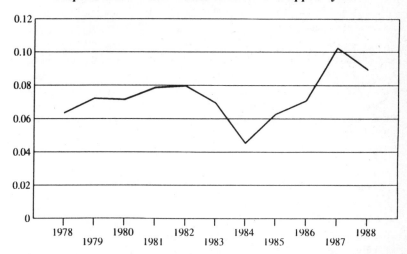

to the extent that later shipments might enable the shippers to qualify for partial subsidies, as many hoped during 1984.[17]

But that land wasn't going anywhere. It was still there and available for farming (or its next best alternative use). Potential farmers simply would not buy or rent the land unless explicit rents charged declined sufficiently to enable them to earn a normal rate of return even in the face of higher grain freight rates. The new farmers could compete internationally just as easily as before. It was the landowners (and to some extent their creditors) who suffered the most when the rates were allowed to rise. It is also possible that in the face of rising rail rates and continuing abandonment of unprofitable branch lines, increasing proportions of wheat were shipped via truck to the major terminal sites.

The effects of trucking deregulation are more mixed and more controversial. In a study of the effects of deregulation in California, Frey, et al., found that

> Real rates have decreased, and rate changes have become somewhat more frequent. We found no significant difference in rate changes experienced by small and large shippers. There is

---

17 The discussions about who would receive what subsidies when is summarized in the autumn, 1984, issues of the *Ottawa Letter*. During these discussions, retired Justice Emmett Hall told the Commons Committee that Canadian farmers needed the subsidy to survive in international competition. The justice was only partly correct: farmers were doomed to lose personal wealth with the de-Crowed rates. Their farm output and hence their implicit rents were expected to fall. Those who had secured large loans based on the former, higher implicit rents faced serious financial difficulties and even bankruptcy.

much less uniformity among rates, but rate information has not become more difficult or costly to obtain. Shippers have experienced some increase in the quality of service, and this increase has been shared by both small and large shippers.
There is no evidence to support the hypothesis that reduced rates will lead to a shift away from private carriers toward for-hire carriers. Carriers have increased their use of non-union employees and subhaulers in an attempt to reduce labor costs. They have also attempted to decrease maintenance costs, primarily by performing more of their own maintenance. Despite their cost-cutting efforts, carriers' profits have decreased since deregulation took effect...There is considerable evidence that competition among the carriers has increased, as expected.[18]

Their major findings, that real rates had declined and become more variable in the face of increased competition, are plausible. Some of their other conclusions are less palatable, however. First, if the rates are less uniform and more variable, it is incomprehensible that information costs would not have risen for at least some shippers. Second, if rates had been regulated to be above some minimum average total cost, then it is likely that the trucking firms engaged more heavily in service and quality competition than they otherwise would have. Third, it difficult to understand why profit-maximizing firms would not cut costs by doing their own maintenance regardless of the regulatory regime if doing so would improve the net worth of the firms. Finally, the move in California to using less unionized labour after deregulation is consistent with the strong opposition that unions have to deregulation in most industries.

In a different study, using data from the Oregon log trucking industry, McMullen obtained results which "suggest that regulatory policy which discourages competitive rate differentials may result in higher motor carrier industry concentration than that found in a competitive market environment."[19] McMullen seems to be arguing that levels of concentration tend to be higher in this industry under regulation than under deregulation. It is difficult to see how he arrived at such a conclusion, but perhaps there are some unique features to the Oregon log trucking industry that do not appear in other trucking industries. It is possible that McMullen thinks concentration is anti-competitive and puts forth his views in support of deregulation and competition. Such a belief about the evils of concentration would be similar to that of Wyckoff and Maister who

---

18 Frey, Krolick, and Tontz (1986) p. 259. The data for their study were collected primarily via surveys.

19 B. McMullen (1985), p. 133.

were horrified that deregulation of the trucking industry in Australia led to its increased concentration.[20]

An alternative view, similar to that of Demsetz in the opening quotation, is that concentration per se is not the issue. In fact, most anti-competitive behaviour persists only with active government support. Instead, one should view the likely increased concentration of the trucking industry that would occur with significant deregulation as a sign that regulation had kept too many trucking firms too small for too long—that increased concentration would enable the larger firms to take advantage of economies of scale in administration and scheduling, generating fewer empty miles and lower average rates.[21] Only when present and potential competition is hindered does concentration become a problem, and then the problem is not with concentration but with whatever hinders competitive behaviour.

Another concern about deregulation in the railway and trucking industries is that "consolidation may lead to rural road deterioration as farmers invest in heavier trucks to move larger loads further to unit train elevators."[22] If indeed deregulation does lead to the use of heavier trucks on rural roads, there will be a problem (depending on one's perspective) only if the increased costs due to road deterioration are externalized to others in society. If instead, through licence fees or gasoline taxes or even tolls, truckers are required to pay according to all the costs their actions cause, then their decision to use heavier trucks will not necessarily lead to an inefficient allocation of society's scarce resources. If, however, tax and licence schemes fail to force truckers to cover all their costs, then deregulation could very well raise some costs to others in society, and these costs are usually ignored in most deregulation scenarios.

A third implication of deregulation that has been put forward by the author and others in the past is that because so many shippers turn to private carriers to circumvent the imposed inefficiencies of trucking regulation, after deregulation there should be a decline in the use of private carriers vis-à-vis for-hire carriers. In this regard, the results of Frey, et al.—that there had been no evidence of a shift away from the use of private carriers—are surprising in the face of this argument. Their explanation of the lack of decline in the use of private carriers is that these firms cut their costs in the face of increased competition by using more non-union labour and subhaulers. Either these firms must not have been profit maximizers or this explanation is incorrect, for surely if it was possible to reduce costs with these methods after deregulation, it should have been possible to do so before deregulation. The only possible exception

---

20 Wyckoff and Maister (1975).
21 See Palmer (1988), chapter 6.
22 MacDonald (1989), n. 39, p. 91. Also see Azzan and Linsenmeyer (1987).

to this argument is that labour union strength deteriorated in the face of deregulation, a not implausible argument.

In Canada it is possible that the effects of trucking deregulation in the 1980s will be so minor that they will not have much of an effect on the private/for-hire trucking mix. By 1985, the trend toward using trucks for shorter, intraprovincial shipments was well under way.[23] And Statistics Canada data for 1986 indicate that this trend was continuing.[24] Furthermore, these data show that an even larger share of private trucking is done on short-haul, intraprovincial routes, the very routes that will remain unaffected by the Motor Vehicle Transportation Act of 1987.

Safety

One separate topic that has received political interest is the potential effect of deregulation on safety. There is some concern that as firms face increased competition, they will sacrifice safety in a cost-cutting move to maintain adequate profit levels. This argument seems to hinge on a satisficing (vs. maximizing) theory of firm behaviour and is somewhat consistent with some early empirical results indicating that satisficing behaviour is more likely to be observed in firms facing less competition than in those facing strenuous competition.[25]

Many people find satisficing theories of the firm unacceptable, however. Nevertheless, even if firms are profit maximizers, they might have incentives to reduce safety under deregulation. In the case of rate regulation, following a Chamberlinian model, one can easily imagine that firms facing a fixed price might choose to compete on service grounds, which might also increase their safety performance. In addition, one can imagine that economists who like to play with δ's could easily construct a mathematical model whereby, given some implausible values for certain bizarre parameters, a profit-maximizing firm would choose less safety when faced with a demand curve of increasing elasticity due to reduced regulatory barriers to entry.[26]

---

23 Palmer (1988), pp. 77-78.

24 Catalog 53-222 (1986).

25 Palmer (1973b), pp. 293-303.

26 It was also suggested during the conference at which this study was first presented that deregulation might lead to the emergence of many smaller firms, each of which would be more open to the risk of bankruptcy and hence have less incentive to take as many safety precautions. These smaller firms, it was argued, could reduce their costs by reducing their safety expenditures. Should a large claim be made against such a firm, it would have few assets, and would be judgement proof (i.e., bankrupt). Such arguments are plausible, but they are inconsistent with the observation that concentration in the trucking industry grows with deregulation, leaving larger, not smaller, firms.

Evidence that deregulation reduces safety is not clear. Table 6 shows Daicoff's recent findings, using U.S. data, of annual average compound rates of decline in involvements per billion of truck miles.

Table 6
U.S. Safety Data*

Time Period	Fatalities	Injuries	Accidents
1974-1985	4.96	5.05	4.52
1974-1980	6.16	6.64	5.10
1980-1985	3.49	3.12	3.81

Source: Daicoff (1988), table 3, p. 182.

As Daicoff emphasizes, the rate of safety improvement could have changed for a variety of reasons. The noticeable decline after the 1980 Motor Carrier Act is consistent, though, with any of the above models which would predict a decline in safety (or its rate of improvement) with deregulation.[27]

Many regulators have expressed concern that deregulation might be undesirable if it leads to declining safety standards. I disagree with this view. Even if we accept that deregulation might lead to slower rates of safety improvement, it does not follow that therefore deregulation is undesirable. In the first place, if safety per se is desirable, it is possible to enact fitness and safety legislation/regulation that addresses these concerns directly. And, in the second place, if fixed freight rates and/or barriers to entry lead to more safety than otherwise, they probably ignore the opportunity costs of using society's scarce resources to provide that safety. It is likely that regulation causes too many resources to be diverted from other valuable uses into the production of safety. While regulators and others may argue for increased safety (at any cost?), Canadians might do well to cheer for deregulation, more efficiency, and less safety.

---

27 Interestingly, a very similar safety pattern is presented for the airlines by another article in this volume, "Will Canadian Airline Deregulation Fail?"

References

Azzan, A.M. and D.M. Linsenmeyer (1987), "The Impact of Volume of Marketings and Distance to Markets on the Choice of Truck Size," *North Central Journal of Agricultural Economics* 9.

Bonsor, Norman C. (1977), *Transportation Rates and Economic Development in Northern Ontario* (Toronto: University of Toronto Press).

Daicoff, Darwin W. (1988), "Deregulation and Motor Carrier Safety," *Logistics and Transportation Review* 24, 2 (June).

Dawson, D.A. and L.P. Parent (1987), "Positive Steps in Transport Deregulation—The Prairies," *Canadian Public Policy* 13, 1, pp. 86-96.

Demsetz, Harold (1974), "Two Systems of Belief about Monopoly," in H.J. Goldschmid, H.M. Mann, and J.F. Weston (eds.) *Industrial Concentration: The New Learning* (Toronto: Little, Brown and Company).

Frey, N. Gail, Reuben H. Krolick, and Jay L. Tontz (1986), "The Impact of Motor Carrier Deregulation: California Intrastate Agricultural Products," *Logistics and Transportation Review* 22, 3 (September), p. 259.

Heavor, T.D. (1981), "Collective Ratemaking by Canadian Railways: An Appraisal," *Logistics and Transportation Review* 17, 1 (March).

Heaver, T.D. and J.C. Nelsen (1977), *Railway Pricing under Commercial Freedom: The Canadian Experience* (Vancouver: UBC Centre for Transportation Studies).

Kahn Alfred E. (1971), *The Economics of Regulation* (Toronto: John Wiley & Sons).

Kahn, Fritz R. (1979), "Motor Carrier Regulatory Reform—Fait Accompli," *Transportation Journal* 19, 2, pp. 5-11.

MacDonald, James M. (1989), "Railroad Deregulation, Innovation, and Competition: Effects of the Staggers Act on Grain Transportation," *The Journal of Law and Economics* 32, 1 (April), pp. 63-96.

McLachlan, D.L. (1972), "Canadian Trucking Regulations," *The Logistics and Transportation Review* 8, 1, pp. 59-81.

McMullen, Stan (1985), "Commodity Specific Rate Differentials in a Competitive Trucking Industry," *Logistics and Transportation Review* 21, 2 (June).

Palmer, John (1988), *An Economic Analysis of Canada's Ground Transportation Sector* (Vancouver: The Fraser Institute).

Palmer, John (1974), "Taxation by Regulation? The Experience of Ontario Trucking Regulation," *Logistics and Transportation Review*, pp. 207-12.

Palmer, John (1973a), "A Further Analysis of Provincial Trucking Regulation," *Bell Journal of Economics and Management Science* 4, 2 (Autumn) pp. 655-64.

Palmer, John (1973b), "The Profit-Performance Effects of the Separation of Ownership from Control...," *Bell Journal of Economics and Management Science* 4, 1 (Spring), pp. 293-303.

Peck, Merton J. (1970), "Competitive Policy for Transportation?", in Paul W. MacAvoy (ed.) *The Crisis of the Regulatory Commissions* (Toronto: W.W. Norton & Co.).

H.L. Purdy (1972), *Transport Competition and Public Policy in Canada* (Vancouver: UBC Press).

Schipper, Katherine, Rex Thompson, and Roman L. Weil (1987), "Disentangling Interrelated Effects of Regulatory Changes on Shareholder Wealth: The Case of Motor Carrier Deregulation," *The Journal of Law and Economics* 30, 1 (April), pp. 53-66.

James Sloss (1970), "Regulation of Motor Freight Transportation: A Quantitative Evaluation of Policy," *The Bell Journal of Economics and Management Science* 1, 2 (Autumn), 327-66.

Wilson, George (1970), "The Effect of Rate Regulation on Resource Allocation in Transportation," in Paul W. MacAvoy (ed.) *The Crisis of the Regulatory Commissions* (Toronto: W.W. Norton & Co.).

Wyckoff, D.D. and David Maister (1975), *The Owner-Operator Independent Truckers* (Lexington: D.C. Heath & Co.).

Discussion of the Palmer Paper

Walter Block

I would like to begin by countering Professor John Palmer's cynical assessment of the economics profession. He sees it as being limited to pushing the rock of Sisyphus up and down the hill. Consider in this regard a statement made by Milton Friedman at a meeting of the Western Economics Association several years ago, expressing a sentiment that really made me proud to be an economist. He said that, and this is just a paraphrase, "because of the work of economists over the many years, the tariff rate is possibly one-tenth of 1 percent less than it would otherwise have been—and with that we've probably paid for our salaries a hundred times over."

Palmer has written an important paper. I agree with virtually all of it, and enthusiastically so. I sense in him a fellow extremist. There are, however, two slight points of disagreement. These prove, if anything, that I am even more out of step with the mainstream of the profession than he. First, Palmer says that anti-trust law is pro-competitive. But it seems to me that the very opposite is true. Anti-trust or anti-combines legislation may well be competitive in the sense employed by the perfectly competitive textbook model. But there is no necessary connection between the concentration of industry, which is the focus of these models, and competition of the real world rivalling sort. Therefore, these laws, which interfere with those voluntary trades between consenting adults that increase industrial concentration, must inevitably restrict, not enhance, competition in the common-sense meaning of that term. Anti-combines law is anti-competitive then, not pro-competitive as maintained by Palmer.

Our author also states that "most anti-competitive behaviour persists only with active government support." I would substitute the word "most" that he employs with the word "all." I offer a challenge: I defy anyone to give an example of anti-competitive behaviour that does not stem from statist interferences with the free market system. (I do not count it as anti-competitive that one person might refuse, for any reason whatsoever, to trade with another; this is logically indistinguishable from the economic analysis of the desire for leisure.)

But these are mere peccadilloes. Apart from these two brief oversights, the Palmer chapter is a stellar one. In particular, his point about the optimal amount of resources to be allocated to safety considerations must be singled out for special mention. His is a courageous analysis. I use this word in the sense it is used in "Yes, Minister." This is the TV show in which whenever the Minister tries to deregulate or privatize, the bureaucrats tell him "it is a courageous step" in an attempt to dissuade him. "Courageous" or not, I support Palmer's view that there is an optimal level of safety and that this is derived from the marketplace. Government regulation in the matter tends to misallocate resources. Often, it promotes greater hazards for society. An example is the U.S. Food and Drug Administration, which has held up the process of approval for new drugs, and thus reduced the health of patients who long had to do without. Sometimes, government intervention can lead to excessive safety. This might sound paradoxical to the layman, but economists all know and appreciate that it is possible to reduce the air flight death rate to zero—by banning air travel, for example—but this is hardly compatible with increasing economic welfare.

I do not intend to comment further on the specifics of the paper. I would find this boring, and so would the reader, because all I would do is reiterate what John said, since apart from the above mentioned exceptions, I agree with his entire analysis. Instead, I shall focus on this idea of safety he brings up, and further elaborate upon it. This also allows me to link my comments with Herb Grubel's insightful point: since there is now more air travel, there is less automobile traffic; as a result, many lives have been saved because highways are ever so much more dangerous per passenger mile than airways.

But why should this be so? Is there any link between the fact that roads and streets are publicly owned and administered and their seeming intrinsic dangerousness? I suggest that there is, and that the solution lies in the direction of privatization and deregulation. I propose to discuss, then, the privatization and deregulation not of trucking or rail or airways, but of streets and highways.

I realize that this is politically unfeasible. There is plenty of opposition to bringing about the advantages of the free market to such transportation industries as buses, trolleys, trains, and planes. To even contemplate privatizing roads, highways, streets, and sidewalks will in some political circles be considered ludicrously extreme. But I am very much out of sympathy with the idea that we should censor ourselves because we think that something is politically impossible. I think we have to seek the truth wherever it may lead us. There may be politicians and bureaucrats who cannot follow economic logic, but the development of important knowledge will be retarded if economists who might otherwise study such a question engage in self censorship out of regard for the political realities.

Not only politicians will recoil in horror from the spectre of private roads. This applies as well to those economists who have long used highways as one of the paradigm cases of a public good. However, for the faint of heart in this matter, I offer up the case of the lighthouse. At one time, virtually the entire community of academic economists would have thrown up their arms in dismay at the suggestion that the market could handle such an enterprise. But then along came Ronald Coase with his seminal article on this topic, and the profession, or at least large parts of it, made an abrupt about-face. Perhaps we can attempt something along this line at present.

Exhibit A in the case for privatizing roads is the number of highway fatalities. In the U.S. there are some 40,000 people a year who die on highways. In Canada the figure is about one-tenth of that; our death rate has hovered around 4,000 on an annual basis for the past dozen years or so. Amazingly, given the level of carnage, there has been no hue and cry at this instance of inhumanity toward mankind.

In sharp contrast, every time there is a little girl lost in the woods, hundreds of people try to rescue her. The news media give such stories big play. At the time of this writing, Hurricane Hugo is now creating a swath of destruction. One cannot turn on the TV without seeing horrendous evidence of this catastrophe. But all of the loss of life due to getting lost in the woods, hurricanes, drownings, industrial accidents, airplane crashes, are as nothing compared to highway fatalities.

I think there is a serious and untoward misallocation of scholarly input in dealing with the problem of safety. We virtually ignore highways and roads—or at least the one meaningful solution to this problem—privatization. There is, of course, a possible explanation for this. Perhaps it is because most analysts see highway fatalities as inevitable, as in the case of death and taxes. In the literature on this subject, the causes of highway fatalities are commonly listed as drunken driving, vehicle malfunction, weather, speeding, etc. Peltzman, for example, lists no fewer than 13 different causes of highway fatalities without mentioning even once the issue of governmental mismanagement in its control of highways.[1] Such analysts confuse proximate cause with an ultimate cause. They are in effect blaming the bullet for the death and not the gun.

Consider the following analogy. If a hotel is forced into bankruptcy, possible explanations are lousy service, broken down plumbing, inedible food, and dirty rooms. But we would all dismiss this out of hand as the arrant nonsense that it is. We would explain the hotel's failure in terms of incompetent management. This is the ultimate cause; those others are merely proximate causes. Management would presumably be replaced and the hotel would be run more efficiently.

It is the same thing with highway fatalities. The managers are ultimately responsible for not weeding out drunken driving, not controlling speeding, and not eliminating vehicle malfunctions to the degree possible. The problem is, we have not focused on the beneficial effects of competition on this area. There

---

1 See Peltzman (1975), *Regulation and Auto Safety* (Washington D.C.: American Enterprise Institute for Public Policy Research), pp. 8, 9.

is no profit and loss in road management. There are no bankruptcies after a fatality occurs. No one automatically loses money whenever a three-car crack-up occurs and five people die. There is no negative feedback mechanism, that is, no one in a position to improve matters loses any money when failure occurs. The Soviet Union and the countries of eastern Europe are now involved in a process of *perestroika* to free up their economies. Yet their highways, and our own, are run on identical principles. We could use a good bit of *perestroika* on our highways.

Let us contemplate an alternative scenario: competitive roads. This would apply not only to limited access highways but also to city streets. My claim is that the competitive process would reduce traffic fatalities to a great degree—the degree desired by the general public, given the alternatives that must be foregone in order to attain this goal. At present, people are now able, at least in principle, to compare the fatality rates on competing air carriers. This cannot help but have a salutary effect on air safety. One benefit of a competitive automobile transport system is that the market could thus do for traffic fatalities what it now accomplishes in the air.

But there are other possible ways in which privatization could enhance safety, some of them highly speculative. For example, private road entrepreneurs might place accident markers, or even cemetery headstones, in the median grass strips which separate the different travel directions. Or perhaps a crashed 'accordianized' automobile might be placed on a gigantic pedestal. If publicizing deaths in this way can really engender more cautious driving, this would certainly bring to people's attention what can happen if they act improperly while driving. This may or may not be the best way of attaining this goal. The point is that a competitive highway industry would at least have the economic incentives to engage in research to this end—a far cry from what obtains at present.

Perhaps the problem with high-speed automobile traffic is not the level of speed itself but its variance. Highway entrepreneurs might experiment with narrowing not the level but the dispersion of legal speeds. Another major reason for contemplating the privatization scenario is highway congestion; this, paradoxically, can also lead to fatalities. California has among the worst congestion in North America and among the worst fatality records. In addition to "ordinary" traffic deaths, there is also, as of late, the quaint California motorist habit of taking pot-shots at each other on the highway. I can't help but believe that the frustration of bumper-to-bumper traffic has led to tempers getting out of hand.

Let us now consider several objections to this very modest proposal. First, there is the claim that free enterprise roads and highways are simply impractical. Natural monopoly problems, insuperable transaction costs, and externalities among other things will render this idea impossible to implement. My research on the matter, however, shows there have been private highways as early as the ninth century A.D. in Great Britain.[2] There were, of course, only dirt roads at that time, but the owners utilized a very sophisticated price mechanism even in those early days. Narrow carriage wheels would allow relatively great speeds, but would damage the roadbed; very wide wheels, in contrast, served much the same road improvement function as a steamroller, but were very slow. The road owners charged a price inversely proportional to the width of the wheel, and transporters chose between saving time and saving money. In this way the negative externalities of highway travel were internalized. There were also price differentials based on weight of the carriage, number of horses used, and other such criteria.

These turnpike companies ultimately failed, not because of any intrinsic incompatibility with reality, but because of what can only be considered to be government failure. The state imposed price ceilings which made the operation economically untenable. When criminals burned the turnpike toll-gates, the government refused to uphold the property rights of the road owners. On the occasions when such government sins of omission and commission failed to ruin the highways market, outright expropriation was employed.

But the market is like a hardy weed, difficult to fully eradicate. There are still private roads, streets, bridges, etc., in operation. Just recently there was a successful proposal made by a private company in Washington, D.C., to build a toll road connecting the city with a local airport.

Nor is there any basic problem with billing for private road services. The universal product code system now used in supermarkets can easily be introduced to automobile transportation. Contrary to the usual brusque dismissal of the proposal, no motorist would have to stop every thirty feet or so to put a penny in a meter placed in front of each house on every road.

Privatization could easily be made to apply to intercity highways, for which we already have an analogy: private railroads. Physically, highways and railroads are very similar: they occupy very long, thin strips of land. If there is no objection in principle to private railways, there should be none for private

---

2   See Walter Block (1983), "Public Goods and Externalities: The Case of Roads," *The Journal of Libertarian Studies* VII, 1 (Spring), pp. 1-34; *idem* (1983), "Theories of Highway Safety," *Transportation Research Record* #912, pp. 7-10; *idem* (1980), "Congestion and Road Pricing," *The Journal of Libertarian Studies* IV, 3 (Fall), pp. 299-330; *idem* (1979), "Free Market Transportation: Denationalizing the Roads," *Journal of Libertarian Studies* III, 2 (Summer), pp. 209-38.

roads. But this applies to intracity streets as well, contrary to the view of transportation theorists such as Gabriel Roth.[3]

Now, consider shopping malls. These ubiquitous phenomena provide the most successful modern instances of private thoroughfares. City streets, in contrast, are a dismal failure: unsafe, cracked, and pot-holed in many urban centres. Malls located in snowbound areas are commonly open for joggers in the early mornings, even before the stores themselves are open. No business is conducted at these times, but great amounts of goodwill are garnered. There is protection from criminal behaviour. With public streets (and this goes for public parks as well) no private individual or firm loses money if a rape or murder occurs. As a result of this irresponsibility, the tendency is for more of these anti-social actions to take place. In contrast, contemplate Disneyland, the West Edmonton Mall, or any other such private venture. Here, there are many private streets. They are relatively safe and efficient because of the usual economic incentives.

One problem, however, is that the courts have attenuated the distinction between public and private streets. Recent cases have established the "right" of people to distribute leaflets on private mall streets because the mall has been designated by the court to be, in effect, a public street. On behalf of the consumer, the market has been attempting to escape invasive government regulations and ownership by setting up its own streets; then the government (court) comes along and denies this option.

Then there is the question of access. The usual critical scenario is that a private road owner will trap people in their homes by not allowing them access to his transportation route. It is difficult to see how entrepreneurs will earn profits by refusing to deal with potential customers. Certainly, shopping mall owners are not in the habit of refusing shoppers access to their tenant store-owners. In any case, before anyone bought a house he would ensure legal access to the highway network.

What of the objection that even though the present thesis is based on sound private property rights analysis, it would be better for it not to be put forth in so public a manner, such as being included in the present book. This is because some people will find it too radical, and it will tend to discredit the more orthodox free market-oriented analyses which inform the other chapters. This comment, in other words, will be an external diseconomy on the other essays. There are difficulties with this position. For one thing, the present contribution may make the others more acceptable, not less, in that they will be rendered more "moderate." For another, the externality relation tends to be reciprocal,

---

3   See Roth (1967), *Paying for Roads: The Economics of Traffic Congestion* (Middlesex, England: Penguin); and *idem* (1966), *A Self-Financing Road System* (London, England: The Institute of Economic Affairs).

as Ronald Coase has long impressed upon the profession. If A harms B, then the suppression of A, on behalf of B, will harm A. In other words, the implication of the externality model is just as much to suppress the A as the B. On a practical note, political-economic public policy decisions usually emerge out of a process of compromise. But if the free market side pulls its punches out of fear of appearing too "radical" while the interventionists suffer no such anxiety, then the result is likely to be skewed in the latter direction. This is surely not a conclusion to be welcomed by those who have made this objection.

Discussion of the Palmer Paper

Richard Schwindt

The previous discussion of the role of economists in encouraging the deregulation process is well illustrated and forcefully presented in John Palmer's paper. Rail and truck shipping are industries that have long provided economists with a rich variety of apparently ill-conceived regulations to criticize. Palmer points out that he was taught even as an undergraduate that these industries were examples of regulatory failure. I don't know how old he is, but I can trace my exposure to these arguments back to the early 1960s. It was then said that a classic agency capture story applied to the United States experience. The Interstate Commerce Commission was set up in order to control the rapacious, monopolistic behaviour of the railways, and the Commission became instead the instrument of the regulated.

Constraints on trucking were a means to curb intermodal competition to protect the regulated. The alleged market failure that was used to justify the foreclosing of intermodal competition was destructive competition in the trucking industry. By the late 1950s, evidence had accumulated that this was wrong. It was recognized that there was intermodal competition that could curb the excesses of the railways in many of the markets in which they were operating. There was evidence that trucking was not "destructively" competitive, and that it could survive in a free market environment.

As this wisdom entered undergraduate economic textbooks, I assume it also entered the public and political consciousness. Now, John attributes the changed regulatory environment to the hostility of the Kennedy Administration to the teamsters union. I hope this isn't true. I hope that John underestimates the accrued effect of the economic evidence that these industries were being misregulated.

Palmer shows fairly significant results coming from deregulation, but certainly no "zingers" as projected for airline deregulation and certainly no massive technological changes as we have witnessed in telecommunications or the other industries under review here. I think that what Palmer has really done is told us a success story. A success story that was built in part upon the analysis that economists provided.

The weakness of this paper is that it is too much a retrospective, a statement of what has happened. I had hoped for more information as to what remains to be done. What are the gains that exist for further deregulation? What should be our position with respect to provincial control over intraprovincial trucking? What are the welfare effects of the provincial regulatory environments? Is further deregulation called for? And, what of privatization? How do we handle institutions like Via Rail?

Chapter 6

Will Canadian Airline Deregulation Fail?

Herbert G. Grubel

This study of the merit of airline deregulation in Canada is motivated by the pervasive criticism and widespread public unease regarding the current and likely future effects of recent deregulation. This style of criticism is exemplified by a book with a title that says it all: *Airline Deregulation in Canada: Why it Failed.* Written by Andrew J. Roman in May 1989, it declares deregulation a failure just 17 months after the adoption of Bill C-18, the bill that deregulated airlines in January 1988.

The U.S. media too have for a long time been blaming airline deregulation for a host of ills that have beset the industry. Alfred Kahn, known as "the father of airline deregulation," was recently quoted in *Reason* as saying,

> When a plane crashes or nearly does, or when congestion, delays, labour unrest, a bankruptcy, accident, price war—or a price increase!—or a rash of lost baggage puts the airline industry in the news, one reporter or another will look up my number and call me to ask if I am sorry for what I did.

Canadian media also associate news about air travel with deregulation. For example, the *Toronto Globe and Mail* (1987) noted that in 1985 a total of 1,534 people died in aircraft accidents world-wide. This record number of accidents was blamed on deregulation.[1]

---

1   This example is taken from Jordan (1989), who points out that all but 174 of the 1,534 fatalities involved planes that were flown by foreign companies and had not been deregulated. Of the U.S. fatalities, 126 involved the Delta Airlines crash in Dallas which was officially attributed to wind shear. Jordan suggests that this

It is difficult to assess the general public's attitude to airline deregulation in Canada. However, one indication is that the views of my friends and colleagues mirror those of the media. Almost all news about air travel is causally linked to deregulation. Typically, concerns over safety and the quality of service carry more weight than the benefits from reduced fares. A substantial proportion of my friends and colleagues prefer the regulated over the unregulated environment.[2]

Scholarly Assessments

By contrast to my friends casual reactions, scholarly analysis has been positive about the economic effects of deregulation in Canada. Jordan (1987, 1989), Moses and Savage (1989a, 1989b), and Stanbury and Tretheway (1987), relying on the U.S. experience, predicted that deregulation of the Canadian airline industry would have large, beneficial economic effects. Concern remains only about the future effects of industry concentration, as expressed by Gillen et al. (1988). Roman's (1989) study is one of the few which roundly condemns airline deregulation.[3]

The following evaluation of Canadian airline deregulation draws heavily on the analysis and data found in Jordan (1987, 1989) and Gillen et al. (1988). However, it superimposes my interpretations and emphasis on their empirical findings. Part 1 presents a conceptual framework for the analysis that follows. Part 2 concerns the effects of deregulation on airline fares and costs. Part 3 deals with safety and other aspects of the quality of service. Part 4 discusses the recent concentration in the industry and assesses its likely impact on efficiency in the future.

---

accident cannot reasonably be blamed on deregulation.

2　It is tempting to suggest that these views are largely due to the fact that most of my acquaintances use aircraft in business travel so that cost is largely irrelevant. Therefore, they have gained nothing and lost through the crowding, congestion, delays, perceived lack of safety, and lower service quality generally caused by deregulation.

3　In fact, the title of Roman's book is highly misleading. The author concludes that safety has not been reduced and that passenger fares have declined. His criteria for assessing failure rests purely on the increased concentration in the industry and the *prospect* that it will lead to the exercise of oligopolistic market power at the expense of consumers in the future. He makes much of the Shepherd (1984) criticism of the Baumol (1981) model of market contestability, which will be discussed further in a later section.

1. What Criteria for Assessment of Merit?

The merit of airline deregulation in Canada will be assessed by the most basic economic criterion—efficiency.[4] More specifically, the issue is whether deregulation is likely to make the airline industry serve better the interests of consumers through lower costs and services with higher quality and greater variety.

It is important to note that by this criterion, it is not necessary that the industry performs as if it were perfectly competitive. The modern theories of regulation and deregulation developed by Stigler (1971), MacAvoy (1979), Peltzman (1976), and others continue to maintain that market failures exist in certain industries like air transport. These failures exist because the technology and market characteristics contain elements of natural monopoly and economies of scale. Therefore, it is not expected that without regulation such industries will have large numbers of competing firms that operate in conditions where prices equal marginal cost.

The central point of the argument for deregulation is that the regulatory process has also proven to be imperfect. It leads to so-called government failures which create inefficiencies and higher costs, to be discussed below in greater detail. It is illegitimate to compare the real world, necessarily filled with market failures, with an ideal world in which an industry can be regulated perfectly to serve the public interest. Instead, we need to compare airline performance in the presence of government failures with its performance in the presence of market failures.

The standard of comparison used here is the U.S. experience with airline deregulation. If it has resulted in lower prices and other benefits to consumers, then an unregulated airline industry is an improvement on the prior regulated service. Because of the similarity of the U.S. and Canadian economies and airline industries, it is safe to infer from such a finding that deregulation will also benefit Canadian consumers. From this analytical perspective, critics of deregulation are left to fight windmills when they seek to prove that the airline industry will never be perfectly competitive.

---

4 The use of the efficiency criterion is suggested by the literature concerned with the rationale for regulation and deregulation, a fine summary of which is found in Breyer and MacAvoy (1987). The economic criterion has been applied to the U.S. airline deregulation experience by Morrison and Winston (1986). It is interesting to note that Roman, the most vociferous critic of Canadian deregulation, does not refer even once to the widely cited U.S. study by Morrison and Winston (1986). Instead, he only refers to Douglas and Miller's (1974) study which was written well before there was any empirical evidence on the effects of deregulation.

Accounting for Other Changes

Any empirical study of industry performance based on actual price develop-ments is complicated by the many influences, other than the regulatory envi-ronment, that determine prices and the quality of service. There are changes in the cost of fuel and capital. The safety of aircraft travel has increased as a result of exogenous technological improvements. Political processes change labour market conditions which also have repercussions on service quality. In the United States, for example, the air controllers' strike and its aftermath has had an important impact on the ability of airports to handle growing traffic. Furthermore, as will be discussed below, other government agencies, like the suppliers and managers of airports, may fail to accommodate an industry driven by Schumpeterian entrepreneurs rather than one of rent-seeking regulated firms.

Jordan (1987) compares conditions in the United States, which has had deregulation at least officially since 1979, with conditions in Canada prior to deregulation. In Canada deregulation came into effect in 1988. This approach makes it simpler to identify the effects of regulation and to distinguish between performance that responds to variations in conditions other than regulation. For example, we'll examine what the effects are of fuel prices being lower in the United States than in Canada. We follow Jordan's methodology to predict the likely effects of airline deregulation on Canadian consumers.

Credit is due to the Canadian government for grasping the political nettle of airline deregulation. By the criteria of public choice models, such a policy on its surface seems to antagonize strong and well-identified interest groups that will show their displeasure on voting day. The main interest groups are the unionized airline employees, the government bureaucracy which has shrunk and lost power, the elite of business and government employees who like to use uncrowded facilities and enjoy the high quality of services provided by regu-lated competitors, and the recipients of cross-subsidies in smaller towns served by airlines as a regulatory requirement. At the same time, the benefits of deregulation are widely dispersed and tend to be low for many individuals. According to theory, the beneficiaries, though numerous, are unlikely to vote in favour of a deregulating government simply because they appreciate the benefits of airline deregulation.

If public choice models predict that deregulation is a political liability, why has the policy been adopted in Canada? One possibility is that strong individuals with an ideological agenda have been willing to put the general public interest before the narrow political agenda of assuring re-election. Many observers of the U.S. deregulation process have credited Alfred Kahn with providing such a driving force. In Canada it is impossible to identify any individual with a similar drive or power. It is true that the benefits enjoyed by U.S. travellers are known to Canadian consumers. That knowledge, however, is also available to consumers of market-board-protected dairy and agricultural products without any apparent political repercussions. More likely, it is industry management and shareholders themselves that have lobbied effectively for deregulation in response to the serious loss of traffic to dynamic U.S. carriers who bussed Canadians to and from near-by U.S. airports in such border communities as Burlington, Vermont, Buffalo, New York, and Bellingham, Washington.

Deregulation has proceeded in a different manner in Canada than in the United States. In the U.S. the Civil Aeronautics Board has been disbanded, while in Canada the gradual process of deregulation has been accompanied by an increase in employment at the regulatory agency. In the long run, therefore, the re-introduction of regulation is much less likely in the United States than in Canada, because in the U.S. there simply are no bureaucrats searching for ways to reintroduce regulation.

Finally, it is important to sound a note of caution about the comparison of the two countries' experiences. For a variety of reasons the levels of price reductions and efficiency gains enjoyed in the United States may not be paralleled in Canada. Deregulation in Canada does not extend to the North. The concentration of the Canadian population in a narrow east-west band may offer fewer savings. Therefore, the empirical evidence presented below should be considered indicative of the nature of potential gains from deregulation, but they provide only a rough guide to the magnitude of such gains.

Types of Deregulation

It is important to differentiate between economic and safety deregulation. U.S. and Canadian deregulation has concerned only economic matters like the freedom to set prices, the right to add or reduce routes and flights, and the authority to compete through the provision of special types of services. The regulation of safety for passengers has not been relaxed in either country. In the next section I consider the effects of economic deregulation alone. Subsequently, I address the alleged linkage between safety and economic deregulation, both in principle and empirically.

A final methodological point concerns the evolutionary character of deregulation. Bill C-18, passed in 1988, is not likely to be the final bill concerned with the regulatory environment of the Canadian airline industry. Instead, the act should be considered as starting an experiment that will be fine-tuned as conditions demand. Thus, it may be necessary to extend deregulation by permitting foreign airlines to compete domestically, privatizing airports, and controlling airspace.[5] It may also be necessary to eliminate the distortion of market incentives created by frequent flyer reward systems through the taxation of the income it creates for their users. Some analysts have suggested that electronic reservation systems be required to operate as common carriers so that they cannot be used to deny access to new competitors. These and other potential areas for further deregulation will be considered in the concluding section of this paper.

2. Effects on Costs and Fares

According to the theory of regulation, the regulatory process raises the costs of airline tickets through two main channels. First, fares are set by the regulatory agency after hearings in which the airlines argue the case for increases on the basis of their operating and capital costs. Then, the agency almost inevitably sets fares at levels that permit the airlines to recoup their cost and earn a "fair" return on capital. This system does not penalize management or stockholders for inefficient operations, and it reduces their resistance to rent-seeking activities of unions since profits are assured whatever their level of costs.[6]

The most important result of this fare-setting practice under regulation has been that pilots, flight attendants, mechanics, and other employees enjoyed higher wages and more favourable working conditions, which affected the number of employment vacancies and applicants. Under regulation, airlines attracted relatively large numbers of job applicants, but since deregulation in the United States, there has been a substantial reduction in the wages and benefits of airline employees and also of applicants for open positions.

The regulatory system blunted entrepreneurial incentives to innovate and take risks by adopting new marketing and operating systems and new capital

---

5   Indeed, at the time of writing, it is being reported that Canada and the United States are on the verge of signing an agreement to allow each other's carriers freedom to operate between any two points within either country. This agreement would be a giant step towards complete deregulation of the Canadian airline industry (the editors).

6   Under this system there are still incentives to maintain efficiency in the short run since cost savings can be used to compete through non-price methods with other carriers. Resultant increases in market share, employment, and capital serve the interests of managers whose pay is an increasing function of the number of people and size of capital they manage. In the longer run, potential entry should restrain the development of excessive costs. However, in practice, the regulatory process has made entry so difficult that scheduled airlines in the United States and Canada faced no entries. Competition was limited instead to the market for charters, where regulation was less stringent and effective.

equipment. Indirect evidence of this is found in the service, marketing, and routing innovations that have taken place in the U.S. industry since deregulation.

The second source of increased costs of airlines under regulation is the requirement that certain routes are served and fares charged even though the airline endures operating losses. The government considers these routes and fares to be in the public interest and permits airlines to recoup their losses on them through higher fares on other routes. In Canada this regulatory program of "cross-subsidized" routes and fares was motivated by the desire to use the industry to tie the country together and thus strengthen national culture and unity.

The U.S. and some recent Canadian experiences show just how great were the inefficiencies associated with cross-subsidization of uneconomic routes. To meet the regulatory requirements of serving small communities, the airlines used equipment optimally designed for long hauls on trunk routes. The use of such equipment on short haul flights resulted in low average capacity utilization and high costs per seat mile. Moreover, consumers were inconvenienced by flight schedules that were geared to assure equipment use on trunk routes during peak demand. Most importantly, the system delayed the development of the hub-and-spoke method for serving large numbers of communities at lower cost and with greater frequency and more convenient departure times.[7]

---

7   The basic problem of serving different communities arises from the fact that the costs of flights between each pair rises very rapidly with the number of communities. Three communities A, B, and C, give rise to three connections, that is, A-B, A-C, B-C. However, in the case of four communities, six flight routes are needed to connect each pair (A-B, A-C, A-D, B-C, B-D, and C-D). Under the hub-and-spoke system, if A is made the hub, all communities can be served by a connection with it. In the case of three communities, persons wishing to fly from B to C take a plane from B to A and from there to C. As a result, only two, rather than three, routes need regular flights and planes to serve the three communities. In the case of four communities, the use of A as a hub reduces the need for interconnections from six to only three. The savings are a rapidly rising function of the number of communities served in this manner. Further savings arise from the fact that the hub is typically a large city from which long distance flights reach other large cities and hubs. This means that customers from the outlying communities all be brought to the hub on flights which minimize delays in transfers to the long distance flights. In practice, the hub-and-spoke system serves the relevant communities well because planes of optimum size can be used. Importantly, the lower cost of the system has made it possible to provide services to communities which even under the regulatory regime did not have scheduled flights. At least in principle it is possible that in the future smaller communities develop into subsidiary hubs and serve surrounding, even smaller communities with specialized planes and convenient schedules. Only the

Development of Passenger Yields

According to the preceding analysis of the cost-raising effects of regulation, deregulation should be accompanied by increased efficiency and reductions in the costs of airlines which in turn should be reflected in reduced passenger fares. To test this hypothesis, it is not possible simply to record changes in published fares. Special discounts, seat sales, and other marketing methods reduce the cost of flying for many passengers so that actual transaction prices must be analyzed. A simpler approach is to study average passenger yields. Such data are calculated by dividing an airline's total revenue from passenger fares by the number of revenue passenger miles flown, where the latter is the product of the number of passengers served times the distances they travelled.

Jordan (1987) has prepared average passenger yields for scheduled Canadian and U.S. airlines for the years 1978 to 1985, both in current and constant price dollars.[8] The passenger yields in constant prices are shown in figure 1, where levels in 1987 are equal to 100. The figure reveals that passenger yields fell 6 percent in both countries between 1978 and 1979, largely as a result of rapidly rising consumer prices and a lag in the adjustment of fares. In 1979 a second OPEC-induced increase in the world price of oil further pushed up the cost of fuel. As a result, during the following two years, yields rose by 13 percent in the United States and 10 percent in Canada. After 1981, fuel prices stabilized and then dropped. This influence, together with the effects of deregulation, resulted in a steep reduction in yields in the United States which reached 20 percent in 1985. Most important for our purposes of analysis is that during the same period, Canadian yields fell by only about 8 percent.

---

future will tell the full limit of such systems and the minimum size of a community warranting scheduled airline service. It should be noted that the deregulation of the airline industry in Canada under Bill C-18 covers only the southern part of the country. Regulators obviously have decided that the competitive system cannot be expected to serve the relatively small northern communities. In the regulated environment and cross-subsidized flight services, market services have only very little opportunity to develop hub-and-spoke systems for the North.

8   He also has estimates for national and regional carriers and, in the case of the United States, for the old airlines and the new ones that were established after deregulation came into effect. Developments in these subcategories of costs shed some interesting additional light on the effects of deregulation, but they are too detailed to present here. In general, they strengthen the results noted in the text.

Figure 1
System Scheduled Passenger Yields
Constant Dollar Values, 1978=100

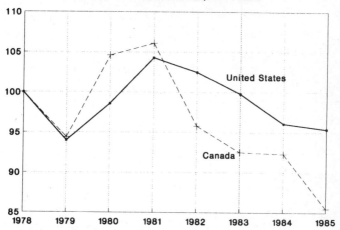

Source: Computed from Jordan (1987), table 2.

Differences in Fuel Costs

From 1982 to 1985, fuel prices in the United States were lower than in Canada, largely as result of Canada's National Energy Policy.[9] To isolate the influence of the different fuel prices on yields in the two countries, Jordan assembled data on total operating[10] and fuel costs of the airlines. I used these data to estimate

---

9 Jordan (1987) also analyzed the effect of divergences in the business cycle peaks and troughs in the two countries. He concluded that these have only negligibly influenced costs and demand. Operating costs of airlines are also a function of the average distance travelled by passengers on each flight. Using data for both Canadian and U.S. carriers, Jordan found a consistent functional relationship between these two variables. By his measure of distance-adjusted costs and revenues, all Canadian airlines perform more poorly than their U.S. counterparts. Differences in the mix of regional and long distance traffic cannot explain the observed differences in the revenue yields and operating costs of airlines in the two countries.

10 Capital costs were excluded since they differ widely between companies in both countries depending on financing and often very complicated leasing arrangements. The capital cost of Air Canada is influenced by its status as a Crown corporation. At the same time, however, real capital costs in the two countries are very similar since the equipment used and interest rates are nearly identical in both.

the development of non-fuel operating costs in constant dollars. These costs were then divided by revenue passenger miles to adjust for the changes in the level of operation. Figure 2 presents the index of real non-fuel operating costs per revenue passenger mile in the two countries, with 1978 set equal to 100.[11]

Figure 2
Operating Costs/Revenue Pass. Mile
Non-Fuel, Real Dollars, 1978=100

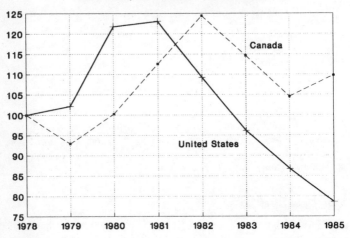

Source: Computed from Jordan (1987), tables 3 and 4. For precise method, see footnote in text.

11 Jordan (1987) provides in table 3 a time series on airline fuel prices in the two countries. In table 4 he presents a time series on fuel and other operating costs. However, the U.S. series on fuel costs in this table does not contain data for 1984 and 1985 because of changes in statistical coverage. To obtain a series for non-fuel costs for the entire period, I combined the index on total operating costs in table 4 with the index in fuel costs from table 3, using a weight of 0.75 and 0.25, respectively. Since this proportion has varied between 20 and 30 percent during the period under observation, my estimates are not exact. However, I believe that the resultant error is minimal and that the data in figure 2 are sufficiently reliable to support the main arguments made in the text.

Since airline activities in the two countries rose at different rates during the period under observation, the indices of non-fuel operating costs had to be adjusted to reflect these changes. My calculations used the index of revenue passenger miles provided by Jordan to produce the data in figure 2. The use of the index of revenue passenger miles may introduce a bias in the result to the extent that airlines in the two countries have changed the mix of passenger and freight services. This bias is likely to be small.

The data strongly support predictions based on the model of deregulation. Non-fuel operating costs per unit of output in the United States in 1985 had dropped 43 percentage points from their peak in 1981 and were 21 percent below the level at the start of deregulation. Canadian costs had risen by 24 percent above their 1978 base in the recession year 1982. They then fell quite steeply as the economy and airline travel recovered. Importantly, by 1985, the Canadian index was 10 percent above its 1978 level. The different developments of non-fuel operating costs predicted by the theory of regulation in 1985 had made Canadian costs 31 percent higher than U.S. costs relative to their 1978 base.[12]

The process that had resulted in the reduction of U.S. costs has been discussed widely in the media. In the deregulated environment new airlines started operations, utilizing non-unionized pilots and other non-unionized personnel. They had lower costs and cut fares without the sacrifice of profits. The lower fares attracted increasing shares of the market. The old airlines, saddled with high labour costs, began to lose money. Some obtained concessions from unions on wages and work practices. Some went bankrupt. Some were bought and their new owners used legal methods to reduce the economic power of the unions. In 1989 unions in some U.S. airlines were holding on to many benefits obtained during the era of regulation. Indications are that these airlines are headed for bankruptcy or merger.[13]

In Canada the maintenance of the regulations eliminated pressures on unions and prevented the drop in non-fuel operating costs, just as the theory implies.[14]

---

12 Airline operating costs per passenger mile are also affected by the average distances travelled. In a regression analysis Jordan estimated a distance-related cost-function from data of about 30 U.S. and Canadian airlines for the year 1985. All of the Canadian airlines have higher costs than U.S. airlines on the basis of this distance-related index. For this reason I consider the data in the text to be a reliable indicator of differences in non-fuel operating costs attributable to deregulation.

13 The creation of new airlines with lower operating costs was profitable only as long as the old airlines had high costs and high fares. After reductions in costs and fares, the creation of new airlines ceased. Many of the new airlines were unable to compete with the reorganized old airlines, most of which had the benefit of economies of scale, long operating experience, and customer loyalty. For this reason, I see no merit in the contention that airline deregulation has failed because the creation of new airlines has nearly stopped and many of them have gone bankrupt or merged.

14 The availability of low-cost flights in the United States resulted in a diversion of some Canadian passengers flying across the continent. This competitive pressure may have resulted in some changes in the behaviour of Canadian airline managers and workers, but it is difficult to quantify this effect. Its operation may well be

Reactions of Consumers

Reductions in the cost of flying on scheduled airlines between 1978 and 1985 resulted in increased demand as measured by the index of revenue passenger miles shown in figure 3. In the United States the initial effects of deregulation on prices and demand were swamped by increases in fuel prices and fares in 1979 and the recession in 1980-81. As a result, passenger traffic stagnated until 1981. Thereafter, the use of airlines rose at unprecedented rates. Total revenue passenger miles increased by one-third in just four years. The 1985 *increase* of 31 billion passenger miles was greater than the *total* of Canadian revenue passenger miles of 22.3 billion that year.

In Canada the increase in revenue passenger miles between 1978 and 1985 was only 22 percent and the level in the last year was still slightly below the peak reached during the 1979-80 economic boom. Of course, the lag in Canadian relative to U.S. travel growth and consumer benefits are due to the fact that fares dropped only about 4 percent here rather than 14 percent in the U.S.

Figure 3
Index of Revenue Passenger-Miles
1978=100

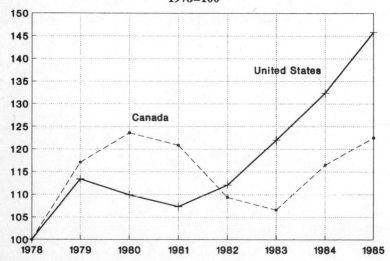

Source: Computed from Jordan (1987), figure 1.

responsible for the constancy of the costs between 1981 and 1985.

Summary and Conclusion

The comparative performance of the Canadian and U.S. airlines between 1979 and 1988 provides an all too rare opportunity to study the effects of changes in an important economic policy. Almost as in a laboratory experiment, one country's industry has continued to operate in the regulated environment while the other faced entirely different government policies. Influences on airline operations and costs in both countries were otherwise very similar or, as in the case of fuel costs, were considered in our calculations.

The data strongly support the theoretical analysis of the effects of deregulation. Increased competition in the United States led to dramatic reductions in both costs and fares relative to those in Canada. As a result, airline travel rose far more rapidly in the United States than in Canada. So dramatic are the results that other differences between the two countries' airline industries cannot account for them. Generally, airline deregulation provides major benefits to consumers.

3. Effects on Safety and Service Quality

Airline deregulation is alleged to reduce the safety of passengers because it raises the probability that airlines lose money to the point where they face bankruptcy. Faced with financial difficulties, airlines are presumed to engage in efforts to restore profitability through a host of measures, including reductions in the quantity and quality of the maintenance of equipment.

This model of the effects of free markets on consumer safety is basically correct. It provided one rationale for regulation in the first place. However, for the debate over the effects of deregulation on safety, the central issue has to be not whether such adjustments affecting safety take place, but how important they are in their effects on accidents. There are two basic influences that suggest airlines in financial trouble tend to skimp only very little on maintenance. First, deregulation covers only commercial aspects of business. In the United States and Canada, regulations concerning the maintenance of equipment remain in effect. Failure to comply with such regulations carries the risk of fines and adverse publicity. Second, safety is one of the most important characteristics of airlines that consumers consider in their purchasing decisions. Airline managers know that accidents and accompanying publicity about problems with equipment maintenance reduce sales and profitability. The publicity accompanying critical reports of inadequate maintenance by the government and the identification of equipment failure as a cause of air crashes immediately reduces sales and thus hastens the bankruptcy of a company already in financial trouble. It is difficult and costly to restore public confidence in an airline's reputation for safety once it has been damaged by such events.

Elaborate theoretical models reviewed by Moses and Savage (1989a, 1989b) incorporate these two arguments and others to consider the effects of deregulation on aviation safety. These models do not lead to a precise conclusion because the results are sensitive to the specification of the model's behavioural parameters. In the end, the issue can be settled only empirically. Rose (1989) related the financial condition of airlines to their accident experience over 30 years. The econometric results are quite poor and suggest that there exists at best a minor influence in the theoretically postulated relationship and then only for smaller carriers.[15]

Figure 4 sheds light on the relationship between deregulation and aviation safety by considering the number of fatal passenger fatalities experienced by scheduled operations of airlines using jet aircraft. The raw numbers on absolute fatalities and adjustments for revenue passenger miles are from Jordan (1989). The data on fatalities are difficult to interpret because fatal accidents in Canada are a rare occurrence, and in the United States the annual rates fluctuate widely because of the rare and occasional large accident. For this reason, I smoothed the annual data on fatalities per billion revenue passenger miles by constructing a time series of three-year moving averages. Each year shown in the graph gives the average for the current and preceding two years.

Figure 4 suggests two comparisons. First, it is instructive to look at the difference in the U.S. fatality rates before and after deregulation in 1978. The graph shows clearly that the fatality rates have been on a distinct downward trend. Though the trend has been interrupted by some large accidents in the middle 1970s, it has continued downward after deregulation. The declining accident trend has been attributed to technological improvements in aircraft. There is no break evident in the years following 1978.[16] For the years 1969 to

---

15   Golbe (1986) found an insignificant but positive relationship between accident experience and the profitability of airlines during the period of regulation, exactly the opposite of the theoretical models' predictions.

16   It is methodologically inappropriate to explain only the nature of causes of interruptions in the trend. Yet it is of some interest to note, as Jordan did, that the 1979 increase was due to the blowing up of an engine on an aircraft in flight. This failure was declared by the Federal Aviation Administration to have been due to changes in maintenance procedures which the airline undertook in 1978 with government approval and before commercial deregulation. The second disruption in the downward trend in 1987 disappears if one excludes from the calculation 38 (out of a total of 47) fatalities which were attributable to a murder/suicide. It may also be noted that between 1969 and 1987, the U.S. airlines experienced only three calendar years during which fatality rates were zero. All of them, 1980, 1984, and 1986, were years of commercial deregulation.

Figure 4
Fatality Rates, Airlines Using Jet Aircraft
Scheduled Operations, Three-Year Moving Average

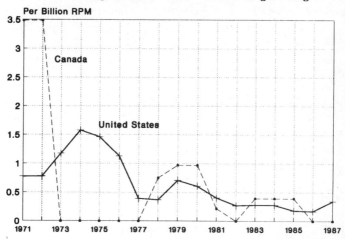

Source: Computed from Jordan (1989), using three-year moving averages.

1978, the fatality rate averaged 0.86, while from 1979 to 1987, it averaged just 0.34.

The second comparison is between the experience of the regulated Canadian and deregulated U.S. airlines after 1978. The graph shows that there is no systematic difference in the safety experience of the two airline systems. One is unable, therefore, to conclude that commercial deregulation results in reduced aviation safety. In sum, the empirical evidence suggests that whatever incentives airlines may have to skimp on the maintenance of equipment during periods of financial distress, they have not been strong enough to affect the historic trend towards greater safety induced by technological improvements. This conclusion has been reached after the consideration of other measures of safety by Jordan (1989), Moses and Savage (1989), as well as Roman (1989), even though Roman is otherwise critical of deregulation.

As an interesting aside it might be noted that airline deregulation is likely to have resulted in reduced road traffic accidents, deaths, and injuries because the lower cost of airline tickets has induced people to switch from car to air travel. McKenzie and Warner (1987) estimated a regression equation where passenger car miles driven in the United States is the dependent variable and income, cost of fuel, speed limits, and other factors are explanatory variables. The coefficients estimated from observations before airline deregulation in 1979 applied to later years overpredicts the actual miles driven by 3.9 percent annually. The authors are convinced that this lowering in the growth of automotive travel is due to the increased use of air travel. They estimate that the reduced use of cars implies a drop in over 600,000 accidents, 1,700 deaths, and economic losses due to accidents of $1.9 billion per year during the 1979-85 period. It is likely that such indirect benefits from airline deregulation exist or will develop in Canada.[17]

Quality of Service

Deregulation has been identified as the cause of a number of inconveniences that have confronted airline users during the 1980s in the Unites States. The most notable of these have been the incidence of lost or misdirected luggage, the overselling of seats, delays in departure and arrival, deterioration in the quality of food and other cabin services, crowding of airport facilities, and difficulties in finding and purchasing low-priced tickets. It is convenient analytically to group these complaints into two categories.

First, there are those that were due to the rapid increase in airline traffic that took place at the same time that ground equipment and reservation systems expanded more slowly due to the normal lags in the production and installation of such equipment. In addition, there were learning problems with the new computer reservation technology by travel agents as well as the old and new airlines. During the late 1980s, most of the complaints in this category have been eliminated or reduced to tolerable levels through experience and the adaptation of new technology, particularly computers and remote access terminals. This is true for the problems of lost luggage, the overselling of seats, the quality of cabin services, and confusion concerning the cost of tickets.

In this category of complaints are also developments that are due to the use of innovative marketing strategies by the airlines, like differences in the quality of food service, the crowding of planes, and the profusion of different fares and classes of service. In my view, these methods of product differentiation and competition used by the airlines are in the interest of most consumers, especially private travellers and price sensitive tourists.

In the longer run, competition will assure the existence of a wide range of choices between quality of services and prices that meet the interests of regular business travellers as well as tourists. Such a state of affairs is likely to have

---

17 Attempts to replicate the McKenzie-Warner study for Canada failed because the government of Canada does not publish a consistent time series on passenger automobile miles driven. Fuel consumption data include use by trucks and buses. Because of the deregulation of the trucking and bus industries in recent years, it is essential that calculations reflect these developments.

some detractors who will argue like J.K. Galbraith that product differentiation results in a wanton waste of resources with small benefits to consumers and often the cost of making choices from many alternatives. Most economists have not taken seriously Galbraith's criticism of imperfectly competitive markets and are unlikely to accept it in this case. It is also conceivable that the quality of service never will return to the levels it had attained under regulation. Such a development may raise efficiency since quite possibly under regulation quality had been too high, relative to the value of alternative uses of those resources committed to the additional service quality.[18]

Complaints about service quality in the second category are those that are caused by the failure of government agencies to respond to growth and change in the airline industry. The most important of these complaints stem from the overcrowding of airport facilities serving passengers and airlines and from the inability of the flight control system to handle increasing traffic. Most analysts consider the solution to these problems to lie in the short run, in the more efficient use of airport facilities. This could be achieved most readily by the appropriate use of prices to avoid congestion of gates, runways, and traffic lanes (Walker and Hoye, 1989). In fact, some U.S. airports have begun to charge different fees for the use of gates and runways at different time of the day. Pressures are rising to charge landing fees for smaller private aircraft which will encourage them to use alternative airports and free runways at major airports for large commercial airliners.

In the longer run, the modernization and expansion of aviation facilities should be undertaken by the private sector. The rationale for privatization is well known (Walker, 1988). There are no convincing reasons why the ownership of airports need be in the hands of governments. Control of such functions as air traffic may remain with government agencies even while operations of the system and ownership of equipment are in the private sector. In cases where facilities cannot be made profitable through user charges but there are believed to be important elements of public service in their provision, government subsidies can be paid to bidders willing and able to contract for their delivery.

In sum, arguments against deregulation based on the deterioration of service quality lack merit. Services provided by U.S. airlines declined initially following deregulation due mainly to rapid growth of demand, lags in the installation of new facilities, and lags in learning to operate in a deregulated environment. Most problems in this category have been or are being solved. However, the ultimate mix of services and prices available will always have critics who

---

18 I owe this point to Bill Stanbury.

dislike the manifestations of imperfect competition and of increased congestion.

The deterioration of service quality associated with the congestion of U.S. and Canadian airports and airways has largely been due to the inefficiency of government agencies that own and operate these facilities. In the short run, these shortcomings can be remedied by the use of price mechanisms for the more rational use of existing resources. In the longer run, the ownership or at least the operation of airports and airways should be turned over to the private sector. Experience with the privatization of other government services suggests that the benefits outweigh the costs of privatization by a large margin.

4. The Threat of Oligopolies

In the United States deregulation was initially accompanied by a large increase in new airlines competing with those that operated previously in the regulated environment. Jordan (1987) shows that between 1978 and 1985 the number of U.S. airline companies using jet aircraft jumped from 27 to 62.[19] Rose and Dahl (1989) note that about 200 new airlines were started during the first nine years of the deregulated environment. However, through mergers and bankruptcies, in 1989 eight giant airlines controlled 92 percent of the market.

In Canada, even before deregulation took place, there was a merger between the second and third largest airlines in the country, Pacific Western Airlines and Canadian Pacific, forming Canadian Airlines International. In 1989 the number of domestic competitors was reduced further by the merger of Wardair with Canadian Airlines International, leaving Canada served by only two large trunk carriers. In addition, Air Canada and Canadian Airlines International have both merged with a large number of regional carriers, which have continued to operate under their original corporate names.

The reduction in the number of airlines through these mergers in Canada and the United States have raised expectations that market power will permit the remaining giants to keep out competition, raise prices for consumers, lower the quality of service, and earn excess profits. Some indications of this process taking place have already appeared. Rose and Dahl claim, for instance, that in the first half of 1989 fares in some U.S. markets have jumped 59 percent. The authors also show data compiled by Airline Economics Inc. according to which

---

19 It is worth noting that during this period the number of U.S. national and trunk
    carriers fell from 11 to 9, and regional and local service carriers (Alaska and Hawaii)
    fell from 12 to 8. All growth has come from intrastate, supplemental, and so-called
    Other New Form 41 carriers.

major U.S. airlines' average fares per passenger mile have risen from 11 cents in 1986 to 14.5 cents in April 1989.

Theoretical Considerations

Economists' views on the need for government control over industrial concentration have changed in recent years. During the immediate postwar years, anti-combines activity by governments was considered essential for the maintenance of competition and the protection of consumers. However, since the 1970s, increasing numbers of economists have expressed the view that competition prevents the development of excessive market power and the exploitation of consumers. This conclusion is based on the proposition that all goods and services have substitutes and no industry is immune from competition. Furthermore, it is believed that increased foreign competition limits market power except where it is maintained by government protection. The lowering of transportation and communication costs contributed much to the reduction of market power enjoyed by local or national oligopolies. It was also argued that even in industries where a small number of competitors has remained unchanged for a long period, power in the industry was constrained by the contestability of markets, that is, the threat of entry by potential rivals.

At the same time that there was a reassessment of the magnitude and effectiveness of market power of oligopolies, questions were raised about the cost of compliance to anti-combines legislation and the hindrances it represented to firms that needed to be very large in domestic markets in order to compete in global markets. Questions were raised especially about the usefulness of concentration ratios as measures of market power in the absence of unique definitions of the market in which the concentration is measured. Product differentiation, low transportation costs, and international competition have increasingly complicated the task of operationally defining the market over which companies are alleged to have control.

During the Reagan administration, anti-trust legislation and enforcement began to reflect these new views on the natural limits to the power of oligopolies and the costs of government anti-trust policies. It is in this atmosphere that the airline mergers of the late 1980s took place without opposition from the U.S. government. In Canada developments paralleled those in the United States, and while the mergers were scrutinized by the Department of Consumer and Corporate Affairs, they were all approved.

Empirical Work

As in the case of arguments over safety, conceptual discussions cannot resolve the issues concerning the potential for exploitation of consumers by airline oligopolies. Empirical work is needed. Useful work has been done by Jordan

(1988) who provides a historical perspective on recent mergers. He shows that they have been preceded by similar moves before deregulation both in Canada and the United States. He also shows that newly merged firms historically experienced higher operating costs than their competitors until they dropped some routes and increased capacity utilization on others.

Caves, Christensen, and Tretheway (1984) found that there are constant returns to scale over a wide range with respect to the size of airlines' networks. On the other hand, they found that significant savings per seat mile exists over a wide range with respect to increasing density of traffic on existing routes. Gillen, Oum, and Tretheway (1986a, 1986b) applied these ideas to the study of conditions in Canada. They concluded that existing travel levels in Canada during the 1980s permitted the efficient operation of only two trunk airlines. These findings imply that breaking up the duopoly would result in higher costs and consumer prices. The unsolved empirical issues are whether the anti-competitive activities of the duopoly under restraint of potential entry, competitive transportation modes, and the use of U.S. carriers and routes result in higher costs to consumers than does an industry consisting of a number of smaller firms operating at less than optimum scales.

Policy Recommendations in the Literature

Increasing concentration in the U.S. and Canadian airline industries have elicited three types of recommendations. First, there are those who recommend that anti-combines policy be applied. In particular, Roman (1989) takes this position and bases his recommendation on a very critical assessment of the new view of industrial organization and contestability by Shepherd (1984). Rose and Dahl (1989) mention that in the United States the reintroduction of regulated fares has been advanced as a policy alternative by some analysts.

Second, there are those who recommend that specific anti-competitive devices of the airlines be monitored and prohibited if necessary. Gillen et al. (1988) single out for such attention the computer reservation system and the frequent flyer programs which they consider to be powerful instruments in efforts to keep out competition. The computer system owned by the major airlines is alleged to charge excessively high prices to smaller companies for inclusion in the listings. In addition, the owners of the system can use discriminatory listing schemes on the displays at travel agents' terminals. The suggested remedy is legislation to make the computer reservation system a public carrier that is forced to sell its services to all customers at non-discriminatory rates reflecting costs.

Frequent flyer programs have the effect of reducing the price elasticity of demand with respect to published prices for services by new carriers since business travellers are keen to accumulate points for private use. New airlines cannot offer corresponding incentives, and in order to gain business, have to undercut not just published prices but those reduced by the implicit value of the bonus travel provided by the established competition. The recommendation here is that these programs be prohibited or at least that the benefits be taxed as personal income of their users.

Gillen et al. (1986a) also recommend that airlines be explicitly covered by the Competition Act so that legal action can be taken in the case of price collusion, market sharing arrangements, and other anti-competitive behaviour prohibited under the act. They also recommend adjustment of Canadian anti-combines legislation to make predatory behaviour illegal, not just with respect to price but also capacity.

The third group of recommendations is most in the spirit of the new view on the need for anti-trust policies. It involves an application of pro-competition rather than anti-combines policies. Of these, the most important is that existing cabotage laws be revoked and foreign competitors be allowed to carry passengers between domestic points of origin. This recommendation has been made by Kahn (1989), Weidenbaum and Penoyer (1983), and Gillen et al. (1986a). Rose and Dahl (1989) note that the proposal is discussed widely in Washington.[20]

In the same spirit are recommendations that Air Canada be privatized so that potential competitors face a level playing field with respect to the cost of capital, which tends to be lower for firms owned by governments (Gillen et al., 1986b).

The existing limitation on foreign ownership in Canada is 25 percent. It should be eliminated.[21] There are no economic benefits to the existence of national flag carriers. To many, the emotional, nationalistic benefits they bring are not worth very much in the modern world. At any rate, in a world without laws regulating cabotage and foreign ownership, it is more likely that at least one Canadian-owned and -based airline would survive to compete successfully on national and international routes. This airline would most likely be the size

---

20 Cabotage laws can be abandoned unilaterally or their elimination made conditional upon reciprocity by other governments. The former process has many advantages, especially simplicity. It may be expected to be costly and time consuming to obtain reciprocity in negotiations from other countries. Moreover, most have few benefits to offer for Canadian and U.S. carriers. Difficulties in obtaining reciprocal concessions may be used to limit foreign competition.

21 Bill Stanbury believes that in the absence of the foreign ownership requirements, Wardair would have been taken over by a foreign airline and that the Canadian consumers would continue to be served by three rather than just two major airlines.

of the average of the eight large U.S. carriers. It would have about 10 percent of the continent's business, matching Canada's relative size.

The privatization of airports and air control functions may also be expected to increase competition. Ready and low-priced access to gates and landing rights at new airports will encourage new entrants on trunk routes as well as for regional service. Ground transportation and shuttle air services between new and old airports would permit integration into the existing network.

Summary and Evaluation

After ten years, U.S. airline deregulation mergers have resulted in U.S. domination of the market for airline travel by eight large carriers. In Canada one year into the era of deregulation, mergers have produced two large carriers. Critics have suggested that the concentration in these markets will eliminate the consumer and efficiency gains from deregulation discussed above.

Not enough empirical data exist to evaluate the merit of these arguments. Airline fares in the United States have risen, but such increases are hardly conclusive evidence of the companies' market power. Even under regulation, fares fluctuated cyclically and it remains to be seen whether this pattern will continue. Profits of airlines have risen, but it is difficult to know what rates of return are consistent with the absence of economic rents. Certainly, the power of unions is much more limited and management incentives to operate efficiently are much stronger under oligopolistic market conditions than they had been under the regulatory regime of guaranteed profits.

Proposals to limit the power of the airline oligopoly by the application of traditional tools of anti-combines policy are not promising. The costs and even conceptual difficulties of enforcement have not changed since their existence was acknowledged as an argument against anti-combines activism. I think that significant legal hurdles exist in attempts to reduce potentially anti-competitive business policies like frequent flyer programs and computer reservation systems. Like regulation generally, such prohibitions are costly to administer and there is always the risk that the bodies regulating them will be captured.

In the final analysis, however, my perception of the need for anti-combines policy is dominated by considerations that some may think are ideological. I believe that abuses of oligopolistic market power will attract entrepreneurs who will exploit them to their own benefit and who in the process protect the consumer. We cannot foresee the ways in which these entrepreneurs will carry out this task. As Hayek has pointed out, by their very nature the activity of these agents involves the discovery of new knowledge that we cannot have in advance.

The further extension of competition through abandoning cabotage laws, removing restrictions to foreign ownership, and privatizing airport and airspace control systems as well as Air Canada represents the best method for protecting consumers from exploitation by carriers with oligopolistic market power. The burden of proof that this approach will not work is on those who suggest alternatives.

6. Summary and Conclusions

The U.S. experience with airline deregulation provides useful information about the likely effects of the Canadian policy changes that were put into place with Bill C-18 at the beginning of 1988. The experience shows that airline deregulation is likely to result in substantial benefits for Canadian consumers through lower prices and more efficient and rational services to customers located away from the major cities.

Airline safety will not be affected by deregulation. The lower airfares are likely to induce a reduction in automotive travel through the greater use of airplanes. This process will reduce overall traffic fatalities and the economic costs of travel accidents in Canada.

The quality of services affecting travellers most likely will remain unchanged. Canadian airlines will be able to benefit from the development of technologies and the experiences of U.S. airlines after the initial rapid expansion of travel after deregulation. They will thus avoid the hassles over lost luggage, bookings, and pricing that had beset U.S. airlines in the early 1980s. It may also be expected that the application of pricing will rationalize airline operations under government jurisdiction, which may reduce airport congestion and delays. In the longer run, such problems will be solved by privatizing these government functions and, possibly, facilities.

The development of oligopolistic market conditions in the United States and Canada may threaten the benefits that deregulation has brought to consumers. The concentration may simply reflect the existence of scale economies which favour the operation of small numbers of airlines. It remains an open question whether it will permit the companies to exercise market power to the detriment of consumers. Arguments have been made that the government needs to curb oligopoly power by strengthening anti-combines legislation and by a series of ad hoc legislation affecting computer reservation systems and frequent flyer points. At this point, the most promising policies seem to be those that would further increase competition through the admission of foreign airlines into the domestic market and limitations on foreign ownership.

In conclusion, it bears repeating that even if market power in the deregulated airline industry results in some inefficiencies and inequities, this constitutes an argument for regulation only if such regulation would improve these conditions. The experience with regulation in the past implies that this is a most unlikely outcome.

References

Baumol, William J. (1981), "Contestable Markets: An Uprising in the Theory of Industry Structure," *American Economic Review* 74, 1, pp. 1-12.

Breyer, Stephen and Paul W. MacAvoy (1987), "Regulation and Deregulation," *The New Palgrave* (New York: The Stockton Press).

Caves, D.W., L.R. Christensen, and M.W. Tretheway (1984), "Economies of Density versus Economies of Scale: Why Trunk and Local Service Airlines Differ," *Rand Journal of Economics* (Winter) 15, 4, pp. 471-89.

Gillen, D.W., W.T. Stanbury, and M.W. Tretheway (1988), "Duopoly in Canada's Airline Industry: Consequences and Policy Issues," *Canadian Public Policy* (March) XIV, 1, pp. 15-31.

Gillen, David W., Tae H. Oum, and Michael W. Tretheway (1986a), *Airline Costs and Performance: Implications for Public and Industry Policies* (Vancouver: Centre for Transportation Studies, University of British Columbia).

————— (1986b), "Entry Barriers and Anti-Competitive Behaviour in a Deregulated Canadian Airline Market," *Proceedings of Canadian Transportation Research Forum 21st Annual Meeting* (Saskatoon: University of Saskatchewan Press) pp. 483-93.

Golbe, D.D. (1986), "Safety and Profits in the Airline Industry," *Journal of Industrial Economics* 34, 3, pp. 305-18.

Jordan, William A. (1987), *Comparative Analysis of Airline Performance in Canada and the United States*, Report for Transport Canada, Submitted to the Standing Committee on Transport, House of Commons, March 13, 1987, mimeo.

————— (1988), "Problems Stemming from Airline Mergers and Acquisitions," *Transportation Journal* (Summer) pp. 9-30.

————— (1989), "Airline Safety: Has Deregulation Made a Difference?," *Transport Review* (forthcoming).

Kahn, Alfred E. (1989), "Surprises, But Few Regrets: A Conversation with Alfred E. Kahn," *Reason* (February) pp. 35-39.

MacAvoy, Paul (1979), *The Regulated Industries and the Economy* (New York and London: W.W. Norton).

McKenzie, Richard B. and John T. Warner (1987), "The Impact of Airline Deregulation on Highway Safety," (St. Louis: Centre for the Study of

American Business, Washington University) Discussion paper OP68, December.

Morrison, S. and C. Winston (1986), *The Economic Effects of Airline Deregulation* (Washington, D.C.: The Brookings Institution).

Moses, Leon N. and Ian Savage, eds. (1989a), *Transportation Safety in the Age of Deregulation* (New York: Oxford University Press).

———(1989b), "Aviation Deregulation and Safety: Theory and Evidence," Discussion paper issued by the Faculty of Commerce and Business Administration, University of British Columbia (no number).

Peltzman, Sam (1976), "Toward a General Theory of Regulation," *Journal of Law and Economics* 19, 2 (August), pp. 211-48.

Roman, Andrew J. (1989), *Airline Deregulation in Canada: Why it Failed* (Ottawa: The Public Interest Research Centre).

Rose, N.L. (1989), "Financial Influences on Airline Safety," in Moses and Savage (eds.) *Transportation Safety in the Age of Deregulation* (New York: Oxford University Press).

Rose, Robert L. and Jonathan Dahl (1989), "Aborted Takeoffs: Skies Are Deregulated, But Just Try Starting a Sizable New Airline," *Wall Street Journal*, Wednesday, July 19, p. 1.

Shepherd, William G. (1984), "Contestability vs. Competition," *American Economic Review* 77, 4.

Stanbury, William T. and Michael W. Tretheway (1987), *Analysis of the Changes in Airline Regulation Proposed under Bill C-18*, submission of the House of Commons Standing Committee on Transport (March), mimeo.

Stigler, George (1971), "The Theory of Economic Regulation," *Bell Journal of Economics* 2, 1 (Spring), pp. 3-21.

Walker, Michael, ed. (1988), *Privatization: Tactics and Techniques* (Vancouver: The Fraser Institute).

Walker, Michael and Lorna Hoye (1989), "Making Canada's Airports Safe," *Globe and Mail*, June 7, A7.

Weidenbaum, Murray L. and Ronald Penoyer (1983), *The Next Step in Regulatory Reform: Updating the Statutes* (St. Louis: Centre for the Study of American Business, Washington University).

Discussion of the Grubel Paper

Walter Block

Herb Grubel's paper is a very important one. On a public policy level, it is important that the arguments of the reregulationists be opposed. The *Wall Street Journal* reports on Thursday, September 21, 1989, that even Republicans are joining the chorus of critics seeking partial reregulation of the airlines in order to "spur competition." This just underscores all the more the value of Grubel's paper. Reregulation is a very practical issue. It affects all of our lives and Grubel makes a signal contribution to the case for deregulation.

I have no criticisms to make of this paper as long as it sticks to the airline deregulation issue. I diverge from it sharply, however, when the author addresses peripheral matters. Before discussing them, let me note several points of appreciation. Grubel shows that due to the increase in air travel use, there has been a cut in automobile usage; since this mode of transportation is associated with many more deaths per passenger mile, airline deregulation has saved many more lives than it is popularly given credit for. Grubel unfortunately calls this an aside. To me this is an absolutely crucial implication of the interconnectedness of economic analysis. We cannot limit our vision to just one industry.

I would also draw our attention to Grubel's point about airline congestion. He quite properly shows that this invites further deregulation, not reregulation. There are all sorts of horror stories, and anecdotal evidence, about people being able to park their airplane on the tarmac more cheaply than they can park their car at the airport parking lot. Surely a market system of peak load pricing, based on actual scarcities, would go a long way toward alleviating airline congestion. We hardly need more central planning; instead, we need a good healthy dose of *perestroika*.

Now to the criticisms. These concern the non-regulation aspects of the paper. Specifically, consider Grubel's views with regard to market failure. Whenever I hear that term, I bristle. "There ain't no such thing," I want to cry out, and I think a strong case can be made for just that position. I appreciate that this terminology has been in some ways a public relations success. Perhaps it is wise to employ it from a strategic point of view. It gives the user an even-handed aura; it might thereby convince some people of the market's merits. But it also has strategic drawbacks. If public policy is to be based on empirical research, market failure might be sometimes calculated as greater than we count government failure, thus making the case for economic regulation. This would be a mistake, given that there ain't no such thing as market failure in the first place. So as a strategy I think it is a double-edged sword.

But I am much more interested in the truth of this concept than in its strategic value. Deep down, the market failure argument is intellectually incoherent. Let me mention in this regard a Harold Demsetz quote than John Palmer cites in his paper: "No good theoretical link has been forged between the structure of an industry and the degree to which competitive pricing prevails, because no good explanation has been provided for how present and potential rivals are kept from competing without some governmentally provided restrictions on competitive activities." This is a magnificent antidote to the "market failure" hypothesis, an antidote that is highly regarded in the current Austrian literature. (The Austrians would go much further, however. In their view, it is not that no good theoretical link *has* been forged, but that no such link *can* be forged because of the very nature of competition.)

Consider Grubel's point that the two Canadian airlines account for 100 percent of the cross-continental traffic, and that eight U.S. airlines account for 92 percent of travel in that market. His analysis? This creates the potential for oligopolistic rip-off of the consumer, the mainstream neoclassical deadweight loss of economic welfare, or exploitation, to put a Marxist twist on it. In this view, we have to contrast this loss with the government rip-off of the consumer via government failure and inefficiencies in the regulatory system.

But as I see things, it is not the case that we must weigh a market failure against a government failure. Rather, there are two different types of *government* failures. The first is the regulation failure considered by Grubel. The other government failure is the law that prohibits such firms as Singapore Airlines, El Al, Aer Lingus, TAP, SAS, British Airways, Mexicana, Aeroflot, Lufthansa, Air France, Iberia, Alitalia, Japan Airlines, Air China, Varig, Ansett, Air India, Aloha, Air Maroc, FinnAir, Air Botswana, BWIA, and scores of others from the internal Canadian and American markets. These carriers would give their eye-teeth to be able to enter the lucrative North American market. I see no reason why repealing this law couldn't add greatly to the competition of the Canadian market.

However, on perfect competition grounds the case for market failure goes much deeper. Herb Grubel and other orthodox economists would presumably agree that tariffs and trade prohibitions are an instance of government failure, and that without them, the industrial concentration would be far lower. But what about the cases of extremely high concentration ratios in which government intervention plays no obvious role?

Take the case of Mike Tyson who at the time of this writing was the current heavy weight champion of the world in boxing. He would have to be considered a monopolist, at least on the basis of mischievous neoclassical theory. Certainly, he is a single seller of Mike Tyson services. Yes, there are substitutes for him, but there are substitutes for everything. It cannot be doubted that he faces a downward sloping demand curve for his very unique services. Surely he can maximize his income, according to the textbook model of imperfect competition, by not fighting as much as he would if he were part of a competitive industry. As a result, he stands guilty of monopolistic withholding of services, the rascal.

What response is open to Mike Tyson to refute these scurrilous charges? He can claim that his leisure is worth more to him than fighting the extra five or six fights per year that might be required of him under the interventionistic neoclassical theory. On what economic basis can the central planner order that Tyson not withhold his boxing services? The mainstream economist would have to argue that the benefit to be derived from watching him take on the extra bouts will be worth more to the general public, when this is all added together, than will his leisure thereby forgone be worth to him. But this argument commits the sin of interpersonal utility comparisons. The irrefutable point is that no public policy whatsoever may be logically deduced from neoclassical theory without opening the Pandora's box of interpersonal comparisons of utility.

Nor need we consider such atypical (for the orthodox economist, that is) cases. The analysis is the same for any industry. Any industry that isn't producing as much as some would-be economic dictator thinks they should be, can make the same point. They can just decide that they don't want to produce that amount, on grounds of leisure. And who can say them nay, without implicitly overriding their utility on the ground? There *is* no "deadweight loss." It is a figment of the overactive imaginations of generations of orthodox economists.

I say there is no such thing as monopoly on the market. Any monopoly power that exists will be found to be caused by government, if analyzed fully. For example, take Ray Croc. He started out with a local hamburger stand and built it up. After a while, he called it McDonald's, and now "controls" a large portion of the fast food market. ("Controls" is the orthodox way of describing this relationship. A far better term is "accounts for," or "serves.") Suppose that McDonald's continues on its present path and in five years forces into bankruptcy Wendy's, Burger King, the Chicken Colonel, Pizza Hut, Arby's, Taco Bell, Roy Roger's and every other present fast food dispenser. McDonald's is then a "monopolist." But notice that this will have been done through a process, no action of which was illegitimate. The way the 100 percent market share will have been achieved is by offering a better product at a lower price, giving better service, etc. According to the logic of anti-combines law, McDonald's will now be a public menace. What will happen? The authorities will pounce, yelling, "monopolist," in much the same way that their intellectual and moral predecessors used to accuse women of being witches. This is certainly incoherent from the process point of view, to say nothing of the moral point of view.

There were three Soviet prisoners in jail, this was before *perestroika* and *glasnost*, of course, and they were comparing their tales of woe. The first one said, "I got to work too early and they accused me of brown-nosing; so they put me in jail." The next one told his fellow prisoners that he got to work too late and they accused him of stealing from the state. The third stated, "I got to work exactly on time and they accused me of owning a western wrist watch." This may bring a rueful smile, but notice that with anti-trust and anti-combines legislation, the same vicious principle of damned no matter what you do is in operation. If the businessman charges a higher price than deemed appropriate by the economic authorities, he is guilty of profiteering and monopolistic withholding. By charging a lower price, he is guilty of cut-throat competition or predation. And if it is the exact same price, he is guilty of collusion. We need a good dose of *perestroika* not only in the Soviet Union but in every country that features this pernicious legislation.

The Fraser Institute has published three books that are critical of the standard neoclassical perfect competition theory upon which anti-combines law is based. They are: Armstrong, *Competition vs. Monopoly*, 1982; Walter Block, *A Response to the Framework Document for Amending the Combines Investigation Act*, 1982; and Walter Block, ed., *Reaction: The New Combines Investigation Act*, 1986. They deserve a wider readership, evidently.

I have some other criticisms of the Grubel paper with regard to its comments about the frequent flyer program and its attempt to promote brand loyalty. If, as Grubel suggests, we legislatively ban frequent flyer plans, to be consistent we shall also have to stop all sorts of other similar attempts by companies to create brand loyalty. For example, my kids (aged 11 and 9) religiously rip off the bottom of their corn flakes boxes because they can get a toy after they accumulate six box tops. After five box tops have been collected, the pressure to purchase a sixth is a tangible element in our household finances. My poor kids are being suckered into this artificial demand and we've got to stop the purveyors of breakfast cereal from this exploitative behaviour. And the same goes for green stamps and McDonald's, that perennial exploiter. My children have to own not one, but a whole set of Ronald McDonald toys, otherwise they can't hold their heads up in the neighbourhood. All these sorts of things have to go by the board. Again, I think this is just legitimate market activity, or, as Robert Nozick calls it, economic acts between consenting adults, or consenting kids in any case. I don't see any problem with it.

And the same analysis applies to computer reservations. If we followed Grubel down this interventionistic path, we would have to prohibit restaurant reservations, car rental reservations, and hotel reservation systems. Why not have a competing reservation system? I don't see these as barriers to entry. The only barriers to entry that are worthy of the name are government inspired ones.

Let us now consider Grubel's point with regard to strengthening the national culture. He fails to pounce on this as voraciously as I would have liked, but concedes that a national airline might well help our national culture. Milton Friedman makes the point that violence is a very precious commodity. If we use too much of it, we rend the very social fabric. Those are not his exact words, I have paraphrased liberally. Well, prohibiting competition is a way of using violence. Prohibiting people from doing what they are otherwise legitimately entitled to do, namely engaging in commercial activity, can only be done with the threat of violence (fines and/or jail terms). Promiscuously and needlessly employing the violence of the state in this way hardly strengthens natural culture and unity. On the contrary, it leads to disunity and fighting.

One last point with regard to air traffic control. I don't see why this is a "public" service. I think that Grubel would be well advised to extend his insight about privatizing airports to privatizing air traffic control. There is nothing intrinsic about air traffic control that makes it unfit for market operation. Contrary to Grubel, there is simply no case for giving it up to the tender mercies of government failure.

Discussion of the Grubel Paper

Richard Schwindt

The title of Grubel's paper, "Will Canadian Airline Deregulation Fail?", raises an interesting point in that "failure" can be viewed from at least two perspectives. On the one hand, failure could mean that deregulation does not generate the net economic benefits that the economics profession almost universally predicts. On the other hand, it could mean failure on the part of policy-makers to carry out the deregulation process. Of course, if deregulation failed on the first count we would have to agree that the failure was deserved. While the evidence indicates that there were very substantial welfare gains attributable to airline deregulation in the U.S., care must be taken in predicting similar gains in Canada. Further, there is a danger that while the net benefits are achievable, the process could become stalled or be reversed. Why would this happen? I think some insights are provided in a recent article by Alfred Kahn where he describes the surprises from airline deregulation in the context of the U.S. experience.[1]

That article is relevant to this discussion because if the unpleasant surprises identified by Kahn hold true in Canada they could weaken the benefits of deregulation and elicit demands for the reimposition of abandoned rules. He groups the unpleasant surprises under four headings: (1) the turmoil which characterized the process, (2) the reconcentration of the industry, (3) the intensification of price discrimination and monopolistic exploitation, and (4) the deterioration of service. Before dealing with each of these, it is important to note one unpleasant outcome that was predicted but did not materialize—the deterioration of airline safety.

It is widely accepted that deregulation in the U.S. did not result in higher accident rates. In fact, Kahn concludes that deregulation was accompanied by a 35 percent or so reduction in accident rates.[2] Grubel's analysis supports these findings, and provides the further insight that regulated Canadian air travel is no less dangerous than deregulated U.S. air travel. This is not surprising, given that airlines know very well that accidents create very bad publicity.

---

1   Kahn (1988), pp. 316-21.
2   Ibid., p. 321.

Kahn did find that deregulation created a good deal of turmoil in the industry. There was a massive restructuring of routes. There was price warring. There was labour strife. There were bankruptcies and there was a dismal profit record over the period of deregulation. To an extent, these symptoms of turmoil are also symptoms of competition, and they have largely been absent from the Canadian scene. However, in the Canadian context, any one of those factors could trigger pleas to the government for reregulation of the industry.

Secondly, he found that there was a significant reconcentration of the industry in the late 1980s. In effect, all the new entrants, including the high profile carriers such as People Express and Piedmont, were gone by 1988. He notes that concentration on a national basis is now higher than it was in the pre-deregulation period. The United States government has in fact taken a close look at reconcentration and has intervened. The Department of Justice was active in the CAB hearings on several proposed mergers and required modifications to those mergers, forcing the sale of slots in particular airports.

The issue of concentration is particularly relevant in Canada. Concentration among the transcontinental carriers has always been high. There were pre-emptive mergers prior to deregulation. Both of the major carriers put into place extensive feeder lines through the acquisition of regional and sub-regional carriers. National concentration was markedly increased by the PWA-CP merger and its successor's subsequent acquisitions of Wardair.

Thirdly, Kahn noted that he was surprised by the intensification of price discrimination and the exercise of market power in the deregulation period. This he had not predicted. While fares did go down on the heavily trafficked routes, they went up considerably on those routes that he considered to be non-competitive. He found this disturbing.

Fourthly, he found that there was a deterioration in the quality of service as reflected by congestion and delay. Some of this degradation in service was attributable to a failure by public authorities to provide adequate airport capacity and to price extant facilities appropriately. However, other changes in the product offering, such as narrower seating, limited on-flight amenities, and queuing, were a response to consumer demand. Consumers were clearly willing to accept lower quality for lower fares.

These were the unpleasant surprises identified by Kahn. He was able to conclude that notwithstanding these unpleasantries, the expectations of the deregulation advocates had been fully vindicated. Deregulation had brought about greater efficiency and lower fares. This raises two questions that bear upon the possibility of airline deregulation failure in Canada. First of all, are we going to enjoy the efficiency gains reaped in the United States? Secondly, if there are efficiency gains, will these be passed on to consumers through lower fares?

It is important to note that the major efficiency gains attributable to deregulation in the U.S. resulted from changed route structures, specifically the adoption of the hub-and-spoke system. Considering this, I think that Grubel's emphasis on reductions in labour costs is exaggerated. In the United States the core long-run cost savings were generated by routing changes, not the suppression of wages. Routing changes had three efficiency enhancing effects. First, adoption of the hub-and-spoke system reduced interlining and increased the proportion of online passengers. Apparently it is more efficient to keep customers on the same airline than switch them from one to another. Second, and importantly, route changes led to a higher capacity utilization of the larger aircraft. Third, hubbing made it possible to offer more final destinations from all originating points.

Given that route restructuring, mainly hubbing, was the major source of efficiency gains in the U.S., can we expect similar gains from deregulation in Canada? There are questions. For example, the Economic Council recognized that our system was quite different from the United States. That is, air traffic is mainly east and west across the country in a linear fashion. This does not lend itself to hubbing which is more appropriate when population is denser and more evenly dispersed.[3] This fact is important to any evaluation of potential gains from deregulation and is relevant to Grubel's performance comparisons of the U.S. and Canadian industries.

Those comparisons are reflected in his figures 2 and 3. Over the 1981-1985 period, the ratio of non-fuel costs to revenue passenger miles declined significantly in the U.S. relative to Canada. This ratio is influenced by two factors: costs and the number of passengers that are travelling. In the United States, because of the cutting of fares, there were many more people flying. The increased passenger loads add to the denominator of the ratio. Judging from the substantial increase in U.S. revenue passenger miles reflected in figure 3, this largely explains the falling ratio. Presumably, costs per aircraft mile, which would reflect lower labour and operating costs, did not decline so dramatically. The point is that if hubbing resulted in greater capacity utilization, and if capacity utilization explains declining costs per revenue mile, then this gain depends on hubbing. If the distribution of the Canadian population is such that hubbing is not as appropriate as in the U.S., then potential gains from deregulation might be less.

Assuming that there are substantial potential gains from deregulation, a second issue is the distribution of those gains. Grubel addresses this head-on when asking whether these cost savings, if they do exist, are going to be passed

---

3 Economic Council of Canada (1981), p. 30.

on to Canadian consumers. This comes down to a question of competition. Kahn noted that studies of airline pricing since deregulation showed that market concentration does matter and that it matters a great deal.[4] Alfred Kahn is by no means a structuralist, yet he puts emphasis on the role of market concentration on pricing in the deregulation period. This should give us serious concern.

Concentration in the Canadian airline industry is high, and has increased substantially in the recent past. The industry is not contestable. There are substantial barriers to entry. There are scale economies in operating a hub system, primarily associated with densities. These will constitute scale barriers in the relatively thin Canadian market. Moreover, such economies argue against the success of cabotage. It is difficult to conceive of a foreign airline successfully implementing a domestic feeder service in the Canadian market.

Furthermore, the two major incumbent Canadian airlines enjoy advantages associated with their reservation services and frequent flyer programs. The merger of the incumbents' computer reservations systems was contested but ultimately allowed, subject to undertakings that improved access to the system for third parties. How effectively this will protect competition remains to be seen.

The frequent flyer programs clearly constitute an effective product differentiation barrier to entry. I can personally attest to the effectiveness of these programs. I was asked by the travel arranger of this conference if I had a preferred airline. I do because I am a few thousand points away from a trip around the world. Unfortunately, I failed to express my strong preference for convenience. Well, after three stops and two changes of aircraft I ultimately reached Lethbridge. I left three hours before Grubel and we arrived at the airport at exactly the same time. But I got my points.

My conclusion is yes, by all means we should proceed with airline deregulation. There are clear benefits out there but we have to remain vigilant in the process. We should prepare the public for whatever turmoil there may be in the short run and, more importantly, we should support pro-competition policies to ensure that cost savings are passed on to the public.

---

4 Kahn (1988), p. 320.

References

Economic Council of Canada (1981), *Reforming Regulation* (Ottawa: Ministry of Supply and Services).

Kahn, Alfred (1988), "Surprises from Airline Deregulation," *AEA Papers and Proceedings* 78 (May), pp. 316-21.

Chapter 7

Deregulation and the Canadian Petroleum Industry: Adolescence or Maturity?

G.C. Watkins

Introduction

Regulation of economic activity involves government controls on the pricing, marketing, and output of firms. The underlying presumption is that left to themselves, firms could act in ways contrary to the public interest.

The petroleum industry—especially in North America—has always attracted regulation. The production sector is subject to extensive surveillance of exploration, drilling, and extraction. Land tenure is at the behest of government, a corollary in Canada of provincial government ownership of petroleum resources. Almost all facets of pipelines are heavily regulated. Controls have been imposed on exports of oil, oil products, and natural gas. Only the refining sector has escaped relatively unscathed. And, of course, petroleum has long been viewed as a strategic commodity, thus inviting policy-makers' attention, both provincially and federally.

Regulation of the industry in the aftermath of the two oil price shocks of the 1970s was particularly intense as governments were directly embroiled in setting prices (whereas previous involvement had been indirect), and controls over output and markets became severe. The apotheosis of these activities was the National Energy Program (NEP) of 1980.

However, the 1980s have seen the dismantling of much of the regulatory apparatus built up over the previous decade. This trend became visible with the change in federal government in 1984. But it would be wrong to see that as the key to deregulation. The latter stages of the Liberal government had already seen erosion of the NEP. It is fair speculation that some clone of the new policies introduced by the Conservative government might have emerged even if the Liberals returned to power.

In this light, the deregulation that has occurred represents the combination of a general disenchantment with regulation as an instrument of public policy and fundamental changes in the world oil market. As we shall see, deregulation is by no means total, and has affected oil and gas in quite separate ways. But it has received additional impetus from the Free Trade Agreement (FTA) of January 1, 1989.

This paper proceeds by first describing the background: defining the point of departure, outlining the agreements made (including relevant features of the FTA), and commenting on the institutional distinctions between oil and gas (section 1). Section 2 reviews what sort of behaviour a more competitive market—the intent of deregulation—might engender. What has happened with oil is examined in section 3. The rather different situation for natural gas is dealt with in section 4. Concluding remarks are made in section 5.

Especially in the case of natural gas, industry jargon has proliferated of late. To assist the general reader, a glossary of terms is appended to the paper.

1. Background

The context in which deregulation took place must be defined. The point of departure was the National Energy Program (NEP).

From Whence We Came—The NEP[1]

The National Energy Program became rather elusive in that by 1984 no single source document could be cited. Instead, there were eight emanations published over a three and one-half year period, beginning with the original October 1980 "missile" and going through various "fall outs" to the "Agreements to Amend" concluded with various provinces from June 1983 to April 1984.

The three main objectives of the NEP as listed in 1980 were security of supply and ultimate independence from the world oil market, increased opportunity for Canadian participation in the petroleum industry, and fairness in energy pricing and revenue sharing.[2] The NEP sought to attain these objectives using four main tools: (1) oil pricing; (2) natural gas pricing; (3) taxes; and (4) incentives and grants.

---

1 For a full description of the evolution of the NEP, see Doern and Toner (1985) and Watkins (1984).

2 Energy, Mines and Resources Canada (1980) p. 2.

Oil prices (1) were initially set under predetermined schedules which basically assumed Canadian oil prices would always be independent of and below world oil prices: the "made-in-Canada" pricing regime. Imported oil was subsidized. Notwithstanding patriotic rhetoric, the 1980 NEP schedules were superseded by schedules expressing oil prices as a direct function of world prices. By the summer of 1984, basically two types of oil were identified— "new" and "old"—according to whether the oil had been discovered before or after 1981. "New" oil essentially received world prices; "old" oil, which accounted for some 60 percent of total production, received about 75 percent of the world price. At the same time, there was a proliferation of oil categories—ten to be precise—on which the "new" and "old" status was conferred.

Natural gas pricing (2) was somewhat simpler, with provision for regular increases at the Alberta border for gas destined for domestic markets, but with the presumption that city-gate gas prices in the main eastern markets would not exceed 65 percent British Thermal Unit (BTU) equivalence with oil. "Vintage" pricing was eschewed. Pending a new agreement, the Alberta government withheld the increase in natural gas prices scheduled for February 1985.

The NEP taxes (3) (excluding incentives and grants) by June 1984 in essence had been reduced to two elements: the Petroleum Compensation Charge (PCC); and the Petroleum and Gas Revenue Tax (PGRT).[3]

The fiscal incentive and grant provisions of the NEP (4) showed the least degree of adjustment over time. The main element was the Petroleum Incentives Program (PIP), whereby exploration and development costs were subsidized at rates that varied according to both the degree of Canadian ownership and the location of the activity, with higher rates for exploration on "Canada Lands" (essentially frontier regions) than for the provinces.

Overall, what constituted the NEP in June 1984 had undergone a very substantial mutation compared with the original proclamation of October 1980. In essence, the June 1984 version consisted of world related "vintage" oil prices, oil related natural gas prices, subsidization of imported oil, federal "royalties" on provincial production, and ownership related cost subsidies. Earlier schedules of future oil and gas price increases and certain new tax instruments had all been overtaken by events not contemplated at the time the NEP was promulgated in 1980, nor even when the main Ottawa-provincial government agreements were signed in the fall of 1981.

---

3   The Natural Gas and Gas Liquids Tax (NGGLT) and the Incremental Oil Revenue Tax (IORT) had been suspended by that time. An additional tax, the Canadian Ownership Special Charge (COSC), had been levied since 1981 on consumers.

In addition to the NEP, several other regulations in place before the NEP were influential. These included export taxes on oil and oil products (to ensure domestic subsidies were not enjoyed by export buyers), oil pipeline subsidies, licensing procedures and surplus tests for exports of oil and gas, and government imposition of natural gas export prices.[4]

It was clear by 1984 that the NEP was too inflexible in a rapidly changing world, and was distorting market incentives.[5] Something had to be done. And the new Conservative government of September 1984 intended to act.

The Western Accord, March 1985[6]

The first main energy measure passed by the new government was the Atlantic Accord of February 1985. This primarily dealt with fiscal and administrative sharing between Newfoundland and the federal government. It is not really concerned with deregulation and need not detain us.

It is the March 29th "Western Accord" between Ottawa and the three oil and gas producing provinces—Alberta, Saskatchewan, and British Columbia—that is of primary importance. The accord emasculated the NEP. Crude oil pricing was deregulated and various federal taxes and grants were eliminated. Resolution of natural gas pricing issues was deferred until later in 1985.

Deregulation of crude oil prices was a fundamental change, marking not only the end of the administered pricing regime upheld since September 1973 but also instituting an open market pricing system of the like not seen since before the inception of the National Oil Policy (NOP) in 1961.[7] Deregulation was effective June 1, 1985. Buyers could purchase oil from Canadian or foreign

---

4 For details on downstream regulation of the oil industry, see Waverman and Watkins (1985); for the evolution of controls on natural gas export pricing, see Watkins and Waverman (1985).

5 For example, the PIP grants ranged as high as 80 percent cash return of a Canadian firm's exploration costs in "Canada Lands." There are clear "moral hazard" problems in these types of cost plus incentive schemes between a principal that cannot go bankrupt (the federal government) and the agents. Federal government officials were "astonished" at the depths drilled, the costs per well, and the total expenditures on the PIP. In turn, economists were astonished by these federal reactions.

6 See Western Accord (1985).

7 The 1961 NOP protected the western Canadian oil producing sector from declining oil prices in the 1960s. The rationale of pricing under the NOP cannot be divorced from the United States Oil Import Program protecting U.S. oil producers (see Watkins, 1987).

sources without volume restrictions and at prices "freely negotiated between buyers and sellers."

Allocation of domestic light crude among eastern Canadian refiners was eliminated. Volume and price restrictions on short-term crude oil and petroleum products exports were removed. However, longer term exports of more than one year for light crude oil and products, and two years for heavy crude, would continue to require authorization by the National Energy Board (NEB). Pipeline subsidies were eliminated. But if supplies to Canadian consumers were jeopardized, export restrictions might return. And if international oil market disturbances resulted in sharp changes in oil prices, the government would take "appropriate measures" to protect Canadian interests. So some potential levers to re-introduce regulation remained.

A more "flexible and market-oriented pricing mechanism" was endorsed for domestic pricing of natural gas, but implementation was to require "extensive consultation."

Two objectives were cited for changes to the fiscal regime: the promotion of industry investment; and taxation on the basis of profits rather than revenues. In true western tradition, several levies "bit the dust." These included the NGGLT, the IORT,[8] the COSC, the Crude Oil Export Charge (COEC), and the PCC. Of great significance was the phasing out of the Petroleum and Gas Revenue Tax (PGRT) by January 1, 1989; moreover, it was not to be imposed on new production after April 1, 1985. The federal government's PIP in large measure was to be terminated in one year.

The governments involved agreed to flow-through benefits to the industry; in other words, there was to be no filching of discarded federal tax revenues by provincial governments. The governments expected the additional funds acquired by the industry to be re-invested; industry actions were to be monitored.

Thus, the accord accomplished two main objectives—it deregulated prices and abolished a whole range of subsidies and taxes. The federal government retained the right to intervene if international oil market disturbances were severe. Provision was made for restriction of exports if supplies to Canadian consumers were threatened—but this has now been superseded by the FTA (see below). Provincial governments retained the right to control production for conservation reasons and to "equitably" share production (prorationing) if spare capacity arose.

---

8   However, the NGGLT and the IORT had been set at zero sometime before the accord was signed.

The Hallowe'en Agreement, November 1985

The Western Accord left certain issues relating to natural gas outstanding, but with the promise of resolution later in 1985. A new agreement was signed on November 1, 1985, between the three western provinces and the federal government.[9] The overall intent of the agreement was to "foster a competitive market for natural gas in Canada, consistent with the regulated character of the transmission and distribution sectors of the gas industry."[10]

Much of the existing domestic gas regime was frozen for one year. But during this time, an "orderly transition" was envisaged to a "market-orientated" pricing system, when prices no longer would be prescribed by governmental fiat. In this vein, effective November 1, 1986, natural gas prices in interprovincial trade were to be determined by negotiation between buyers and sellers, but under the umbrella of protecting "reasonably foreseeable" domestic requirements of gas.[11] During the transition year, any negotiated prices would be endorsed as a matter of course within the administered price system.

Domestic Gas Sales

Provision was made for gas consumers to buy additional supplies at prices negotiated directly with producers, as long as "contract carriage" transportation arrangements were made. Such provision also applied to consumers seeking release from existing distributor contracts if producers and distributors agreed.

The National Energy Board (NEB) was requested to review the allocation of pipeline charges on volumes of gas switching between categories (from distributors to direct sales) and the basis for sharing any take-or-pay levies. Provision was also made for Competitive Marketing Programs (CMPs) negotiated between distributors, shippers and producers.

Gas prices under existing contracts were frozen at the prevailing Alberta border price of $3.00/MCF until October 31, 1986. However, negotiations were to commence between distributors, shippers, and producers on prices for gas under existing contracts, with such negotiated prices to be effective November 1, 1986. Thereafter, arbitration under the Alberta Arbitration Act would apply if the parties could not agree.

The Alberta government was committed to amend its Arbitration Act to ensure the act operated in a way consistent with market responsive pricing by allowing arbitrators to take into account all factors, not just "commodity value"

---

9   Agreement (1985).
10 Ibid., p. 1.
11 The term "reasonably foreseeable" was no doubt inspired by the wording in the National Energy Board Act.

(which treats the market value of natural gas as a function of the value of competing fuels).[12]

Export Gas Sales

Reviews of "surplus" tests then underway by the NEB and promised by provincial authorities (Alberta and British Columbia) were anticipated to result in reduced protection and freer access to domestic and export markets. Moreover, the federal government was committed to eliminate both the "incrementality" test[13] and the "competing fuels test" relating to negotiated export prices for spot sales; short-term exports (less than two years) were to be licensed without volume limitations.

Export price criteria were set:

"i) the price of exported gas must recover its appropriate share of costs incurred;

ii) the price of exported natural gas shall not be less than the price charged to Canadians for similar types of service in the area or zone adjacent to the export point;

iii) export contracts must contain provisions which permit adjustments to reflect changing market conditions over the life of the contract;

iv) exporters must demonstrate that export arrangements provide reasonable assurance that volumes contracted will be taken; and

v) exporters must demonstrate that producers supplying gas for an export project endorse the terms of the export arrangement and any subsequent revisions thereof."[14]

Criteria (i) was straightforward in the sense it was the same as previous provisions, and related mainly to the allocation of pipeline charges to export volumes. Criterion (ii) effectively replaced the Toronto city-gate price with regionally variable adjacent domestic prices as the floor price for exports. Criterion (iii) repeated an earlier provision and echoed the flexibility demanded by U.S. import regulations. Criterion (iv) was delightfully vague, but reflected the demise of firm take-or-pay arrangements. Criterion (v) was to ensure producers were aware of commitments to which they subscribed!

---

12 The Arbitration Act, chapter 10, 1986.

13 This test involved demonstrating that short-term sales to the U.S. were not displacing other Canadian export sales.

14 Agreement (1985, p. 4). Note that these criteria were five of seven conditions already in place by virtue of modifications made to the federal government's export pricing policy in November 1984.

Other Aspects

The agreement recognized that natural gas pipelines and distribution companies would continue to be regulated. Although consuming provinces were not signatories to the agreement, it was anticipated their governments would "make changes to ensure effectiveness of a market-sensitive gas pricing regime," provide "direction to provincial agencies to provide consumers with alternative sources of supply through the availability of transportation services or distribution systems," and provide "distributors with greater flexibility in determining prices for gas sold by them."[15] Thus, downstream regulatory actions were expected as part of the overall deregulation process.

Government Measures After 1985

Although producing provinces retained their rights to regulate removal of gas, these were not to be exercised in a way that would frustrate the agreement. Specifically, Alberta and British Columbia reviewed their "surplus" tests, and Alberta reviewed its interpretation of the Gas Resources Preservation Act in terms of "incrementality" of new sales.[16] Moreover, Saskatchewan—which hitherto had banned gas sales outside the province—allowed limited exports and direct sales within the province between end-use customers and producers.

NEB Policies

Since 1985, the NEB's natural gas "surplus determination" procedures for regulating exports have undergone two reviews. The first was in 1986 and resulted in a significant loosening of the NEB's mandated surplus test.[17] The former "reserves" test which set aside supplies to satisfy 25 years of domestic requirements was dropped. In its place a reserves to production (R/P) ratio procedure was established. The stipulated R/P ratio was set at 15. However, a second review in 1987 abandoned the *mandated* surplus formula altogether. In its place, a "market-based" procedure was established providing for a broader assessment of export applications which was still intended to satisfy the legislative imperative of only exporting gas "surplus to foreseeable requirements."[18]

---

15 Ibid., p. 5, item 26.
16 The "incrementality" test was intended to avoid a permit displacing markets served by LDCs (local distribution companies) under contracts in force on October 31, 1985, unless there was an "operational demand" reduction.
17 NEB (1986).
18 NEB (1987).

Under the new procedure the NEB reviews applications to export natural gas only for contracts longer than two years. A "complaints" process is intended to protect access of Canadian users to supplies of gas under the same terms proposed for an export sale. The board will use this complaints mechanism in determining whether the proposed export is surplus. And gas will not be authorized for export "if Canadian users have not had an opportunity to buy gas for their needs on terms and conditions similar to those of the proposed export."[19]

Exporters must also submit an "impact assessment" demonstrating the effect of the proposed export on natural gas markets. This will allow the board to determine "whether a proposed export is likely to cause Canadians difficulty in meeting their energy requirements at fair market prices."[20] As well, exporters must provide evidence that the proposed sales are in the Canadian public interest, typically by submitting benefit-cost analyses (dropped in March, 1990).

The market-based procedure also requires the NEB to monitor Canadian energy markets on an ongoing basis. And the board conducts periodic studies of natural gas supply and demand to see whether Canadian gas requirements will be met.

Satisfaction of the export price criteria as a condition to granting an export licence is no longer the concern of the NEB. The 1985 agreement provided for a joint federal-provincial committee to monitor and assess trends in domestic and export prices.

In 1988 the NEB recently approved construction of the St. Clair Pipeline to link eastern Canadian gas users with major American gas producing regions. Now operational with a capacity of 200 million cubic feet (MMCF) per day, this pipeline offers new supply options to consumers in eastern Canada. This is consistent with fostering market-oriented pricing in the domestic market.[21]

Alberta Policy

Before deregulation, Alberta's surplus test protected current Alberta markets for 25 years. This policy was relaxed to a 15-year period of protection for Alberta "core" (residential, commercial, and small industrial) markets plus protection of "non-core" (large industrial and electric utilities) contracted requirements.[22]

---

19 Ibid., p. 24.

20 Ibid., p. 25.

21 NEB (1988a).

22 See ERCB (1987).

The policy inherently assumes that to ensure adequate protection the core market must be served by long-term contracts. The government has requested Alberta gas utilities to continue using long-term contracts for protection of "core" market customers. And, although no formal core market policy for Alberta has been unveiled yet (March 1990), the government appears to be leaning towards recommendations made by the ERCB and Alberta PUB in late 1987.[23] The core market was defined in this report as comprising residential and commercial users; their protection was to be provided through long-term contracts with local distribution companies (LDCs) or producers for ten to 15 years.

The Alberta government would like to see similar protection accorded to domestic core customers east of Alberta. Thus far virtually no removal permits have been issued for short-term direct sales to non-industrial domestic customers or for relatively small volume industrial customers (those consuming less than 35,000 gigajoules (GJ) per year).

The conditions that the Alberta government currently attaches in whole or in part to removal permits include satisfaction of the prevailing surplus test for longer term commitments, and market specification. A no "self-displacement" condition[24] for domestic LDCs contracts was imposed until recently. It was dropped after conclusion in late 1988 of the new Western Gas Marketing Ltd.

Amendments to the provincial royalty system were made in January 1988 which imposed a floating "floor" royalty reference price of 80 percent of the Alberta average gas price. This provision acts to discourage direct sales of "low" priced non-system gas.[25] The averaging process for system gas sales tends to preclude such royalty penalties on low priced system gas.

Protection of the public interest is cited by the government as justification for using removal permits to extend its within Alberta core market policy to domestic core markets beyond Alberta. Prices for gas removal from Alberta are monitored, but no specific price test exists.

British Columbia Policy
New British Columbia surplus determination procedures were adopted in 1987; they bore a close resemblance to the current Alberta policy. Dubbed the "Market-Based Formula," 15 years of proven reserves were to be put aside for the current core market of residential, commercial, and small industrial users.

---

23 See PUB/ERCB (1987).
24 Self-displacement means the purchase of gas by an LDC to displace gas it would otherwise obtain under its contracts with TransCanada PipeLines (TCPL).
25 Non-system gas means gas other than that contracted to supply a pipeline.

Protection was also given to contracted firm non-core domestic market requirements.

Subsequently (June 1988), British Columbia announced a "Core Market" policy. This market has been defined as all residential, commercial, institutional, and industrial customers not engaged in direct gas purchase. LDCs are to contract for a ten- to 15-year reserve assignment. Local consumers with more flexible requirements (for example, large industrials with access to other sources of energy) can make less stringent supply arrangements.

The mandatory surplus test was eliminated on November 1, 1990, as was the border price test which had intended to prevent natural gas from being removed at prices below those paid by domestic customers. A monitoring system has been set up to review the status of provincial natural gas reserves and prices. A "complaints" procedure has been instituted to provide B.C. customers with the opportunity to contract gas on terms and conditions similar to those for exports.

Exports from Saskatchewan

Until recently, Saskatchewan had no surplus test since production was insufficient to support extra-provincial sales. This situation has since changed—an estimated 40 petajoules (PJ) of gas was exported from the province in 1988—which led to the development in 1987 of a formula to determine Saskatchewan's gas surplus. It provides 15 years' protection for the equivalent of "core" markets plus protection for direct purchase volumes. In short, the formula is a clone of that in Alberta.

Prices for removal gas must not be lower than those paid by Saskatchewan consumers for similar types of sales. Further, removal permits will not be issued for schemes which displace Saskatchewan sales presently under contract (shades of the former Alberta "incrementality" test).

Ontario Energy Board

The role of provincial regulatory agencies in consuming provinces has assumed more importance with the growth of direct sales into the interprovincial gas market. New measures have been adopted by these provinces in the last few years to accommodate direct sales to end-users. And Ontario as the largest consumer of natural gas in Canada has taken the lead in this market restructuring.

The Ontario Energy Board (OEB) has addressed several issues in determining the role of the LDCs and what range of services they should offer to new users. Specifically, the OEB has made recommendations on the appropriate role of brokers and unbundling rates for separate distribution services.[26]

As well, the OEB has conducted a major hearing addressing the question of appropriate purchasing requirements for the LDCs. Subsequently, the board recommended that all direct purchasers be required to hold supply and transportation contracts for a minimum of three years.[27] No recommendation was made requiring LDCs to protect core market customers by entering into long-term purchase contracts. The OEB decided that each LDC should be responsible for determining its optimal supply portfolio provided that at least a three-year supply was under contract.[28]

The reader will have observed this position is contrary to Alberta's. Discussions between the Ontario and Alberta governments on whether "core" markets should receive special long-term protection have been ongoing for some time, but resolution of this issue remains elusive.

The Free Trade Agreement (FTA)

The Free Trade Agreement will likely have minimal impact on the petroleum industry in the short term. This is simply because free trade in oil and gas between the two countries is already tantamount to reality, given the impetus behind deregulation on both sides of the border. It is in the long run that the FTA will likely have its greatest impact, especially if future events conspire to resurrect protectionist sentiments.

Chapter Nine of the FTA prevents explicit protectionism and direct government-induced price discrimination in energy trade. Article 902 affirms the same rights and obligations on bilateral energy trade that Canada and the U.S. already have under the General Agreement on Tariffs and Trade (GATT). Examples of these obligations are prohibitions on minimum export and import price requirements. Article 904 provides that, where energy export restrictions are imposed under GATT provisions—including temporary, critical shortages of essential products, conservation of exhaustible natural resources, and as part of a domestic price stabilization program—then the restriction may not reduce the proportion of total supply available for export below that prevailing in the most recent

---

26 OEB (1988).

27 OEB (1988a).

28 Legislation passed by the Quebec government in 1989 stipulated that direct purchases must offer the same kind of security of supply to the end-user as that offered by the distributor. And the Régie de l'Electricité et du Gaz has the authority to reject a direct sale if the transaction would adversely affect other users on the distribution system.

36-month period. This is the so-called "proportionality" clause. Article 905 provides for direct consultations between the respective energy departments about regulatory actions of the Federal Energy Regulatory Commission (FERC) or the NEB that are considered questionable.

To conform with the FTA, the NEB Act has recently been amended to require that "in exercising its powers and performing its duties, the Board shall give effect to the Canada-United States Free Trade Agreement Implementation Act."

Thus, the board's decisions in such areas as pipeline certification, toll regulation, and particularly the regulation of exports and imports are to pay heed to "let-the-market-work" philosophy to ensure consistency with the FTA. Thus, the FTA reinforces the trend towards deregulation of natural gas by attempting to eliminate in large measure the 49th parallel as a determinant of movements of natural gas between two nations.

It remains to be seen how the FTA will actually operate. Will the NEB complaints mechanism be upheld? Will any restrictions flowing from public interest aspects be challenged?[29] Will price monitoring, if it bites, be seen as contravening the FTA, or will it be seen as preventing "dumping"? And will provincial surplus tests trigger proportionality? Only when a "case history" of disputes emerges will the full extent of deregulation made under the FTA be revealed. But it certainly eliminates repetition of some past controls, such as export taxes.

2. Implications of Competitive Market Behaviour

The 1985 "agreements" outlined above were intended to foster a more flexible and market-oriented pricing regime for domestic markets. In short, movement towards a more competitive market structure was endorsed.

Pursuit of "market-oriented pricing" conjures up visions of the emergence of a fully competitive market. Recall that the criteria for a "pure" competitive market are strenuous, including sufficient buyers and sellers so that their own actions have little effect on market prices, identical consumers from a seller's point of view, complete knowledge held by buyers and sellers of prevailing prices, total freedom of entry and exit, and no government intervention. In combination these conditions are formidable and therefore it is not surprising

---

29 Midland Cogeneration Venture Ltd. referred an NEB decision to the Federal Government Court of Appeal, protesting among other things the NEB's benefit-cost analysis of its application. The benefit-cost requirement was dropped in March 1990.

that an impersonal "pure" market remains a vision—not only for oil and natural gas, but for almost all other commodities as well.

But the criteria of pure competition underlie the more tractable concept of "workable" competition. Workable competition is a "second best" proposition: modifications of the tenets of pure competition to reflect constraints caused by cost conditions inherent in the industry, government policy, other structural characteristics, and the realities of the marketplace.

Long-term Contracts and Market Structure

The later discussion on natural gas (see section 4) will make clear that it is here that deregulation has proven difficult. One hurdle has been the way long-term contracting practices have governed the evolution of the Canadian natural gas industry. Many contend they should continue to do so today—at least for what is termed the "core" market—notwithstanding nascent changes in industry structure. Long-term arrangements are viewed as vital for the exploration and development of new natural gas supplies.[30]

But it can be argued that the role of long-term contracts cannot be divorced from the prevailing degree of market competition, and that insofar as the October 1985 agreement seeks to promote a more competitive natural gas market structure, the inherent need for long-term contracting correspondingly diminishes.

In more detail: much of the (economics) literature on long-term contracts has stressed the importance of situations where a small number of parties make investments that are specified to them (idiosyncratic).[31] Such transaction-specific durable capital is typified by pipeline and gas production assets. When there is just one buyer (say a pipeline) and one effective seller (a unitized reservoir or group of reservoirs), the situation is tantamount to bilateral monopoly. Each party will wish to avoid "opportunistic" behaviour of the other. Once large up-front investments are made, their costs become sunk, and relatively low marginal costs of operation may erode a party's bargaining position.[32] One solution is vertical integration, favoured historically in the oil industry. Another is long-term contracting that allows each party to amortize his investment with confidence.[33]

---

30 For example, see CPA (1988).

31 See Williamson (1979).

32 Low spot prices witnessed recently are perhaps evidence of relatively low short-run costs in relation to full-cycle sunk costs.

33 It can be shown that efficient contracting under demand uncertainty and with a bilateral monopoly is characterized by a fixed payment (typically take-or-pay) and

In the case of Alberta, long-term supply commitments also were required simply to underpin the financing of large scale long distance pipeline investments. These required dedication of supply; an important aspect here was the role of long-run removal permits issued by the Alberta government. The historical emergence of long-term contracts along the chain of gas supply between LDCs with a monopoly on local gas distribution, between pipelines acting under a purchase and resale regime, and between pipelines and producer groups, therefore, was a natural response.

But the rationale for long-term contracting changes was a function of market structure. To see this, suppose the natural gas market were to become fully competitive. In a fully functioning "faceless" market, buyers and sellers meet to exchange goods at equilibrium prices. The market always clears. Transactions are standardized and do not require a special structure. New trading relations are easily arranged. Such unspecialized transactions pose few hazards. Buyers can easily switch to alternative sources. Suppliers can easily sell to other buyers. Large numbers competition is continually self-policing.[34]

This sort of market structure does not apply now in the Canadian natural gas industry. Nor is it likely to emerge in the foreseeable future. Nevertheless, the conclusion is clear: the more the gas market takes on a competitive mantle and the greater its flexibility, the less the need for long-term contracts.[35]

Long-term contracts are often justified on the grounds of security of supply. But, again, the legitimacy of this argument depends on the nature and state of market competition. In a fully competitive market, supply can always be purchased—at a price. This is how markets provide security. The lesser the

---

a flexible payment covering marginal costs. Analysis of a large number of U.S. gas contracts in the relatively unregulated 1950s confirms the importance of transaction-specific "small numbers bargaining" issues in explaining contract price variations, rather than market power influences; see Hubbard and Weiner (1987).

34 As the size of the market grows and the number of suppliers increase, an exchange that was "transaction-specific" loses this characteristic and greater reliance on markets becomes feasible. Thus, developments over time may well progress from vertical integration to "obligational" contracting and then to fully functioning competitive markets; see Williamson (1979, p. 260).

35 Modelling analysis of spot and forward (i.e., longer term) contracts suggests the distinction between spot and forward prices would merge as the number of buyers increases (see Parsons, 1989). Parsons analyzes the possible spread between forward and spot contracts for a large field, such as Venture attracting three buyers, and a smaller Alberta field assumed to attract five buyers. He finds the estimated strategic value of forward contracts to be significantly greater for Venture because more competition among buyers for Alberta gas makes the capacity installation decision less important in terms of a seller's bargaining power.

degree of competition, the greater the role for long-term supply contracts to secure access to supply. Long-term contracts can also be viewed as affording some protection against precipitous price rises. Such rises may well be felt by users relying on spot markets, which display much more volatility than term markets.[36]

Thus, while in a competitive market the price will determine the quantity of gas offered for sale, a risk faced by gas buyers is the probability that the price will vary. And to the extent "core market" customers are price risk averse, one vehicle to mitigate price swings is long-term contracts. It follows that the "core" would pay a risk premium to induce producers to enter an arrangement that moderated price swings—always assuming producers are not as price risk averse as the core. But if producers have an equal interest in mitigating price fluctuations, no risk premium would be imposed on buyers.[37]

Whether a long-term contract affords any general price protection other than from spot market style volatility depends on the pricing and other terms embedded in it. The more frequent the price renegotiation period, the more a long-term contract—at least in terms of pricing—begins to look like a series of short-term contracts, in terms of affording little protection against price swings.

In summary, given that in a competitive market supply would be available at *some* price, one of the main functions of long-term contracts would be to provide a degree of pricing certainty for price risk averse parties. But the shorter the price renegotiation period, the less this applies.[38]

Long-term contracts have always been impeded by limitations on the ability to take uncertain events into account (bounded rationality). Drawing up contracts that took all contingencies into account would be prohibitively costly. Incomplete long-term contracts—and there must be some open ends—predictably pose the potential for conflicts of interest between parties.

Routine price adjustments should relate to easily verifiable, external events. Where uncertainties lead to provision of pricing flexibility in long-term contracts—the situation that holds now—third party assistance in the form of arbitration has advantages over litigation in resolving disputes.[39]

---

36 Also see later discussion.

37 There is little or no market evidence at this time on suitable premiums for price security.

38 Price renegotiation terms can provide for stability. Note that using prices that prevail around the time of delivery at least relieves buyers and sellers of the need to outguess the future.

39 See Fuller (1963) cited in Williamson (1979, p. 238).

Long-term contracts are also motivated by the desire to insure against changes in market conditions other than those registered by changes in price. Some customers may well prefer long-term contracts as a hedge against political uncertainties.

Market Pricing Spectra

The development of spot and short-term sales for natural gas during times of market weakness (typified by the gas "bubble" in the United States and the gas "surplus" in Canada) conveys the impression that spot gas prices would always be below term prices. Any such impression is mistaken. Spot prices tend to act as a leading indicator. When markets tighten, such prices would jump ahead of term prices and drag the entire term price structure upwards over time.

Thus, whether "going short term" is cheaper depends on the underlying market conditions. Over the past few years, short-term and spot contracting has meant less expensive gas, but the seasonal volatility of spot prices in the United States indicates how quickly this market reacts to changes in pressures. And price patterns may be confused if long-term upward pressures exerted by the cost of new supplies contradict short-term downward pressures emanating from spare capacity.

The main motive to switch from longer term to shorter term contracts at any one point in time is of course price. However, recurring spot transactions incur additional costs of renegotiation and, moreover, can involve uncertainties about the cost and availability of transportation capacity. Longer term contracts can offer some reductions in transaction costs—buyers and sellers save the costs of shopping around and making new agreements for successive deliveries.[40] And buyers with risk averse consumers will be willing to pay some premium for the security of supply inherent in long-term contracts. Thus, a workably competitive commodity market may offer a spectrum of prices constituting buyer and seller preferences expressed by different terms and conditions of sale.

Tanker transportation is a good example of a market with no one competitively determined price of transportation services. Rather, a mix of rates is offered depending on various conditions of service: firm spot (single shipment) rates to term charters of several months or longer. But all rates are interdependent because each can be substituted for the other. Term charter rates reflect an average of *expected* spot charter rates over the term of the contract, and in

---

40 But long-term contracts also involve additional costs, for example, those associated with deciding how to deal with unanticipated outcomes and with writing the contract in clear and unambiguous language.

equilibrium would normally be below the expected spot average, since spot rates would reflect costs of search and negotiation and compensation for prospective idle capacity.[41]

If and when natural gas markets come into balance, longer term contracts may become more attractive to direct purchasers who do not wish to take the risk of reserves not being developed and made available on a timely basis. There is some evidence of U.S. natural gas buyers shifting to long-term contracts in expectation of tighter markets.

3. Oil Deregulation: Quick and Easy

The March 1985 Western Accord (see section 1) deregulated crude oil pricing and virtually eliminated all controls on oil exports, especially in the short run. The major refiners have "posted" prices at Edmonton, the prices at which they would purchase any oil presented to them. After the long period of administered pricing, oil companies found the need to sell their oil a novel and, for some, a chastening experience.

If deregulation were effective and a "workably" competitive market were established, what kind of pricing behaviour might be observed? First, the price of Alberta crude posted at Edmonton by refiners would be set within a narrow band at any one point in time. A significant spread in posted prices for crudes of the same quality would suggest price discrimination—behaviour not sustainable in a competitive market. Second, the level of posted prices would be closely related to "netbacks" from the main market interfaces where Alberta crude competes with international supplies, namely Montreal and Chicago.[42] Or, to put it another way, the delivered price (laid down cost) of Alberta crude in

---

41 The operation of copper markets has some interesting features in the context of spot and term contract relationships. A two price system evolved over the period of price decontrol following the Second World War to mid-1978. Major U.S. producers used term contracts to set producer prices. The price of other production was governed by London Metal Exchange (LME) spot prices. Differences between the two prices were often substantial. But customers under term contracts were often retained even when producer prices exceeded LME spot prices, because term customers were supplied at below LME prices when the latter exceeded producer prices. However, the two-price system eventually broke down when such a large fraction of the world copper trade took place on a spot basis that buyers no longer saw relying on the spot market as risky (see Weiner and Hubbard, 1988). Note also that typically the variance of spot prices is larger the greater the fraction of trade conducted through term contracts (tests have been carried out for both oil and copper; see Weiner and Hubbard, op. cit.).

42 This is not to suggest the aggregate world oil market satisfies all competitive criteria: OPEC is still attempting to operate as a cartel.

market regions where Alberta faces competition would correspond closely to the delivered prices from other sources. Third, refiner postings would be sensitive to changes in world prices. If world prices were quite volatile, correspondingly frequent changes would be seen in posted prices.

To what extent do refinery postings satisfy these tests? August 1989 postings at Edmonton by three major refineries—Esso, Shell, and Petro-Canada—were $21.61 per barrel, $21.29 per barrel, and also $21.29 per barrel, respectively, for 40 degrees American Petroleum Institute (API) gravity crude (0.5 percent sulphur).[43] The spread in prices is minimal.

Estimated netbacks in July 1989 for international crudes at Montreal and Chicago are shown in table 1. The upper panel develops the Edmonton netback for North Sea Brent crude delivered to Montreal; the lower panel develops Edmonton netbacks for West Texas Intermediate (WTI) crude delivered to Chicago (WTI is the most popular "bench-mark" crude in the United States). The spread in netbacks is about $1 per barrel, suggesting that Chicago (the nearer market) is a more attractive one for Alberta crudes.[44] More importantly, the actual light crude oil price prevailing was $22.98 per barrel (CDN$), straddling the two netbacks. This confirms that Alberta crudes are competitively priced with international crudes.

Finally, over the period July 1988 to June 1989, one refiner—Shell—registered eleven changes in postings: precisely the kind of volatility expected in light of the frequent changes in world oil market conditions. Parallel changes were registered by other refiners.

Thus, all three competitive pricing criteria have been met: deregulation has been effective. A competitive market exists for the sale and purchase of Canadian crude, interfacing with the world oil market. And the world oil market is more competitive and volatile than in the 1950s and 1960s, when the majors ruled the roost, than in the 1970s and early 1980s, when OPEC was ascendant.

Formerly, the supply of Alberta crude was governed by prorationing (quota allocations). Prorationing reduces incentives for direct price competition, and it remains on Alberta's legislative books. But in large measure deregulation has induced changes in administration of the prorationing scheme which allow producers to sell any shut-in oil on the spot market,[45] although, for technical reasons, control is retained on maximum production rates. This flexibility

---

43 See Esso, Shell Canada, and Petro-Canada Products, *Crude Oil Price Bulletins*, August 1, 1989 (Shell's Bulletin is dated July 30, 1989).

44 Note that tentative proposals by Interprovincial PipeLine (IPL) to expand capacity are directed towards the U.S. Midwest.

45 ERCB (1987).

Table 1
Alberta Netbacks From Foreign Crudes*

Netback for Brent Crude from Montreal, July 20, 1989	$/bbl
Representative Price (spot) Brent 38.0° API	18.25 (U.S.$)
Plus Tanker Charge	0.81 (U.S.$)
Plus Portland-Montreal Pipeline Tariff (includes terminalling charge)	0.96 (U.S.$)
Laid Down Cost at Montreal	20.02 (U.S.$)
Laid Down Cost at Montreal	23.80 (CDN$)
Less IPL Tariff to Edmonton	1.53 (CDN$)
Netback at Edmonton	22.27 (CDN$)
Quality Adjustment for 40° API	0.30 (CDN$)
Netback for 40° API, Equivalent Type Crude	22.57 (CDN$)

Netback for WTI Crude from Chicago, July 20, 1989	$/bbl
Representative Price (spot), West Texas Intermediate at Cushing, 40° API	20.35 (U.S.$)
Plus Pipeline Tariff, Cushing to Chicago	0.39 (U.S.$)
Laid Down Cost at Chicago	20.74 (U.S.$)
Less IPL U.S. Tariff	0.46 (U.S.$)
Border Price	20.28 (U.S.$)
Border Price	24.11 (CDN$)
Less IPL Tariff to Edmonton	0.51 (CDN$)
Netback at Edmonton	23.60 (CDN$)
Quality Adjustment at 40° API Netback at 40 degrees, Equivalent Type Crude	23.60 (CDN$)

*based on exchange rate of $0.84 U.S./$1 CDN

enables producers to offer discounts on incremental production. Beforehand strict quota control kept the prices of oil from a reservoir uniform.

Of course, pipeline transportation remains federally regulated, but common carrier legislation provides for open access. However, the pricing mechanism has yet to fully intrude on the "menu" of pipeline services offered.

Deregulation has also affected the disposition of Canadian production. With the removal of federal transportation subsidies, Atlantic refineries no longer use Canadian oil, and the share of refinery runs held by imports in Quebec has risen. At the same time, the share of Canadian output absorbed by more proximate (Midwest) export markets has tended to increase. This more efficient distribution of Canadian production is what would be expected if deregulation were effective.

The 1986 price collapse when the spot price of North Sea oil fell into single digit figures provoked proposals for reregulation of prices (not the least from some in private industry). These included import tariffs, floor prices, income stabilization plans, and the like. Admittedly, most proposals stressed that assistance would be temporary. However, the federal government resisted the temptation to introduce price supports, and confined itself to certain tax reliefs and incentives.

In sum: deregulation has resulted in a more competitive market structure for the oil industry than at any time since the Leduc discovery of 1947.

4. Natural Gas Deregulation: Protracted and Arduous

The transition from intense regulation to a competitive pricing and market sensitive environment for natural gas has been difficult. And while there has been a substantial increase in market flexibility, impediments to competitive market structures remain, and are likely to continue to do so.

Before the 1985 agreement, virtually all interprovincially traded gas was sold as system gas under a few sales contracts between TCPL and the local distribution companies (LDCs). The agreement allowed consumers to contract directly with producers for new gas supplies as their existing contracts terminated. And LDCs could enter into direct purchase arrangements for volumes additional to those committed under existing contracts.

The introduction of direct sales into the gas market has created an array of purchasing options for consumers. These range from typical direct sales between producers and end-users to buy/sell arrangements between end-users and distributors and system gas resales (SGRs) and between end-users and Western Gas Marketing Limited (WGML)—the marketing arm of TCPL.[46]

The 1986 Distributor Agreements

After the one-year transition period, the prices in existing LDC contracts renegotiated to take effect on November 1, 1986, provided for substantial discounts to large industrial customers and progressively smaller discounts to lower volume industrial customers and commercial and residential customers. In particular, the base price for these contracts with the exception of Manitoba was $2.59/GJ at the Alberta border, $0.20/GJ less than the previous frozen Alberta border price.[47] This price would apply to residential and commercial customers. Price discounts at the Alberta border of as much as $1.00/GJ would be offered to large industrial users under competitive marketing programs (CMPs). These discounted prices were to be flowed-through to end-users served by the distributors.

Regulatory boards in consuming provinces were to decide whether or not to approve these arrangements. And, because the prices were predicated on a netback formula, they require a finding of producer support. At least 51 percent of the producers supplying a minimum of 70 percent of the contract volumes is necessary for approval of a netback sale.[48]

---

46 A buy/sell arrangement involves the end-user purchasing gas at a negotiated price from a producer in Alberta, reselling the gas to an LDC immediately east of the Alberta border at the LDCs average gas purchase price and repurchasing the gas from the distributor at the point of delivery. An SGR arrangement is similar except that the end-user purchases gas from WGML just inside the Alberta border at a negotiated price and immediately resells the gas to TCPL for the average cost of gas to the distributor. TCPL then sells the gas to the distributor for this average price plus TCPL's tolls and finally the end-user repurchases the gas from the distributor at the point of delivery. What is the purpose of these machinations? A buy/sell arrangement enables an LDC to avoid quoting individual rates for services on their system. An SGR enables TCPL (or WGML) to avoid quoting a price for an individual customer at the Alberta border that might attract regulatory attention by consuming provinces.

47 The base price for sales to Manitoba remained at $2.79/GJ. No reduction was offered in light of the Manitoba government's imposition of a tax on compressor fuel used in the province for transporting gas to eastern Canadian and export markets.

48 Alberta Natural Gas Marketing Act, chapter N-2.8, 1986. The volume requirement has recently been reduced to 60 percent.

Price Discrimination

These "system gas" contracts showed appreciable Alberta border price differentials between various categories of end-users. Such a degree of price differentiation is not compatible with a competitive market pricing regime unless sustained by variations in the nature of service offered.

It is unlikely that differences in load factors or other service features between customers were sufficient to account for the degree of "discount differentials" shown. Moreover, the award of discounts reflected the price of competitive fuels and the ability of large users to contract quite easily for non-system gas—criteria that have little to do with service characteristics. It follows that the differentials that emerged under TCPL's pricing scheme suggest market power.

TCPL occupies a very strong market position by purchasing about 85 percent of the gas sold in domestic markets east of Alberta. Moreover, more than 40 percent of all established natural gas reserves in Alberta are currently contracted to TCPL. This represents the largest pool of contracted reserves in North America.

Falling demand and increasing gas supplies—both elements characteristic of the North American gas market in the early 1980s—placed severe pressure on pipeline companies with take-or-pay commitments to producers.[49]

The legacy of take-or-pay arrangements was particularly serious for TCPL since it had entered into area-purchase contracts committing the company to purchase a proportion of *all* reserves developed in a relatively large geographical area. By 1983, TCPL could not meet its take-or-pay obligations, and they were taken over by a consortium of banks (the TOPGAS I and II Agreements).

The speed and extent of deregulation has been affected by the existence of TOPGAS. The agreements obligate TCPL to try to maximize sales of "system" gas. Therefore, it is not in TCPL's interest to have system gas sales displaced by direct sales. And hence TCPL's marketing subsidiary, WGML, has fought to maintain market share. An important tool here has been WGML's access to transportation capacity.

However, since deregulation, deliveries of non-system gas to the domestic market served by TCPL have grown from 6 percent to a level of nearly 23 percent of total gas sales by 1988.[50] And this increase in non-system gas sales has been largely at the expense of system gas, since overall growth in natural gas demand has been quite modest.

---

49 Take-or-pay, as the term implies, is a provision in gas supply contracts for payment to be made for gas whether it is taken or not.

50 NEB (1988b, p. 30).

The combination of loss of markets to other producers making direct sales and falling gas prices have adversely affected the revenues of TOPGAS producers. Any decline in sales volume increases the proportion of the TOPGAS producer's prepaid to total deliveries, leaving a diminishing share of deliveries yielding current revenue. Moreover, if the revenue-yielding deliveries were at lower net prices at the wellhead, the decline in net revenues would be compounded.

The TOPGAS prepayment schedule also has implications for netback prices in light of Alberta regulations requiring that negotiated prices in netback sales contracts receive producer approval. These prices will tend to be sticky since any deficiencies incurred by producers on the sale of prepaid gas would be recovered from the proceeds on other gas sales. Thus, TOPGAS producers will be reluctant to approve any negotiated netback sale that at a minimum would not cover the amount owing on the prepaid gas.[51]

Indeed, the average plant gate price of around $1.50 per GJ from recent sales by WGML's producers is likely slightly below what is owing on the tranche of prepaid gas presently recovered. Thus, TOPGAS producers and TCPL are reluctant to indulge in price cutting unless compelled and especially not in a way that would involve reducing prices to all customers—the competitive market solution.

Downstream Reactions to Upstream Discrimination

The Manitoba government objected vehemently to the segmentation of markets under the renegotiated 1986 gas price agreements. In May 1987 it directed the Manitoba Oil and Gas Corporation (MOGC) to act as purchasing agent for the province's gas utilities. The MOGC contracted directly with a group of producers to supply gas to these utilities which would have usurped the WGML supply. The MOGC then applied to the NEB for an order requiring TCPL to transport MOGC's gas purchases. In its decision, the board noted that the gas volumes to be transported under this application "in essence displace all volumes presently being purchased by each of the distributors—ICG and GWG—to serve markets in Manitoba. This would effectively result in the total replacement of the distributor's contracted firm supply."[52] The Board denied this application on the grounds that the MOGC's proposed gas supply arrangements constituted a

---

51 Recovery of the principal is generally on a first-incurred/first-recovered basis in that prepayments for gas made, say, in 1979 are recovered before prepayments made in 1980. The monies are to be repaid over a ten-year period which is to end by November 1994.

52 NEB (1987a).

form of "self-displacement" which was seen as contrary to the intent of the 1985 agreement.[53] Without transportation access, it was rather difficult to move the gas to market!

The Ontario Energy Board's decision in 1986 on the two-year gas price agreement between WGML and Ontario distributors focused on the board's jurisdictional mandate to determine rates for all customers in Ontario. In particular, the OEB wanted all natural gas purchased by utilities delivered to Ontario without "streaming" to specific customers and groups. The board approved these flow-through prices on an interim basis but asked that they be renegotiated in a manner which would restore the board's authority for setting distributor rates.[54]

The Ontario contracts were renegotiated for the 1987-88 gas year, and, although they failed to address the OEB's concerns, they were nevertheless approved—albeit reluctantly—by the board. In its decision, the board listed several factors constraining the development of a fully competitive market.[55]

Upstream Reactions

Alberta government policy on the removal of gas from the province was described in section 1. What is the reason for Alberta's apparent policy of using the award of removal permits to extend its within Alberta core market policy to domestic core market customers beyond Alberta? The short answer might be to keep the price up, but this interpretation would be superficial.

The Alberta government is committed to making deregulation work to maintain the enhanced access to the United States market that the relaxation of federal export controls affords. It sees deregulation as threatened if domestic core customers elsewhere were to suffer supply exigencies. There is concern that since shortages for such customers would not be tolerated, they may be "opportunistic" in their contracting practices in the belief that any negligence on their part would be corrected by government intervention.

It is precisely the resurrection of intervention by the federal government that the Alberta government seeks to avoid by ensuring the core market is served by long-term contracts. Such policy would achieve consistency within and beyond Alberta, and would assist in emasculating any complaints that may arise under the federal government's new market-oriented export policy (and possibly under the Free Trade Agreement).

---

53 A year later, the NEB reversed its position on self-displacement; see NEB (1988c).
54 OEB (1986).
55 OEB (1988b, p. 38).

The 1988 Distributor Agreements

In late 1988 new long-term gas sales contracts were concluded between Western Gas Marketing Ltd. (WGML) and the LDCs. They provide for a two-year pricing agreement under which a $0.60/GJ demand charge and a $1.60/GJ commodity charge applies to "core" market customers in Ontario and Quebec, yielding an Alberta border price of $2.20/GJ at a 100 percent load factor. The price to Manitoba core market customers is a straight $2.20/GJ commodity charge, irrespective of load factor.

"Non-core" volumes are ostensibly also priced at a commodity charge of $2.20/GJ. But since most of these volumes flow under system gas resales (SGRs) arrangements, industrial users end up paying a discounted price for the gas at the Alberta border. Recall this manipulation avoids overt "streaming" of system gas by price to different classes of end-users.

These contracts were subsequently approved by the regulatory boards in Manitoba and Ontario. The OEB said it "had regard" for the circumstances under which the $2.20/GJ price was negotiated. And these circumstances would not produce a fully competitive price.[56] Constraints identified by the board included capacity limitations on the NOVA, Transgas, and TCPL systems; volumes to be purchased by the LDCs could only be supplied by WGML; the LDCs were prevented from self-displacing volumes supplied under long-term contracts that were in force at the time the 1985 agreement was executed; and the Alberta government's removal permit policies.[57] The OEB noted that these constraints were beyond its jurisdiction and prevented distributors from obtaining supplies other than by negotiation with WGML.

The Array of Prices for Alberta Natural Gas

Since deregulation, a wide range of natural gas prices at the Alberta border has emerged. To the extent that the market was competitive, such price differences can be attributed to variations in the nature of the product offered. Product variations are such aspects as the point of delivery (transportation costs), manner of delivery (storage costs), reliability of services (continuous or interruptible supply), length of service (short- or long-term contracts), different specifications (heating content of gas), and the like. In a fully competitive market, the array of prices would demonstrate how the market values different service qualities.

---

56 OEB (1989).
57 Ibid., pp. 50-51.

Domestic Prices

Table 2 shows selected natural gas prices under short-term direct sales contracts to domestic markets at the end of 1988. Short-term contracts typically run from one to two years; the load factor is usually high, running from 90 to 100 percent.

Short-term direct sales from Alberta were confined to industrial customers, reflecting the province's prohibition on short-term sales to "core" markets. In contrast, the majority of direct short-run sales made by Saskatchewan producers were to core market customers in Ontario—a niche that these producers are able to supply in large part because of the Alberta policy restrictions.

Short-term sales of Alberta gas to industrial customers in eastern Canada for the 1988 contract year commanded a price at the Alberta border ranging from $1.45 to $1.60/GJ and from $1.50 to about $1.65/GJ in the second contract year. This pattern (presumably) reflects an expectation of modestly rising prices. And in December 1988, SGRs (direct sales of system gas by WGML) for a one-year term were being made at a price of 1.40/GJ. Saskatchewan prices for direct sales were somewhat higher, as would be expected for core market customers requiring backstopping arrangements. These prices ranged anywhere from $1.60 to $1.80/GJ in the first year of the contract and from $1.75 to $1.90/GJ in the second year.

The prices in long-term contracts negotiated for the first two years (up to 1990) between Canadian LDCs and Alberta suppliers are shown in table 3. All contract prices shown in this table are at the Alberta border. As well, all the contracts are assumed to be operating at high load factors—80 percent or better. And all are assumed to provide for firm service. However, the price differential between the WGML and the eastern LDC contracts with other Alberta sources is a very considerable $0.55 to $0.70/GJ, depending on the contract year. What differences between the contracts might warrant the price variations displayed?

One difference between the WGML contracts and those for the Ontario LDCs with other suppliers is their term. The WGML agreements generally run for 15 years while some others are effective for a primary term of ten years. Some recent work on cost differentials suggested that going from a ten- to 15-year contract term can increase the price by as much as $0.25/GJ.[58] Thus, allowing for a generous term differential such as this would reduce the initial price difference between the WGML and other supplier contracts to $0.30-$0.45/GJ.

Part of the remaining premium can be interpreted as reflecting the broad based security represented by the diverse WGML pool. But it is unlikely that such a large premium could be justified by the improved quality of supply

---

58 However, such a differential has not been tested in the marketplace—it is based on costs that the market may or may not underwrite.

Table 2
Domestic Gas Prices—Short-term Contracts

Short-term Contracts (1-2 years)	Alberta Border Prices (CDN$/GJ)
Ex-Alberta (to Eastern Canada) (a)	
Call for Tenders (b) (end November, 1988)	
1st year	1.45-1.60
2nd year	1.50-1.60
Call for Tenders (c) (December, 1988)	
1st year	1.54-1.58
2nd year	1.59-1.63
WGML (SGR) industrial sales (December 1988)	
one-year basis	1.40
Ex and intra Alberta (d) (December, 1988)	
one-year contract	1.60-1.80
two-year contract	1.65-1.70
Ex-Saskatchewan (to Eastern Canada) (e)	
Call for Tenders (b) (end November, 1988)	
1st year	1.60-1.80
2nd year	1.75-1.90
Call for Tenders (c) (December, 1988)	
one-year basis	1.65-1.75

(a) To industrial customers, at 100 percent load factor.
(b) Third party negotiated price (excluding mark-up) between customers and producers and based on volumes of about one Bcf/year.
(c) Brokers prices to customers include a mark-up of 3 to 4 cents/GJ.
(d) Based on field prices at inlet to NOVA Pipeline.
(e) To core market customers—note that Saskatchewan gas prices are equivalent location wise to Alberta border prices; gas comes into the TCPL line at Success or Liebenthal, Saskatchewan. These points are within the same "zone" as Empress; therefore transportation costs are the same.

Source: Confidential industry information.

Table 3
Domestic Gas Prices—Long-term Contracts with Canadian Distributors

	Alberta Border Price ($/GJ)	
	1988/89 Contract Year	1989/90 Contract Year
WGML—Manitoba and Eastern Zone Distributors (Block A volumes)	2.20	2.20
DEM—Consumers	1.49	1.54
Unocal—Consumers	1.51	1.61
Unigas—Union	1.53	1.53*
Northridge—Union	1.61	1.67
Petro-Canada—Union	1.50	1.65*
PSR—Union	1.65	n.a.
Pan-Alberta—GMi	2.20**	2.20**

* to March 31, 1990.
** less discounts to commercial and small industrial users as well as to the non-core market.
n.a. = not available

vis-à-vis the other distributor contracts. There is no firm evidence to suggest how the market would value the security associated with diversified supply.

Since contract features probably cannot account for all of the WGML premium, the implication is that structural aspects of the market and other influences contribute. Such influences would include Alberta's restrictive gas removal policy essentially precluding eastern zone distributors from attracting alternative sources of supply for their base core market loads. And even if they could have done so the sheer size of the Ontario market compelled the Ontario LDCs to deal with WGML. Moreover, WGML was the only supplier to hold firm capacity on TCPL and NOVA to accommodate the volumes.

Thus, eastern LDCs were hardly in a proper arms-length bargaining position. It is not surprising, then, that the initial WGML-eastern LDC price of $2.20/GJ was not what might be predicted if LDCs were free to purchase and transport gas from whomever they wished. More competitive conditions held for the incremental purchases by eastern LDCs. They were able to tender for this supply and so had access to many sellers.

Export Prices
Natural gas prices for September 1988 under selected long-term export contracts are provided in table 4. Adjustments were made for transportation load factors less than 100 percent for gas exports shipped on TCPL's system.

Table 4
Export Gas Prices—Long-term Contracts
(September 1988)

Company	Point of Export	Export Price (CDN $/GJ)	Pipeline Costs[1] (CDN $/GJ)	Alberta Border Price (Empress) (CDN $/GJ)
A&S	Kingsgate	2.40	0.36	2.04
Pan-Alberta	Kingsgate	2.14	0.36	1.78
	Monchy	2.15	0.21	1.94
Consolidated	Emerson	1.99	0.27	1.72
	Monchy	1.93	0.21	1.72
Kanngaz[2]	Niagara	3.68	0.74	2.94
Niagara Gas	Cornwall	2.81	1.41	1.40
ProGas	Emerson	2.31	0.45	1.86
	Monchy	1.54	0.21	1.33
TCPL	Emerson	1.85	0.45	1.40
	Niagara	2.35	0.63	1.72
	Philipsburg	3.03	1.36	1.67

1 Firm Contract Service at 100 percent load factor unless otherwise specified. (Load factors: Consolidated at Emerson—79 percent; Niagara—42 percent; ProGas at Emerson—45 percent; TCPL at Emerson—45 percent; Philipsburg—44 percent.)

2 Kanngaz normally has been taking 98 percent of authorized take but for September the percentage dropped to 38 percent and thus the demand component effectively more than doubled the price.

Source: NEB, *Monthly Export Statistics*; Friedenberg (1988).

Although lack of data precluded adjusting load factors on the ANG and Foothills lines, it is known that both systems were operating at close to capacity in September 1988 (which makes adjustments for load factor minimal). Indeed, one-half of the total volumes exported in September were high load factor sales to California via the Kingsgate exit point.

A very wide spread of long-term prices at the Alberta border prevailed in September 1988—from $1.33 to $2.94/GJ—representing substantial differences in contract terms and conditions. The $2.94/GJ price reflected a low level of take which had the effect of more than doubling the demand component of the price; the $1.33/GJ reflects indexation provisions. Most of the prices were under $2.00/GJ. But note that the Alberta average border prices for firm export sales, the majority of which would be made under long-term contracts, averaged $2.00/GJ for September 1988.[59]

Since deregulation, long-term export prices have fallen by as much as $0.50/GJ. Overall, the weighted average long-term firm export price at the Alberta border for the 1987-88 (November 1, 1987 to October 31, 1988) gas year declined by $0.20/GJ to $1.98/GJ from $2.17/GJ in 1986-87.[60]

Domestic-Export Price Comparison

For all sales (short-term, long-term, and interruptible), domestic prices have generally been lower than export prices. However, there is evidence that the differential between domestic and export prices is narrowing: in 1987-88 the differential was $0.13/GJ compared with $0.22 for the previous gas year.[61] The convergence of export and domestic prices demonstrated increasing competition in North American gas markets.

Provision of Transportation Service on TCPL

With the 1985 agreement providing for direct sales in interprovincial markets, attention focused on the terms and conditions of access to the TCPL system. If non-system gas sales were to compete with system sales in these markets, the TCPL pipeline would have to be accessible to all shippers. Indeed, the signatories to the 1985 agreement requested the NEB to review TCPL's tariff policy with respect to displacement of system sales by non-system sales.

---

59 NEB, Natural Gas Exports and Imports, *Monthly Statistics*, September 1988.
60 EMR, *Natural Gas Price Monitoring Report*, March 1989.
61 Ibid.

In a May 1986 decision[62] the NEB decided that inappropriate duplicate demand charges would result from a displacement purchase by an end-user.[63] The LDCs obligation to pay a demand charge was reduced by an amount equivalent to the displacing direct purchase—the so-called "operating demand" mechanism.

The NEB also recommended that Alberta require non-system shippers to share the TOPGAS charges since their sales would be eroding TCPL's market share. Alberta subsequently passed legislation implementing such sharing.[64] To date, the non-system shippers' share has been maintained at 10 cents per GJ; this arrangement extends to 1994. In effect, all gas producers are paying for a portion of the TOPGAS payments, whether they enjoyed prepayments or not.

A major issue in recent years has focused on whether LDCs should be allowed to "self-displace," that is, whether LDCs could replace some portion of its gas purchases from TCPL with purchases from an alternative supplier. The NEB has deliberated on this issue on four occasions since 1985. The first three times it ruled against LDCs self-displacement, citing the need for an orderly transition to a market-sensitive pricing regime. However, after the 1988 WGML/LDC contracts were negotiated, the NEB reversed itself. As of November 1, 1989, distributors would no longer be prevented by pipeline regulation from self-displacing system gas.[65] But, in effect, this came about after the stable-door was locked; the WGML-Distributor contracts had already been negotiated, if not approved.

The convoluted picture of deregulation of the Canadian natural gas industry described in this section demonstrates the difficulty of changing an institutional framework so attuned to regulation. Yet the changes made have been very considerable. Neutral transportation is an important ingredient in developing competitive markets, and TCPL's (and Westcoast's) merchant and transportation roles have been "unbundled." Mechanisms have been put in place to accommodate direct sales. LDCs can (now) shop around for supply. Brokers and other agents have emerged to facilitate flexible supply arrangements. Producing companies have set up marketing departments. Alberta has shown a

---

62 NEB (1986a).

63 The duplication of demand charges arose as follows: when a customer previously purchasing gas from an LDC arranged an alternate supply through a direct purchase, he was required to pay the demand toll directly to TCPL for T-service and to the LDC for demand charges which it was still liable to TCPL. TCPL would have been paid twice for rendering the same service.

64 *Take-or-Pay Cost Sharing Act*, chapter T-0.1, September 30, 1988. This document is deemed to have come into effect on November 1, 1986.

65 NEB (1988c).

commitment to fostering a competitive market despite price weaknesses (although it has also sought to restrict access terms, for reasons described above). Although a buyers' market prevailed, consuming provinces have tolerated a quite extensive transition to deregulation. And various regulatory agencies have put a lot of effort into modifying rules and regulations to better accommodate market sensitivity.

However, the degree of concentration of Alberta supply, notwithstanding a multitude of producers, remains high. Three aggregate suppliers—WGML, Pan-Alberta, and Alberta & Southern—account for around 70 percent of all sales. And the special treatment of core markets raises the spectre of a form of institutional price discrimination, with certain market segments prevented by regulation from full participation in competitive gas supply purchases.

Concluding Remarks

The length of the preceding discussion on natural gas compared with oil visibly illustrates fundamental differences in the ability to deregulate. Yet there are strong similarities in the provision of oil and gas. Both involve risky exploration and development and less risky production (and include conditions of joint supply), large up front investments, pipeline transportation, and economies of scale in distribution. But in contrast with gas, oil industry transactions have not typically been conducted under a long-term (15 to 20 years) contract regime. At present all Alberta oil is sold effectively on a spot basis. There is no array of prices posted by refiners for different contract terms.

Why are the circumstances for oil and gas so different? The main reason is that the basic structure of the oil market—notwithstanding the earlier predominance of integration—is more competitive than that for gas. At present about 50 refineries buy Alberta oil. Producers are many, and regulation awards all of them market access. Oil pipelines are common carriers, required to serve any legitimate customer; they operate, then, on the equivalent of "transportation" service. This quite flexible and competitive market structure tends to suppress the need for long-term contracts for both buyers and sellers.

The institutional structures for handling natural gas have developed quite differently from those for oil, with long-term contracts predominating. Pipeline transportation is required from the field to the burner tip. Natural monopoly prevails for gas distribution, in contrast to the delivery systems for refined petroleum products. Canada has ready access to world oil markets which afford a lot of visible pricing information—spot, futures, and posted prices. Information on natural gas prices is much more obscure. And the main marginal market for Canadian gas, the United States, is complex and itself trying to surmount the ramparts of regulation. In this light it is not surprising that deregulation of natural gas has offered a stark contrast with that for oil.

Is it all simply a matter of timing, that after a few more years many of the present impediments will vanish, and the market structure for gas will become similar to oil? Certainly, access to markets within the United States will ease as deregulation continues to gather impetus, and if, as many believe, the demand for Canadian gas grows. The institutional structures to handle significant volumes of shorter term sales, direct purchases, and the like have been created and will continue to develop. Pricing information will become more widespread while more comprehensive spot markets and nascent futures markets will better enable deregulation to flourish.

Yet it is not clear that the big gas pools in Alberta will be significantly eroded. Legislation governing surplus gas—and for "surplus" read "constraints"—remains on the books. The NEB's market-based procedures have yet to be tested in circumstances where supply availability is less generous. The Alberta government will remain suspicious that enhanced access to U.S. markets will be somehow undermined in the event of any perceived domestic gas "shortage," notwithstanding the FTA. And the ramifications of the FTA itself remain vague until it is seen how disputes are resolved.

Above all, it is crucial to recognize that the circumstances in which deregulation has taken place have been favourable to consumers—soft markets and lower prices. The acid test will come when and if markets tighten and prices rise. Oil markets may be quite relaxed in the 1990s. However, many anticipate North American natural gas to tighten (for "tighten" read "clear") by the mid-1990s. Then we shall see whether deregulation is robust or fragile. To revert to the question posed by the title of this paper: I believe oil deregulation is mature; gas deregulation is in late adolescence, but achieving its majority may prove elusive.

Glossary

Broker   A gas broker is an entity other than an LDC that brings together buyers and sellers of gas and may or may not take title to the gas. Thus, the broker acts as an agent or consultant.

Bundled Rate   A single charge that covers a number of services provided by a pipeline or distributor. Examples of such services are gas sales, transportation, storage, and load balancing.

Buy/Sell   In this arrangement, the end-user purchases its own supply of gas and arranges for transportation, generally to the distributor's delivery point. The distributor purchases the gas and commingles it with the balance of its supplies, and then sells gas to the end-user as a sales customer under the appropriate rate schedule.

Commodity Charge   A commodity charge is a charge payable by a gas purchaser in a sales contract for each unit of gas purchased. The unit charge generally covers the commodity component of the applicable pipeline toll and cost of gas, and may include a portion of the fixed costs of the seller.

Competitive Marketing Program (CMP)   A mechanism by which WGML (Western Gas Marketing Limited) has provided specific discounts to individual end-users of gas. Generally, the distributor sells to the end-user under the approved sales rate schedule. The distributor advises the pipeline of volumes sold each month. The pipeline rebates to the distributor the agreed upon discount for the preceding month's volumes and the distributor flows the rebate through to the end-user. (WGML replaced CMPs with SGRs on January 1988).

Consuming Provinces   Those provinces of Canada that consume more natural gas than they produce—Manitoba, Ontario, and Quebec.

Core Market   Generally, that part of the gas market that does not possess fuel switching capability; typically, residential, commercial, and small industrial.

Demand Charge   A demand charge is a fixed, usually monthly, obligation of a gas purchaser in a sales contract. It may cover some or all of a seller's fixed costs and is payable regardless of volumes actually taken.

Direct Sale   Natural gas supply purchase arrangements transacted directly between producers or brokers and end-users at negotiated prices.

Displacement Volume   A direct purchase volume is a displacement volume when, assuming the absence of such direct purchase, the LDC could supply the account on a firm contract basis without its contracting for additional firm volumes to accommodate the demand.

Firm Service A relatively higher priced service for a continuous supply of gas without curtailment except under extraordinary circumstances.

LDC A local distribution company.

Load Factor The ratio of the average load over a designated period of time to the contracted maximum load expressed in percent.

Non-system Producers Gas producers other than those contracted to supply a pipeline.

Open Access The non-discriminatory access to transportation services.

Operating Demand Volumes Volumes specified in a distributor's CD contracts with a pipeline less the volume deemed to have been displaced by direct sales, as determined under the NEB's rules established for defining displacement volumes.

Peak Demand The maximum amount of gas required by a customer or LDC over a short period of time (typically one day).

Producing Provinces Those provinces of Canada that annually produce more natural gas than they consume—British Columbia, Alberta, and Saskatchewan.

Remaining Established Reserves Initial established reserves less cumulative production.

R/P Ratio Reserves to Production ratio = remaining reserves divided by annual production.

Self-displacement The purchase of gas by an LDC to displace gas it would otherwise obtain under its contracts with a pipeline.

System Gas Resales (SGRs) A form of buy/sell arrangement wherein the end-user purchases gas from WGML immediately east of the Alberta border at a discounted price, then resells the gas to TCPL at the Alberta border at the average cost of gas to the distributor. The distributor then sells the gas to the end-users under its normal rate schedule.

System Gas Sales Gas sold by pipeline companies or their affiliates, e.g., WGML's sales.

Take-or-pay A clause or provision in a contract requiring that gas contracted for, but not taken, will be paid for.

Unbundled Rate A rate for an individual, separate service offered by a pipeline or distributor.

References

Agreement (1985), Among the Governments of Canada, Alberta, British Columbia and Saskatchewan on Natural Gas Markets and Prices (October).

Brent Friedenberg and Associates (1988), *Canadian Natural Gas Focus* (November).

Canadian Petroleum Association (1988), *Submission* to the OEB Gas Supply Hearing (June 23).

Doern, G.B. and G. Toner (1985), *The Politics of Energy* (Toronto: Methuen).

Energy, Mines and Resources, Canada (1980), *National Energy Program* (October).

Energy, Mines and Resources, Canada (1989), *Natural Gas Price Monitoring Report* (March).

ERCB (1987), "Gas Supply Protection for Alberta, Policies and Procedures" (March).

Hubbard, R.G. and R.J. Weiner (1987), "Natural Gas Contracting Practices: Some Evidence from the United States" in Golombek/Hoel/Vislie (eds.) *Natural Gas Markets and Contracts* (New York: North Holland Publishing).

National Energy Board (1986), *Reasons for Decision* in the Matter of Phase 1, the Surplus Determination Procedures Phase of Gas Export Omnibus Hearing 1985 (April).

National Energy Board (1986a), *Reasons for Decision* in the Matter of TransCanada PipeLines, Availability of Services (May).

National Energy Board (1987), *Reasons for Decision* in the Matter of Review of Natural Gas Surplus Determination Procedures (July).

National Energy Board (1987a), *Reasons for Decision*, Manitoba Oil and Gas Corporation, Application Dated 25 May 1987, as Amended, for Orders Directing TransCanada PipeLines Limited to Receive, Transport and Deliver Natural Gas and Fixing Tolls, MH-1-87 (September).

National Energy Board (1988a), *Reasons for Decision* St. Clair Pipelines Ltd. and TransCanada PipeLines Ltd., Pipeline Facilities, GH-3-88 (October).

National Energy Board (1988b), *Natural Gas Market Assessment* (October).

National Energy Board (1988c), *Reasons for Decision* TransCanada PipeLines Ltd., Tolls, Phase 1, RH-1-88 (November).

Ontario Energy Board (1986), *Partial Reasons for Decisions* EBRO 414-1 (November 28).

Ontario Energy Board (1988), *Decisions with Reasons* in the Matter of a Hearing Respecting the Sale of Gas in Ontario by Brokers (May 8).

Ontario Energy Board (1988a), *Interim Report on Gas Supply* (August 19).

Ontario Energy Board (1988b), *Decisions with Reasons* EBRO 410-111, 414-11, 417 (January 22).

Ontario Energy Board (1989), *Decisions with Reasons* in the Matter of the OEB Act and in the Matter of an Application by Union Gas for Rates and in the Matter of Gas Costs, EBRO 456-4 (April 14).

Parsons, J.E. (1989), "Estimating The Strategic Value of Long-Term Forward Purchase Contracts Using Auction Models," *Journal of Finance* (forthcoming).

PUB/ERCB (1987), *Gas Supply and Transportation Service Inquiry* (December 29).

Watkins, G.C. (1984), "The National Energy Program—or Pogrom," Paper presented to the Convention of the Canadian Society of Exploration Geophysicists and the Canadian Society of Petroleum Geologists, Calgary, June 17-20.

Watkins, G.C. (1987), "Living Under a Shadow: U.S. Oil Policies and Canadian Oil Pricing," in R.L. Gordon, H.D. Jacoby, and M.B. Zimmerman (eds.) *Energy Markets and Regulation* (Cambridge, Mass.: MIT Press).

Watkins, G.C. and L. Waverman (1985), "Canadian Natural Gas Export Pricing Behaviour," *Canadian Public Policy* XI, Supplement.

Waverman L. and G.C. Watkins (1985), "The Regulation of the Canadian Downstream Oil Industry: Nature, Impact and Remedies," (Toronto: Institute for Policy Analysis, University of Toronto) Policy Study 85-1 (January).

Weiner, R.J. and R.G. Hubbard (1988), "Contracting, Spot Trade, and Price Stability: Evidence from International Copper and Oil Markets," (Waltham, Mass.: Department of Economics, Brandeis University) Paper no. 209 (May).

Western Accord (1985), *Agreement* Between the Governments of Canada, Alberta, Saskatchewan and British Columbia on Oil and Gas Pricing and Taxation (March).

Williamson, O. (1979), "Transaction Cost Economics: The Governance of Contractual Relations," *Journal of Law and Economics* (October).

Discussion of the Watkins Paper

Herbert G. Grubel

This paper contains a fine record of the National Oil Policy (NOP), which I hope will remain a unique episode in Canadian history. It shows how private economic rents can be dissipated, even when they are generated by exogenous and unpredictable events. The government simply expropriated them, allegedly to serve the public interest, but quite obviously also to provide benefits to interest groups with voting power. Of equal importance is that Watkins's analysis illustrates that rules and regulations once in effect will endure often for a long time, even after the disappearance of circumstances that originally led to their creation.

I have nothing to add to or criticize in Watkins's historic account and analysis of the changing regulation of the petroleum industry. Instead, I wish to raise several points and questions concerning the turbulent years that began with the National Energy Policy.

Economic Analysis and the National Energy Policy

The reading of the sordid history of energy regulation in Canada reminds me of the importance that "scientific" economic analysis played at its conception. Large-scale economic computer models were used to estimate the present value of the derivable rent from existing petroleum reserves and these estimates were extremely large. The benefits from the expropriation of this rent were therefore considered to be so big that they warranted disregarding all traditional concerns with the morality of breaking contracts and blatantly taxing one region of the country in favour of the rest.

While the computer simulations generated many useful insights and may have contributed to a marginally more rational design of policies, they were deficient in one fundamental respect. They accepted as given and apparently without further research the estimates of future energy prices. These estimates were based on the consideration of price elasticities of demand and supply during periods of small price changes. Even cursory examination of history and economic principles should have suggested that these estimates could not be relevant under the then prevailing circumstances. Every previous attempt to create a cartel has failed ultimately because price elasticities of demand and supply become larger the longer the applicable time period and the larger are the price changes.

In this case, economists should have been reluctant to entertain, no less base policy simulations on, the forecast that a cartel driven rise in a relative price can reach 30 times over 15 years. There were plenty of dissenting views on this matter. They could and should have been used to create doubts about the true size of the rents.

What Did the NEP Do to Expected Investor Returns?

The historic account reminded me of an analysis that I had presented with a colleague in 1975 when the National Energy Policy was introduced.[1] We argued that investments in energy, exploration, and production are made with certain expectations about future returns. These expectations can be represented by a normal distribution with a mean equal to the risk-adjusted rate of return needed to attract capital into the activity. The auctioning of exploration rights may be expected to create this outcome for the industry on average.

Prices for energy diverge regularly from the level considered most likely, that is, a price that generates the mean of the expected returns. At times, energy prices are such that actual returns are above the mean, and at other times they are below. The industry is satisfied to play the game by the normal rules of investment in free market economies and operates expecting the variation of returns around the mean.

We postulated in our paper that the National Energy Policy fundamentally and forever changed these traditional rules of the game. The policy amounted to saying to investors in the natural resource industry in Canada that "You take the risk of investing in a world of uncertain prices and accept wide variations in returns, including large losses. However, if the outcome provides you with very large profits, we take them from you." An analogy to the change in policy suggests itself. The government for a long time has sold lottery tickets (auctioned off drilling rights) with the understanding that there is a wide distribution of gains and losses. A few large prizes are included to make the lottery program attractive. However, when the large prizes were drawn, the government decided that they were in conflict with some other of its policy objectives and it made the winners give them back.

In our paper we argued that such a change in the rules of the game must inevitably result in different investor attitudes in the future. In particular, we would expect exploration to be undertaken only if the expected return was raised sufficiently to compensate investors for the absence of the upper tail of the distribution. I wonder whether there is any empirical evidence that investors

---

1 Grubel, Herbert and Sam Sydneysmith (1975), "The Taxation of Windfall Gains on Stocks of Natural Resources," *Canadian Public Policy* 1, 1 (Winter).

in Canadian oil exploration have indeed changed their behaviour in the way we had postulated?

Importance of Alternative Energy Sources

Oil and gas encounter competitive substitutes in various forms including electricity generated by atomic power, coal, water, and even exotic methods like windmills. During the last few years, there have been wide swings in the popularity of these alternative sources of energy. The use of atomic power, once considered too hazardous, looks much better after the discovery that coal-fired stations contribute to acid rain and the greenhouse effect. I expect that within a few years the supply of water-generated electricity will increase sharply in western Canada as investors take advantage of new legislation that enables them to build dams privately and sell them to the regional electricity monopolies. In British Columbia, where Energy Minister Jack Davis has passed legislation encouraging co-generation, several such projects are on the drawing boards.

I wonder what influence these developments in alternative energy producing industries have had and are likely to have on the markets and regulation of the oil and natural gas industries discussed by Watkins.

Are Core-contracts Needed?

I was intrigued by the new form of regulation which requires that exports of gas are permitted only after long-term contracts have been signed by suppliers; this is done in order to assure security of supply of domestic users over periods as long as 15 years. I wonder whether such regulation is needed.

Long-term contracts are very much in the interest of both users and producers of natural gas. They reduce substantially the risks from uncertain prices, demand, and supply. For any given set of expectations, there should be one price (or set of prices through time), at which both parties would be better off than under a spot-price regime alone. If my ideas are correct, the regulation requiring the security of Canadian supplies is not needed, it interferes unnecessarily with freedom, its administration wastes resources, and the length of the required contracts does not permit the kind of flexibility private markets are likely to generate.

What is the historic evidence on this matter? Were there such long-term contracts before the energy crisis of the 1970s? Has the natural gas industry accepted the regulation without complaints? If the answers to these questions are yes, then core-contracts may be nothing but an exercise in public relations. If they are, they should be exposed as such.

Discussion of the Watkins Paper

Michael Walker

The Fraser Institute has just released a book, edited by Campbell Watkins and titled *Petro-Markets: Probing the Economics of Continental Energy*. It is a marvellous book, which includes among its authors some of the top energy economists in North America. I always refer to Watkins as Canada's leading energy economist, so you wouldn't expect me to be highly critical of the paper. We have also previously produced two other books at the Fraser Institute on energy, which Watkins and I edited. The first one is called *Oil in the Seventies* and the other, *Reaction: The National Energy Program*. There is significance in the fact that Watkins edited *Petro-Markets* by himself because I no longer felt competent in energy economics. Of course, this is not going to stop me from making some remarks about Watkins's paper.

The paper is a wonderful summary, as only Watkins can produce, of where we are in energy regulation. I have no comment about that, but I would like to comment on why we observed the evolution of petroleum regulation that we did. In this perspective, the National Energy Program was simply the crowning absurdity in a long line of ill informed energy market intrusions. What I want to do is track five threads that led to the kind of energy regulation that we ended up with. Some of these threads are the kind we have already discussed, but others relate more to the ideology of regulation which primarily concerns me.

I think the first and most important development that led to the National Energy Program and the associated intrusion of the federal government into the energy sector was the calculation and observation in Ottawa and elsewhere of the huge rents, as they were then called, and windfall profits that were being generated in the petroleum sector and their regional distribution. (I am reminded of Herbert Stein's definition of a "windfall" profit as being a profit that was earned by somebody who had more foresight than you and who had invested in a product whose price had subsequently gone up.) There was, both at the technical advisory level and at the political level, a great deal of concern about the windfall profits being earned in the energy industry and a consideration in some vague way whether this was socially desirable. We all remember scientific papers of the day making projections of the rents and whether this was really something the government should be permitting. Against this background, the National Energy Program was not a purely technical exercise. There were very strong priors in Ottawa about what was an acceptable distribution of petroleum income and most people at the time shared the views of people like Ian Stewart and Ed Clark. The NEP was popular for that reason.

A second thread, to which I was exposed after I left Ottawa, was a concern by Canadian nationalists about ownership. Canadian nationalists in the oil industry, in particular Bob Blair of Nova, worried and pondered about the impact the cash flows that were being generated in the oil sector would have on the ownership structure of the industry. (The point being that foreigners who had invested in the Canadian energy industry in the past now had all these windfalls to further increase their concentration.) You can see from Blair's point of view why he was worried about that, but of course it had to be cloaked in a broader way before it could be a background for policy. Incidentally, the history of that as I understand it is that American companies in particular had been given a leg up by the fact that under U.S. law the capital they invested in Canada was pre-tax dollars because they could deduct drilling expenses and other investment costs from other income, whereas Canadians couldn't. So as a consequence, much of the early capital that was used for development and drilling was American capital. Now, when large increases in prices occurred, the cash flow from the industry was being used to secure, as Bob Blair would have put it, "a foreign grip on the industry." So that was another thread that was leading up to the formation of the National Energy Program. It was not true that everybody in the oil patch disagreed with the National Energy Program.

Third, Ottawa observed that very little energy development activity was occurring on federal lands. An important aspect of this stemmed from the fact that there would be no need to worry about energy sharing agreements or energy revenue sharing agreements about oil that was discovered on federal lands, but unfortunately, no development was occurring.

Fourth, there was a firmly held view that the provision of energy was something that should not be left entirely up to the private sector, that there should be a strong public sector presence to act as a window on the industry. While there were a lot of discussions of a very technical nature about the dangers of allowing prices to overshoot and undershoot, in the minds of the people who were ultimately going to write the policy there was a very definite notion that this was not something that could be left to the private sector. It had nothing at all to do with technical considerations. It was something that was just too important to be left to the private sector because of the ideological preferences that were then popular in Ottawa.

Fifth, many of the ministers and the senior deputy ministers at the time were firmly convinced that the market economy was dead and that it was in need of replacement by the more reliable hand of the public sector. I think it is important to remember that the National Energy Program had a precursor in a general economic policy discussion paper called "The Way Ahead," which was meant to map out what was going to happen to Canada after the Wage & Price Control Program. The document, "The Way Ahead," was, although consultatory, essentially an unreconstructed Keynesian view of Canada's future.

In sum, I think the National Energy Program and the regulations that Watkins has been discussing were first intended to implement the abandonment of the price system as a resource allocator in the energy sector in line with the redistributionist "Way Ahead" thinking, indeed in line with thinking that was increasingly prevalent in Ottawa. Secondly, they were intended to tax all of the windfall cash flows that were generated in the energy sector. The work of John Helliwell had enormous impact in convincing people that the cash flows being generated were essentially rents that could be taxed away with no effect whatsoever on the structure of the industry and on the functioning of the industry. Third, having done that, they would reflow some of this, via federally controlled programs, to those companies who could pass the maple leaf test. This was to accomplish two things: to assuage the people like Bob Blair and their concerns about foreign ownership; and, of course, to target those programs on the federal lands in the form of PIP grants so that the federal government would get the development on federal lands they wanted. Fourth, impose a huge regulatory tax on Alberta via made-in-Canada oil prices to offset what was then popularly felt to be a regional imbalance. As you know, the estimates Brian Scarfe and Campbell Watkins have made suggest that tax was in the order of fifty billion dollars, depending on what you think might otherwise have happened. And fifth, establish a strong planning and public ownership presence in the energy industry in areas ranging from exploration for petroleum to the installation of insulation.

The energy regulation regime that we adopted in the decade following the oil embargo of 1973 was as much a conceptual error as it was a political boondoggle. The weight of intellectual opinion behind such policies as the NEP was firmly rooted in a mistrust of the market process, a conviction about an appropriate regional and income class distribution of petroleum "rents," and a xenophobic concern about the ownership of the petroleum industry. In the end, deregulation is as much about expunging the ghosts of these faulty premises as it is a matter of technical adjustment.

Chapter 8

Regulatory Change in Canadian Agriculture

R.M.A. Loyns, Colin A. Carter, and Eric E. Peters

The Government of Canada has been a strong supporter of freer trade in agriculture and has been active in the Uruguay Round of the General Agreement on Tariffs and Trade (GATT) negotiations while working towards the goal of liberalized agricultural trade. Canada was also instrumental in the formation of the Cairns group of so-called "free traders," which has been particularly critical of farm policies in the European Common Market (EC) and the U.S. It has been argued by some that the Canadian position at GATT and with the Cairns group is a classic case of the "pot calling the kettle black." At the present time, Canadian farmers are as heavily regulated and protected as their counterparts in the U.S. and possibly the EC. Throughout the 1980s, Canadian farmers have received anywhere from $4 to $6 billion per year in the form of direct and indirect subsidies and protection. As a percent of the value of production, Canadian farm policy transfers averaged 31 percent from 1982 to 1986. This exceeded the U.S. level of 25 percent and was almost as high as the 35 percent in the EC over the same five-year period.[1] Between 1986 and 1989, Canadian support exceeded 40 percent and may have reached 50 percent in grains. We will argue in this paper that these latter levels of support are transitory and not true measures of regulation in Canadian agriculture. However, support to the industry is substantial, and deregulation may not be the most suitable term to use to describe regulatory change that has occurred over this decade, although events occurring in late 1989 may indicate policy change toward less regulation in years ahead.

---

1   United States Department of Agriculture (1988).

We have two objectives for this paper. First, we provide a discussion of major aspects of Canadian farm regulation and highlight recent (1980s) policy initiatives. An effort is made to delineate where Canada currently stands in the "deregulation" process. Second, we attempt to empirically determine whether or not regulation over time and across commodities can be explained by the Peltzman and Becker theory of efficient redistribution. For the latter purpose, we examine events since the mid-1960s.

Results and conclusions presented in this paper are somewhat tentative because we recognize further work is required on both objectives. The complexity of Canadian agriculture, measured in terms of commodities, regions, programs, and federal-provincial relationships, requires more than a few pages to describe what has occurred in the regulatory process. We have focused on federal initiatives because of time and space constraints. As a result, provincial initiatives are underrepresented here.

Framework for the Paper

What is and what is not regulation is debatable. For example, at the conference for which the first draft of this paper was prepared, a variety of views were expressed. Kurt Klein preferred the definition used by the bureaucracy, i.e., that regulation is equivalent (only) to "regulations" (by government). Stanbury opted for the Institute for Research on Public Policy (IRPP) definition, "imposition of rules by government, backed by the use of penalties that are intended specifically to modify the economic behaviour of individuals and firms in the private sector."[2] The authors of this paper adopt the "redistributionist" camp for a definition of regulation, which includes any intervention through policy and fiscal instruments that produces aspects of a non-market solution. For example, Posner said of "economic regulation" that "properly defined, the term refers to taxes and subsidies of all sorts as well as the explicit legislative and administrative controls over rates, entry, and other facets of economic activity."[3] Stigler's earlier paper appears to agree with this definition when he referred to taxation on whisky and playing cards as "acquired regulation."[4] Despite the apparent simplicity of the "redistributionist" interpretation of the term regulation, and its derivatives "reregulation" and "deregulation," the alternative models pose insurmountable difficulties for accurately describing regulatory change in Canadian agriculture. The need for a broad definition of regulation may not be unique to agriculture, but the scope and complexity of

---

2   Priest, et al. (1981), p. 5.
3   Posner (1974), p. 335.
4   Stigler (1971), p. 3.

both the agriculture industry and government intervention in agriculture certainly favours the broad definition of regulation for agriculture.

In what follows, we consider income transfers, subsidies, restrictive and facilitative regulation, and taxation to be encompassed by the definition of regulation. *Reregulation* is considered as any significant change in regulation that alters the original regulated situation. *Deregulation* is a form of reregulation that is anticipated to produce a more market-oriented situation.

There is a rather compelling pragmatic reason for viewing regulation in Canadian agriculture in this way. Regulations,[5] subsidies, deficiency payment schemes, shared (subsidized) insurance and stabilization programs, and taxation are all very much part of the structure and performance of the Canadian agricultural industry. To limit discussion to "regulations" issues would be to miss a great deal of agricultural policy and its structure; it would also be to ignore the major changes that have occurred in the 1980s. To treat regulatory change in a constrained manner appears to us to be a rather incomplete and inadequate analysis so long as policies are good substitutes for one another.

The 1970s in Canada were undoubtedly the most active legislative and regulatory period in Canada's agricultural history—at a time when farm population continued to decline and dropped below 5 percent of the total population. In the early years of the 1970s, direct agricultural expenditures by the federal government in real terms increased at an average annual rate of almost 10 percent,[6] and was augmented in many provinces by similar rates of increase. During the 1970s, stabilization programs and supply management were the primary policy instruments for effecting transfers. Some provinces (Quebec, maritime provinces, and Saskatchewan) opened their treasuries to use the agriculture and food sector as tools of economic development. Federal initiatives during the 1970s were consistent with an alleged but undocumented policy decision by the Liberal government, reached sometime after the 1968 election, to ensure that Canadian farmers captured a larger share of the national pie.

---

5   Several examples of private regulations exist in Canadian Agriculture. For example, the Winnipeg Commodity Exchange, although "regulated" by the Grain Futures Act, is really regulated by the rules determined within the organization itself. The extensive changes implemented within this Exchange in the past two years, in response to trading irregularities, were primarily, if not solely, sourced in the Exchange, not the Grain Futures Act. Similarly, although all marketing boards exist under umbrella legislation, much of what boards really do have are significant aspects of private, self-interest regulation because of the wide latitude of powers granted. Contracting implies some element of choice. Anyone dealing through the Winnipeg Commodity Exchange or with marketing boards knows that there is no choice vis-à-vis operating rules, except to be in or out.

6   Forbes, Hughes, and Warley (1982), p. 13.

Beginning the discussion on the first objective at 1980 is, therefore, interesting for the following reasons:

- it coincides with completion of the Regulation Reference work undertaken by and for the Economic Council;
- the 1980s have been an extremely stress filled decade for much of the Canadian farm sector (Russian grain embargo, 1980; high interest rates, 1980-82; drought, 1985 and 1988; U.S./Canadian countervails, 1987-89; U.S./EC grain price wars 1986-88; and free trade discussions, 1986-88); and
- fiscal restraint has been a major stated policy objective of federal and provincial governments.

We were tempted to strive for completeness by analyzing the entire food industry, i.e., agriculture and food. There have been major changes implemented in competition policy that impact on agriculture and could be reviewed. We were also tempted to include some discussion of the consumer's role in regulatory change during this period, including the apparent decline of the Consumers' Association of Canada (CAC) and the federal department of Consumer and Corporate Affairs (CCAC) as significant players in policy formulation. In addition, there are several important changes that appear to be evolving and will likely be reflected in regulatory change in the next few years. Finally, a major regulatory change occurred in 1991 in the form of the Goods and Services Tax; the effect on agriculture may be significant. Despite these additional areas that could be analyzed, this paper is restricted to the traditional notion of farmers and the markets in which they participate, and most of the examples are at the federal level. Even within this restricted context, it is necessary to limit our analysis to the major regulatory changes that have occurred and are influencing the agriculture sector now.

Review of ECC Recommendations on Regulatory Reform

A logical starting point for this paper are the results of the studies done for or by the Economic Council of Canada (ECC) since 1979. The major results from those studies are reported below.[7] The final report of the Economic Council on the Regulation Reference (1981) did not get much beyond analysis of, and recommendations on, marketing boards. There were eleven recommendations presented, most of them relating to supply management boards. The essence of the recommendations were to:

---

7 There are several of these reports: Economic Council of Canada (1981); Forbes, Hughes, and Warley (1982); and a set of reports on the grain crisis of the mid-1980s, including Economic Council of Canada (1989).

- improve board accountability and appeal mechanisms; governments should exercise caution in extending powers or scope of boards;
- make quotas less restrictive and use production expansion to limit quota value;
- replace quantitative controls with tariffs; and
- review dairy policy.

The report by Forbes et al. (1982) included marketing boards and managed to examine other important areas of regulation:

- their recommendations on marketing boards were similar to and consistent with the above;
- they recognized the "second generation effects" of supply management; and
- they recommended greater accountability and no new supply management programs.

In the area of western grains, this report:

- promoted expanded production capacity, improved market signals to ensure the required product mix, and improved incentives;
- identified the need to upgrade handling, storage, and transportation;
- identified the need to co-ordinate grains transportation policy with overall transportation policy; and
- argued for improved stabilization programs and a reduction in distortions among regions and commodities.

For livestock, it was argued that:

- the Agriculture Stabilization Act (ASA) required restructuring to achieve increased effectiveness;
- reductions were required in regional production distortions; and
- support was given (reluctantly) for the then proposed Beef Import Law.

In general, this report promoted a "food industry, developmental" approach to policy formulation and regulation in agriculture, i.e., to view agriculture as a component of the food industry, to promote productivity enhancement and market development, and to reduce structural rigidities. A 1984 ECC Working Paper prepared by Loyns and Carter[8] reinforced these recommendations as they related to the grains industry in western Canada.

Regulatory Change in Canadian Agriculture in the 1980s: The Global View

This section summarizes the major regulatory changes disaggregated by commodity group. Before providing this detail it is useful to overview the changes

---

8   Loyns and Carter (1984).

within agriculture during the 1980s. We provide two versions of this overview. First, Alston, et al. (1989) [9] provide a program classification for the U.S. related to form and level of intervention, i.e., output or input subsidy, border control, etc. We have modified this classification system to reflect Canadian programs[10] and we summarize the results in table 1. Second, table 2 provides a financial measure of government intervention in the form of Producer Subsidy Equivalents (PSE) as measured by USDA for the five years 1982-86. Producer Subsidy Equivalents are a trade related measure of intervention. They are only one of several possible measures of intervention and they are used here despite their limitations because they are readily available.

In general, the major areas of increased intervention are in the ad hoc output subsidies on grains (table 1) for which PSEs have more than doubled (table 2).[11] Dairy has the largest relative PSE terms and is an ongoing program; the increase from 1982-86 exceeded $1 billion (table 2). Among the important commodities, cattle and hogs have the smallest PSEs. As later analysis will show, regulatory change in the supply managed areas has been limited but with very differential impacts on PSEs. As measured by PSE, dairy shows increased support while poultry shows a large decline. Interestingly, in 1986 and 1987, because of high poultry (chicken) prices in the U.S., the supply management program for chicken in Canada (which did not change) shows an almost zero PSE and is actually negative for part of that period. This difference between dairy and poultry illustrates the care that must be exercised in using PSEs to analyze regulatory changes. The difference in these measures is primarily due to changed price relatives between Canada and the U.S. rather than any change in actual regulation or support to the dairy and poultry sectors in Canada.

Overall, both measures indicate increased intervention (from a PSE of 20.4 in 1982 to 43.1 in 1986), and a significant increase in subsidization (steady growth which likely continued into 1987 and 1988). On the other hand, higher grain prices, formula based reductions in the Western Grain Stabilization Program (WGSP) payouts, a cap on the Western Grain Transportation Act (WGTA) payout, and the reduced likelihood of drought payments for the 1989

---

9   Alston, et al. (1989).

10 We make a distinction between "legislated" and "ad hoc" output subsidies. Although the terminology is imprecise and better descriptive terms may exist, the notion is that a major portion (and much of the growth) in agriculture intervention in the 1980s has been reactive, after-the-fact, and outside of the mandate of the existing programs, i.e., much of the Canadian intervention has been unplanned or ad hoc. This is a very important characteristic of Canadian agricultural policy in the 1980s.

11 These data understate the amount of support to grains because there were large payments in 1987 and 1988 under WGSP, SGP, and Drought Relief. Some experts suggest grains PSE's topped 50 percent but these data are not yet publicly available.

(continued on next page)

Table 1

Illustrative Regulatory Change by Program Category
1980-89

	Economic Function	Commodity Illustrations	Level[a]	Activity[b]
1.	Supply Management	Dairy, Poultry, Eggs	F/P	0
2.	Supply Management	Hatching Eggs, Tobacco	F/P	+
3.	Output Subsidy			
	- legislated	CWB Initials,	F	+
		ASA, Provincial "Stabilization"	F,P	+
		Transportation	F	-
		SGP,[c] Drought Relief	F	++
	- ad hoc	Saskatchewan Crops, Alberta Crow Offset	P	+
4.	Import Controls			
	- tariffs	where applicable with U.S.	F	-
	- countervail	corn	F	+
	- quantitative	supply management	F	+
		grains	F	-
	- other	health, safety, label	F	-
5.	Stabilization	provincial	P	+
		Tripartite (cattle, hogs, sheep and lambs, sugar beets, honey)	F/P	+

Table 1 (continued)

	Economic Function	Commodity Illustrations	Level[a]	Activity[b]
6.	Government Purchase	CIDA	F	0
		Disposal under ASA	F	+
7.	Input Subsidy	Credit/Foreclosures	F,P	+
		Crop Insurance	F/P	+
		Taxation	F	-
		Tax Rebates	P	0
8.	Infrastructure	Research	F,P	-
		Extension	P	?
		Market Development/Promo	F,P	?
		Trade Offices	F	?
		Faciliative	F	-

[a] F, P, F/P denote federal, provincial, or federal-provincial intervention, respectively.

[b] Activity indicates increase (+), decrease (-), or no change (0) in regulation or subsidization during the 1980s, and (?) indicates the direction of change is unknown.

[c] Special Grains Programs.

Source: Compiled by the authors.

Table 2

Producer Subsidy Equivalents (PSE) for Thirteen Commodities

1982-86

Item	1982	1983	1984	1985	1986	1982-86 Average
1. Policy Transfers (mil CDN$) by Commodity:						
Wheat	681.7	1007.9	1413.9	1452.3	2575.3	1426.3
Barley	171.3	214.5	280.3	563.0	890.5	423.9
Oats	7.2	13.5	22.2	32.7	50.3	25.2
Rye	9.7	15.7	19.1	14.3	37.9	19.3
Corn	54.6	66.5	79.3	84.6	129.8	83.0
Rapeseed	105.0	172.5	317.1	418.8	609.7	324.6
Flaxseed	15.8	31.2	41.2	69.0	119.5	55.3
Pork	135.8	121.9	206.7	176.4	200.2	168.2
Poultry	234.0	195.7	152.0	107.8	35.3	145.0
Sugar Beets	3.0	9.4	15.6	17.1	15.4	12.1
Dairy	1720.2	2193.1	2470.1	2705.6	2796.6	2377.1
Soybeans	16.2	29.0	22.6	37.2	70.6	35.1
Beef and Veal	271.4	269.9	308.9	353.7	320.3	304.8

(continued on next page)

Table 2 (continued)

Item	1982	1983	1984	1985	1986	1982-86 Average
2. PSE (percent) by Commodity:						
Wheat	14.1	20.2	34.2	33.9	49.9	30.4
Barley	12.7	16.5	22.1	42.1	65.8	32.1
Oats	2.4	5.3	8.5	12.6	23.2	9.7
Rye	12.0	16.7	29.0	25.9	63.6	27.2
Corn	7.5	7.0	8.0	9.8	21.4	10.0
Rapeseed	17.5	16.9	24.3	36.8	54.1	29.9
Flaxseed	8.5	20.9	17.6	25.5	48.5	25.5
Pork	8.6	8.8	12.6	11.7	11.8	10.7
Poultry	29.6	24.9	16.7	11.8	3.7	16.7
Sugar	7.1	20.4	40.1	105.3	48.7	34.6
Dairy	56.9	69.6	75.4	83.5	81.3	73.7
Soybeans	7.5	10.8	8.5	13.8	25.4	13.5
Beef and Veal	8.8	9.1	10.0	11.2	10.5	9.9
Total policy transfers (mil CDN$)	3425.9	4340.8	5349.0	6032.5	7851.6	5399.9
Value to producers (mil CDN$)	16795.1	17386.3	17482.6	17315.2	18214.0	17438.6
13-commodity PSE (percent)	20.4	25.0	30.6	34.8	43.1	31.0

Source: United States Department of Agriculture, (1988). OECD estimates of PSE provide different numbers but similar relationships.

or 1990 crops imply significant reductions in Canadian PSEs over the next two or three years. The potential exists for significant crop insurance payouts since program benefits (and premiums) have been increased but this is entirely a question of participation rates in these programs and weather conditions. These aggregate measures reveal some other important characteristics of the changes. However, the conditions underlying the changes are probably more important than their increase, particularly when much of the increase is due to what might be considered extraordinary circumstances in the grain market (international price warring in 1986-88, and widespread and severe drought conditions in 1988). The next section attempts to analyze some of these changes in more detail by looking at major program changes by commodity groups.

Regulatory Change by Commodity Group

Table 3 summarizes the major regulatory changes that have occurred (or are about to occur) in several commodity programs. As indicated earlier, these changes are selective and far from exhaustive although they represent the important changes that could be documented for the period 1980-89. "Nature of Change" is intended to reflect the criteria for increased regulation, reregulation, or deregulation as defined above but sometimes the designation is oversimplified. "Causal factors" are an effort at identifying why the changes occurred. "Economic effects" and "Initiators" are also generalizations of effects and source of change.

Livestock

There have been two major changes in regulation of livestock in Canada in the 1980s. In 1982 a Meat Import Act was implemented limiting imports of fresh, chilled, and frozen forms of beef and veal into Canada according to a formula. To meet GATT commitments, there is a minimum global amount established. The act also establishes a Meat Import Advisory Committee made up of representatives of the meat industry and consumers. The act, in effect, amends the Export and Import Permits Act. The Meat Import Act certainly represents increased regulation (quantitative border control).

Tripartite Red Meat Stabilization, in the process of implementation at present, is the important regulatory change in the Canadian livestock industry. On the one hand, since producers and the signatory provinces undertake financial commitments under the Tripartite plan, and it is accompanied by more rules and bureaucracy, the change could be termed increased regulation. On the other hand, the plan should reduce provincial top-loading and production distortions and improve production and market planning by producers. Consequently, the plan has important aspects of a change in the direction of more

Table 3

Major Agricultural Regulatory Changes
Canada, 1980-89

Commodity Group/Program	Nature of Change	Causal Factors	Economic Effects	Initiators
I Livestock				
1. Red Meat Stabilization (cattle, calves, sheep and lambs, hogs)	Reregulation (phase in, 1988-91)	Fiscal implications provincial conflicts	Extended commodity coverage; producer participation; F/P co-operation; increased market orientation	Federal and prov'l governments; producer groups
2. Meat Import Act (beef and veal)	Increased regulation (February 1982)	Imbalance in trade conditions in meat	Limited protection against increases in imports; establishes Meat Import Advisory Committee	Producer groups

(continued on next page)

Table 3 (continued)

Commodity Group/Program	Nature of Change	Causal Factors	Economic Effects	Initiators
II Grains				
1. Plant Breeders' Rights (1990)	Increased regulation	R&D initiative; declining gov't research exp.	Inconclusive; (patent-like protection for plant breeding); higher cost of administration and policing seed use	Private sector breeders; Agriculture Canada (Research Branch)
2. Western Grains Stabilization Program (WGSP) (1985)	Deregulation	Huge positive fund balance	Reduce producer cost; faster payout	WGSP Farmer groups
WGSP (1988)	Increased regulation	Huge fund deficit	Increased producer cost (two times); debt write down ($700 m); easier entry	Gov't of Canada
3. Corn Countervail (1987-)	Increased regulation	U.S. corn subsidies	Higher feed gain prices within Canada (magnitude inconclusive)	Canadian corn producers

(continued on next page)

Table 3 (continued)

Commodity Group/Program	Nature of Change	Causal Factors	Economic Effects	Initiators
4. Deficiency Payments				
- Russian Embargo (1980)	Increased regulation	International diplomacy	Reduction in sales to Russia established @ $81 m	Gov't of Canada
- Special Grains Program (1986, 1987 crops)	Increased regulation	International price wars	Deficiency payment 1986 crop ($1 b) 1987 crop ($1.1 b)	Producer groups Provincial gov'ts
5. Two-price Wheat (1988)	Deregulation	Processor pressure; Ontario wheat production; free trade	Remove discriminatory wheat prices (market distortion); decrease producers returns	Millers Gov't of Canada
6. Canola Cash Call Market (1988)	Increased regulation (or reregulation)	Future/cash price distortions; existing regulation	Eliminate producer cars; reduce payoff to individual producer marketing efforts; reduce competition in rapeseed marketing; create new market distortions	Elevator Cos.

(continued on next page)

Table 3 (continued)

Commodity Group/Program	Nature of Change	Causal Factors	Economic Effects	Initiators
7. Remove Quotas on Off-board Grains	Deregulation	Unknown	Reduced quota constraints on rye, canola, flax; move toward more open market	Unknown
8. Removal of Oats from CWB	Deregulation	Private sector/producer pressure; changing oat market	Private trade handling and sale of oats; possibly market expansion	Private sector; some producers; CWB indifference to oats
9. Crop Insurance Revisions (1989, 1990)	Reregulation	To make crop insurance more attractive as a risk management tool	Increased level and scope of coverage; increased participation	Federal and provincial governments
10. Increased Handling Tariffs Under CGC (1989)	Application of tariff setting authority	Held down for several years; volume year anticipated	Significant increases in handling, elevation and cleaning charges	Elevator Cos.

(continued on next page)

Table 3 (continued)

Commodity Group/Program	Nature of Change	Causal Factors	Economic Effects	Initiators
11. Western Grain Transportation Act (WGTA) (1983)	Deregulation	Inadequate grain transport system	Increased capability to move grain; higher freight rates; declining relative subsidy	Railways; Gov't of Canada; some producer groups
12. Prairie Grain Advance Payments (1989)	Eliminate subsidy (deregulation)	Unknown (fiscal implications)	Remove interest free loans on farm stored grain	Gov't of Canada
III. Credit				
1. Farm Loans Interest Rebate Act (1981-84)	Increased regulation	Farm debt problems high interest rates	5 percentage point interest rebate on selected loans under Special Farm Financial Assistance Program	Farm groups
2. Farm Debt Review Act	Increased regulation	Farm debt problems	Debt review process through formal Review Boards	Farm Groups

(continued on next page)

Table 3 (continued)

Commodity Group/Program	Nature of Change	Causal Factors	Economic Effects	Initiators
IV **Supply Management** Amended to include tobacco	Increased regulation	Drop in tobacco demand	Extends SS management provisions to tobacco	Tobacco growers
Regulation on hatching eggs	Increased regulation	Imports of hatching eggs	Regulate hatching egg sector consistent with broiler regulation	Poultry producers; Hatcheries
V <u>Taxation</u> - $500,000 Cap Gain Exemption	Deregulation	Cap gains/transfers issues	Some increase in flexibility in disposing of farm assets	Farm groups
-Reduction in Machinery Tax Credits	Deregulation	Fiscal implications	Increase cost of new machinery	Gov't of Canada
-Part-time Farming	Deregulation	Equity issues	Some additional flexibility for part-time and beginning farmers	Farm groups

(continued on next page)

Table 3 (continued)

Commodity Group/Program	Nature of Change	Causal Factors	Economic Effects	Initiators
- Trend to Accrual vs. Cash Accounting	Increased regulation	Unknown	Less flexibility in accounting	Gov't of Canada
VI Free Trade (1988)	Deregulation	Varied	SS management exc. processing product and global quota; breweries exc. some increased import competition	Business sector, Limited producer groups; some provincial gov'ts
VII The Environment Tightened pesticide regulations	Increased regulation	Environmental quality; food and personal safety	Deregistration; longer test periods; banned chemicals	Public pressure, some farm groups

Source: complied by authors from various sources, including a draft copy of *Acts and Regulations*, prepared by Agriculture Canada (1988) market-orientation; in the context of problems of cattle and hog stabilization since the mid-1970s, economists likely would place greater weight on these (positive) characteristics of the change. This is one instance in which we have difficulty characterizing the nature of the regulatory change—we have tentatively called it reregulation.

Grains

As listed in table 3, there have been many changes in intervention and regulation in the grains economy. In terms of the changes listed, there are about an equal number of increases and decreases in regulation. Changes in crop insurance programs (1989 and 1990) are in some respects similar to Tripartite Red Meat Stabilization changes; consequently, we have identified these as reregulation. The changes to the Western Grains Stabilization Program do not categorize easily, partly because in 1985 there was a significant aspect of deregulation offset by (more) opposite changes in 1988, and partly because the federal government is making the WGSP (and crop insurance) more attractive to producers to attempt to avoid any further special grains programs like those used from 1986 to 1988 in response to severe price or drought problems. This approach is consistent with ECC recommendations in *Handling the Risks*, and overall, would imply a more market-oriented form of agricultural policy than the programs that were replaced.

Most of the big ticket items in table 3 (Special Grains Programs, Drought Relief, and Canadian Grain Commission tariffs) are all forms of increased regulation. On the other hand, the WGTA represents an important example of deregulation that retains a large element of government-to-farmer transfer (approximately $700 million in current terms). Many of the examples of deregulation (two-price wheat, oats, and off-board quotas) are significant within their own context but they do not have much financial significance.

An interesting effect of most of these changes (measured in 1989) is that they imply either reduced support or increased costs to farmers over time, and reduced absolute or relative government expenditures. As of 1989, WGTA, WGSP, the tariff increases under the CGC, termination to two-price wheat, and most importantly, termination of the special grain programs imply greatly reduced transfers to grain producers. Superficially, one may be inclined to refer to all of these as deregulation but that is only a partial description of the changes.

We have not attempted to impute value to these reductions in transfers to grain producers, but measured in terms of PSEs (table 2) we expect that by the 1990 crop, the PSEs for grains will fall significantly; PSEs for the early 1990s could approach those of the early 1980s. This would reduce the overall PSE in Canada to the 30 percent level or below (depending on relative prices and intervention elsewhere). It is important to note that much of the reduction in support to grain producers is mandated within existing programs. A similar mandated reduction in government expenditure may accompany the Tripartite program in red meats. This point is often overlooked when Canada's record is assessed according to the support levels experienced in 1986, 1987, or 1988. In effect, Canada already has in place the instruments that will allow it to meet some of the international commitments associated with its role in the Cairns Group. It is important in this context to make the distinction between ongoing and ad hoc programs as we did in table 1. Assessed this way, Canada's kettle may not be so black even though the pot has been drained.

There is another characteristic that we suggest is associated with many of the changes in grain. The locus of influence in decision making in grains policy appears to be shifting away from farm groups. If we have correctly attributed the sources of change, a common thread is that program cost (government) and the agribusiness sector (elevator companies, the railways, and millers) have become major players in determining the direction of grains policy. Some might argue that this is simply a return to earlier times, but we submit that it was not characteristic of the era of the 1970s. It is our view that this change is occurring, and that it explains some of the shift in policy initiatives of the 1970s from a larger share of the national pie going to farmers via regulatory means, to an era when a process characterized as "deregulatory" will reduce transfer to at least some farmers. The policy review process initiated in 1989 and described at the end of this section also appears to be similarly motivated.

Transportation

The most significant change in transportation of agriculture products was the passage of the Western Grain Transportation Act in November 1983. The purpose of the WGTA was to replace the Crow Rates on grain transportation with rates that would be compensatory to the railways in order to remove the capacity constraints that had developed over almost three decades. Rates of grain transportation are now annually determined and adjusted to maintain incentive for the railways to move grain. Prior to the WGTA, rates were fixed, railways had limited incentives to move grain, and the rolling stock was depleted except for provincial, federal, and Canadian Wheat Board purchases of cars. Also, throughout the 1970s and 1980s the federal government made large subsidy payments to the railways.

The magnitude of the "Crow benefit" was established as $695 million in 1981-82 dollars, and was applicable to the 1981-82 volume of movements of 31.5 mmt. The subsidy is currently paid to the railways, but this method of payment is under review with support appearing to grow for a change to "pay the producer." The WGTA also extended the commodity coverage for which the subsidy could apply, thereby reducing some of the inter-commodity distortions that existed under the Crow Rates. The most important extension was to canola oil. The most important effects of the WGTA are summarized as:

1. Increased transportation charges paid by farmers for grain shipments, but which are still far less than the variable cost of moving the grain because of the federal subsidy. Example (for 901-925 mile shipping distances paid by the shipper):
    *   the Crow Rate was $4.85/mt;
    *   on August 1, 1988, the rate was $7.27/mt; and
    *   on August 1, 1989, the rate was $9.71/mt.

2. The railways now have some increased flexibility in pricing and increased incentives to move grain:
    *   they are paid the estimated cost of moving grain; consequently, there are incentives to provide rolling stock;
    *   the transportation constraint to grain movement is manageable; and
    *   volume rates are beginning to appear at large shipping points.

3. The "method of payment," i.e., payment of the subsidy to the railways or to the producers, or some other method of allocating the Crow benefit remains to be settled. This regulatory issue is partly a question of political-administrative complexity, and partly an issue of regional (East versus West) and commodity (grains versus livestock) readjustment to changed grain price relationships.

This process of regulatory change occurred over a period of at least ten years and involved several public inquiries in various forms. The primary motivation for change can be summarized as the intolerable lack of transportation capacity created by the existence of the Crow Rates. It is unclear at this stage that the WGTA is in any significant manner meshed with, or otherwise integrated into, other aspects of national transportation policy.

Credit

The farm debt problems that characterized the early 1980s produced some regulatory efforts at the federal level: an interest rebate program, debt review and debt moratoria, and increased funding for the federal credit agency. Most provinces developed counterpart activities in some form. Obviously, these changes indicate increased regulation, probably most accurately identified as "ad hoc." The overall effect is difficult to assess. One is tempted to conclude that in a stable credit environment the significance of the changes will be limited, but some of the changes somewhat complicate the life of lending agencies; on balance, the changes are not likely to significantly alter the entry or exit rates of farmers, nor to alter the basic structure of the industry.

Supply Management

This sector of Canadian agriculture has had the least regulatory change of any, despite the attention and prescriptions offered by economists and others. In response to the drop in tobacco demand, and capital losses occurring on tobacco land (quota), the National Farm Products Marketing Agencies Act (NFPMAA) was amended in 1986 to include tobacco. As well, orders were issued to exercise supply management on hatching eggs. Consequently, our conclusion is "increased regulation." We suggest that these boards have not modified their operation in line with improving overall economic efficiency or in terms of increased accountability. The boards themselves were excluded from the FTA, although processed product will now be allowed greater access to Canada and this could alter board operations in the longer term.

Taxation

There have been several major changes in tax policy affecting farmers. At present there is a $500 thousand capital gains exemption for farms—we suggest that this is deregulation because it provides some improved flexibility to farmers and farm corporations in transferring or disposing of capital assets. The reduction, then removal, of the machinery tax credit will increase costs to farmers in a taxable income position by removing a form of implicit subsidy. There appears to be some increased flexibility occurring in the treatment of "part-time" farmers which suggests decreased regulation. Finally, there is a trend occurring that may become law whereby farmers must use accrual accounting instead of having the choice of cash or accrual. Based strictly on the consideration of limitations-of-choice, this would be considered increased regulation.

Free Trade

The Canadian-U.S. Free Trade Agreement (FTA) reduces regulation in agriculture, with the exception of the supply managed commodities and breweries which received exemptions. The impact of these changes is beyond the scope of this paper, but the regional impacts of the FTA could be significant. As well, the FTA has already helped generate significant modifications in some programs (two-price wheat) and could in others (supply management). It is our view that the FTA was as much sourced in the motivation to remove structural rigidities within Canada as it was to enhance trading conditions between Canada and the U.S. As such, it would have to be viewed as a significant element of deregulation, the significance of which will take years to document.

The Environment

The major regulatory change we have been able to identify in this area is the tightening of registration requirements, deregistration of some products, and banning of other chemicals. This result may be the most interesting (lack of) change in the entire sector given the public awareness and apparent concern over environmental issues. Despite the perceived groundswell of support for environmental protection, and experiences with soil drifting, hazardous wastes, animal waste odours, and pollution of ground water, there has been remarkably little activity at the federal level to alter these circumstances. Provincial initiatives appear as well to be extremely limited.

Federal Policy Initiatives in 1989

We conclude that not much deregulation has occurred in Canadian agriculture during the 1980s, and there are several instances of large increases in support to the industry. The federal paper addressed by Mr. A.C. Campbell at the Deregulation Conference, *Regulatory Reform: Making it Work*, confirms this conclusion. The references to agriculture and food regulation in that paper are minimal and all references are to "regulations" except for identification of a "study of the operations of supply management."[12]

Consequently, the regulatory environment within agriculture during the 1980s has been very different than in most of the other areas covered by the conference. Subsequent to the September Deregulation Conference, however, a policy process has been initiated by the federal government that could produce significant changes in the years ahead. A brief summary of that process is presented here because it indicates an effort to achieve some degree of deregulation in Canadian agriculture.

In November 1989 a White Paper, *Growing Together: A Vision for Canada's Agri-Food Industry*,[13] was released and circulated widely. On December 12 and 13, 1989, a Policy Conference was held in Ottawa, hosted by the Federal Minister of Agriculture, the Minister of State for Grains and Oilseeds, and the Minister of State for Agriculture. The White Paper and the Policy Conference were the first steps in a policy process that is intended to effect significant changes in agriculture policy. The paper emphasizes four basic market-oriented objectives:

1. to achieve a more market-oriented industry, from production to consumption;
2. to develop a more internationally competitive industry;

---

12 Government of Canada (1988), pp. 51-56.
13 Agriculture Canada (1989).

3.   to reduce interprovincial trade barriers; and

4.   to "decouple" programs and provide market neutral safety nets.

The next step in the process is the establishment of task forces to present recommendations for action. In the case of safety nets, the government has a tight deadline (late 1990) for implementation. This process, even if it is only partially successful, is likely to produce more significant examples of deregulation than we have observed to date. But it is unlikely that anything close to the experience of communications, airlines, or petroleum deregulation will be observed in agriculture. This is because the industry structure is very different (size and number of firms and nature of demand); interest group pressures are extremely diverse; the mix of regulation is extremely varied, complex, and overlapping; and the international market in which most Canadian exports must compete is heavily subsidized.

Consequently, we anticipate that deregulation in Canadian agriculture will be incremental, some of it disjointed, with a redirection of public funds and through increased sharing of costs by farmers and the provinces. In the foreseeable future, returning federal support to the general level of about $2.0 billion annually (half of recent levels), achieving some increased free trade among provinces, and reducing provincial treasury competition would be an ambitious achievement regarding deregulation in this industry. Supply management programs will be altered modestly in the next few years, probably in the direction of some flexibility in pricing, some reallocation of quota between regions, and some form of safety net on the income side, but these changes will occur in response to competition of processed product from the U.S. rather than domestic restructuring directly. Our view is that major, or comprehensive, deregulation in any absolute sense within Canadian agriculture in the next decade is unlikely to occur.

Theory of Efficient Redistribution

Beginning at this point and throughout the rest of this paper we use aspects of public choice theory to analyze some of the forces contributing to the regulatory changes identified above. Although the theory used in these sections has been tested on U.S. data,[14] this represents its first application to Canadian agricultural policy. The results appear promising, but we are continuing the analysis because this first effort unavoidably will contain some weaknesses.

---

14 Gardner (1987), pp. 290-310. His original paper was published as "Efficient Redistribution Through Commodity Markets," *American Journal of Agricultural Economics* 65 (May 1983), pp. 225-34.

The theory of efficient income redistribution, developed by Peltzman[15] and Becker,[16] treats the political process as a clearing house, which trades off political pressures among interest groups. These models have been used to explain why some sectors receive protection and others do not and they have been formulated to explain protection (or lack thereof) among domestic sectors or across international boundaries.

The Peltzman/Becker/Gardner framework explains policy as being the outcome of interest groups using the government (as a clearing house) to either maximize net gains or minimize net losses resulting from income transfers. Government policies subsidize some groups and tax others in the redistribution process. This political "game" is zero-sum in influence and negative-sum in taxes and subsidies (due to deadweight costs). This model can be expressed as follows:

$$-I_{ti}(T) = n_iF_i(R_{ti}) = n_jG_j(R_{sj}) = I_{sj}(T)$$

where $i = 1,...,q$ and $j=1, ..., v-q$. I_{ti} is the influence function of the ith taxed group and I_{sj} is the influence function of the jth subsidized group. R_{ti} is a vector of taxes paid by the n_i members (n_i is the size of the ith group) and F_i determines the deadweight losses associated with taxes. Similarly, R_{sj} is the vector of subsidies to the n_j members and G_j represents the deadweight loss of the subsidy.

Becker's comparative static results give the following results:

> ...pressure tends to be greater by more efficient groups, by subsidized groups with smaller deadweight costs, by taxed groups with larger deadweight costs, by groups with intrinsically more influence, and by subsidized groups whose benefits are financed by a small tax on many persons.[17]

Applying the Becker framework sheds light on two questions—the choice of policy instrument and the level of protection. Theoretically, these factors will be a function of commodity characteristics. If we consider just two interest groups (e.g., farmers gain and consumers lose) it can be shown (see Miller, 1989 or Gardner, 1983) that there are two factors at work that make the net farmer gain less than the total consumer cost. These two factors are: (a) deadweight costs associated with the price distortion (G_j in the above equation), and (b) the collection costs of taxes used to pay for the policy (F_i in the equation). Determinants of the levels of G_j and F_i include the type of policy selected, the amount of intervention, and the elasticities of supply and demand.

---

15 Peltzman (1976), pp. 211-40.

16 Becker (1983), pp. 371-400.

17 Ibid., pp. 390-91.

With two interest groups the choice of policy becomes quite straightforward. Farmers desire a higher price and their only concern is the ratio of net gains to total costs at the margin. As explained by Miller (1989), they

> will want the government to choose a policy that gives them a high level of net gains per dollar spent on political pressure, while minimizing the marginal costs of policy and therefore the incentive to spend on political pressure by the other group (p. 13).

The Peltzman-Becker model of government intervention can be depicted as in figure 1. Assume two interest groups, farmers and consumers, and a single policy variable that redistributes income from consumers to farmers. The surplus transformation curve (STC) in figure 1 traces out efficient combinations of producer surplus (PS) and consumer surplus (CS) that are attainable from varying the amount of government intervention. The shape of the STC depends on the underlying commodity characteristics.[18] The STC can also be represented as the cost of redistribution because its slope equals dPS/dCS. The demand for redistribution determines the final redistribution point on the STC, such as point A in figure 1. The competitive equilibrium is at point CE, where the slope is equal to -1.0. To the left of CE the slope of STC<1, which means a dollar given up by consumers transfers less than $1 to producers.

Figure 1
Peltzman-Becker Model of Efficient Redistribution

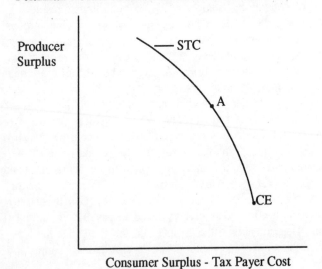

Consumer Surplus - Tax Payer Cost

---

18   See Gardner (1983) for a thorough discussion of the relationship between underlying commodity market characteristics and the positioning and shape of the surplus transformation curve.

In his 1983 paper, Gardner suggested that the theory of efficient redistribution has two general applications in agricultural policy, one positive and one normative. The positive application relates to whether or not policies over time and across commodities can be explained by the theory of efficient redistribution. Alternatively, the normative application deals with the ranking of prospective income redistribution programs. In his 1987 paper, Gardner employed the positive application to study U.S. farm programs over the 1912-1980 period. A similar approach was followed by Miller on international agricultural programs. Gardner and Miller consider only two interest groups, consumers and producers, and they test the predictions of the Peltzman-Becker model. Gardner aims to explain differences in the levels of protection for 17 U.S. farm commodities over 69 years. Miller analyzes protection levels in an international cross-section of 34 countries and ten different commodities. Gardner combined his cross-sectional and time series data and regressed the level of protection on 14 "explanatory" variables. He obtained reasonably good regression results and was able to conclude that (a) greater deadweight losses per dollar transferred reduces intervention, (b) there is an "optimal" interest group size, and (c) import competing goods receive more protection than export goods, *ceteris paribus*. Unlike Gardner, Miller also considered cases where farmers are taxed, rather than subsidized. He regressed the level of protection on ten "explanatory" variables. Like Gardner, Miller concludes that his results are consistent with the Peltzman-Becker model of income redistribution, but his statistical results were not as good as Gardner's.

An Application to Canadian Agriculture

In this study we use the Peltzman-Becker model to explain the generally different levels of supports for cattle, hogs, chickens, eggs, dairy, wheat, corn, rapeseed, and sugar beets over the 1965-87 period. The above commodities are representative of the major Canadian agricultural policy tools varying from supply management to stabilization programs to no (or very little) intervention, and with substantial geographic distribution of commodities. The 1965-87 period is reflected because it spans the era of active intervention in Canadian agriculture.

The Model

In general, the theory of efficient distribution indicates that the level of support afforded a commodity will depend upon:
- the characteristics of the commodity in terms of production and consumption response;
- societal values as they relate to producer groups;

- characteristics of groups which attempt to extract benefits from public support; and
- conditions of organization which influence ability to effectively lobby.

Reflecting these factors into hypotheses for quantitative analysis is not a precise process. We have adapted the Gardner model to our commodity and data requirements and propose a linear model to estimate by a combination of cross-section (nine commodities) and time series (annual, 1965-87) data:

$$Y_{it} = \beta_0 + \sum_j \beta_j X_{jit} + U_{it}$$

where $i = 1, 2, ..., 9$ commodities; $t = 1965, ..., 1987$; and $j =$ independent variables. Following are the specific variables used, the rationale for their inclusion, and the anticipated direction of association. It is noted that the data requirements for this analysis are significant. First, the data set is large, but more importantly, there are many instances for which the required data are not reported, necessitating building estimates or using proxies.

The dependent variable, Y_{it}, is the ratio of domestic price to world price for each commodity i, measured implicitly by ratios of value to volume series. In most cases, these series were obtained from estimates of farm cash receipts. The impact of government intervention or support to a commodity should show up in higher ratios of domestic to world prices. This measure has the advantage that it should reflect the impact of federal and provincial intervention, even though most of our previous discussion has understated provincial intervention, and it reflects non-price transfers. A weakness of this variable is that it will not allow lagged or non-price effects to be picked up, but this is one of the limitations of applying a simple economic model to complex social analysis. The variable is indexed to a 1981 base to achieve comparability among commodities.

The first two explanatory variables, X_{1t} and X_{2t}, represent the share of the commodity (relative to domestic production) imported and exported, respectively. Following Gardner, the expectation is that both variables will be positively correlated with the price ratio. Highly competitive imports displace domestic production and local producers can be expected to lobby for import restrictions or other regulatory measures to keep the domestic market to themselves. The obvious Canadian cases are the supply managed commodities. For exported commodities, Gardner attributes the positive association to the fact that the burden of protection is shifted to importing countries. In addition, there has been stiff competition in export markets in recent years, and to keep or gain market shares, most exporters chose to subsidize their exports (a good example is the export restitution of the EEC, the Export Enhancement Program, and the U.S. public law, PL 480). Countries like Canada and Argentina chose to compensate their farmers for loss of export revenue either by direct cash payments or a decrease/termination of export taxes. Finally, agriculture is a major foreign exchange earner for Canada; most countries intervene to protect foreign exchange earnings. Therefore, we should expect the model to reflect these situations through positive coefficients.

The next variable, X_{3t}, is the ratio of farm income to non-farm income. It is introduced to reflect societal values that perceive farm incomes to be low relative to incomes of other Canadians, resulting in the use of intervention to achieve an improved measure of "parity." As a result, the expectation is that the relationship between this measure of income and the dependent variable will be negative, i.e., the lower farm incomes are in relation to non-farm incomes, the greater the support. The variable is lagged one year to allow response time by government. Estimates of net farm income by commodity do not exist. Consequently, proxies were calculated by adjusting per capita cash receipts by the ratio of farm prices received (output price index) to farm prices paid (input price index) for each commodity. This proxy appeared to track market conditions in each commodity reasonably well even though the levels were questionable, and should reflect changes in farm income by commodity. Non-farm income was measured by per capita disposable income.

Related to the parity argument is the potential that differences exist among political parties in their inclination to support agriculture. We said earlier that the Liberals were understood to have made a policy decision in the earlier 1970s to transfer a greater share of the national pie to farmers. The present government appears to prefer more market solutions, whereas the Liberals were more interventionist. The variable X_9 is a dummy variable which picks up the effect of the Liberal majority governments between 1974 and 1984, ignoring the short period of Conservative government in 1979. The expectation is that support would be greater, other things constant, during that era.

Factors affecting organizational ability and effectiveness of lobbying are reflected in variables: X_{4t}, a Herfindahl index of regional concentration of production; X_{6t}, a measure of the growth of production over time; and X_{7t}, a measure of the variability in production by region. One hypothesis (Gardner, 1987) is that the more concentrated the production, the cheaper the lobbying effort, and the greater the support, i.e., X_4 and Y should be positively related. A counter-hypothesis is that the more dispersed the production, the broader the base for legislative support, implying a negative relationship. In Canada there is a natural tendency for commodities to be concentrated: grains on the Prairies, specifically Saskatchewan; livestock, dairy, and poultry in the East; cattle in

Alberta; and fruits and vegetables in British Columbia, Ontario, and the Maritimes.

Rapid production growth should mean greater organizational problems which would imply a negative relationship between X_6 and the dependent variable. An alternative hypothesis is that rapid growth creates the perception of oversupply and the need for controls or support. In this case the relationship may be positive. The arguments on geographic variability of production, X_7, are similar but opposite to those for output growth; the greater the variability, the more incentive to organize, and subsequently, we expect a positive relationship between X_7 and the dependent variable.

The effect of middlemen on producers' support, measured by a proxy for the marketing margin X_5, may also be argued to be positive or negative.[19] The variable is measured as the ratio of retail price of the product to farm price for the commodity. On the one hand, the larger the margin, the smaller the farm share and the less sensitive commodity prices would be to raising farmers prices, implying a positive relationship. On the other hand, if farmers and middlemen are viewed as adversaries in the market (as we suggest they have been, reinforced by intervention based upon the countervailing power thesis), there should be a negative relationship between size of the marketing margin and producer support. We favour this latter hypothesis and suggest the sensitivity issue is measured with the elasticity of demand variable.

Supply and demand elasticities representing product characteristics are incorporated into a single variable (X_8) in the model. As shown by Gardner (1983), relatively efficient redistribution is achieved when either the supply or demand elasticity is near zero, and the other elasticity is large. X_8 is, therefore, the absolute difference between supply elasticity and (the absolute value of) demand elasticity. Begging the question of the appropriate transfer instrument depending on which elasticity is greatest, the relationship between X_8 and the dependent variable should be positive. Estimates of demand and supply for each commodity (appendix 2) were taken from a recent USDA report, "A Database for Trade Liberalization Studies."

A time trend variable (X_{10}) is included in the model specification under the assumption that the constant term in the equation is increasing steadily over time, i.e., general increase in support over time.

Whether the model yields acceptable results depends partly on the specification of the stochastic term. One consideration in this particular case might be to base the characterization of the error term with reference as to how support

---

19 Gardner (1987) and Miller (1989) ignore middlemen, or implicitly lump them with consumers. Alston et al. (1989) argue that the market should be considered at least three dimensionally, including middlemen. We share this view.

levels for commodities are determined. It is a common practice in Canadian agricultural policy to set support levels based on averages and moving averages of production income or price levels. For example, ASA stabilization programs relate the support price to moving averages of preceding years prices, or to production costs. The Western Grains Stabilization Program makes payouts in relation to a moving average of the previous three years prairie-wide cash flow. Under supply management programs, provincial production was originally allocated on the basis of historical production, and dairy prices are determined by a process of indexation.

These methods of supporting agriculture would suggest specifying the error term as a moving average process. However, examination of when either ASA or WGSA payments were made for each commodity suggests that the frequency of payments may not have been sufficient to significantly affect returns in this way. During the 1965-87 period, cattle producers received ASA payments (exclusive of tripartite payments) in six years, mainly in the mid-1970s. Payments to the poultry and egg sectors occurred mostly in the middle 1960s. Wheat producers received ASA and WGSA benefits only in the late 1970s and 1980s. The canola sector did not realize any ASA benefits at all in the period of this study. Dairy payments are the only ASA payments that are both significant and continuous.

As a result, alternative specification for the error term which is appropriate to analysis of pooled time series and cross-sectional data is used. Three assumptions are made regarding the variance of the error term. First, due to the cross-sectional components in the model, we must allow for heteroscedasticity. Second, the covariances of the error terms for commodities i and j are not equal to zero, i.e., support levels for different commodities may be interdependent. Third, due to the time series component, the error term follows an autoregressive process within each commodity unit i. Therefore the cross-sectionally correlated and time-wise autoregressive model is estimated using a two-step process assuming the existence of contemporaneous correlation between cross-sections and first-order autoregressive error term.[20]

Results and Conclusions

The results of the estimated model are reported in table 4. In general, the results were stable in response to variation in the specification of variables and to variable inclusion or exclusion. Also, except for the share of exports variable (X_2), the standard error of the regression coefficients was low enough in relation to the magnitude of the coefficients to give t-values significant at the 95 percent level of confidence. We anticipate that the problem of a negative sign on the

---

20 Kmenta (1971), pp. 512-14.

import variable, X_1, and the non-significant estimate of the export variable may result from identification problems. For example, the negative results on the import variable may only reflect the fact that a major policy instrument utilized in the 1970s and 1980s (supply management) has produced lower imports and higher domestic prices. Similarly, our higher internal prices have reduced exports. If these are the reasons for the failure to generate the expected sign on the variables, they suggest the need for a more complete (multi-equation) specification of the intervention process. Similarly, the sign on the supply/demand elasticity variable is wrong and indicates the need for further analysis.

The lagged ratio of farm to non-farm income (X_3) and the measure of the magnitude of the marketing margin (X_5) generate the expected sign and are statistically significant. The concentration of production index (X_4) and the rate of output growth (X_6) are consistent with Gardner's (1987) results. The coefficient on variable X_7 supports the hypothesis that production variability by region motivates organization and support, and is also consistent with Gardner's results. The majority Liberal government variable (X_9) produced a negative parameter coefficient that was not consistent with a priori expectations. As expected, the coefficient for the time trend variable (X_{10}) had a positive sign. In other words, the massive injections into agriculture in the 1980s override those made in the 1970s.

The elasticity coefficients associated with the estimates provide a measure of the relative importance of each variable. Assessed this way, the marketing margin variable has the greatest impact at -0.643, production concentration is next at 0.112, and the time trend is third at 0.154. The shares imported and exported which are insignificant or have the wrong sign are relatively unimportant measured this way. These latter results (time trend and seemingly unacceptable results on imports and exports) suggest the need for further analysis. The results on demand and supply elasticity provide a relatively weak (-0.032) relationship with the level of support. This area, as indicated above, also requires more refined analysis.

In general, this preliminary investigation of support for Canadian agricultural products agrees with Gardner's analysis in the U.S. and appears to support the public choice arguments on support to Canadian agriculture. At this stage of the analysis, the evidence does not appear to support the efficient redistribution hypothesis. Further analysis will be undertaken to pursue these results with more refined modelling and more complete specification of some variables such as demand and supply elasticities. Obviously, particular policy instruments should be investigated, and there appears to be latitude for comparing and contrasting policy approaches in the two countries.

Table 4

Factors Explaining Producer Support in Canadian Agriculture 1965-87
(Dependent Variable: Ratio of Canadian to World Price)

Variable	Coefficient	T-value	Elasticity[a]
Intercept	1.348	21.12	—
1. Share Imported	-0.554	-3.39	-0.045
2. Share Exported	0.0313	0.84	0.007
3. Ratio of Lagged FI to NFI	-0.298	-2.89	-0.046
4. Production Concentration Index	0.270	2.87	0.112
5. Retail/Farm Price Ratio	-0.485	-15.42	-0.643
6. Rate of Output Growth	-0.001	-2.98	-0.003
7. Production Variability Index	4.504	9.00	0.026
8. Elasticity of Demand Minus Elasticity of Supply (Absolute Difference)	-0.128	-2.38	-0.032
9. Party in Power	-0.061	-2.25	-0.032
10. Time Trend	0.012	3.82	0.154
Minimum Sq. Error (MSE)	0.9692		
Degrees of Freedom	196		

[a]Measured at the mean of the variables.

Source: Estimated.

Appendix 1
Farm Cash Receipts
(Including WGSA, ASA, and Dairy Subsidy Payments)
1983-87

Commodity	1983	1984	1985	1986	1987
			millions of dollars		
Cattle	3,146.5	3,229.7	3,257.3	3,237.9	3,387.8
Wheat	5,091.1	5,170.2	3,946.8	3,848.8	4,031.9
Corn	598.5	572.9	585.5	399.5	412.9
Eggs	485.3	510.4	503.2	494.2	492.6
Poultry	766.6	896.6	911.1	977.7	1,014.2
Hogs	1,718.6	1,882.3	1,889.8	2,143.8	2,127.2
Dairy Products	2,718.4	2,977.1	3,000.4	3,088.9	3,165.9
Canola	736.5	940.9	899.6	675.2	722.0
Sugar Beets	45.4	37.2	22.5	20.2	23.1

Source: Canada Grains Council, *Statistical Handbook*, 1989; *Annual Reports of the Agriculture Stabilization Board*, 1964-75 to 1986-87.

Appendix 2
Selected Commodity Characteristics: Averages 1965-1987

Commodity	Share Imported	Share Exported	Ratio of Farm to Non-farm Income	Herfindhal Concentration Index	% Change in Output	Variability Index	Supply Elasticity	Demand Elasticity
Cattle	0.085	0.10	0.264	0.26	-0.50	0.003	0.50	-0.80
Canola	0.0006	0.61	0.045	0.38	3.31	0.005	0.85	-0.77
Corn	0.204	0.044	0.023	0.79	6.10	0.009	0.23	-0.21
Dairy	0.138	0.009	0.216	0.29	-0.74	0.001	0.45	-0.18
Eggs	0.025	0.022	0.044	0.22	0.55	0.0004	0.50	-0.30
Hogs	0.046	0.114	0.150	0.24	2.35	0.008	1.50	-0.86
Poultry	0.040	0.005	0.071	0.24	2.24	0.001	0.70	-0.67
Sugar	0.035	0.055	0.005	0.43	-5.71	0.035	0.30	-0.24
Wheat	0.000	0.757	0.320	0.44	-1.36	0.003	0.50	-0.20

References

Agriculture Canada (1988), *Acts and Regulations*

————— (1989), *Growing Together: A Vision for Canada's Agri-Food Industry* (Ottawa, November).

Alston, Julian M., Colin A. Carter and Michael K. Wohlgenant (1989), *Who Determines Farm Program? Agribusiness and the Making of Farm Policy*, International Agricultural Trade Research Consortium, Working Paper (January).

Becker, Gary S. (1983), "A Theory of Competition Among Pressure Groups for Political Influence," *Quarterly Journal of Economics* 98 (August), pp. 371-400.

Carter, Colin, Alex F. McCalla, and Andrew Schmitz (1989), *Canada and International Grain Markets: Trends, Policies, and Prospects*, Economic Council of Canada.

Economic Council of Canada (1981), *Reforming Regulation* (Ottawa: ECC).

————— (1988), *Handling the Risks: A Report on the Prairie's Grain Economy.*

Forbes, J.D., R.D. Hughes, T.K. Warley (1982), *Economic Intervention and Regulation in Canadian Agriculture*, (Ottawa: Economic Council of Canada).

Furtan, W.H., T.Y. Bayri, R. Gray, and G.G. Storey (1989), *Grain Market Outlook*, Economic Council of Canada.

Gardner, Bruce (1983), "Efficient Redistribution Through Commodity Markets," *American Journal of Agricultural Economics* (May), 65, pp. 225-34.

————— (1987), "Causes of U.S. Farm Commodity Programs," *Journal of Political Economy* 95, pp. 290-310.

Government of Canada (1988), *Regulatory Reform: Making it Work*, (Ottawa: Office of Privatization and Regulatory Affairs, September).

Kmenta, J. (1971), *Elements of Econometrics* (New York: Macmillan).

Loyns, R.M.A. and Colin A. Carter (1984), *Grains in Western Canadian Economic Development to 1990*, Discussion Paper No. 272, (Ottawa: Economic Council of Canada).

Miller, T.C. (1989), *Explaining Agricultural Price Policies Using a Model of Competition Between Interest Groups*, (Waco, Texas: Baylor University), mimeo.

Peltzman, Sam (1976), "Toward a More General Theory of Regulation," *Journal of Law and Economics* 19 (August), pp. 211-40.

Posner, Richard A. (1974), "Theories of Economic Regulation," *Bell Journal of Economic and Management Science* 5, pp. 335-58.

Priest, Margot, et al. (1981), "On the Definition of Economic Regulation," in W.T. Stanbury (ed.) *Government Regulation: Growth, Scope, Process* (Montreal: The Institute for Research on Public Policy).

Stigler, George J. (1971), "The Theory of Economic Regulation," *Bell Journal of Economic and Management Science* 2, pp. 3-21.

United States Department of Agriculture (1988), *Estimates of Producer and Consumer Subsidy Equivalents*, Government Intervention in Agriculture, 1982-86, ERS, ATAD (Washington, D.C.: USDA, April).

DATA SOURCES

Agriculture Canada. *Canada's Trade in Agricultural Products*, various issues.

————. *Annual Report of the Agricultural Stabilization Board*, 1986/87.

————. *Handbook of Food Expenditures, Prices and Consumption*, 1988.

Bank of Canada. *Quarterly Review*.

Canada Grains Council. *Canada Grains Industry Statistical Handbook*, 1975, 1976, 1982, 1989.

Commodity Research Bureau. *Commodity Year Book*, New York, 1988.

International Wheat Council. *World Wheat Statistics*, 1986.

Statistics Canada. *Agricultural Economics Statistics*, Catalogue No. 21-603.

————. *Consumer Prices and Price Indexes*, Catalogue No. 61-010.

————. *Dairy Market Review*, Catalogue No. 23-001.

————. *Farm Input Price Index*, Catalogue No. 62-004.

————. *Field Crop Reporting Series*, Catalogue No. 22-002.

————. *Handbook of Agricultural Statistics*, Catalogue No. 21-516.

————. *Historical Statistics of Canada*, Catalogue No. CS11-516E.

————. *National Income and Expenditure Accounts*, Catalogue No. 13-201.

————. *Prices and Price Indexes*, Catalogue No. 62-002.

————. *Production and Stocks of Eggs and Poultry*, Catalogue No. 23-003.

————. *Trade of Canada and Summary of External Trade*, Catalogue No. 65-203.

Sullivan, J., J. Wainio and V. Roningen. "A Database for Trade Liberalization Studies," USDA, ERS, March 1989.

USDA. *World Agriculture Situation and Outlook Report*, ERS, 1965-1988.

————. *Foreign Agricultural Trade of the United States (FATUS)*, May 1975.

Discussion of the Loyns, Carter, and Peters Paper

K.K. Klein

Carter, Loyns, and Peters presented a comprehensive analysis of government involvement in Canadian agriculture. This involvement has been substantial in recent years. Although a large part of government interference in Canadian agriculture during the past few years has been one of reaction rather than proaction, no one can deny that the federal and provincial governments in Canada have been vigorous in their protection of the agricultural sector. Indeed, as the authors have noted, the total subsidization level of Canadian agriculture in recent years, on a percentage basis, is of the same magnitude as that in the U.S. or in the highly protectionist European Community.

The focus of the authors' attention was clearly on subsidies and regulations in Canadian agriculture that distort trade. This was made obvious by their extensive use of producer subsidy equivalents to measure the impacts of government programs in agriculture. As useful as this approach is for comparing subsidization levels among countries, it can lead to some confusion in the analysis and interpretation of regulations. For example, everyone agrees that the poultry industry is highly regulated in Canada. I can't raise chickens and start selling eggs without first purchasing a supply quota. Yet the authors state that "in 1986 and 1987...the supply management program for chicken in Canada...shows an almost zero PSE and is actually negative for part of that period."

The difficulty is in the authors' definition of regulation. They have combined subsidies and regulations to present an overall picture of government involvement in Canadian agriculture. However, subsidies and regulations are different concepts and should be discussed separately.

The need to regulate an industry has its basis in micro-economic theory. When market solutions do not lead to desirable outcomes, we say there have been market failures. Three broad classes of government policies can be used to correct the market failures: taxes, subsidies, and regulations. Economists generally prefer the use of taxes or subsidies to deal with market failures; lobby groups and politicians seem to prefer regulations. Taxes and subsidies change the price signals received by producers and consumers, thereby encouraging them to make decisions that differ from what they would make in the absence of the taxes or subsidies. Regulations put outright constraints on the activities of producers or consumers, restricting the freedom of individuals.

It is well known that a market failure occurs in most types of agricultural research. Since revenues that result from agricultural research cannot usually be appropriated, there is insufficient incentive for private companies to invest in this activity. In areas where private companies can appropriate the rewards (e.g., where new chemicals or machine components can be patented and thus protected), there is no good argument for government involvement, except perhaps to regulate the process and keep it orderly. The Government of Canada has provided large and continuing subsidies for agricultural research to correct this market failure. Many economic studies have documented high rates of return to agricultural research that has been performed by public agencies. But should we define this subsidy for research as a regulation in agriculture?

The economic rationale for a regulation is to correct a market failure. The hope is that a regulation will result in improved resource allocation. Many regulations in the agricultural industry clearly improve the overall welfare of Canadians and are well supported by the populace:

- Enforcement of control of noxious weeds ensures that farmers don't impose extra costs on their neighbours by failure to control weeds on their own property.
- Production and marketing of agricultural products are subject to a vast array of health, sanitation, and labelling regulations. These regulations not only limit consumers' exposure to dangerous chemicals, they also provide consumers with knowledge about nutritional content of foods they buy in the grocery store.

Unfortunately, not all regulations on Canadian agriculture provide such clearly recognized benefits. A few examples follow:

- Supply restricting marketing boards for poultry, dairy, and tobacco. These certainly restrict the freedom of entry into the industry. Furthermore, they restrict the freedom of consumers to purchase these commodities from competitive suppliers in other provinces or countries.
- The Canadian Wheat Board is the sole export agency for Canadian wheat and barley. Private farmers or organizations of producers are not permitted to export these commodities from Canada.
- In some provinces of Canada, a number of zoning regulations have been effected. These include restrictions on the location of feedlots, requirements for building permits to alter existing or construction of new buildings, and the Agricultural Land Reserve in British Columbia. The latter restricts future uses of land that is presently agricultural. In some areas of the prairie provinces, growth of Hutterite colonies has been restricted by local regulations.

As is well known by the authors, regulations that restrict the freedom of economic actors can result in large distortions to a market economy. Unfortunately the costs to society of many of these regulations are not easy to tabulate. It is much easier to calculate the level of subsidization.

Some regulations probably don't result in large distortions in the market, but they do affect the freedom of producers. In some cases, these regulations seem almost silly. Currently in Alberta, there is a government regulation that makes compulsory the control of warble flies on cattle. All producers are required to treat their cattle every fall with an insecticide that will kill this pest. For over a decade, less than four percent of all cattle in Alberta have been infested with warbles. Not only does this regulation impose a cost on producers for a pest that causes very little damage at current infestation rates, it requires the application of a dangerous pesticide to animals that will soon be slaughtered for human consumption.

The Canadian Grain Commission licenses varieties of grain before they can be legally grown in Canada. This agency has adopted tough regulations so that the high quality of Canadian grains are not contaminated with varieties of what they consider to be lower quality. The objective of these regulations is noble. Unfortunately, the international demand for the lower quality wheats has grown rapidly in the last two decades, while the international demand for Canadian high quality wheat has stagnated. The lower quality wheats are much higher yielding than are the high quality wheats. Many economic studies have shown considerable potential gains to Canadian agriculture if Canadian farmers were allowed to produce the lower quality wheats.

During the 1960s, I farmed in Saskatchewan. It is hard to believe now, but regulations in my district prevented me from growing mustard as a crop; the rationale for this regulation was that mustard seed would be hard to separate from rapeseed and we were trying to develop a rapeseed market. This regulation existed in spite of the fact that much wild mustard grew in the district, and neighbouring districts permitted the planting of mustard alongside their rapeseed crops. Also, no one in my rural municipality was permitted to have an uncastrated male calf older than six months on his farm unless that calf was pure-bred and duly registered with one of the established breed associations.

Have regulations in Canadian agriculture increased in recent years? Recent inclusion of tobacco and hatching eggs in supply-controlled marketing boards restrict the freedom of producers and do not improve the welfare of Canadians. Also, recent regulations that control the import of meats into Canada and that eliminate producer cars of canola at Vancouver are undesirable restrictions in the marketplace. On the other hand, economic pressures have led to the removal (albeit slow removal) of many regulations in Canadian agriculture:

- at least one variety of lower quality wheat is permitted to be grown on the prairies;
- oats has been removed from the jurisdiction of the Canadian Wheat Board;
- quota constraints on off-board grains have been removed;
- mustard can now be grown on my land in Saskatchewan;
- farmers in my rural municipality can now have bulls of any breed and colour combination (and some of them look very strange, indeed).

In addition, the federal government is in the process of reviewing and simplifying most regulations that cover agriculture.

A final comment: increased regulation is partly the nature of a more complex society that is continually increasing its knowledge base of effects on third parties from decisions made by producers. The objective should not be to remove all regulations from agriculture, but to develop an appropriate set of regulations that improve the welfare of society.

Discussion of the Loyns, Carter, and Peters Paper

George Lermer

I have a couple of points to make about this excellent paper. One, it is amazing that in one industry you can actually get enough data to do cross-sectional studies on the degree of regulation. That in itself speaks volumes about Canadian government policy. The other thing is that, having been involved with marketing board discussions and trying to figure out the American schemes for regulation and subsidy of agriculture for about three or four months, I thought I knew a fair amount about agriculture regulation, but every time I turn to these guys, Loyns, Carter, and Klein, I learn more about it all the time. I didn't know about warble fly regulation.

Despite the authors' encyclopedic knowledge of agricultural regulation, there is a problem with the type of empirical research they present in this paper. I remember trying to do similar work about rent-seeking behaviour using variations in Canadian tariff rates. That work was reported to a Canadian Economics Association meeting. I had doubts about that work then and I continue to worry about it today. The problem is that we are not looking at the *ex ante* decision to regulate or benefit the interest group or even the interest groups' expectations of what they are going to get. What we in fact observe in the numbers are *ex post facto* outcomes that are influenced by a lot of unforseen factors. For example, the 1981 U.S. agricultural legislation was designed with the producers and everyone else involved agreeing on the Denis Meadows-Club of Rome model, to the effect that food and agricultural prices were going to go up forever and the United States economy was going to boom as a result. The object of policy was to encourage production and to assist the producers with storage costs because private speculators were allegedly too short sighted. So the program had all kinds of incentives to produce, produce, produce. By the time the act came into effect in 1981, of course energy and agricultural prices had fallen. As a result, the elements in the act turned around and worked the other way, and the United States ended up with subsidies amounting to 30 or 40 billion dollars a year. These subsidies were not forecast. When the program was put in, it wasn't believed that it was going to subsidize so lavishly. After the fact, Gramm-Rudman and some other program changes attempted to ratchet down the cost to the taxpayer a little, but the fact is no one believed that they were subsidizing to such an extent when they put the program in place and it is difficult to remove an integrated program quickly. It came into effect one day and the world changed the next day. You usually get stuck with it for four or five years. This illustrates the danger of ascribing motives and measuring levels of subsidy from *ex post facto* numbers.

I agree with Klein's comment about the paper mingling tax subsidy and regulations together. As Loyns and Carter explain, government policies that redistribute income to a special interest group are substitutes. Nevertheless, it is useful to separate regulation from other interventionist mechanisms even if we know that they are good substitutes, and that creates a problem for this type of work. There are tax and direct subsidy considerations as well as indirect regulatory mechanisms of conferring a benefit on an interest group. But though they are substitutes from the point of view of the recipient, they also differ in the deadweight losses they impose and the incidence of the "tax" that is used to effect the redistribution.

I have another brief comment to make about an issue I learned from Darrell Kaft, one of Loyns's colleagues, who keeps emphasizing it. What we do in Canada that is different from what others do when it comes to regulating agriculture is that we force the farmers to produce the stuff. They do not get the subsidy unless they produce the product, whereas in some other parts of the world, farmers don't have to produce, but, in fact, are supposed to take the land out of production and there is a price to be paid in the form of reduced production for entering the program. As a result, we have some distortions peculiar to Canada because people produce to gain subsidies in those areas where they are available. We might achieve the same benefit in terms of income transfer if we said to people, here is your income transfer and you don't need to produce anything, do whatever you want with your land.

Are research subsidies a response to market failure, special interest group lobbying, or governmental failure? Since we don't allow plant breeders' rights, I am not sure what comes first, and I have no idea what the optimal amount of protection would be for plant breeders' rights, that is, for patents for plants. But I am told that a lot of Americans love the fact that we don't have plant breeders' rights because they follow very carefully every development of our government stations in Canada and then market those products in the U.S.

I had the same reaction as Klein on the t-values, and I have a number of other comments about the equations because they use elasticity estimates. When I looked at supply elasticity and demand elasticity for agriculture products, I reviewed estimates from at least forty studies. I found estimates that ranged from .05 to 2.0 or higher, so I could pick virtually any number I wanted to use. I don't know what you make of those sorts of things.

My final comment is that you cannot appreciate how complicated these agricultural programs are until you get deeply involved in studying them. For instance, I didn't think the U.S. program was too bad at first glance, because farmers had to take substantial chunks of land out of production in return for getting a benefit. But after checking on this, it turned out that the farmer can get in and out of a program at no cost. If he stays out for a little while, he can come in and start up again at no cost and with any amount of land he had previously devoted to a program crop. This point is the key to understanding the American program. Before realizing this point, I wasn't able to figure out why it is that there was such a large percentage of people out of the program. Clearly, those people who thought prices would go up chose to stay out of the program, despite its immediate benefits, in order to put more land into production. They made that decision knowing that they were free to join the program after a delay of just one crop year when they thought prices would turn around. So there are many nuances in these programs that are difficult to capture in a numerical scale of regulation levels. Another example is that there is a limit on the maximum subsidy that can be paid on any one crop. That would certainly limit production. After phoning around, I found that this provision is ineffective because everyone incorporates their farm, and no single farm is larger than a size that ensures maximum access to the subsidy. The farmer may own as many farms as he or she chooses to own. It is just like deposit insurance with a 60,000 dollar limit per deposit, which allows one to have as many deposits as one likes. So I caution people about the risks of doing this kind of work. Though valuable, it is awfully time consuming and difficult to know how much subsidy there really is, and how much was intended ahead of time as opposed to the actual subsidy after circumstances having changed.

Chapter 9

Rent Control and a Program for Decontrol in Ontario

Lawrence B. Smith

You can't win;
you can't break-even; and
you can't even quit the game.
—Ginsberg's Theorem

It is better to have a horrible ending
than to have horrors without end.
—Matsch's Law

Quoted from A. Block (1979), *Murphy's Law and Other Reasons Why Things Go Wrong* (Los Angeles: Price Stern, Sloan).

Rent controls, in the form of a rent review system, have existed in Ontario since 1975. Although the regulations have undergone numerous changes, the controls continue to jeopardize the viability of the private rental sector and to foster a severe shortage of rental housing. Moreover, as the duration of the controls has increased the economic distortions have intensified, increasing both the need for some form of rent decontrol and simultaneously the political obstacles to it. This paper examines the consequences of rent control and other rent control induced regulations in Ontario, and then develops a program for rent decontrol.

Introduction: A Summary of Rent Controls in Ontario

Rent controls have existed in Ontario since October 1975, when they were introduced as a temporary measure in the midst of an election campaign. During their existence, rent controls have undergone numerous changes, with the most substantive ones occurring in 1986.[1] The basic approach, however, has remained essentially a cost pass-through system with provisions for the elimination of financial and/or economic loss and for the amortization of capital expenditures. Prior to 1986, the system provided for the pass-through of nominal costs, so that net rent was basically fixed in nominal terms; after 1986, the system provided for the pass-through of real (including inflation) costs so that net rent is basically fixed in real terms. When empirical evidence is presented in this paper pertaining to the pre-1986 period, the results and conclusions are also applicable to the current rent control regime.

The central feature of the rent control system in Ontario is that rents may be increased only once in any 12-month period by a percentage not to exceed that set by statute (the statutory increase). The statutory percentage increase was originally set to enable the typical landlord to approximately recover any cost increases. Prior to 1986, if the statutory increase was insufficient to enable a landlord to recover his cost increases, a formal rent review hearing was permitted to determine the permitted rent increase. The statutory increase from July 1975 to October 1977 was 8 percent, from October 1977 to August 1985 was 6 percent, and from August 1985 to December 1986 was 4 percent.

In late 1986 the cost pass-through approach was modified. The statutory increase was tied to inflation by a formula which generated rent increases of 5.2 percent, 4.7 percent, and 4.6 percent for 1987, 1988, and 1989, respectively. The provision for a rent review hearing if the statutory increase was insufficient for a landlord to recover his cost increases was respecified in terms of abnormal cost increases. In a world of steady state inflation, the formula generates a statutory increase equal to the inflation rate if inflation is 6 percent, in excess of the inflation rate if inflation is below 6 percent, and less than the inflation rate if inflation exceeds 6 percent.[2]

---

1   Rent controls were introduced in October 1975 and made retroactive to July 29, 1975. The controls were to self-destruct on July 31, 1977, but prior to this date, they were extended to December 31, 1978. In October 1978 it was announced that controls would be extended, and in June 1979 revised controls became permanent. Controls were tightened in November 1982, and were expanded and considerably revised under Bill 51 which was passed in December 1986 (although the major terms were announced in August 1985).

2   The statutory increase is two-thirds of a three-year moving average of increases in

Initially, all existing rental dwellings in Ontario except government assisted housing were subject to controls, although new dwellings completed after the controls were introduced and previously non-rented dwellings were exempted from controls for five years after they were first rented. In 1979 the exemption for newly constructed dwellings was extended indefinitely and units with rentals in excess of $750 a month were decontrolled. In 1982 controls were reimposed on units with rentals in excess of $750; and in 1986 controls were extended to the previously exempt units constructed after 1975, and to units to be constructed in the future.

In addition to the statutory rent increase (or prior to 1986, to the increase set by rent review on account of cost increases), rent increases are permitted to eliminate financial or economic loss[3] and to reflect capital expenditures. Prior to late 1982, if a landlord experienced a financial loss he could seek a rent review hearing to obtain additional rent increases sufficient to eliminate the loss over a three-year period. In late 1982 rent increases associated with a financial loss were reduced to the lesser of the amount sufficient to eliminate the loss over a five-year period or 5 percent of the gross rent; and in 1986 the financial loss increase was set at 5 percent of the gross rent. In 1986, when controls were imposed on units constructed after 1975, the concept of economic loss was introduced by recognizing rate of return on equity as an economic cost for units constructed after 1975.[4] An additional rent increase was allowed for these units to eliminate the economic loss on a phased-in basis.

Capital expenditures are recognized as a reason for an additional rent increase, the increase allowed being the amount necessary to amortize an expenditure over its expected future life at the rate of interest paid on borrowed funds used to finance the expenditure (or the prime first mortgage rate). After 1986, if capital expenditures were used to obtain an additional rent increase, the permitted statutory rent increase was reduced by 1 percent of the gross rent, which substantially reduced the effective return on capital expenditures.

---

the building operating cost index, plus 2 percent.

3   A financial loss occurred if the sum of the operating costs, financing costs (including normal principal payments on mortgages) up to 85 percent of the acquisition or construction cost, and annual amortization write-offs for capital expenditures exceeded the total revenue.

4   An economic loss occurs when the cash flow rate of return on invested equity and capitalized losses is less than a specified rate (which was set at a three year average of the yield on ten-year and over Government of Canada bonds plus 1 percent). (See Bill 51, section 80.)

The major implications of these regulations are as follows:

Prior to 1987:

- Net rents on units constructed prior to 1976 were essentially fixed in nominal terms, which meant that net and gross rents declined in real terms (unless additional rent increases were justified by financial loss or capital expenditures) because permitted rent increases were only sufficient to allow for the passing through of cash flow cost increases.
- Gross and net rents on units constructed after 1975 were uncontrolled.

After 1986:

- Rents on all units were controlled, but allowed to rise more or less at the inflation rate, assuming inflation was close to 6 percent, which allowed net rent to increase in nominal terms and remain relatively fixed in real terms.
- Rents were allowed to increase more quickly in cases where financial or, for post-1975 units, economic loss existed.
- Post-1975 units were permitted to earn a return on invested capital but pre-1976 units were not.
- Landlords were permitted to set the initial rent on newly constructed and previously unrented units.

Impacts of Rent Controls[5]

Rents and Capital Values for Controlled Units

Rent controls have clearly had a deleterious effect on the rental housing market in Ontario. Studies presented at the Thom Commission in the mid-1980s[6] found that the real monthly gross rent on pre-1976 controlled apartment units fell by approximately 7.5 to 11 percent from the inception of controls in 1975 to the early 1980s,[7] and suggest that this fall was primarily attributable to the controls. Since operating costs were approximately 50 percent of gross revenue in these buildings, and since the majority of these costs are unaffected by controls (vacancy loss, advertising, repair, and maintenance expenditures being the exceptions), the reduction in gross rents translates into approximately a 20 percent reduction in net operating revenue. Table 1 supports these findings. It indicates that monthly real gross rents declined approximately 10 percent, and

5   The analysis in this section draws heavily on Smith (1988a).

6   The Commission of Inquiry into Residential Tenancies in Ontario. See Thom (1987) p. 16.

7   See, for example, Muller (1985), Stanbury and Vertinsky (1985), Steele and Miron (1984), and Slack (1986). See also Fallis and Smith (1985a).

estimated real net monthly rent exclusive of financing costs declined approximately 25 percent from the 1974-75 pre-control period to 1988 for a typical pre-1976 one bedroom apartment in the City of Toronto. After taking into account the depreciation of the rental housing stock during the control period (approximately 1.5 percent on buildings, 0.7 percent on land and buildings) and the estimated rent adjustment necessary to restore equilibrium in the rental market at the time controls were introduced,[8] rent controls have likely reduced rents on pre-1976 units by approximately 5 to 8 percent.

However, table 1 also indicates that the decline in both real monthly gross rent and real monthly net rent was not continuous. Rather, real gross and net rents declined steadily until 1982, but then increased until 1988. The post-1982 increases were a consequence primarily of the high interest rates in the early 1980s which triggered financial losses and financing cost increases, of the statutory increases slightly exceeding inflation between 1982 and 1986, and of the rental formula that generated rent increases slightly higher than inflation after 1986.

The capital value of an income producing property is the discounted value of its expected future income stream, as set out in equation 1.[9] Rent controls significantly depress capital values because they depress the current and expected future rental stream and/or increase the appropriate discount rate by increasing the risk associated with an expected real income stream. In a 1981 study Peter Tomlinson and I (Smith and Tomlinson, 1981) found that the real per unit price of rental apartments in 1980 was 39 percent below the 1975 level, and the capital value of rental apartment units was 29 percent lower than 1975 relative to the Multiple Listing Service (MLS) value of all residential dwellings in Metropolitan Toronto. A rough comparison of apartment prices based on a sample consisting of sales provided by Glenn M. Haskett Realty Inc. is shown in table 2 and indicates that the real per unit price of rental apartments was still 34 percent below the 1975 level in 1986, but that the capital value of apartments rose rapidly in 1987 and 1988. By 1988 real capital values had returned approximately to their pre-rent control levels, (although compared to the MLS index capital values were still 30 percent below 1975 values).

Although the increase in the real price of apartments appears to have coincided with the 1986 alterations in the rent controls legislation, the timing is largely coincidental. The 35 to 40 percent increase in real values is likely a consequence of the sharp (20 to 25 percent) increase in real net rent since 1982,

---

8   See Fallis and Smith (1985b) for a calculation of this adjustment. Arnott (1981) discusses a similar adjustment.

9   For a discussion of the valuation of rental apartments, see Smith (1985).

Table 1
Gross and Net Monthly Rents for a Rent Controlled (pre-1976) One Bedroom Apartment in Toronto

| | Average Monthly Rent | | Estimated Net Monthly Rent[1] | |
| | Current[2] | Constant[3] | Current | Constant |
	$	1975 $	$	1975 $
1988	502	205	208	85
1987	476	202	195	83
1986	457	202	187	83
1985	436	201	176	81
1984	408	195	155	74
1983	387	193	141	70
1982	361	191	130	69
1981	328	192	125	73
1980	310	204	130	85
1979	292	211	120	94
1978	276	218	126	100
1977	256	220	119	102
1976	230	214	107	100
1975[4]	217	217	109	109
1975[5]	238	238	119	119
1974	197	218	99	109

[1]Calculated by assuming operating costs (excluding financing) were 50 percent of pre-control gross rent, and that operating costs increased according to the "household operating cost component" of the CPI after 1974.

[2]Calculated from CMHC Toronto Office "Rental Apartment Vacancy Survey." Data to 1977 were based on vacant units only, while data after 1977 were based on a survey of all private rental dwellings in buildings of six units or more. To compensate for the upward bias in pre-1978 data the series was spliced by assuming an 8 percent rent increase in 1978 and adjusting pre-1978 data accordingly. 1974 rent was an interpolation of survey results for other months. Rent for 1988 supplied by CMHC, Toronto Office.

[3]Based on the consumer price index.

[4]After rent control rent roll back. The rent reflects the rent roll back to July 1975. Since the 1974-80 increase was 57 percent and the allowed 1975-80 increase after adjusting 2.74 percent for average rent review awards was 42.7 percent (see Fallis and Smith, 1984), the effective 1974-75 increase was 10 percent. Hence the 1975 controlled rent was estimated to be $217.

[5]October 1975 rent before rent control and rent roll back.

Equation 1

$$V = \sum_{t=1}^{n} \frac{R_t - E_t - T_t}{(1 + d)^t} + \frac{SV_n - TC_n - ST_n}{(1 + d)^n}$$

where

d	=	$\alpha\, dm + (1 - \alpha)\, de$
V	=	present value of the property
R_t	=	gross revenue in period t
E_t	=	operating expenses, including property taxes, in period t
T_t	=	income taxes in period t
SV_n	=	selling value in period n
TC_n	=	transaction costs associated with selling in period n
ST_n	=	income or capital gains taxes associated with selling in period n
d	=	discount rate
dm	=	cost of mortgage or debt capital
de	=	opportunity cost of (or required after-tax return on) equity capital
α	=	the proportion of debt to debt and equity capital, expressed as a decimal (assuming a constant debt to debt and equity ratio)

most of which occurred prior to the 1986 rent control changes and which were primarily the consequence of the high interest rates in the early 1980s (although the 1986 changes increased awareness of these gains and raised expectations that they would continue) and the sharp decline in interest rates since mid-1984.[10]

Since the residential complex cost index (RCCI) formula used to establish the statutory rent increase is based on a three-year moving average and the current 1989 statutory rent increase is only 4.6 percent compared to a current inflation in Toronto of approximately 6.5 percent, the probability is high that real rents and the real price of apartments will decline somewhat during the next two years.

It will be argued that the reduction in net operating revenue and in capital values substantially impacts on the housing market by accelerating deterioration of the existing stock, encouraging conversion of the stock to alternative

---

10 From mid-1984 to mid-1988 the three-year mortgage rate declined from approximately 14.8 percent to approximately 11 percent.

Table 2
Average Per Unit Price for Rental Apartment
Buildings of 6 or more suites, Toronto

	Current $	Constant 1975 $
1974	15,407	17,062
1975	18,903	18,903
1976	17,617	16,388
1977	16,766	14,441
1978	17,730	12,238
1979	16,901	12,238
1980	17,429	11,459
"	"	"
"	"	"
"	"	"
1986	28,579	12,486
1987	34,226	14,326
1988	48,664	19,568

Source: 1974-80: L.B. Smith and P. Tomlinson (1981), p. 96; 1986-88: Calculated from data provided by Glenn Haskett Realty Inc.

uses, and discouraging new construction. The reduction in gross rents alters the tenure decision, encourages household formation, and contributes to a shortage in rental housing.

Rents and Capital Values for Uncontrolled Units

In a 1984 paper George Fallis and I (Fallis and Smith, 1984a) argue that the imposition of rent controls in one sector of the housing market is likely to cause the price for the uncontrolled housing substitute, in our case post-1975 rental buildings (under the new construction exemption prior to 1986 and the regulation permitting landlords to set the initial rent for new construction thereafter) and owner-occupancy housing, to rise above the equilibrium price that would have existed in the absence of controls. Table 3 indicates that in October 1988 in the Toronto Census Metropolitan Area (CMA) in buildings of 6 or more units, the rents for post-1975 bachelor, one bedroom, two bedroom and three bedroom units were respectively 38 percent, 52 percent, 44 percent, and 26 percent higher than for the equivalent pre-1976 units, and as a weighted average the rent for post-1976 units was 46 percent higher than for pre-1976 units.

The basic explanation for increased rent on uncontrolled substitutes is that rent rises both from demand effects—the depressed rent in the controlled sector generates increased household formation (Smith, 1984; Smith et al., 1984) and likely increased demand for housing services per household—and supply effects—the imposition of controls reduces the quantity of housing services by accelerating deterioration and conversion in the existing stock (Arnott, 1981; Thom, 1987), and likely discourages new construction. Since the increased demand can be made effective only in the uncontrolled substitute sector, the price in the uncontrolled sector likely will rise above the equilibrium price in the absence of controls.

The impact of rent controls in Ontario on the rental price of the uncontrolled rental substitute (the post-1975 units) was examined by George Fallis and me (Fallis and Smith, 1985a) for the Toronto CMA using a hedonic index approach. We found that in 1982 approximately half of the difference in rent between post-1975 and pre-1976 units (approximately 40 percent in 1982) reflected quality differences, and half reflected the pure price effect of rent control. The difference attributable to the pure price effect was split almost evenly between depressing controlled rents (10 to 12 percent) and elevating uncontrolled rents (8 to 10 percent above the level in the absence of controls). Assuming the proportion attributable to quality differences has increased slightly (by approximately 10 percent),[11] the 1988 rent differentials imply rents on post-1975 units are approximately 11 to 15 percent higher than they would have been in the absence of controls. Moreover, since landlords are able to set the initial rent on newly constructed units and post-1975 units have been subject to controls since 1986, the rent differentials with respect to newly constructed units are likely to be even greater. If the rents on vacant units can be used as a proxy for the rents on newly constructed units, the rent on newly constructed one bedroom, two bedroom, and three bedroom units exceeds the rent on post-1975 units by 5 percent, 24 percent, and 19 percent, respectively (shown in table 3).[12]

The impact of higher rents on capital values in the uncontrolled sector and on the volume of new construction is ambiguous. The capital value of an asset

---

11 The difference attributed to quality differences likely increased slightly since rent controls accelerate deterioration and the average age differential has increased. The calculation assumes the proportion increased 10 percent, so that 55 percent of the differential is attributable to quality differences and 45 percent to the pure price effect of rent control.

12 This proxy was suggested by Nancy Thomson at CMHC, Toronto region. Since vacant units cover all age categories but are predominantly newly constructed, vacant units may be of superior quality, but the quality difference with respect to post-1975 would be slight.

Table 3
Rent Differences in the Toronto CMA, (6 units and over) October, 1988

	Bachelor	1 Bedroom	2 Bedroom	3 Bedroom
Between Post-1975 and Pre-1976 Units				
Post-1975 units	$ 537	$ 710	$ 798	$ 871
Pre-1976 units	388	467	556	691
Difference	$ 149	$ 243	$ 242	$ 180
Difference (%)	38%	52%	44%	26%
Between Vacant Units and Post-1975 Units				
Vacant Units	N/A	$ 751	$1053	$1082
Post-1975 units	537	710	798	871
Difference	N/A	$ 41	$ 255	$ 211
Difference (%)	N/A	5%	24%	19%
Between Condominium Units (City of Toronto, May 1988) and Post-1975 Units (Toronto CMA)				
Condominium Units*	$457	$849	$1282	$1441
Post-1975 Units	537	710	798	871
Difference	$ -80	$ 139	$ 484	$ 570
Difference (%)	-15%	20%	54%	65%

* Based on $.95 per sq. ft.

Source: Data supplied by CMHC, Toronto Office. Data for condominiums from City of Toronto, Planning and Development Department, "Condominium Monitor, 1988," Toronto, December 1988, p. 29.

depends not only on the level of the current rent but also on its expected growth path and the applicable discount rate. Although the imposition of a rent control regime may increase the rent in the uncontrolled sector in the short run, the impact on rents in the longer run is uncertain given the probability that controls may be tightened by extension to the uncontrolled sector. This tightening did occur in Ontario in 1982 when the exemption on units with rents in excess of $750 a month was removed, in 1986 when the exemption on post-1975 units and future new construction was removed, and in 1988 when some regulations (eg., with respect to financial loss for post-1976 units) were tightened. It is thus quite consistent for rent controls to increase the current rent on exempt newly constructed units above the equilibrium level in the absence of controls, and to simultaneously depress the capital value of these units. If controls depress the expected capital value of newly constructed units, the volume of new construction will be less than in the absence of controls and the equilibrium housing stock will be reduced.[13]

Home-ownership and Housing Prices

Rent controls also have spill-over effects on the home-ownership housing market. The rental bargain on pre-1976 units encourages sitting tenants to postpone their home purchase. This encourages higher income tenants to occupy relatively lower rent housing, and reduces the demand for home-ownership housing and home-ownership house prices. However, as the vacancy rate on pre-1976 housing declines, the increased demand created by the reduced rent and the reduced supply of rental apartments forces prospective tenants, especially newly formed or newly arrived households, into the post-1975 rental market, into the lower end of the home-ownership market, and into less traditional forms of rental housing (such as single rooms, flats, basement apartments, rooming houses, condominiums, and single family housing).

The shift into the home-ownership market exerts upward pressure on home-ownership prices, especially at the lower end (which includes condominiums, co-operative housing, row housing, and lower priced single family housing). The shift into less traditional forms of rental accommodation creates a viable rental market and raises returns in these housing forms. This in turn creates a revenue source for some home owners and draws investors into the formerly predominantly home-ownership market, which further exerts upward pressure on prices of home-ownership type housing. Consequently, once rent

---

13 Even if new construction increases, the equilibrium stock might be reduced via accelerated deterioration of the existing stock.

Table 4

Housing Prices, Vacancy Rate, and Three-year Mortgage Rate

	MLS Average Residential Price Toronto		Vacancy Rate Metro Toronto	Three-year Mortgage Rate
	$ (000)	% change	%	%
1988	229.6	21.4	0.1	11.35
1987	189.1	36.0	0.1	10.71
1986	138.9	27.3	0.1	10.88
1985	109.1	6.9	0.4	11.65
1984	102.3	0.6	0.6	13.23
1983	101.6	6.5	1.0	12.66
1982	95.5	5.8	0.7	17.85
1981	90.2	18.7	0.3	18.15
1980	75.7	—	0.5	14.32
Annual average				
1970-74	38.0	—	3.9	—

controls reduced the vacancy rate in traditional rental housing close to zero, they exerted upward pressure on prices of traditionally home-ownership housing. The Toronto real estate board Multiple Listing Service (MLS) house prices and the vacancy rate are shown in table 4.

Some impressionistic evidence of the increased flow of non-traditional investment generating higher prices in the traditionally ownership sector of the housing market is provided by the large number of ads of traditional ownership housing for lease and by the number of renter occupied condominiums. On September 3, 1988, the *Toronto Star* had ads for leasing 896 houses and townhouses and 321 condominiums, numbers that have increased substantially in the last few years despite a tightening rental market. Table 5 indicates that at the end of 1987, 32 percent of condominiums in Metro Toronto were renter occupied, and the increase in tenant occupied condominium units between 1981 and 1987 was 50 percent of the increase in condominium units over this period.

Table 5
Renter Occupied Condominiums in Metro Toronto

	total occupied units* (000)	tenant occupied units (000)	percentage tenanted %
1987	84.4	26.8	32
1986	75.0	24.5	33
1985	70.9	22.9	32
1984	67.4	20.5	30
1983	62.7	16.9	27
1982	60.3	15.9	26
1981	53.9	11.7	22

* row and apartment condominiums.

Source: Ontario Ministry of Housing (1988), p. 13.

New Construction

An indication of the impact of rent controls on new construction can be seen from table 6. Table 6 indicates that total rental apartment and row housing rental starts fell from 22,260 units in 1974 (the year immediately preceding the implementation of controls), and an average of 36,846 starts annually during 1971-74, the four years immediately preceding controls, to 10,394 units in the year controls were implemented and to an average of 14,509 starts annually during the next five years of controls. Moreover, rental starts remained de-

Table 6
Ontario Housing Starts by Categories 1969-88

	Total Housing Starts	Single Detached, Semi-Detached, & Duplex Starts	Total Row & Apartment Starts (Condominium and Rental)	Total Condominium Starts	Total Rental Starts[1]	Rental Starts	
						Unassisted[2]	Government Assisted
1988	99,924	59,531	40,393	24,014	16,379	9,072	7,307
1987	105,213	67,560	37,653	21,965	15,688	7,370	8,318
1986	81,470	58,746	22,724	11,950	10,774	4,849	5,925
1985	64,871	45,436	19,435	6,355	13,080	3,478	9,602
1984	48,171	33,726	14,445	5,032	9,413	2,455	6.958
1983	54,939	34,967	19,972	3,325	16,647	n/a	n/a
1982	38,508	19,927	18,581	2,606	15,975	n/a	n/a
1981	50,161	29,973	20,188	5,822	14,366	n/a	n/a
1980	40,127	23,321	16,806	5,164	11,642	3,842	7,800
1979	56,887	36,160	20,727	7,328	11,938	7,711	4,227
1978	71,710	36,556	35,154	11,781	21,105	6,935	14,170
1977	79,130	38,263	40,857	22,020	15,402	5,382	10,020

(continued on next page)

1976	84,682	40,754	43,928	26,992	12,457	3,691	8,766
1975	79,968	42,212	37,756	24,309	10,394	3,775	6,619
1974	85,503	39,944	45,559	20,920	22,260	15,094	7,166
1973	110,536	50,701	59,835	19,794	37,047	25,933	11,114
1972	102,933	46,169	56,764	8,427	46,134	39,097	7,037
1971	89,980	38,483	51,497	7,652	41,945	31,873	10,072
1970	76,675	26,201	50,474	9,881	38,561	23,982	14,579
1969	81,446	35,484	45,962	3,586	39,897	27,543	12,345

[1] Rental Starts include private NHA financed co-operative starts and syndicated rental condominiums.

[2] Starts without any form of explicit assistance from government, including CRSP, CORSP, Renterprise, Convert to Rent or Assisted Housing, ARP, etc. 1984-86 also excludes MURB units.

n/a The unassisted-assisted breakdown on a consistent basis is not available. Privately owned apartment starts, including government-assisted starts under the CRSP, CORSP, ARP, and MURB programs, were 9,760, 9,600, and 10,814 units in 1981, 1982, and 1983, respectively. For 1984-86 these starts were 4,975, 7,106, and 7,611 units, respectively. Data supplied by CMHC Ontario Region from local office manual registers.

Source:
1969-86 data for columns 1 and 2, CMHC *Canadian Housing Statistics*, various years.
1969-80 data for columns 3-7 from Smith and Tomlinson (1981).
1981-86 data for columns 3-5 supplied by CMHC Ontario Region from Ottawa data files.
1984-86 data for columns 6-7 from CMHC Ontario Region "Ontario Housing Market Report" June 1986 and December 1986, Toronto.
1987 data from CMHC Ontario Region "Ontario Housing Market Report" December 1987, pp. 44, 47, and 49.
1988 data estimated from CMHC Ontario Region "Ontario Housing Market Report" January 1989, tables A40, A45, and p.2.

pressed, averaging only 13,376 units annually during 1981-86, a 64 percent decline from 1971-74, before increasing to 16,034 units in 1987-88.

An even larger percentage decline occurred in the purely private sector as non-government subsidized rental apartment and row housing starts declined from 15,094 units in 1974 and an average of 27,999 starts annually during 1971-74, to 3,775 starts in 1975 and an average of 5,512 starts annually during the next five years. These starts continued to remain very depressed at an annual average of 3,594 units during 1984-86, an 87 percent decline from 1971-74, but rebounded to 8,221 units in 1987-88. On the other hand, government subsidized rental starts and condominium starts remained strong and even rose during the early control period, but this strength was primarily a function of federal and provincial housing subsidy programs introduced at this time.[14]

Despite these programs, total apartment and row starts declined with the implementation of controls, plunged in 1979-80 with the phasing out of a number of government subsidy programs, and remained low throughout the 1980-85 period. They then rebounded in 1986-88 with the boom in condominium starts. The timing and severity of the decline in rental housing starts, and especially in government unassisted rental starts, suggest rent controls substantially reduced the volume of new rental construction in Ontario.[15]

This suggestion is supported when the decline in rental starts is contrasted with the pattern of single detached, semi-detached, and duplex starts in Ontario, and with the performance of rental starts in the rest of Canada and the U.S. Single detached, semi-detached, and duplex starts remained relatively strong in the early control period, plunged in 1980-82 with the termination of the Assisted Home-Ownership Program and steep increase in interest rates, and then rose sharply in the mid-1980s with the buoyant Ontario economy and the declining and low interest rate. In the U.S. rental housing starts in 1984-86 were only 19 percent below 1972-74 starts compared to a 50 percent decline in Ontario; and apartment starts (condominium and rental) in the rest of Canada

---

14 The federal government in 1975 reformulated and greatly liberalized its Assisted Home-Ownership Program (AHOP) and introduced its Multiple Unit Residential Building (MURB) tax shelter program. The Ontario government responded with the Ontario Rental Construction Grant Program (ORCGP) in 1976. For details of these programs and their impacts, see Smith (1981) and Smith and Tomlinson (1981).

15 A number of other factors were also exerting downward pressure on rental housing starts. For a discussion of some of these factors see Slack (1986), Smith (1983), and Stanbury and Vertinsky (1985).

Slack concludes rent controls probably depressed housing starts from 8,000 to 10,000 units in 1984 in Ontario.

were only 29 percent lower compared to a 60 percent decline in Ontario over the same period.

Rent controls were extended to new construction at the end of 1986 under a system in which landlords can establish the initial rent. Assuming the initial rent is set at a level no greater than that which allows an initial cash flow return competitive with ten-year Government of Canada bonds, a 1986 study by Andrew Muller indicates that internal nominal rates of return of approximately 22 to 31 percent (and real rates of return of 13 to 21 percent) are possible over a ten-year holding period under the assumption of moderate 4 to 8 percent inflation.[16] Since this essentially makes controls on new construction non-binding, the negative impact of rent controls on housing starts should be substantially ameliorated if it is believed these controls will not be altered[17] and if the implicit permitted rents are attainable in the market.

This anticipated increase in rental starts may be occurring. Total rental starts in 1987 and 1988 increased approximately 45 percent from the 1984-86 average, and unassisted rental starts more than doubled compared to their 1984-86 average. However, since CMHC includes syndicated rental condominiums as rental starts, an investment form which essentially first became viable in 1987, the growth in rental starts is somewhat overstated. Moreover, rental starts continue to remain substantially below the level required to restore equilibrium to the rental housing market.

Housing Quality and Conversions

A major implication of the depressive effect of rent controls on the net operating income and capital value of controlled units is the incentive provided to landlords to collectively disinvest in controlled housing by converting their units to alternative non-controlled uses or by allowing their properties to deteriorate more quickly.

Conversion to other uses is encouraged because the imposition of controls reduces the expected return in the existing use, which provides incentive to convert the property to alternative uses (condominium, commercial, co-operative housing, offices, etc.) rather than realize the reduced return via a con-

---

16 Muller (1986) calculates the internal rate of return under various inflation and other scenarios. Real internal rates of return were 13.2 percent, 17.2 percent, and 21.2 percent for projected inflation rates of 0 percent, 4 percent, and 8 percent, respectively.

17 There are good reasons for not believing this. These include the history of controls being tightened and exemptions removed, and the large and increasing differential in the rent on these units and pre-1976 units.

strained cash flow or depressed selling value. Deterioration is encouraged because reduced expected returns also encourage the replacement of existing structures by new construction,[18] because rent control regulations usually reduce the expected return to repairs and maintenance expenditures, capital expenditures, or both, and because controls constrain the cash flow for landlords which reduces their capacity to finance repair and maintenance and/or capital expenditures. Prior to 1987, Ontario rent controls discouraged both forms of expenditures because higher expenditures for repairs and maintenance usually were not rewarded with higher rents (nor lower expenditures with lower rents),[19] and the yield permitted on capital expenditures was considerably below that justified by the risk, illiquidity, and long-term aspect of the investment. After 1986, both forms of expenditures continued to be discouraged because adjustments for operating cost increases (which include repair and maintenance expenditures) were covered by a formula, and the yield on capital expenditures[20] was lowered by the provision that reduced the statutory rent increase by one percentage point if capital expenditures were used to justify a rent review.

Condominium conversions were prohibited in many municipalities in Ontario before 1986, and throughout Ontario in 1986 by the Rental Housing Protection Act (RHPA).[21] Nevertheless, substantial loss of rental units occurred through conversion to co-operatives, single family units, and non-residential uses. Between January 1978 and April 1985, approximately 10 percent of the moderate rental stock in the City of Toronto was lost through conversion, demolition, or renovation requiring tenant eviction,[22] significantly reducing the availability of this form of housing. Although the RHPA prohibits these activities, the large and growing disparity between the value of housing as a provider of owner-occupied housing services and as a generator of investment income ensures that there will be continued pressure on the controlled rental stock from these sources.

---

18 This occurs if controls depress the capital value of the land and building in the controlled use below the land value for an alternative use.

19 Higher expenditures could generate higher rents if they were sufficiently large to justify a rent increase under a rent review hearing (and under some circumstances if the higher level of expenditure was maintained). Lower expenditures could generate lower rents if they could be shown to reduce the level of housing services.

20 Usually the prime first mortgage rate.

21 See Smith (1988b) for a discussion of its economic implications.

22 CMHC, Toronto Office (1985).

Numerous studies also indicate that the quality of pre-1976 rental housing in Ontario is deteriorating, and that its long-term viability is severely threatened. These studies indicate that under a continuation of the pre-1986 rent control policies and in the absence of the RHPA, approximately 30 percent of the low-rise rental stock in Ontario cities could be lost within the next ten years through physical deterioration (16 percent) and market pressures (an additional 14 percent),[23] and that major expenditures in the order of $11,690 per high-rise apartment unit in 1982 dollars are required over the next 20 years to preserve the typical high-rise apartment building.[24] These studies all identify rent control as a major factor impeding the expenditures necessary to preserve and maintain the existing rental housing stock. It is still too early to determine the impact of the 1986 legislation on this deterioration, although it is unlikely to reverse it.[25]

Rental Housing Availability

Rent controls have contributed to a severe shortage of rental housing, and especially moderately priced rental housing. In October 1988 the vacancy rate in buildings containing six or more rental units in Metro Toronto was 0.1 percent or 303 units[26] and, except for a brief period in 1983, the vacancy rate has been below 1.0 percent since 1980 (see table 4). In contrast, the vacancy rate for Metro Toronto during 1970-74, the five years immediately prior to rent controls, averaged 3.9 percent; and I estimated the natural vacancy rate to be 5 percent during 1961-71 (Smith, 1974).

In a normally functioning, uncontrolled housing market a vacancy rate below the natural (or equilibrium) rate triggers an increase in real rents and real capital values. This in turn stimulates increased expenditures on the existing stock and increased new construction (Rosen and Smith, 1983). Rent controls break this connection between low vacancies and large housing expenditures, and thereby impede the market adjustment necessary to satisfy the excess demand. It is thus not the low level of vacancies at a particular (single) point in time but the persistence of the extremely low level over a prolonged period that indicates the market failure generated by rent controls and the true severity of the availability problem. The prolonged period of a below 1.0 percent

---

23 Ekos Research Associates Inc. (1985), and Peter Barnard Associates (1985).
24 Klein and Sears, et al., (1983).
25 To encourage revitalization of the housing stock, Ontario introduced the Low-Rise Rehabilitation Program.
26 CMHC, Toronto Office (1988).

vacancy rate thus indicates a complete market failure in the rental housing market in Toronto and most of Ontario.

In addition to the hardship provided by the unavailability of rental housing for new or newly arrived households, the virtually zero vacancy rate is responsible for numerous other problems. These include the widespread emergence of key money, sharply constrained tenant turnover, "reverse filtering" of housing units in which lower quality housing units are increasingly occupied by higher income households (forcing lower income households, and especially single parent households, into severe overcrowding, homelessness, and permanent use of temporary shelters), and increased need for public housing and use of foodbanks.[27]

Key money, a payment made by a prospective tenant usually to a sitting tenant to induce the sitting tenant to transfer the property right associated with a below market rent tenancy,[28] is a natural consequence of controls.[29] Rent controls generate key money by creating a below equilibrium rental price, and the larger the rental advantage created by controls, the more prevalent and larger will be the payment of key money. Anecdotal and other evidence presented at the Thom Commission indicated that key money is widespread, especially in prime and intermediate locations in Toronto[30] The negative effects of key money include breeding cynicism and disrespect for the law, disproportionately handicapping moderate and low-income households who do not have the cash for the key money necessary to acquire a rent controlled apartment, eroding the rental price protection for new tenants, and diverting funds paid by tenants from landlords who might otherwise utilize these funds to maintain or improve the quality of their buildings.

Income Distribution and the Rationing Process

Rent controls affect income distribution and welfare not only by constraining controlled rents but also by elevating uncontrolled rents and home-ownership housing prices. Consequently, the incidence of rent controls depends upon a comparison of controlled and uncontrolled rents and house prices with the rent

27 The increased demand for these services could also be a reflection of a growing income problem.
28 Another reflection of the rental bargain and need to induce a tenant to move is the reduction in tenant turnover under rent control. Stanbury (1984) indicates that the rate of tenant turnover declined almost 30 percent since rent controls were introduced.
29 Bill 51 specifically prohibits "key money," but is unlikely to be successful.
30 See the testimony of Michael Mascall before the Thom Commission.

and house prices that would have occurred in the absence of controls, and the rationing process allocating the controlled housing stock. Most analyses on income distribution have focused on the impact of rent controls on tenants. However, if one considers the impact of controls on home-ownership prices, which confers a benefit in the form of a capital gain for home owners and/or land owners and a loss in the form of a higher entry price for prospective home owners, then the income redistribution is likely to be even less progressive or more regressive.

Given the income distribution of tenants in the controlled and uncontrolled sectors, the housing consumption of these tenants, the impact of controls on controlled and uncontrolled rent, and the relative size of these sectors, George Fallis and I concluded that the overall impact of controls on tenants in 1982 was moderately progressive, but the magnitude of the net redistribution by income class was rather small (Fallis and Smith, 1985b). The gain to lower income tenants in the controlled sector was significantly offset by the loss to lower income tenants in the uncontrolled sector, and the loss to higher income tenants in the uncontrolled sector was significantly offset by the gain to higher income tenants in the controlled sector.[31] Stanbury and Vertinsky (1985) indicate that the bulk of the benefits from lower rents accrues to tenants in the higher income categories, and a study by the Ontario Ministry of Municipal Affairs and Housing (1982) indicates that only 34 percent of the benefits of rent control go to low-income households.

Because households of similar income, age, and size receive markedly different treatment depending on the market in which they reside, rent controls create severe horizontal inequities among tenants. Benefits are conferred on those tenants occupying rental units at the time controls are imposed. However, because over time the vacancy rate in the controlled sector approaches zero, landlords are able to ration units and appear to do so by favouring "desirable" low cost tenants such as households without children, older households with lower turnover rates, and higher income households.

This is discussed in Steele and Miron (1984). Newly formed households, new entrants to the community, low-income households, and especially households with children are clearly disadvantaged by rent controls if they are not the original sitting tenants from the inception of the controls. Controls thus impact very differently on households depending on their original tenure situation, and adversely affect an important segment of the low-income households that the controls were designed to assist.

---

31 If these categories are further refined to reflect household size and life cycle position, the effective progressiveness of income redistribution is further reduced.

Government Revenue and Expenses

Although rent controls appear to be relatively costless from a government budgetary perspective, they in fact exert a substantial impact on government budgets. Rent controls generate a substantial tax loss for all levels of government and induce additional government expenditures in Ontario.

The tax loss occurs primarily in three forms. First, controls reduce income tax, both individual and corporate, by reducing gross rents, and hence the taxable income of landlords. This loss is partially ameliorated by increased taxes generated by additional consumer spending as a result of their reduced rental costs, although this amelioration is in turn partially offset by reduced landlord consumer expenditures due to their reduction in net after tax income. Second, controls reduce property taxes by lowering the volume of new construction and the upgrade and maintenance expenditures on existing housing stock. In localities using market value assessment they also reduce property taxes by lowering the capital, and hence assessed, value of residential rental properties. Third, controls reduce capital gains taxes by reducing the market value of rental dwellings, and hence of the capital gain realized on the sale of these dwellings. Tax expenditures, shown in table 7, were estimated by Slack

Table 7
Government Tax Loss and
Expenditure Costs of Control, ($ mill)

	1984	1988
Foregone tax revenue:		
Income and corporate tax	77	
Property tax	75	
Capital gain tax	43	
Provincial capital tax	3	198	200
Administrative costs		7	40
Increased cost of other government programs	32	60
(ORCLP; CRSP; ARP; ORCGP; LRRP; Rent Supplement; MURB; etc.)		
Total costs		237	300

Source: 1984—mid point of estimates by Enid Slack; 1988—rough estimate by L. Smith.

(1986) to be approximately $200 million in 1984,[32] and I estimate they are still approximately that amount.

In addition to the foregone tax revenues, government budgets are impacted by increased expenditures. These expenditures occur both in the form of the administrative costs of controls and of induced additional government expenditures to mitigate the rental housing supply effects (on both new construction and deterioration) of controls. Induced government expenditures are very difficult to quantify because the degree to which any government program can be attributed to any specific cause is unclear. The appropriate specification of the cost of any program is also uncertain because the costs can be specified on a cash expenditure basis, on a carrying (or debt service) cost basis, or on a notional cost basis reflecting the amount necessary to amortize the expenditure over the expected life of the capital asset being financed. Many federal and provincial programs, such as the Assisted Rental Program (ARP), the Ontario Rental Construction Grant and Loan Programs (ORCGP and ORCLP), the Canada Rental Supply Program (CRSP), the Assured Housing for Ontario Program, the Low-Rise Rehabilitation Program (LRRP), and the Multiple Unit Residential Building (MURB)[33] tax shelter program fall into this category. On a carrying cost basis, in 1984 expenditures under these programs that were attributable to rent control were estimated by Slack (1986) to be approximately $30 million, and I estimate these expenditures to be now approximately $60 million. The administrative cost of rent controls was $7.4 million in 1984, and is now approximately $40 million.

The total annual cost of rent control in Ontario to all levels of government (the sum of all cost components) appears to have been approximately $237 million in 1984, and to be now approximately $300 million. Rent controls thus impose a substantial opportunity cost on society through higher alternative taxes and/or through reduced government funding of other programs.

Finally, the magnitude of the fiscal costs of rent control may be placed in perspective by comparing them with estimates of the cost of a shelter allowance program for Ontario. A 1985 study on shelter allowances by John Chant estimated a comprehensive shelter allowance program for Ontario would have cost approximately $200 million in 1984, or approximately 20 percent less than the 1984 cost of rent control estimated by Enid Slack (1986). Marion Steele

---

32 Foregone tax revenues for 1980 were estimated by Smith and Tomlinson (1981) to be approximately $114.7 million, and by the Ontario Ministry of Municipal Affairs and Housing (1982) to be approximately $88 million.

33 This is really a tax expenditure program but is included here for consistency with Slack (1986).

(1986) estimated a somewhat less comprehensive program would have cost approximately $100 million in 1980,[34] or approximately 30 percent less than the estimate of the 1980 cost of rent control by Peter Tomlinson and me (Smith and Tomlinson, 1981). Rent controls are thus an expensive policy both absolutely and relative to alternative housing programs.

Ancillary Regulations

The effectiveness of a rent control regime depends to a considerable extent upon the ease with which its regulations may be avoided. Because the imposition of controls inevitably leads to circumventing behaviour by those adversely affected, additional regulations often are imposed. In Ontario these regulations include revisions to the Landlord and Tenant Act, the imposition of the Rental Housing Protection Act, the introduction of a rent registry, and the introduction of the Residential Rental Standards Board.

Landlord and Tenant Act

The Landlord and Tenant Act underwent substantial revision upon the imposition of controls. The thrust of the revision was to improve security of tenure for tenants—a necessary adjunct to make rent controls effective in the absence of a rent registry.[35] The grounds for tenant eviction were restricted to non-payment of rent or malconduct (eg., causing undue damage, interfering with the reasonable enjoyment of the premises by other tenants, conducting illegal activities on the premises) by the tenant, or because the landlord needed to obtain possession for demolition, conversion, or major renovation purposes, or because the landlord or a member of the landlord's immediate family wanted to occupy the unit.

In addition to severely limiting the landlord's grounds for eviction, the revisions further constrained landlords by prohibiting security deposits and by increasing notice provisions for rent increases, termination of tenancy by the

---

34 Chant (1985) assumes a take up rate of 80 percent of those households with incomes below 150 percent of the poverty line with a rent supplement equal to 93 percent of the average gap between average rent and 25 percent of income; Steele (1986) assumes a take up rate of 70 percent for a shelter allowance equal to 75 percent of the gap the between actual rent paid (to a maximum equal to the 33rd percentile of rents) and 30 percent of income. I estimate the cost of a shelter allowance program in 1984 would have been $192 million assuming a 100 percent take up rate, or $135 million assuming a 70 percent take up rate, for an estimated 180,000 household in core housing need for a shelter allowance equal to 75 percent of the gap between actual rent and 30 percent of income.

35 For a discussion on security of tenure issues see Makuch and Weinrib (1985).

landlord, and right of access to tenant premises. An effect of these changes was to increase the cost of management for the landlord.

The Rental Housing Protection Act

The Rental Housing Protection Act (RHPA) was introduced in 1986 on a temporary two-year basis. It was extended for one year in 1988 and was revised and made permanent in 1989.[36] The RHPA prohibits the demolition, conversion, or renovation requiring tenant eviction of rental residential properties containing five or more units unless the municipality in which the property is located gives its approval. Municipal approval under the 1986 act was based on a number of criteria. In the case of demolition or renovation control, municipal approval required the building to be unsafe, and the owners were to provide similar accommodation at a similar rent or give evidence that the supply of affordable rental housing would not be adversely affected in the municipality. In the case of conversion control, municipal approval required the owner to provide similar accommodation at a similar rental range or give evidence that the supply of affordable rental housing would not be adversely affected.

The primary criterion for municipal approval was that the demolition, conversion, or renovation did not adversely impact on the supply of affordable rental housing (the "affordability exemption"). This, however, was a very difficult case to make since, by definition, anything that anyone buys is affordable. To give meaning to the exemption, the concept of affordable must be defined, and this was done by the Ontario Municipal Board (OMB).[37] The OMB ruled that if the annual rent was equal to or less than 25 percent of the income of the 66.67 percentile household in Metro Toronto, the rental unit was affordable and not eligible for exemption. This eliminated the vast majority of the rental stock from this exemption, especially those units with the largest economic advantage in being demolished, converted, or renovated, and thereby virtually eliminated the exemption.

The economic consequences of the RHPA are thus to reduce the economic value of pre-1976 rental apartment buildings by eliminating the value associated with the potential for demolition, renovation, or conversion of these buildings, and to accelerate the deterioration of these buildings by this reduction in value and by removing incentives to maintain their quality.

---

36 The discussion in this section is drawn from Smith (1988b).
37 Decision of the OMB, M 870009, May 11, 1987, in the case of 400 Walmer Road, Toronto.

Rent Registry

The 1986 revision to the rent control legislation provided that a rent regisu y bc established to record rents for units in buildings of six or more units. The date for the first registered rent was to be July 1975.

Since, in Ontario, rent controls reside with the unit, the possibility of circumvention by illegally increasing rents on tenant turnover existed in the system. The rent registry was introduced to prevent further illegal rent increases and to try to roll back some past illegal increases. The problems associated with attempting to retroactively register rents on approximately 540,000 units, notify and seek verification of accuracy from 540,000 tenants, and also check rents against past rent review orders have been enormous. Not only has a large bureaucracy been created but errors in the process have further strained landlord and tenant relations and generated a flood of rent rebate applications by tenants.[38]

Residential Rental Standards Board

The 1986 Residential Rent Regulation Act also provided for the establishment of a Residential Rental Standards Board (RRSB).

One method of ameliorating the effects of rent controls for landlords is to disinvest in rental housing by curtailing repair and maintenance expenditures since this increases net cash flow at the expense of capital value. Over time, this reduces the quality of housing services and partially frustrates the controls with respect to the quality adjusted rental price. In an attempt to prevent this and preserve the quality of the existing rental stock, the RRSB was authorized to establish minimum standards of maintenance, repair, health, and safety.

The RRSB has the authority to determine whether there is substantial noncompliance under a municipal property standard (done by monitoring municipal standards orders), and to set provincial maintenance standards for municipalities with no standards or inappropriate ones. The RRSB thus can establish and monitor property standards in the province. Where standards are not met, the board can initiate actions resulting in rental penalties. Moreover, tenants are permitted to challenge a guideline (statutory) rent increase on the basis that a rental unit does not comply with the maintenance standards established by the RRSB, thereby making the RRSB standards applicable to all units in the province (in addition to appropriate municipal property standards). An indication of the potential impact of the RRSB is that in just over a year of operation it received 7,400 deficiency orders covering 160,519 rental units and

---

38 Of course, many rebate applications have been justified by the situation.

found in 2,328 of these cases that there was a substantial standard violation. In 66 cases there have been rent penalty orders.[39]

Administrative Efficiency

In addition to its economic deficiencies, rent control in Ontario has become an administrative nightmare. During 1988, there was a backlog of over 25,000 applications for rent review, covering approximately one-quarter of all tenants in private rental units in Ontario. A landlord filing an application for a full building rent review can anticipate a two-year wait before receiving an order. Since there is no obligation for tenants to pay rent above the statutory amount until a rental order is received, landlords may sustain considerable cash flow difficulties while awaiting an order and the collection of back-rent. Landlords may also experience difficulties in collecting back-rent over such a lengthy period and in obtaining sufficient finance on their buildings while awaiting a rental Order.

Because rental orders are retroactive and may cover two or more back years, the retroactive payment can be quite substantial and create considerable financial hardship for tenants.[40] Tenants may also be faced with extended periods of uncertainty during which they do not know the amount of rent for which they are responsible. Since landlords may request higher rents than will be awarded, tenants may be subjected to prolonged periods of concern about rents higher than they will be required to pay.

The administrative backlogs thus have created considerable uncertainty, distress, and financial hardship for tenants, while creating cash flow, financing, and retroactive rent collection problems for landlords.[41]

Rent Decontrol

The preceding discussion indicates that the major effects of rent controls in Ontario have been:

- to reduce rents on pre-1976 controlled units, but to increase rents on post-1975 units;

---

39 Figures taken from Doumani (1989).

40 Average rental awards in 1988 were 11.4 percent, or approximately 7 percent above the statutory rent increase. If these were granted for two years and the tenant paid only the statutory rent, the retroactive rent due on an initial $600 rent would be over $1500.

41 For common perceptions of these problems see the *Toronto Star*, May 13, 1989, D4, "Rent Review System Pleases Next to No One" by David Israelson.

- to increase prices of home-ownership housing;
- to reduce new rental and total apartment construction;
- to jeopardize the quality and survival of the existing rental housing stock by accelerating deterioration, encouraging conversions of rental residential dwellings to other uses and other tenure forms, and fostering demolitions;
- to contribute to a severe rental housing shortage;
- to impact adversely on an important segment of the low-income group, such as newly formed households, new entrants to the community, and low-income households with children;
- to exacerbate the government budgetary deficit by reducing government tax revenues and inducing increased government housing expenditures;
- to breed additional layers of ancillary regulations and controls; and
- to create administrative and bureaucratic chaos.

Although some of the consequences of rent control appear to have been reversed (most notably the erosion in real net rent and capital values) or mitigated (the decline in unassisted rental housing starts) since the 1986 changes in the rent control legislation, the general deleterious impact of rent controls remains. Moreover, the improvements in capital values and rental housing starts since 1986 are largely the outcome of a favourable economy (strong economic growth and immigration in Ontario, and lower interest rates) and the consequence of the previously begun upward trend in real net rents.

It is clear that under the rent control system in Ontario the viability of the private rental sector is in doubt. A program for decontrol is thus a requirement if the private rental sector is to survive and provide affordable rental housing in decent accommodation for future generations in Ontario.

Options for Decontrol

Numerous strategies exist for rent decontrol. Richard Arnott (1981) lists seven such strategies which may be followed separately or in combination:

- vacancy decontrol: decontrol when units become vacant;
- vacancy rate decontrol: decontrol when the vacancy rate in an area reaches some target level;
- rent-level decontrol: decontrol when the rent on a unit reaches some target level;

- floating up and out: gradual relaxation of controls, i.e., gradually increasing the statutory or guideline rent increase;[42]
- contracting out: where a landlord and tenant may negotiate a rent or rent increase usually in conjunction with other considerations;
- local option: where the province passes jurisdiction over controls and their retention to the municipalities;
- blanket lifting: complete decontrol at one time.

Because a blanket lifting of controls could be extremely disruptive in a period of excess demand, causing major adjustment problems for tenants and possibly leading to a political reversal of the decontrol, Arnott (1981) recommends a policy of gradual decontrol, and, in particular, floating up and out.

Muller (1987, p. 23) also prefers a gradual decontrol program of the floating up and out variety proposed by Arnott, possibly in combination with income supplements. However, Muller (1989) indicates that in five of the six decontrol episodes in Canada, controls were "phased out" through some combination of vacancy decontrol, vacancy rate decontrol, and rent-level decontrol, followed by blanket lifting of controls (Alberta 1980, British Columbia 1983, Manitoba 1980, New Brunswick 1980) or replacement by a rent arbitration scheme (Saskatchewan 1983).[43] No province has attempted a floating up and out strategy, which Muller (1987) considers an indication that this option may not be viewed as politically viable. Nevertheless, these episodes do not indicate that a form of floating up and out would not be appropriate or viable for Ontario because the appropriate decontrol strategy depends upon the specifics of the rent control regime and the particular housing market conditions.

A Summary of Rental Housing Market Conditions in Ontario

As discussed earlier, the private rental housing sector in Ontario, and especially in the Toronto CMA, is in crisis. The vacancy rate in buildings of six units and over in Metro Toronto was 0.1 percent, or 303 units, in October 1988; and the vacancy rate has been at or below 1.0 percent since 1980, and at 0.1 percent since 1986, indicating a prolonged period of excess demand and market failure. This excess demand is manifest in the differentials in rent between the rent on pre-1976 and the rent on post-1975 units, on newly constructed units, and on

---

42 In Ontario this could mean altering the rent formula annually to allow for a larger statutory rent increase each year.

43 Categories taken from Muller (1987). New Brunswick decontrolled twice. Controls were reimposed in 1983 and then removed in a straight blanket decontrol in 1985. Manitoba also reimposed controls in 1982. Thus, only British Columbia, Alberta, and New Brunswick have no controls.

condominium units. In the case of two bedroom units in the Toronto CMA, the rent for post-1975 units is 44 percent above the rent for the pre-1976 units; the rent on vacant units, which may be taken as a rough indicator of the rent on newly constructed units, is 89 percent above the rent for pre-1976 units and 24 percent above that for post-1975 units; and the rent for condominium units is approximately 130 percent above the rent for pre-1976 units (see table 3). Newly formed households and new-comers who have relatively little access to lower rent pre-1976 units are thus faced with rents that are considerably above average and above equilibrium. The excess demand has also spilt over into the home-ownership market, contributing to the upward pressure on house prices. In the three years from 1986 to 1988, the MLS average residential house price rose 110 percent (see table 4).

Despite the almost zero vacancy rate and high rent level for newly constructed units, rental housing starts have remained depressed. Total rental starts in Ontario, including private and National Housing Act (NHA) financed co-operative starts and syndicated rental condominiums, were only 16,379 units in 1988 and averaged only 14,280 units in 1986-88, and private unassisted rental starts, including syndicated rental condominiums, were only 9,072 units in 1988 and averaged only 7,183 units in 1986-88 (see table 6). During this period, the growth in demand was strong, propelled not only by natural domestic forces but also by net interprovincial migration and international immigration which averaged 91,300 persons annually in 1986-88.[44] Moreover, since the demand for rental housing has been partially met in recent years by condominium and other traditionally home-ownership type housing, an increasing segment of the rental supply is vulnerable to attrition via tenure shift. Finally, the quality of the existing stock of housing has been jeopardized by accelerating deterioration.

Consequently, the Ontario rental housing market is suffering from severe shortage, deteriorating quality, and low levels of new construction. Prospective tenant households face long queues for affordable rental housing and rents on new housing above those that would have existed in the absence of controls. The backlog for public housing has increased significantly and housing costs are often cited as a cause for the increased need for foodbanks.

A Program for Rent Decontrol in Ontario

The market failure in the rental housing market, the scarcity of rental housing, the distorted structure of rents, the negative expectations of developers and

---

44 See CMHC, Ontario Region, "Ontario Housing Market Report," December 1988, p. 5.

landlords, and the depressed volume of new construction and maintenance expenditures clearly demonstrate the need for rent decontrol; while the extreme tightness of the rental market, especially in the Toronto CMA, dictates that the decontrol be on a gradual but certain basis.

To be effective, a decontrol program must redress those areas that controls impact upon while providing protection for tenants against rapid and excessive movements in rent. In particular, a decontrol program should seek to alter rents and prices, and expectations about them, to spur new rental construction and to encourage the preservation and upgrading of the existing rental stock without creating serious affordability problems for tenants.

A rent decontrol program for Ontario should thus contain the following three elements:

- rents must be free to seek their equilibrium level;
- tenants must be protected from market excesses by restraints on the speed of rental adjustments and, where appropriate, rental assistance; and
- the program must be sufficiently certain that it eliminates doubts as to its viability and longevity, and thus restores landlord and developer confidence.

Such a program is set out below.

1. Statutory annual rent increases should be tied to the rate of inflation by a formula that generates rent increases 2 to 3 percent above inflation. The selected percentage is essentially a political decision, but it is likely that anything much less than 2 percent would be ineffective and in excess of 3 percent would generate excessive adjustment costs for tenants. The lag in the rent increase formula must be minimal, so that the rent increase should either be based on inflation in the previous year, or on an anticipated rate with a forecast error adjustment in the next year. For simplicity in what follows, I shall arbitrarily assume a rental increase x percent above inflation. Illustrative formulas are set out in equations 2 and 3.[45]

---

45 A refinement in the formula would replace the $\overset{o}{CPI}$ by $.5\ \overset{o}{BOCI}$, where $\overset{o}{BOCI}$ is the rate of inflation in the index of building operating costs as presently used in Ontario, for example,

$$\overset{o}{R} = .5\ \overset{o}{CPI} = .5\ \overset{o}{BOCI} + x, \text{ s.t. minimum } \overset{o}{CPI}, \overset{o}{BOCI} = 0$$

The advantage of this refinement is that it explicitly compensates for variations in price changes in building operating costs. A weight of .5 is used for the BOCI because operating costs typically approximated 50 percent of gross rent, and this

Equation 2

$$\overset{o}{R}_t = \overset{o}{CPI}_{t-1} + x, \text{ s.t. minimum } \overset{o}{CPI} = 0, \text{ or}$$

Equation 3

$$\overset{o}{R}_t = \overset{o\ e}{CPI}_t + x - (\overset{o\ e}{CPI}_{t-1} - \overset{o}{CPI}_{t-1}) \text{ s.t. minimum } \overset{o}{CPI} = 0$$

where

$\overset{o}{R}_t$ = the statutory rent increase allowed in year t,

$\overset{o}{CPI}_t$ = the rate of inflation in the CPI in year t, and

$\overset{o\ e}{CPI}_t$ = the expected rate of inflation in the CPI in year t.

2. No rent increases in excess of the statutory increases should be permitted except with respect to upgrade capital expenditures. An additional rent increase should be permitted to enable the expenditures to be amortized at an interest rate appropriate for risk and investment characteristics associated with the expenditures.[46] Because the investment is long term, illiquid (since it cannot be recovered except through the amortized payment or by sale of the entire project), and essentially subordinate to the prior debt and equity in the project, the risk and investment characteristics suggest an interest rate at least equal to the long-term

---

variable would compensate for direct operating cost increases. A weight of .5 is used for the CPI to compensate for the erosion in net operating income caused by the current inflation.

46 The appropriate definitions of capital and amortization period are theoretically difficult. At one extreme, it could be argued that the appropriate amortization period is the expected life of the building. In this case, any rent increase should apply over the lifetime of the building and the "cost no longer borne" concept would have no meaning. Replacement expenditures would then be additional expenditures giving rise to additional rent increases. At the other extreme, it could be argued that the appropriate amortization period is the expected life of the item on which the expenditure is made. This approach would justify a larger rent increase, but also the "cost no longer borne" concept. The choice of interest rate, definition of capital, and selection of the appropriate amortization period are interconnected. If these variables are specified consistently, various combinations will produce equivalent outcomes.

second mortgage rate. In order to mitigate adjustment costs for tenants, the annual rent increase generated by these expenditures should be phased in,[47] for example, by specifying a cap at 5 percent of gross rent annually until the total permitted increase is in effect.

3. A rental assistance program, preferably in the form of rent supplements or shelter allowances, for tenants in greatest need should be introduced to mitigate the impact on low-income tenants. The assistance program can be financed out of revenue savings generated by the dismantling of rent controls.

4. The rent on newly constructed buildings would not be subject to control for some period, eg., three years.[48]

5. Development agreements should be entered into between the province and developers and builders, at the request of the developers and builders, whereby the province agrees to indemnify the developers and builders against any loss suffered by the reimposition of a more stringent rent control regime. This indemnification could take various forms, including a put option granted to the developer, a lump sum indemnification payment, an annual rental loss compensation payment, or a forgivable mortgage loan.

6. A rent registry should be maintained.

7. The Residential Rental Protection Act should be phased out over some predetermined period, e.g., over a two or three years.

The preceding program contains all the elements necessary for viable rent decontrol. Rent increases in excess of inflation permit rents to gradually approach their equilibrium. Rent increases would be constrained initially by the percentage increase allowed in excess of inflation, and then by market forces as the equilibrium is approached. Given the estimated 5 to 8 percent reduction in real rents on pre-1976 units generated by controls, rents on a substantial portion of the stock should approach their long-run equilibrium within three years, although the adjustment period for the entire market would be longer because the rent on a significant portion of these units is more deeply depressed.[49] It would, moreover, take considerably longer for rents to approach

---

47 The costs associated with the phase-in (i.e., the additional carrying costs) should be factored into the permitted rent increase.

48 It is not sufficient to allow only the initial rent to be set by the developer because lease-up costs, and hence overall building costs, are reduced by providing initial rent concessions. If developers and landlords are precluded from offering these concessions because they would be locked into them, lease-up and overall project costs would be increased, resulting in a reduced level of new construction.

49 In 1986, 5.5 to 7.0 percent of the pre-1976 buildings and 1.0 to 2.2 percent of the

their short-run equilibrium, and hence for the market constraint to operate, because of the reduced supply of rental housing as a result of the controls

The decontrol program not only provides protection for tenants but also increases equality within the system. Under the present rent control system in Ontario, there is no cap on the maximum rent increase that may be justified. This has lead to a large dispersion in annual rent increases, with many tenants experiencing increases in excess of three to four times the statutory increase. The elimination of all factors other than capital expenditures, the allowance for which would be capped, augmenting the statutory rent increase means that an effective cap would be imposed on the maximum rent increase, and that no tenants would be faced with unusually large rent increases. Consequently, although the statutory rent increase would be higher under the decontrol program, the dispersion in rent increases would be reduced. Thus, additional protection against abnormally large rent increases would be provided, large deviations in rent increases would be prevented, and the equitableness of the system would be substantially increased.

Low income tenants would be further protected by a rental assistance program. This assistance could be financed from the increased government revenues and expenditure savings arising from phasing out controls. As indicated previously, a shelter allowance program was estimated to cost between 20 and 30 percent less than the budgetary costs of rent control. Although some regulatory costs would remain to administer capital expenditure reviews and the rent registry, the majority of government costs and revenue losses would be eliminated in the decontrol program, enabling a rental assistance program to be financed without significant additional budgetary cost.[50]

New construction would be encouraged by allowing the rent on newly constructed dwellings to be exempt from controls for some initial period, by permitting annual rent increases in excess of inflation, and by utilizing development agreements. The development agreement would solidify builder and developer expectations that controls would not be tightened or reinforced, and raise the costs of such a policy reversal for government. Since any policy reversal would entail large indemnification costs, such a policy reversal would

---

pre-1976 units were renting at more than 20 percent below the average rent on equivalent units, based on a sample of buildings in London, Ottawa, Thunder Bay, and Toronto (Institute for Social Research, 1986).

50 A qualification is that the tax loss applies to all three levels of government and consequently some intergovernmental cost sharing arrangement would be necessary to effect this budgetary balance.

be politically less likely because an explicit vested interest would be created for all beneficiary taxpayers.

Maintenance and upgrade expenditures would be encouraged by phasing out controls (which would improve cash flows to finance the expenditures), the provision for a rate of return on capital expenditures appropriate for the risk characteristics of the investment, the possibility of a development agreement with respect to major capital expenditures, and the termination of the Residential Rental Protection Act.

The program would therefore provide for a gradual movement of rents to the market equilibrium, enabling a return to market determined rents while continuing to maintain tenant protection against excessive rental adjustments by the statutory rent increase formula, the rent registry, and the rental allowance program. The movement to market determined rents and adoption of development agreements to solidify landlord and developer expectations should remove the impediments to new construction and maintenance and repair expenditures, eliciting a supply response that would enable restoration of a normally functioning market.

Comparison with Alternative Decontrol Programs

For a variety of reasons, the preceding program is preferable to the alternative decontrol programs:

- **Blanket decontrol** would be inappropriate given the amount of excess demand in the rental market. This demand would generate a very rapid and large rent increase driving rents beyond their equilibrium because of the rent control-induced shortage of supply. The market distortions this would generate and the excessive adjustment costs this would cause tenants would increase the likelihood of a reimposition of controls, and expectations of this would inhibit new construction and maintenance expenditures.

- **Vacancy decontrol** is inequitable and slow, and not likely to reverse developer expectations. Because binding controls in one sector of the market increase rents above the equilibrium for the uncontrolled substitute, vacancy decontrol causes rents on uncontrolled vacant units to exceed the equilibrium (Fallis and Smith, 1984). This raises rents substantially for incoming tenants, and the discrepancies in rent between vacated and occupied units is inequitable. This discrepancy will reduce tenant turnover, perpetuating a continuation of controls in a large segment of the market. The continuation of controls prevents the dismantling of the rent control bureaucracy, maintaining the costs to government and increasing the probability of the reimposition of controls.

- **Vacancy rate decontrol** is a non-viable option. Rent controls artificially stimulate demand (and household formation) by depressing rents below their equilibrium in the controlled sector, and they reduce supply by discouraging new construction and maintenance expenditures and encouraging conversion to other uses. Consequently, controls generate rental shortages that will persist under normal macro-economic conditions as long as the controls are in existence. Hence, this decontrol program would not be triggered. Moreover, this program would not generate a significant supply response because developers would be fearful of a reimposition of controls if the vacancy rate were to decline below the threshold rate.

- **Rent-level decontrol** is inappropriate for many of the reasons applicable to vacancy decontrol. Since the rent-level decontrol threshold would not be reached simultaneously by all units, decontrolled rents would exceed the equilibrium, creating inequitableness and substantial hardship for tenants in decontrolled units. Because lower rent units would be the last to be decontrolled, there is a high probability that decontrol might be stopped prematurely, leaving a large component of the market under controls. The gap between the rent on the decontrolled and controlled units would generate pressure to fully restore controls, and expectations of this would deter a supply response. Moreover, the creation of two classes of tenants, decontrolled and controlled, in the same building would be fractious. Finally, the rent control bureaucracy could not be dismantled because of the continuation of a controlled component in the market.

- **Local option and contracting out** are not viable decontrol alternatives. Local option is not viable because it simply passes the political responsibility to a different level of government and increases the probability that controls will remain in part of the market. Contracting out is not viable because its associated uncertainty for landlords and developers would inhibit any supply response. The bargaining process would lead to different outcomes across buildings and across tenants, thus being quite inequitable. The retention of controls would require a continuation of the full rent control administrative apparatus. Thus, neither local option nor contracting out are workable decontrol programs.

Summary

This paper analyzes the effects of rent controls in Ontario and outlines a program for decontrol. It indicates that rent controls have jeopardized the viability of the private rental sector in Ontario, introducing major market distortions, impeding new supply, accelerating the deterioration and conversion of the private rental stock, contributing to a severe rental housing shortage, and impacting adversely on a large component of low-income tenant households.

The paper presents a program for gradual rent decontrol tailored for the market conditions and rent control regime in Ontario. The program is designed to revitalize the private residential rental sector by freeing the market from excessive regulation while maintaining tenant protection against excessive market adjustment.

References

Arnott, Richard (1981), *Rent Control and Options for Decontrol in Ontario*, (Toronto: Ontario Economic Council).

Canada Mortgage and Housing Corporation (1988), Ontario Region, "Ontario Region Housing Market Report" December, and earlier issues.

Chant, John (1985), *Complimentary Policies to Rent Regulation*, Paper prepared for the Commission of Inquiry into Residential Tenancies, Toronto.

Doumani, R.G. (1989), "Extra Thorns in Landlords' Sides: Bill 211 and the Maintenance Standards Board," Paper presented at Insight Conference on Rent Controls and Related Legislation, Toronto, February 22.

Ekos Research Associates Inc. (1985), "Report on the Study of Landlords and the Ontario Rent Review Process," Paper prepared for the Commission of Inquiry into Residential Tenancies, Toronto.

Fallis, George and Lawrence B. Smith (1984), "Uncontrolled Prices in a Controlled Market: The Case of Rent Control", *American Economic Review* 74 (March), pp. 193-200.

Fallis, George and Lawrence B. Smith (1985a), "Price Effects of Rent Control on Controlled and Uncontrolled Rental Housing in Toronto: An Hedonic Index Approach," *Canadian Journal of Economics* 18 (August), pp. 652-59.

Fallis, George and Lawrence B. Smith (1985b), "Rent Controls in Toronto: Tenant Rationing and Tenant Benefits," *Canadian Public Policy* 11 (September), pp. 543-50.

Institute for Social Research, York University (1986), "Study on Abnormally Low Rents: A Study of Landlords and Tenants," Report for the Ministry of Housing, mimeo, Toronto.

Klein, J. et al. (1983), *Study of Residential Intensification and Rental Housing Conservation*, Study prepared for the Ontario Ministry of Municipal Affairs and Housing, and the Association of Municipalities of Ontario, Vol. 9, Toronto.

Makuch, S. and Weinrib, A. (1985), *Security of Tenure*, Research Study #11, The Commission of Inquiry into Residential Tenancies, Toronto.

Muller, R. Andrew (1985), "Rent Regulation and the Supply of Rental Housing," Paper prepared for the Commission of Inquiry into Residential Tenancies, Toronto.

Muller, R. Andrew (1986), "The Effect of the Recommendations of the Rent Review Advisory Committee on New Rental Construction," Report for the Ministry of Housing, mimeo, (May) Toronto.

Muller, R. Andrew (1987), "Ontario's Options in the Light of the Canadian Experience with Decontrol," in R. Arnott and J. Mintz (eds.) *Policy Forum on Rent Controls in Ontario* (Kingston, Ontario: John Deutsch Institute).

Muller, R. Andrew (1989), "The Experience with Rent Regulation in Canada," (Hamilton, Ontario: McMaster University) mimeo.

Ontario Ministry of Municipal Affairs and Housing (1982), "The Impact of Rent Review on Rental Housing in Ontario: A Staff Research Report" (July) Toronto.

Ontario Ministry of Housing (1988), "Rental Housing Protection Act: Future Directions, Toronto, mimeo.

Peter Barnard Associates (1985), "Under Pressure: Prospects for Ontario's Low-Rise Rental Stock," Study prepared for the Ministry of Municipal Affairs and Housing, Toronto.

Rosen, Ken and Lawrence B. Smith (1983), "The Price Adjustment Process for Rental Housing and the Natural Vacancy Rate", *American Economic Review* 73 (September), pp. 778-86.

Slack, Enid (1986), "The Costs of Rent Review," Paper prepared for the Commission of Inquiry into Residential Tenancies, Toronto.

Smith, Lawrence B. (1974), "A Note on the Price Adjustment Mechanism for Rental Housing," *American Economic Review* 64 (June), pp. 478-81.

Smith, Lawrence B. (1981), "Canadian Housing Policy in the Seventies," *Land Economics* 57 (August), pp. 338-52.

Smith, Lawrence B. (1983), "The Crisis in Rental Housing: A Canadian Perspective," *Annals of the American Academy of Political and Social Science* 465 (January), pp. 58-75.

Smith, Lawrence B. (1984), "Household Headship Rates, Household Formation and Housing Demand in Canada," *Land Economics* 60 (May), pp. 180-88.

Smith, Lawrence B. (1985), "Rental Apartment Valuation: The Applicability of Rules of Thumb," *The Appraisal Journal* (October), pp. 541-52.

Smith, Lawrence B. (1988a), "An Economic Assessment of Rent Controls: The Ontario Experience," *Journal of Real Estate Finance and Economics* (November), pp. 217-31; revised and reprinted in R. Arnott and J. Mintz (eds.) *Rent Controls, The International Experience* (Kingston: John Deutsch Institute, 1988), pp. 57-72.

Smith, Lawrence B. (1988b), "Economic Implications of Ontario's New Housing Legislation: Bills 11 and 51," *Canadian Public Policy* (December), pp. 290-98.

Smith, Lawrence B., Kenneth T. Rosen, Anil Markandya, and Pierre Ullmo (1984), "The Demand for Housing, Headship Rates and Household Formation: An International Analysis," *Urban Studies* 21 (November), pp. 407-14.

Smith, Lawrence B. and Peter Tomlinson (1981), "Rent Controls in Ontario: Roofs or Ceilings?" *American Real Estate and Urban Economics Association Journal* 9 (Summer), pp. 93-114.

Stanbury, William T (1984), "The Normative Basis of Rent Control, Volume I," Paper prepared for the Commission of Inquiry into Residential Tenancies, Ontario.

Stanbury, William T. and Ilan B. Vertinsky (1985), "Design Characteristics of Systems of Rent Regulation and Their Effects," Paper prepared for the Commission of Inquiry into Residential Tenancies, Toronto.

Steele, Marion and John Miron (1984), "Rent Regulation, Housing Affordability Problems and Market Imperfections," Research Study #9, prepared for the Commission of Inquiry into Residential Tenancies, Toronto.

Steele, Marion (1986), *Canadian Housing Allowances: An Economic Analysis* (Toronto: Ontario Economic Council).

Thom, Stuart (1987), *Report of the Commission of Inquiry into Residential Tenancies: Vol II* (Toronto: Queen's Printer).

Discussion on L.B. Smith Paper

Denton Marks

Despite widespread agreement among economists on the expected effects of simple rent control (RC) (e.g., Kearl et al., 1979; Block and Walker, 1988), the task set for Larry Smith was not an easy one—an analysis of the expected and actual effects of RC in Ontario and formulation of a program for decontrol (or deregulation). Isolation and measurement of the effects of actual RC legislation have often proven to be difficult if evidence from the economics literature can be accepted. This is important because analyses of RC—including Smith's—are often motivated to a significant degree by an interest in assessing RC's desirability according to some reasonable criteria. They seek to answer the question: Do theoretical arguments and empirical evidence lead a dispassionate audience to support or oppose the policy? In light of this, there are four themes stemming from Smith's paper which I wish to pursue briefly: (1) the challenge posed by the continuing use of RC as a policy instrument, (2) the difficulty of knowing the effects of actual RC legislation, (3) the role of measurement and size of effects in forming opinions about RC, and (4) the development of policy in this area.

Smith provides a comprehensive and critical discussion of the provisions of Ontario RC as it has evolved since 1975 as well as a survey of the types of distortions one expects from RC. These range from the textbook problems of reduced supply of rental housing and capricious distribution of costs and benefits (by reasonable standards of vertical and horizontal equity) to the more subtle problems of administrative inefficiency and the effects on house values and government revenues. Most objections arise from these effects. Yet professional objections must deal with the fact that RC is, and has been for decades, a popular public policy around the world. It existed in some form in all Canadian provinces during much of the 1970s and still exists in some form in all provinces but New Brunswick, Alberta, and British Columbia. More than 200 communities in the U.S. (where RC is usually under local jurisdiction) have some form of RC; they are all in five states (New York, New Jersey, Massachusetts, Connecticut, and California) and the District of Columbia. In contrast, 14 states have outlawed RC (Downs, 1988). However, the states (and district) where RC is widespread represent almost one-third of the 1988 U.S. population in metropolitan areas and over 40 percent of rental housing in U.S. urbanized areas (1980 Census).

Economic analyses generally conclude that RC is an inefficient policy for preserving access to housing, especially for low-income households. However, while its popularity rises and falls, it shows no signs of disappearing, especially in North American jurisdictions which are among the most sophisticated in public policy development and liberal in resources devoted to policy making. In fact, the analysis of Ontario policy under the Thom Commission during 1983-86—arguably the most thorough scrutiny of RC policy ever undertaken—seems to have been largely disregarded (Gooderham, 1988). Few would agree that economic analysis and opinion have led to the demise of RC, though some non-economists have been converted (Thom, 1989).

The analysis of RC also begs a question about the role of the economist in the analysis of public policy. Is it sufficient for one to analyze a policy and simply recommend against it (on efficiency grounds, for example)? Is there a role to be played in realizing that a government is going to adopt an "impure" policy and then turning one's efforts toward the design of a best second-best policy? A particularly interesting feature of Smith's paper is his willingness to go beyond a critical analysis of the current Ontario legislation and its effects and propose a method of decontrol that allows some of the features of RC to continue.

The Problem and Importance of Measurement

One of the most important lessons from the paper is the central role played by measurement. One must bear in mind that, as with all regulation, the actual and predicted effects of RC are sensitive to the provisions of the particular law (Arnott, 1981). Anthony Downs's recent analysis (1988, pp. 17-28) emphasizes this point: available evidence supports theoretical predictions of the effects of RC in the case of "stringent" controls, but the evidence of detrimental effects from "temperate" controls is not strong. By Downs's criteria, Ontario RC in its various forms has embodied elements of both caricature policies. Currently, it has stringent characteristics (e.g., no exemptions, no vacancy decontrol, and severe restrictions on conversion) as well as temperate ones (e.g., statutory increases which allow constant or slightly increasing real rents, increases to prevent loss including an allowed rate of return on equity, and unregulated initial rent on new and newly rented units).

Of course, effects also depend upon the market conditions to which the law is applied (and which, in turn, also affect the evolution of the law). A 5 percent limit on annual rent increases may have very different effects on the rental housing market, depending, for example, on its tightness. Decontrol becomes virtually painless if housing markets became so slack that the existing legislation is no longer binding (especially if the legislation is changed over time to make it less binding). This characterizes at least some of the decontrol experience in Canada (Muller, 1987).

It is often difficult to measure the effects of RC. There are conceptual problems of knowing what to measure (e.g., a unit of housing services, transaction costs); there is usually a lack of data on the variables of interest; it is difficult to control for the effects of other market forces; and RC provisions change, making it difficult to isolate the effects of any particular regime, especially since effects may emerge with different lags.[1] Addressing these issues directly goes beyond the scope of this discussion; suffice it to say that they represent significant challenges.[2] Downs (1988, p. 41) observes:

> Considering both the importance of rent controls and their highly controversial nature, there is surprisingly little hard empirical evidence about how controls have actually affected housing conditions. Hundreds of articles and many books have been written about rent controls, but most are based entirely upon either theory or opinions or both rather than upon carefully gathered and well analyzed relevant data.

Given the aforementioned consensus of opinion on the effects of RC, this lack of measurement of RC's effects is sobering.

Furthermore, like all regulation, the effect of RC depends on the completeness of enforcement and the penalties for noncompliance. Indeed, evidence from Ontario indicates that noncompliance and lack of enforcement have probably had a significant effect on the impact of RC (Social Planning Council of Metropolitan Toronto, 1983, p. 10) and were a fundamental reason for the introduction of a rent registry in 1986.[3] However, there is very little literature that measures the impact of enforcement and penalties on the ultimate impact of the regulation (e.g., Ashenfelter and Smith, 1979, on minimum wages; Graves et al., 1989, on speed limits).

There are a number of measurement issues suggested by the Smith analysis, which relies upon straightforward comparisons and published evidence rather than new econometric work. It seems clear that RC has distorted real rents and rental property values for pre-1976 units, but one cannot tell how much from

---

1 Stanbury and Todd (1989) describe and analyze the three periods (so far) of Ontario RC.

2 A number of these issues are discussed in the recent survey paper by Smith, Rosen, and Fallis (1988) and the earlier surveys they cite.

3 Stanbury and Todd (1989, ch. 4) discuss the increased penalties for noncompliance contained in the 1986 legislation. However, it is difficult to know the extent of noncompliance in the Ontario system, which depends upon tenant complaints.

the simple comparisons in the paper. For example, unit sale prices fell much more rapidly than unit rents from 1975 to 1978 but seem to have risen more rapidly than rents since 1980 (sale price data from 1981 to 1985 are omitted). The possible effects of RC upon capitalized values look more severe than upon rents during the first period and more benign during the second (especially the 56.7 percent rise in sale price from 1986 to 1988). While recent rents and prices may reflect only the most recent (1986) changes in Ontario's law, it is difficult to rely upon such mixed effects as evidence of an oppressive RC regime. Also, some or all of the differences in rent and price movements may result from the difference in value between an existing rental unit and a new development resulting from the sale of a property (due, for example, to demolition and the exemption of new construction until the 1986 RC revisions or perhaps to a change in use). The data on annual rental housing starts show a significant decline since the introduction of RC in 1975, but, without further analysis, one cannot know how much of this is attributable to RC. Other jurisdictions (e.g., British Columbia) have experienced dramatic declines in rental starts in recent years in the absence of RC (probably due to a depressed regional economy in B.C.'s case). While one expects that RC has discouraged construction in Ontario, there are numerous local factors that may have contributed to the decline; the effect of RC has not been isolated from these factors. It is difficult to find reliable data tying maintenance levels to RC; in fact, one author (Olsen, 1987) has shown that the commonly held view that RC reduces maintenance expenditures is neither theoretically certain nor empirically confirmed. That same analysis reminds us that tenant maintenance may increase under RC; yet that behaviour is even more difficult to assess.

Isolating the effects of RC on the value of ownership or conversions out of the rental market is also difficult in a market like Toronto's where numerous factors have been affecting market behaviour dramatically and the RC law itself is changing regularly. Finally, determining the effect of RC upon government revenue requires consideration of adjustments in other markets (e.g., property values and rents in the uncontrolled sector, and altered tenant expenditures and producer income in other markets). These adjustments also affect government revenue in opposing directions, and one is unlikely to capture the ultimate revenue effect without a general equilibrium model.[4] However, it is worth noting that the welfare loss from RC can be greater when it is imposed upon a market already distorted by various taxes.

---

4 This part of Smith's analysis relies in part upon analysis by Slack (1986), but her analysis relies, in turn, upon earlier "back of the envelope" calculations by Smith and Tomlinson (1981).

Most of the evidence suggests that rates of return on controlled rental housing should have fallen since the beginning of RC; this would certainly confirm theoretical prediction. However, evidence presented elsewhere suggests that even this result has not been apparent (Ministry of Municipal Affairs and Housing, 1982). Like much evidence on the effects of public policy, evidence on effects of Ontario RC suffers from the difficulty of holding other things equal.

Consideration of such measurement problems does not correct the distortions that RC (or any form of price control) introduces and perpetuates. However, it does press one to reconsider the bases on which RC is objectionable as a form of regulation if its effects seem to be small, especially in light of the pressure on decision makers to address, at least symbolically, widespread housing affordability problems. It seems that professional opinion is usually conditioned to some extent on the magnitude of distortions (certainly referees' reports suggest that this is the case) as well as predictions of their existence.

Dealing with Decontrol

The analysis of decontrol is no less complex than that for RC itself. Underlying many of these comments has been a concern about our ignorance of the circumstances in which RC is adopted in light of considerable professional opinion against it. One also needs a knowledge of those circumstances in dealing with the issue of decontrol. In the other discussion of the Smith paper, Stanbury provides the kind of analysis of the political economy of RC that might also help in developing an effective plan for decontrol (see also Stanbury and Thain, 1986). For example, recall that the limited literature on decontrol indicates that decontrol often occurs after a significant loosening of the rental housing market; of course, this is a positive and not a normative proposition.

The particular provisions of Smith's decontrol plan raise interesting issues. First, the plan does not literally remove controls. There is still an allowable increase (inflation plus 2 to 3 percent plus an increase to amortize capital upgrading); such a provision wisely recognizes "excessive adjustment costs for tenants." While this does not remove controls, it means they are binding only when the relative price of rental housing is rising rapidly. Second, decontrol does not apply to two significant pieces of ancillary regulation in Ontario: the Landlord and Tenant Act, which places severe restrictions on the form of tenancy agreement that can exist in order to increase security of tenure; and the maintenance of the Residential Rental Standards Board which monitors and enforces maintenance standards. There is no evidence of the impact that the former regulation has on the market (though provisions such as prohibition of security deposits and severe constraints on eviction are costly to landlords), but the latter represents a substantial intervention. The continuation of a rent registry seems reasonable for policy analysis and research purposes, but true decontrol should not require it.

A third concern is the feasibility of requiring a government to indemnify landlords against future RC. While governments can make contracts, it would seem to be difficult or impossible for a government to bind itself either not to pass contrary regulations which are constitutional or to pay damages if it does. However, the intent of that recommendation is appropriate: credible commitments not to intervene in the future would have a significant effect upon the restoration of market efficiency by reducing developers' and landlords' risks of new constraints on their rents. Finally, economists have long supported Smith's recommendation that a shelter allowance be used instead of RC to address the housing needs of low-income households (barring the adoption of a more comprehensive negative income tax). However, once again ignorance of the true model of policy choice prevents us from knowing whether such a policy would in fact be a substitute for RC and not a complement (especially because shelter allowances tend to leave the risk of price increases with the tenant for some period). While it is beyond the scope of his paper to provide details of a shelter allowance policy, it is worth remembering that the particular provisions of such an allowance are important: it is not the case that any shelter allowance Pareto dominates all possible RC schemes.

I have suggested that an analysis of the political process and conditions from which RC emerges is also relevant to the decontrol issue. However, the same analysis must apply to the evolution of RC in a given jurisdiction. For example, can we say that the evolution of RC in Ontario provides support for a rent-seeking (or rent-control-seeking!) theory of public policy choice? Does the Ontario example show de facto a pattern of groping less inefficient policies that contradict a public choice analysis? While it is difficult to isolate the effects of the current (and past) RC policy, the current provisions that allow for "reasonable" rates of return, rent increases to avoid losses, constant real rents at a minimum, and freedom to set initial rents on newly rented units are less burdensome than some earlier provisions, albeit more burdensome than others. Smith is willing to conclude that "some of the consequences of rent control appear to have been reversed (most notably the erosion in real net rent and capital values) or mitigated (the decline in unassisted rental housing starts) since the 1986 changes in the rent control legislation…"

Conclusion

Smith's paper, along with his and others' extensive research on the topic, make a strong case that rent control has significantly distorted the operation of Ontario housing markets (notably Toronto) and imposed significant costs as a result. However, rent control differs from a number of the most prominent forms of government regulation because its form and effects are much more localized. As a result, numerous schemes may be operating simultaneously in a country, and critical analysis of one scheme may be of limited value in assessing the impact of others; indeed, the same scheme may have differential impacts across local markets. This characteristic of the policy, its ability to confer diffused but significant benefits quickly at little immediate public expense, and the lack of a policy alternative that is clearly a close substitute in the eyes of the relevant level of government (provinces in Canada, municipalities in the U.S.) probably means that rent control will persist as a popular public policy (relative to housing allowances or income maintenance). This need not weaken one's conviction that it is poor public policy. It means that it may be worth expanding our traditional focus (i.e., opposition to the policy) to incorporate our understanding of the economics of the political process into the analysis of RC. This should yield potentially interesting work on policy designs that capture the political appeal of rent control while minimizing the market distortions and administrative burden it represents.[5]

---

5   Some initial work in this direction is in Marks (forthcoming).

References

Arnott, Richard (1981), *Rent Control and Options for Decontrol in Ontario*, Policy Study Series (Toronto: Ontario Economic Council).

Ashenfelter, Orley, and Robert S. Smith (1979), "Compliance with the Minimum Wage Law," *Journal of Political Economy* 87 (April), pp. 333-50.

Block, Walter, and Michael A. Walker (1988), "Entropy in the Canadian Economics Profession: Sampling Consensus on the Major Issues," *Canadian Public Policy* 10 (June), pp. 137-50.

Downs, Anthony (1988), *Residential Rent Controls: An Evaluation*, (Washington, D.C.: Urban Land Institute).

Gooderham, Mary (1988), "Ontario Will Disregard All of Four-Year Rent Study Despite $3 Million Cost," *Globe and Mail* (January 29), p. A1.

Graves, Philip E., Dwight R. Lee, and Robert L. Sexton (1989), "Statutes Versus Enforcement: The Case of the Optimal Speed Limit," *American Economic Review* 79 (September), pp. 932-36.

Kearl, J.R. et al. (1979), "A Confusion of Economists?," *American Economic Review* 69 (May), pp. 28-37.

Marks, Denton (forthcoming), "On Resolving the Dilemma of Rent Control." *Urban Studies*.

Muller, R. Andrew (1987), "Ontario Options in the Light of the Canadian Experience with Decontrol," in Richard J. Arnott and Jack M. Mintz (eds.) *Policy Forum on Rent Controls in Ontario* (Kingston, Ont.: John Deutsch Institute for the Study of Economic Policy).

Olsen, Edgar O. (1987), "What Do Economists Know About the Effect of Rent Control on Housing Maintenance?" in Richard J. Arnott and Jack M. Mintz (eds.) *Rent Control: The International Experience* (Kingston, Ont.: John Deutsch Institute for the Study of Economic Policy).

Ontario Ministry of Municipal Affairs and Housing (1982), *The Impact of Rent Review on Rental Housing in Ontario: A Staff Research Report* (Toronto: Ministry of Municipal Affairs and Housing).

Slack, Enid (1986), *The Costs of Rent Review in Ontario*, Research Study No. 26 (Toronto: Commission of Inquiry into Residential Tenancies).

Smith, Lawrence B., Kenneth T. Rosen, and George Fallis (1988), "Recent Developments in Economic Models of Housing Markets," *Journal of Economic Literature* 26 (March), pp. 29-64.

Smith, Lawrence B. and Peter Tomlinson (1981), "Rent Controls in Ontario: Roofs or Ceilings?" *American Real Estate and Urban Economics Association Journal* 9:2 (Summer), pp. 93-114.

Social Planning Council of Metropolitan Toronto (1983), *Brief to the Commission of Inquiry into Residential Tenancies* (Toronto: Social Planning Council of Metropolitan Toronto, February).

Stanbury, William T. and Peter Thain (1986), *The Origins of Rent Regulation in Ontario*, Research Study No. 17 (Toronto: Commission of Inquiry into Residential Tenancies).

Stanbury, William T. and John Todd (1989), *Rent Regulation in Ontario*, Unpublished manuscript, Faculty of Commerce and Business Administration, University of British Columbia.

Thom, Stuart (1989), "The Rent Regulation Rip-Off," *Policy Options* 10 (July/August), pp. 16-18.

Discussion of the Smith Paper

W.T. Stanbury

Introduction

I would like to comment on an important perspective not addressed in Dr. Smith's paper, namely the politics of rent regulation. Regulation of all kinds is born in the political arena. Creating a regulatory regime is a political act, no matter how technical the legislation may appear.[1] It is political because it almost certainly alters the distribution of income—even if its objective is to remedy market failures and so improve allocative efficiency. Based on the analysis of its effects, the central objective of almost all direct or industry-specific regulation is to redistribute income (Stanbury and Lermer, 1983). Moreover, regulatory reform—including outright deregulation—is also a political act.[2] As such, it must meet political criteria. These criteria may well be different from, and in conflict with, criteria endorsed by economists.

My starting point is the following observation and question. While rent regulation has been universally condemned by economists, it has been legislated in a variety of jurisdictions in North America and elsewhere.[3]

Anthony Downs (1988, p. 12) states that as of 1986 more than 200 communities in the U.S. had enacted some form of residential rent controls. "All but one were located in the five states of New York, New Jersey (which

---

1   The political and economic forces that resulted in rent regulation in Ontario in 1975 are described in Stanbury and Thain (1986). The forces that may lead to rent regulation in B.C. are described in Hamilton and Stanbury (1990).

2   Generally, see Derthick and Quirk (1985) and Stanbury (1987).

3   It should be noted that unlike some other forms of government regulation, the control of residential rents is by no means universal. Indeed, it is a minority—albeit a substantial one—of jurisdictions that have rent regulation. In Canada, only B.C., Quebec, and Newfoundland had some form of rent regulation prior to the federal anti-inflation program announced in October 1975. Then all provinces agreed to establish controls as part of the national effort to reduce the rate of inflation. Most provinces "phased out" their rent controls: Alberta, Manitoba, and New Brunswick in 1980; B.C. in 1983; while Saskatchewan replaced controls with a rent arbitration scheme (Muller, 1989). Ontario, which agreed to impose rent controls in response to political pressures in the context of a general election in mid-1975, made controls "permanent" in 1979 (Stanbury and Todd, 1990a, ch. 2).

contains over half of all rent-controlled localities), Massachusetts, Connecticut, and California. The other jurisdiction is the District of Columbia." Downs points out that as of mid-1988, 14 states have passed laws or have constitutional provisions prohibiting their local governments from adopting rent controls. Why is it that "economists have been notoriously thorough in convincing themselves of the destructive effects of rent control and notoriously inept at convincing anyone else?" (Hazlett, 1982, p. 278).

But are politicians unaware of the adverse consequences of rent controls? Stigler (1982, p. 14) argues that "when the society imposes a price ceiling that prevents a market from clearing...that is not an act of defiance against the law of demand. Rather, it is a decision based upon a preference for another system of assigning goods and distributing income." He concludes that "it will not do to say that rent control...[is] adopted out of ignorance of [its] effects." Stigler goes even further. He argues that all important public policies

...take account of whatever established knowledge economists possess and perhaps of some that we do not yet possess...If rent ceiling laws were not anticipated to have the effects they do have, many of their aspects would be mysterious. If it were not expected that landlords would seek to escape the controls—that is, if the elasticity of supply of rental housing were really thought to be insignificant—then the laws would not include controls over conversions and demolitions. If the chilling effect of rent controls on new construction had not been anticipated, the promise—however badly kept—to leave uncontrolled the rents of premises built thereafter would not have been made. If queuing had not been expected, rent control laws would have paid little attention to the rights of tenants to sublease controlled properties (Stigler, 1982, p. 14).

Rent controls, like scores of other public policies, actually reduce aggregate income, but are adopted and persist because they produce a redistribution of income desired by some politically effective group. In legislating rent controls, according to Stigler, society is insisting on "taking into account the realities of a political process which economists persisted in viewing as an all-powerful God who shared their preoccupation with efficiency" (1982, p. 16).

In its simplest terms, rent regulation is clearly the triumph of politics over economics. The purpose of these comments is to explain why the conventional economic analysis of the effects of rent controls such as that provided by Smith is likely to have little influence in having them removed.

Politics of Rent Controls

Public Choice Perspective

According to U.S. Senator William Proxmire, a politician for several decades, the politics of rent control are simple:

> Rent control has the most obvious kind of political appeal. There are more tenants than landlords. Every tenant likes to have his rent held down. No tenant wants to have his rent increased. So the political arithmetic is straightforward and deadly. Fix rents by law (quoted in Hazlett, 1982, p. 296).

This explanation suggests that rent regulation should be ubiquitous since the political calculus upon which it is based is essentially the same in every jurisdiction.[4] But rent regulation is in existence in a minority of local jurisdictions. In order to explain this, economists and political scientists turned to the public choice approach.[5]

Fallis (1987) provides a convincing argument that the public choice approach to understanding rent controls is incomplete.[6] He suggests that when the relative costs of organization and the pecuniary and political resources (except votes) of landlords and tenants are taken into account, it is not clear why tenants' interests dominate those of landlords so as to result in rent controls. A fuller explanation, he contends, lies in the ideas that housing is a necessity with a low elasticity of supply and that all participants are concerned with fairness in making public policy.[7]

Fallis suggests that fairness in rental housing involves four notions: specific egalitarianism regarding the necessities of life (as per Tobin, 1970); fairness in respect to the gains from owning land (e.g., it is not fair to increase rents due to an increase in demand but it is appropriate to do so if costs increase); security of tenure for tenants; and general egalitarianism (1987, pp. 166-68).

---

4 Downs (1988, p. 12) notes that in the U.S. several of the communities with rent controls have certain common traits: a high proportion of tenant households, a relatively high percentage of college and university students, relatively low vacancy rates when controls were adopted, and strong barriers to the creation of more rental units within their boundaries.

5 See, for example, Stanbury and Thain (1986), Hartle (1984), and Di Canio (1982).

6 Fallis (1987, p. 164) states that in positive public choice analyses, "homo economicus" and "homo politicus" are the same: they are rational, utility maximizing individuals subject to budget and institutional constraints.

7 See, for example, Knetsch et al. (1984), Kahneman et al. (1986).

While Fallis indicates that a belief in fairness is not consistent with self-interest strictly construed, he says its existence is manifest in "the language of the political debate" over rent controls.[8] It is only the fetish of some economists (e.g., Hirshleifer, 1985) that rejects the idea that one person's self-interest cannot include the welfare of others. While the acceptance of interdependent utility functions makes the mathematics of optimization a nightmare, there is no *logical* reason to rule out the idea that person A's utility can be increased by actions that reduce A's wealth while increasing the utility of certain other persons that A deems to be important.

Politics has its own logic. If economists, as citizens, are going to achieve their normative objective of increasing society's economic welfare by improving efficiency, they need to better understand the nature of political logic.

The Tyranny of the Worst Case

As in many other policy issues, the politics of rent control is driven by the well-publicized worst case example. While economists tend to focus on what is happening *on average* or changes in aggregate income, politicians have to deal with the outlying cases, particularly those adversely affected by some change. Leone (1986) emphasizes that equity in public policy matters has come to focus on the adverse consequences for some individuals (or firms) of virtually any change from the status quo whether exogenous to government or created by government. It is clear that tangible losses have greater salience to the "losers" as compared with the value of gains to the "winners." The aggregate benefits of efficiency-increasing policy actions may be large, but they are widely diffused and not easily identifiable and "connectable" to a particular policy action.

To increase their political impact, tenant activists and/or their political allies, or even political entrepreneurs,[9] focus on individual cases of large rent increases for those deemed to be least able to pay (e.g., the poor and old age

---

8 Fallis (1987, p. 167). See also Stanbury and Thain (1986) and Stanbury and Todd (1990b).

9 By political entrepreneurs I refer to individual politicians (candidates or office holders) who spot an issue that they believe will be of concern to a significant group of voters. When an issue is latent or at the early stages of salience such individuals seek to both "create an issue" and offer a policy "solution" that they believe will attract votes for themselves and/or their party. A political entrepreneur may even increase the probability of becoming party leader by such behaviour. The point is that politicians need not be seen as merely weighing and responding to interest group pressures. They can, in some cases, create or channel the demand for their own services. See below.

pensioners). Large increases for such people are characterized as "gouging" by landlords. To prevent large percentage increases in rent, tenants and their allies call for general rent controls.[10]

Rudimentary concepts of justice in a democracy emphasize that every individual is to be treated "fairly." A tiny percentage of households hit by a large increase in rent can amount to thousands of individuals. Their cries of alarm when heard by the vast majority who are not directly experiencing a problem can create feelings of fear and insecurity in the latter. Losers or potential losers ask government to act to ensure they are not hurt.

The political problem of attending to the few most adversely affected is exacerbated when the legislature is located in a city that is both a media centre and an area experiencing an unusual combination of forces that make rent controls most attractive: greater excess demand, tighter zoning/building controls, the issue has been more politicized, there is greater racial/ethnic diversity, and there is the greatest contrast between conspicuous wealth and poverty. Rent regulation in Ontario is driven by economic pressures—which become political pressures—in Metro Toronto.[11] To deal with the "hot house" condition of Metro (and the City of Toronto in particular), the entire province has been made subject to the same set of extensive rent controls.

Timing, Adjustment Costs, and Political Imperatives

When he was prime minister of the U.K., Harold Wilson is said to have remarked that "in politics a week is a long time." Economists' lags during which markets move from one equilibrium to another (or at least toward it) are a politician's nightmare.

It appears that demands for rent control usually originate during periods of excess demand and sharply rising rents (or at least the perception of the latter). Economists grossly understate the political significance of the rather long lags in supply in response to rising rents in the housing market. Even if price is left

---

10 It is hard to imagine rent controls being imposed when the rental market is "slack," i.e., when there is a high vacancy rate and rents are stable or falling in nominal terms. Political action almost always requires that there be "losers" who demand that government act to help them. Political pressures to obtain regulatory protection usually stem from changes in economic conditions that are or appear to be making a politically salient group worse off. See Stanbury and Thain (1986) and Hamilton and Stanbury (1990).

11 Further, note that the 1986 Census indicates that 42.1 percent of households in Metro Toronto were renters versus 36.3 percent for Ontario as a whole. In the City of Toronto, however, 60.5 percent of households in 1986 were renters.

free to do its job as a signalling device, movement to the new equilibrium takes a long time in "human" terms. Paying 20 or 30 percent higher rent for two to three years while supply expands to satisfy the increase in demand and reduce rents to close to their previous level is hardly a pleasant experience. No wonder the losers demand immediate protection and ignore the costs of misallocation.

Economists often ignore the problems involved in the process of equilibration because they use comparative statics analysis. In the "real world" people live their lives constantly coping with disequilibrium. The process of adjustment is often difficult and costly. In their praise for the role of price changes as signals to adjust quantities to equilibrate the forces of supply and demand, economists probably underestimate the adjustment costs borne by tenants. They either have to adjust other expenditures or move. It is tenant mobility that prevents landlords from "gouging" in the sense of charging "discriminatory rents" or trying to raise all their rents above the market-clearing level. The real costs to tenants of moving are far higher than the sum of payments to the moving company, and the imputed value of one's time finding another unit, packing, and unpacking. This is made clear by Knetsch et al. (1984) who have measured the large amounts people would require to get them to move. (Of course, the tenant can inflict costs on the landlord by moving, the biggest being the loss of rental income if the unit is vacant for a period.)

Timing of the Costs and Benefits of Rent Controls

The benefits and costs of rent controls occur at largely different points of time. This fact goes a long way in explaining why various rational, self-interested actors support rent controls. For politicians, the major benefit of imposing controls is that it is possible to stop rents from rising "out of control" *now*. They will be able to demonstrate to voters that the law can prevent undesirable economic events, i.e., the noble art of politics can triumph over the relentless grinding of market forces motivated by greed. Even if politicians fully appreciate the adverse consequences of binding rent controls, they recognize that the worst effects will only be significant and visible some years in the future. The odds are high that the adverse effects won't become apparent until after the next election. Politicians are driven by the rhythms of the electoral-oestrus cycle and problems are examined in terms of their effects within this cycle. The politics of re-election aside, the present value of a burden that won't be borne for five or ten years is small at conventional discount rates, e.g., 10 to 15 percent. Because uncertainty is high in political markets, the discount rate is much higher.

Economists, if they are familiar with the housing market, will appreciate that while the level of maintenance expenditures may drop quite quickly and plans for new units may be cancelled almost immediately, the real effects of the supply of rental housing occur several years after controls are imposed. There is, in effect, a "honeymoon period" in which the predicted evils have not made themselves felt and rent increases can be held below increases in income or inflation.

When, to mix a metaphor, the chickens do come home to roost (reduced supply, lower vacancy rates, higher search costs, key money, and widespread conversions to get out of controls), they do not have the force economists expect them to have in the political arena. Why? First, a lot of other political and economic circumstances have changed so it is difficult for many citizens to link the new evils to actions taken several years earlier. Second, even within a few years, many of the individuals directly involved in the decision to enact controls no longer hold the same positions. New members of the cast seldom have the same sense of history as do the longer serving ones. Third, the advocates of controls misconstrue certain facts and claim that controls have nothing to do with the present problems. In Ontario, they emphasized that only a small number of new rental units were built despite the fact such post-1975 buildings were exempt from controls, and despite the fact that vacancy rates were low suggesting a strong demand for rental housing. To the advocates of controls, this was proof that controls were not responsible for the drop in the rate at which new units were built. Their explanation is that the private housing market— driven by greed—does not work except to supply single family homes or condominiums for the rich. Private developers can't or won't (some activists accused them of "going on strike") provide "affordable" housing. The reduction in the rate of new supply of rental units is variously "explained" by higher interest rates, rising land prices, and higher construction costs. The solution is seen as larger government subsidies for non-profit housing organizations or more government-owned units with rents geared to the tenants' income.

"Clear" and "Fuzzy" Prices

Economists need to appreciate the political significance of the difference between "clear" and "fuzzy" prices. A conventional money price is a clear price, particularly when exactly identical goods or services are being compared. Therefore, it is easy to compare offers for a Brand-X refrigerator, model 102B (delivered, with a two-year warranty) if one dealer quotes $999 and the other asks $1079. Fuzzy prices, however, are those things for which there is no easily defined common metric or for which the exchange value, *ex ante*, is uncertain. For example, under rent control, would-be tenants personally experience the higher search costs of finding a "bargain" rent controlled unit. They simply can't pay a certain number of dollars and skip the agony. Instead, the price of finding a unit must be paid in time, travel, telephone calls, and frustration. Moreover, the price is not only in kind, but it is uncertain: the searcher might "luck out" and find a good deal after only an hour of search, but they might spend 100 hours before they find a comparable deal. Rent controls are replete with costs that are fuzzy to the average person, even if economists can put some hard numbers on them (see Slack, 1987).

Not surprisingly, politicians prefer forms of intervention that inflict costs that are fuzzy than those where the costs are clear because it is much more difficult for voters to fully appreciate what they are doing and because clear costs are more real or tangible than fuzzy costs. Fuzzy costs are easy for economists to ignore as being of little significance precisely because they are fuzzy. Moreover, such costs may have politically attractive distributional consequences. For example, there is such a huge backlog of rent review applications in Ontario that decisions are often delayed more than two years. Landlords must forgo interest on large retroactive rent increases. Tenants heartily dislike both the uncertainty and the fact they may end up owing several thousand dollars for which they have not budgeted. Some refuse to pay and move out, thus increasing their transaction costs (see Stanbury and Todd, 1990a). Landlords, in practice, are unable to collect the retroactive increases from such tenants. To both landlords and tenants these costs are real, but in the policy making (political) arena, they are fuzzy because it is difficult to put a dollar figure on them using a method most people would understand. Hence they are less likely to result in political action. In politics, opportunity costs don't count and what economists call sunk-costs are often highly relevant psychological "investments."

Restrictive rent controls are an example of what Kornai (1986, p. 7) calls "the reproduction of shortages" which is characterized by fuzzy prices or consequences. The general effect of such shortages is to create a seller's market in which "the buyer feels defenceless and subordinated, while the seller develops a consciousness of power and dominance" (op. cit., 1986, p. 63). Because the role of price as an equilibrating mechanism is suppressed, buyers have to compete with each other in other ways to ensure that they are served rather than a competing purchaser. Among the ways this is done, to use Kornai's words, is "to please the seller, not only by what he gives him, but also by what is not demanded. He [the buyer] is humble and submissive, so as not to annoy the seller by expressing dissatisfaction, let alone by making a complaint" (ibid.). Further, in the world of planned shortages, buyers are forced to adjust in a number of ways: by purchasing inferior substitutes (lower quality), and by higher search costs. In short, "the buyer adjusts himself to the chronic shortage situation" by compromise and conformity. The buyer is deprived of certain choices and must accept second or third best. "Shortage keeps on making the choice instead of you." Price signals are replaced in part by grumbling, complaints, and protests (op. cit., 1986, pp. 65, 67, and 68).

Adapting to Rent Controls

Even when the predicted adverse economic consequences of binding rent controls do appear in full force, the "misery" is very seldom sufficient to result in their repeal. Why? Because democratic political systems are remarkably adaptive. They adapt in several ways. First, more legislation is passed to deal with the problems engendered by controls, e.g., Ontario passed the Rental Housing Protection Act in 1986 as a "temporary measure" and then made it permanent in 1989. It requires municipalities to restrict efforts by landlords to shift their rental buildings out of controls (Stanbury and Todd, 1990c). There is no end to the number of political patches than can be piled upon each other.

Second, pressed by the same interest groups that support rent controls, governments increase direct subsidies to overcome the worst effects of controls, namely to increase the supply of rental units. Unfortunately, the average taxpayer doesn't associate these expenditures and higher taxes he must pay with rent controls.

Third, those most directly affected adapt to the realities of rent controls in a wide variety of ways:

- Some landlords try to "escape" from controls by demolition or conversion. When their efforts become apparent, tenant groups lobby for legislation to prevent such actions. (See Stanbury and Todd, 1990c.)
- Landlords "shirk," i.e., they try to reduce the quantity and quality of rental services supplied to tenants to reflect the constrained price. They do this by eliminating amenities (swimming pool, cable TV, the doorwoman) and by reducing maintenance (if you want the apartment painted, do it yourself).
- Some landlords and tenants (usually in small buildings owned by an individual or family who manage it themselves) agree to "opt out" of controls and negotiate illegal rents for renovations or continued high levels of maintenance.
- Some tenants and landlords engage in illegal behaviour. Tenants demand key money for subletting their unit. Landlords raise rents above the legal level.
- Over time, more landlords learn to fully utilize all the opportunities for increasing rents and thereby reduce their cost. In other cases, rental buildings are sold to individuals better adapted to dealing with rent controls, i.e., more willing to try to "beat the system."

Human perception depends heavily on personal experience and nearby bases of comparisons. Landlords, but particularly tenants, adapt so well to the benefits and costs of rent regulation that they fail to recognize that there are other ways to deal with rental housing. People who grow up under the system take it for granted. Having no comparisons in their personal experience, they "play it as it lays." Moreover, since the benefits of eliminating rent regulation are widely diffused (as are the costs) and amount to a public good, individuals have little incentive to change the system.

Political Criteria for Reform

If rent regulation is to be changed, as Smith suggests, to allow rents to gradually rise to the long-run market-clearing level, the proposal must not be inconsistent with political rationality and the forces operating in political markets. These include the following in the case of Ontario. There is intense competition among all three political parties for the tenant vote (about one-third of all voters). All have supported rent regulation in some form since mid-1975.[12] While two of the three parties' support for rent regulation may be purely pragmatic, one party (the NDP) appears to have a strong ideological commitment to stringent rent controls. There are numerous tenant interest groups and the most important one (Federation of Metro Tenants 'Association) has close connections with the NDP which has frequently been willing to introduce bills to change the legislation embodying rent regulation and related provisions (e.g., security of tenure and control over conversions and demolitions; see Stanbury, 1989). Home owners, even though they very likely pay higher taxes due to the policy, are not opposed to rent regulation. Indeed, a majority support it. The worst effects of persistent highly restrictive rent controls have yet to be seen, e.g., severely under-maintained buildings, abandoned rental buildings, widespread illegal rents or "key money," extremely low tenant mobility, and sharp contraction of the private ownership of rental buildings (and corresponding expansion in public housing). If tenant groups are sufficiently strong to not only keep rent controls in place but also extend them to previously unregulated units (post-1975 buildings), why would they ever agree to a plan like Smith's?[13] If they did, why would they not be strong enough to subsequently reduce the allowable annual rate of increase to the CPI or even less? (It is not at all clear that the type of contract Smith proposes to bind the government would be enforceable.) The boom conditions in Ontario in the late 1980s resulted in excess demand for all types of housing. Moreover, it seems likely that, even when the boom abates, Metro Toronto will continue to enjoy greater demand for rental housing than other areas of the

---

12 The only antidote to such competition is for the parties to form a "cartel" to phase out rent controls. Unfortunately, the NDP would never join such a cartel or would defect if it did. It is ironic that the adoption of an efficiency-promoting policy can only be achieved if the political market is cartelized.

13 For an alternative plan, see Stanbury and Todd (1990b).

country. Continued pressure on this all important housing market will dominate the politics of reforming rent regulation.[14]

The choice of rent regulation over alternative policy instruments (such as shelter allowances) to help low- to moderate-income tenants should force economists to ask why is this the case. An examination of the political characteristics of shelter allowance indicates it has a number of notable disadvantages from the perspective of self-interested politicians (and they are the people who make the key decision). It would make redistribution explicit in terms of target, amount, and cost to the treasury. Middle-class activists argue that such subsidies "stigmatize" the recipients. Government budgets are already under fiscal strain and a shelter allowance program would be costly. Further, a shelter allowance is inconsistent with Aaron Director's "law of public redistribution," namely that most public programs are designed to benefit the middle class at the expense of the poor and/or rich. Finally, a shelter allowance, being in cash, give the recipients a choice as to how to use the benefit—they could live in a cheaper unit and buy more beer. While economists value choice, many interventionist middle-class social activists have a highly paternalistic attitude toward the disadvantaged. They would not want housing grants spent on other things (except perhaps more milk or orange juice for children).

It appears that it may be easier to pass a camel through the eye of a needle than to meet these criteria for reforming Ontario's system of rent regulation.

---

14 It seems more likely that controls will be removed when the period of excess demand has passed so there is no longer an excuse to retain "temporary" controls designed to deal with a crisis. Indeed, controls are easiest to remove during a recession in which there is an excess supply of rental housing in the sense of no sharp upward pressure on rents and there is a healthy vacancy rate. Alternatively, it might be that the original control regime was not highly restrictive, hence the size of the distortions caused by controls was small so that when the next normal downturn of the cycle comes about, it is easy to conclude that controls are no longer needed and can be removed.

References

Derthick, M.J. and P. Quirk (1985), *The Politics of Deregulation* (Washington, D.C.: Brookings Institution).

Di Canio, Stephen (1982), "Rent Control Voting Patterns, Popular Views and Group Interests," in M. Bruce Johnston (ed.) *Resolving the Housing Crisis* (Cambridge, Mass.: Ballinger Publishing), pp. 301-18.

Downs, Anthony (1988), *Residential Rent Controls: An Evaluation* (Washington, D.C.: Urban Land Institute).

Fallis, George (1987), "Rent Control: The Citizen, the Market and the State" in R.J. Arnott and J.M. Mintz (eds.) *Rent Control: The International Experience* (Kingston, Ont.: John Deutsch Institute for the Study of Economic Policy), pp. 163-74.

Hamilton, S.W. and W.T. Stanbury (1990), "Demands for Rent Regulation in British Columbia and the Relevance of the Ontario Experience," in W.T. Stanbury and John D. Todd (eds.) *Rent Regulation: The Ontario Experience* (Vancouver: Canadian Real Estate Research Bureau, Faculty of Commerce and Business Administration, University of British Columbia), pp. xv-xliii.

Harney, K. (1982), *The Invisible Tax: What Home Owners Pay to Support Local Rent Controls* (Washington, D.C.: Harney Corp.).

Hartle, D.G. (1984), *The Political Economy of Residential Rent Control in Ontario* (Toronto: Research Study No. 12, Ontario Commission of Inquiry into Residential Tenancies).

Hazlett, Thomas (1982), "Rent Controls and the Housing Crisis," in M. Bruce Johnson (ed.) *Resolving the Housing Crisis: Government Policy, Decontrol and the Public Interest*, Pacific Studies in Public Policy (San Francisco: Pacific Institute for Public Policy Research; Cambridge, MA: Ballinger Publishing), pp. 227-300.

Hirshleifer, Jack (1985), "The Expanding Domain of Economics," *American Economic Review* 76, pp. 728-41.

Kahneman, D., J. Knetsch, and R. Thaler (1986), "Fairness as a Constraint on Profit Seeking," *American Economic Review* 76, pp. 728-41.

Knetsch, Jack L., Daniel Kahneman, and Patricia McNeill (1984), *Residential Tenancies: Losses, Fairness and Regulations*, Research Study No. 14 (Toronto: Commission of Inquiry into Residential Tenancies).

Kornai, Janos (1986), *Contradictions and Dilemmas: Studies on the Socialist Economy and Society* (Cambridge, Mass.: MIT Press).

Leone, Robert (1986), *Who Profits: Winners and Losers and Government Regulation* (New York: Basic Books).

Muller, R. Andrew (1989), "The Experience With Rent Regulation in Canada," (Hamilton, Ont., McMaster University), mimeo.

Slack, Enid (1987), "Ontario's Experience With Rent Regulation," in R.J. Arnott and J.M. Mintz (eds.) *Policy Forum on Rent Controls in Ontario* (Kingston: John Deutsch Institute for the Study of Economic Policy, Queen's University), pp. 7-20.

Smith, Lawrence B. (1987), "The Economic Assessment of Rent Controls: The Ontario Experience," in R.J. Arnott and J.M. Mintz (eds.) *Rent Control: The International Experience* (Kingston: John Deutsch Institute for the Study of Economic Policy, Queen's University), pp. 57-72.

Stanbury, W.T. (1987) "Direct Regulation and its Reform: A Canadian Perspective," *Brigham Young University Law Review* 2, pp. 467-539.

Stanbury, W.T. (1989), "The Politics of Rent Regulation in Ontario, 1975-1989" (Vancouver: Faculty of Commerce and Business Administration, University of British Columbia, July), mimeo.

Stanbury, W.T. and George Lermer (1983), "Regulation and the Redistribution of Income and Wealth," *Canadian Public Administration* 26, 3, pp. 378-401.

Stanbury, W.T. and Peter Thain (1986), *The Origin of Rent Regulation in Ontario*, Research Study No. 17 (Toronto: Commission of Inquiry into Residential Tenancies).

Stanbury, W.T. and John D. Todd (1990a), *Rent Regulation: The Ontario Experience* (Vancouver: Canadian Real Estate Research Bureau, Faculty of Commerce and Business Administration, University of British Columbia).

Stanbury, W.T. and John D. Todd (1990b), *The Political Economy of Rent Regulation* (unpublished book manuscript under review).

Stanbury, W.T. and John D. Todd (1990c), "Landlords as Economic Prisoners of War," *Canadian Public Policy* 16, 4, pp. 399-417.

Stigler, George J. (1982) "Economists and Public Policy," *Regulation* (May/June), pp. 13-17.